The Rural World
1780–1850

Social change in the English countryside

Pamela Horn

Hutchinson

London Melbourne Sydney Auckland Johannesburg

Hutchinson & Co. (Publishers) Ltd
An imprint of the Hutchinson Publishing Group
24 Highbury Crescent, London N5 1RX

Hutchinson Group (Australia) Pty Ltd
30–32 Cremorne Street, Richmond South, Victoria 3121
PO Box 151, Broadway, New South Wales 2007

Hutchinson Group (NZ) Ltd
32–34 View Road, PO Box 40–086, Glenfield, Auckland 10

Hutchinson Group (SA) (Pty) Ltd
PO Box 337, Bergvlei 2012, South Africa

First published 1980

Set in Monotype Garamond

Printed in Great Britain by The Anchor Press Ltd
and bound by Wm Brendon & Son Ltd
both of Tiptree, Essex

British Library Cataloguing in Publication Data
Horn, Pamela
    The rural world.
    1. England – Rural conditions
    2. England – Social conditions – 18th century
    3. England – Social conditions – 19th century
    I. Title
    301.29'42   HN385
ISBN 0 09 141880 1 cased
       0 09 141881 x paper

Contents

6 CONTENTS

Illustrations and tables

Illustrations

Tables

Acknowledgements

I should like to thank all those who have helped in the preparation of this book, either by providing material or in other ways. My thanks are due, in particular, to Lady Lucas for permission to quote from the Wrest Park papers at Bedford Record Office and to the Duke of Bedford and the Trustees of the Bedford Settled Estates for permission to quote from the Russell papers at the same Record Office. Lord Coke has kindly allowed me to quote from the Holkham estate papers; I have used the microfilms of the Holkham archives published by E.P., East Ardsley, Wakefield, Yorkshire. I am also grateful to the Hampshire and General Friendly Society at Winchester for generously making their records available to me.

I have received much help from the staff at the libraries and record offices in which I have worked. These include the Bodleian Library, Oxford; the British Library; the Museum of English Rural Life, Reading; Reading University Library; Christ Church and Nuffield College, Oxford; the Public Record Office; the Cathedral Archives and Library, Canterbury; and the county record offices for Berkshire, Bedfordshire, Buckinghamshire, Cambridgeshire, Dorset, Hampshire, Northampton and Oxfordshire.

As always, I owe a great debt of gratitude to my family for their help and support – particularly my husband, who has helped in so many ways and without whose assistance neither this nor any of my books could have been written.

Time, like an ever-rolling stream,
  Bears all its sons away;
They fly forgotten, as a dream
  Dies at the opening day.

ISAAC WATTS

The inhabitants of the country, dispersed in distant places, cannot easily combine together. They have not only never been incorporated, but the corporation spirit never has prevailed among them. No apprenticeship has ever been thought necessary to qualify for husbandry, the great trade of the country. After what are called the fine arts, and the liberal professions, however, there is perhaps no trade which requires so great a variety of knowledge and experience. . . . Not only the art of the farmer, the general direction of the operations of husbandry, but many inferior branches of country labour require much more skill and experience than the greater part of mechanic trades. . . . The common ploughman, though generally regarded as the pattern of stupidity and ignorance, is seldom defective in . . . judgment and discretion. He is less accustomed, indeed, to social intercourse than the mechanic who lives in a town. His voice and language are more uncouth and more difficult to be understood by those who are not used to them. His understanding, however, being accustomed to consider a greater variety of objects, is generally much superior to that of the other, whose whole attention from morning till night is commonly occupied in performing one or two very simple operations.

ADAM SMITH, *The Wealth of Nations* (1776), vol. I

Dairymaid churning butter, 1805

I The rural community at the end of the eighteenth century

... agriculture is the grand product that supports the people. ... Both public and private wealth can arise only from three sources, *agriculture, manufactures,* and *commerce.* ... Agriculture much exceeds both the others; it is even the foundation of their principal branches.
ARTHUR YOUNG, *A Six Months' Tour Through the North of England* (1771)[1]*

As for poverty, rags, and misery, they should not exist in my village; for the cottages should not be only comfortable and low-rented, but attached to each should be, at least, 2 acres of ground, which on first possession the hirers should find well cropped with potatoes, and planted with fruit trees; – teach them how to proceed, redeem the poor from misery, make a large public enclosure at the end of the village, for their cows, &c.; and then poverty would soon quit your neighbourhood.
HON. JOHN BYNG, *The Torrington Diaries* (1789)[2]

The economic life of Britain in the 1770s and 1780s was dominated, as it had always been, by agriculture and its associated trades. Indeed, as late as 1811 agriculture, forestry and fishing contributed over one-third of the gross national product – more than any other sector – and it was the state of the harvest which was still the most significant factor in determining change in the national income between one year and the next. Admittedly, northern industrialism was beginning to challenge that pre-eminence by the final quarter of the eighteenth century, thereby foreshadowing the eventual decline of the landed interest, while country people in many places were being drawn into manufacturing production by the expansion of cottage industries like framework knitting, nailmaking and woollen clothmaking. There were villages which specialized in manufactures, like Shepshed in Leicestershire, which, thanks to the growth of framework knitting, became in the course of the eighteenth century 'the most intensively industrialized

*Superior figures refer to the notes on pages 271–309.

rural community' in the county. By 1812 there were about 1000
knitting frames for a population of around 3000.[3] But most people
were little affected by such changes. They continued to live in rural
communities and to gain their livelihood, either directly or indirectly,
from the soil. Nearly half the total labour force worked on farms, while
in the middle of the eighteenth century it is unlikely that more than
one in six of the British lived in towns – and a high proportion of them
were found in London. Even in 1831 only about a quarter of the people
lived in towns with populations of over 20,000.[4]

In the countryside attachment to the local community played a
significant role in day-to-day life. As T. S. Ashton has written:

Men lived their lives in a provincial or parochial setting. The territorial
aristocrat wielded more power over his neighbours than the sovereign state
operating from London; the justice of the peace, on the spot, mattered far
more than the civil servant in the metropolis. The market town where local
produce was sold, local incomes spent, and local prices determined, was of
more account than Smithfield or Mark Lane. If men wanted to improve a
road or a river, construct a harbour, build a hospital, or initiate a new
business enterprise, it was on local, rather than central, resources that they
drew. Loyalties attached to the country house, the county regiment, and the
regional hunt; affections were centred on the parish church, the village
green, and the local inn.[5]

Even migration to seek fresh employment was rarely beyond a ten-
mile radius from a worker's place of origin. Instead people 'milled
about' within a given group of villages, moving from one to the other
as employment opportunities – or fancy – took them.[6] Equally, those
fast-expanding industrial areas like south Lancashire and Warwickshire, which relied on immigration to meet their labour needs, drew
people from a relatively short distance only. The growth of population
in the northern industrial counties took place not by any dramatic
long-distance movement, but rather by a series of short migrations –
and by the above-average fertility rates of the native population in
most of the affected areas.[7]

Allied to this, in many districts, were strong ties of kinship, with
much intermarrying within a small geographical compass. Thus at
Colyton in Devon between 1765 and 1777 more than three-quarters
of the wives who appear in the baptismal registers (that is, those of
childbearing age) were born in that parish or within a five-mile radius
of it, while in a group of Oxfordshire villages around 65 per cent of
marriages contracted in the second half of the eighteenth century
involved partners who lived in the same parish.[8] In remoter communi-

ties outsiders were viewed with deep suspicion. On the Isle of Portland the Hon. John Byng noted that people often intermarried because they dreaded 'the alliance of foreigners'. For them kinship served as a useful frame of reference, enabling them to decide whether a person was 'suitable' to know, at a time when old prejudices and superstitions were slow to crumble.[9]

Among such villagers proper names were little used. Instead they referred to one another by nicknames or, as in parts of rural Lancashire, by combinations of their own Christian name and that of their father – like 'Tum o' Charles o' Billy's', or 'Jone o' Isaac's' – a way which indicated neatly just where the man or woman concerned fitted into the community network.[10]

Even at the upper end of the social scale, among the aristocracy and gentry, kinship ties were important. The landed estate

belonged less to the individual than to the family: it was the source of income not only of the man who, by law or custom, was termed the owner, but, through jointures and portions, of the women related to him by blood or marriage. Entails, made between father and son, were commonly renewed, generation after generation; and hence continuity of the union between the family and the land was assured.[11]

Poor communications were a major factor in this survival of localism. Despite the growth of the canal system and the improvement in roads which followed the wider development of turnpike trusts, in many areas it was still possible for villages to be cut off from the nearest town for months at a time by the impassability of winter roads due to mud and flooding. William Marshall drew attention to the poor condition of the roads around Statfold on the Warwickshire–Staffordshire border during the 1770s, when the principal route from Tamworth to Ashby-de-la-Zouch lay in a state 'almost impassable, several months in the year. Statfold Lane had long been proverbial. In winter it was unfrequented; the riding and driftways . . . being on trespass, thro the adjoining inclosures. Waggons were dragged on their bellies through it: to a coach it was impassable, during the winter months.'[12] Even the turnpikes left a good deal to be desired in some districts, as the writings of Arthur Young demonstrate. On the road from Newport Pagnell to Bedford his indignation knew no bounds as he condemned the

cursed string of hills and holes by the name of *road*: a causeway is here and there thrown up, but so high, and at the same time so very narrow, that it was at the peril of our necks we passed a waggon with a civil and careful driver. This is a pernicious and vile practice; it might be expected if thrown up at the expense of the farmers alone; but when found in *turnpikes*, deserves every unworthy epithet which frightened women or dislocated bones can possibly give rise to.[13]

Parson Woodforde's diaries confirm that a journey from East Anglia to the West Country or even to London was not to be undertaken lightly. In July 1778 he noted that his 'poor dear Sister shook like an aspin leave [*sic*]' as she and her husband left Norwich for their Somerset home, for this was the first time she had ever travelled in a stage coach.[14]

In such circumstances, when a visit to London was a great adventure for most people, the social life of even the gentry tended to centre for much of the year on country house parties and the amenities of the county or market town. Here subscription balls and musical recitals were held in the local assembly rooms; firework displays were organized; and travelling players would provide entertainment at the theatre.[15] Cardplaying, too, featured prominently in the leisure activities of the well-to-do, while heavy drinking was normal among the men. In Herefordshire Henry Gunning recalled that country gentlemen regularly took 'in addition to their wine, a copious draught of the real *Steyre* cider, a huge tankard of which was always placed at each end of the table'.[16]

However, as readers of Jane Austen's novels will appreciate, this was only one aspect of gentry life. Study of the classics imparted learning and discrimination to many. The art of conversation – as that of letter-writing – was highly prized. And even at less elevated levels a gentleman would converse, like Mr Rushworth in *Mansfield Park*, about his day's sport, his dogs, his neighbours and his 'zeal after poachers'.

Nevertheless, the strength of these traditional aspects of rural life should not disguise the degree of change which was taking place, not merely in the industrial field, which has been touched upon, but in the overall acceleration in the size of the population and the character of land cultivation itself. During the years 1750 to 1800 the population of England and Wales grew from just over 6,000,000 at the earlier date to around 9,000,000 by the later; the sharp upward movement continued thereafter at least until the 1820s.[17] The reasons for this expansion have been the subject of some controversy: certain writers have emphasized the drop in mortality rates, thanks to a decline in the virulence of former killer diseases like smallpox and the effect of inoculation in preventing the latter's spread;[18] other, more recent, commentators have tended to place most stress on the growth in the birth rate and the accompanying drop in the age of marriage. This has been attributed to the decline in importance of apprenticeship in many traditional crafts and industries and to an ending of residential farm service in favour of day labour by a growing band of large capitalist farmers. Both trends removed what had formerly been barriers to early marriage and freed people to set up homes of their own – for in England at least the extended or multiple household, in which various generations lived together, was rare.[19] In expanding, industrialized communities like Shepshed, where employment opportunities were growing rapidly, the changes were particularly apparent. But virtually all communities came to share in them, and in the long run this was to create serious problems of poverty and underemployment in the less dynamic parts of the country. Indeed, even in places like Shepshed 'the tendency for population growth to outstrip work opportunities kept labour costs low'. The trend was also intensified by the fact that those groups who married early became proportionately more important within the village, while the smallholders and artisans, who continued to display prudent attitudes towards marriage and childbearing for property or apprenticeship reasons, grew less significant.[20]

The same process of change was apparent in agriculture. Under the impact of the 'agricultural revolution', arable rotations were improved, and a wider recognition was given to the importance of fodder crops like clovers, sainfoin, lucerne and turnips. More attention was paid to the breeding and rearing of stock, and there was an increase in the intensity of cultivation of the soil.[21] Although village communities were still basically self-sufficient, the expansion of the larger towns, particularly London, had already created a growing market for food which was being exploited by the bigger, more commercially minded farmers with surpluses to sell. Therefore within the overall pattern of mixed holdings a measure of agricultural specialization was apparent. Grain production was the prerogative of East Anglia and Essex; barley was grown extensively in Cambridgeshire, Hertfordshire, Berkshire, Wiltshire and parts of Yorkshire; there were orchards and hop gardens in Kent and Worcestershire; and cider was produced in most of the West Country. A similar specialization was apparent among livestock producers. Thus store cattle bred in Scotland were fed on Norfolk meadowland before being sent to market, while animals raised in Brecknock and Radnor were fattened on the Essex marshes. In Leicestershire the larger tenant farmers and yeomen bred and fattened cattle on their own pastures before dispatching them to the town markets. Dairy farming was characteristic of Cheshire, as well as parts of Wiltshire, Glamorgan, Huntingdon, Suffolk and the Vale of Pickering in Yorkshire. Geese and capons were raised in Sussex and Surrey, while turkeys and geese came to London from Norfolk and Suffolk.[22]

To cater for this movement of farm produce, widespread distribution networks were established. Fairs and markets played an important part in these. William Marshall, for example, commented in October 1784 on Fazeley Fair in the Midlands, which he described as the largest fair 'in this country, for *fat* cows, and, lately for sheep'. On that occasion about 500 head of cattle and 3000 sheep were offered for sale, their purchasers being butchers from Birmingham, Wolverhampton and other manufacturing towns. A number of bulls were also bought up 'chiefly for the collieries, going off in droves; many of them completely ugly'.[23] Stourbridge Fair in Cambridge was even more impressive. As Henry Dunning remembered, at the end of the 1780s it was the great mart 'at which all the dealers in cheese from Cottenham, Willingham, with other villages in the county and isle [of Ely] assembled; there were also traders from Leicestershire, Derbyshire, Cheshire and Gloucestershire'. Vast quantities of farm produce were bought up for dispatch to London, though at other booths there were smaller retail outlets, where villagers could buy woollen cloth, earthenware, leather goods, linens, furs and toys.[24] Alongside these were the statute and mop fairs which were used as impromptu labour exchanges. Men and women seeking work would stand together, often wearing some distinguishing mark to indicate their trade. Cooks wore a red ribbon and carried a basting spoon, while a carter would have a piece of whipcord attached to his hat, and a shepherd a wisp of wool.

The shipment of goods by river, canal or coast from the producing counties to urban consumers was a still more important aspect of the distribution network, and it is significant that when landed estates were offered for sale it was common for the vendor to stress their proximity to navigable waterways, if such were the case.[25] Clearly, this increased the value of the property concerned. In his tour of the southern counties Arthur Young observed that the price of veal and butter in Wales was influenced by the great quantities of provisions bought up

in all the little ports of the *Severn*, by the *Bristol* market boats. As I drove from *Cardiff*, I met such numbers of butchers, with calves, that I inquired if that little town could consume such a quantity of veal; (it was a market-day) they told me the boats were ready in the river to buy for Bristol. And this was doubtless the case with butter, &c.

Wheat prices, on the other hand, were affected 'everywhere' by the demands of London.[26]

Norfolk, through its port of Kings Lynn, had a well established grain trade with the capital. At the end of the eighteenth century this town was the outlet for more inland navigation than any other port in England, with the exception of London itself.[27] From south Buckinghamshire, too, surplus corn was sent to London by Thames barges, though the north of the county supplied the rapidly growing population of the Black Country towns. At first the grain was carried as return freight by carts bringing northern manufactured goods to London, but later, after the opening of the Grand Union Canal in 1806, it travelled by barge as part of the regular trade.[28] In the heavily populated West Riding of Yorkshire, corn was brought in from Lincolnshire as well as from the county's agrarian North and East Ridings, while Lancashire drew supplies from Cumberland, Cheshire and North Wales.

All through the century livestock was driven to London by road. Geese either travelled on foot from August until October, when the mud became too deep for their short legs, or else they were carried in specially constructed carts. Cattle came on the hoof. William Marshall described a settling up at Walsham market by one drover who had sold bullocks at Smithfield market on behalf of local graziers:

What a trust! A man, *perhaps*, not worth a hundred pounds, brings down twelve or fifteen hundred, or, perhaps two thousand pounds, to be distributed among twenty or thirty persons, who have no other security than his honesty for their money: – nay, even the servant of this man is entrusted with the same charge; the master going one week, the man the other: but so it has been for a century past. . . . The business was conducted with great ease, regularity, and dispatch. He had each man's account, and a pair of saddle-bags with the money and bills, lying upon the table: and the farmers, in their turns, took their seat at his elbow. Having examined the salesman's account; received their money; drank a glass or two of liquor; and thrown down sixpence towards the reckoning, they severally returned into the market.[29]

In Wales the drovers were often part-time farmers and innkeepers, who collected the black cattle, sheep, pigs or geese they were to drive to England from nearby farms. The cattle had to be shod for their long journey (the shoes were frequently renewed along the way), while pigs sometimes wore a kind of boot made from a woollen sock with a leather sole. As in Norfolk, the drovers took the cattle on credit and reimbursed their owners when the beasts had been sold. Some also carried with them bales of knitted garments for sale at English fairs, while well-to-do families regularly asked them to undertake financial commissions on their behalf in London. In remoter Welsh communities these men would often be the only source of information about events in the outside world.[30]

In the sale of wool marketing arrangements were equally far-flung; Norfolk's short fleeces were purchased by Yorkshire manufacturers to be made into woollen cloth, and Norwich worsted makers bought in their supplies from Yorkshire, Westmorland and even Ireland and Scotland.[31]

Yet, despite such networks of markets, at village level strong elements of subsistence agriculture still survived. Lives were ruled by the demands of agriculture and by the changing seasons. The daily concerns of these smaller men are brought out in surviving farm diaries – like that of Peter Pownall, who farmed near Stockport in Cheshire. The following are extracts from his diary for 1784:[32]

March
13 Sent Cheese into the Market. Bought two store pigs.
14 Sent 32 Measures of Barly [*sic*] to the Malt Kiln.
16 Got done threshing oats.
19 Set Geese [that is, put them to sit on eggs for hatching].
20 Set Peas and Beans.
25 Stockport fair.
31 First Ewe Lambed.

August
2 Went into Derbyshire a looking [at] colt.
3 Got done leading hay.
4 Plucked Geese.
6 Got done seling [*sic*] Meal.
9 Sowed Cabbage seed.
12 Went to the Moors a Shooting.

Joseph Lamb, a Quaker farmer from Sibford Ferris, Oxfordshire, likewise noted the minor events of his life – as on 21 June 1798, when he was 'plowing at Scotch Hedge with two Teams . . . finished weeding Corn. Boght a Poney of John Wilkes £2 18s. & a new Wagon from J. Enoch.' Apart from this buying and selling between villagers, they also lent money to one another. On 15 January 1775 Lamb recorded that he had 'Lent Jane French . . . £4 4s.', while on 3 March 1798: 'John Enoch paid in Twenty Pounds the property of Lydia Kerby with 11s. Interest.' Enoch was a carpenter and wheelwright.[33]

The most important event of the farming year in arable and mixed-farming counties was, of course, the corn harvest. Once gathered, the

THE END OF THE EIGHTEENTH CENTURY 21

grain was normally ground into flour by the village miller, and for families unable to make their own bread this task would be undertaken by the local baker. Poorer families would normally be allowed to glean once the main crop had been carried, though in William Marshall's view this was a concession which should be confined to children, cripples and 'superannuated reapers': 'There are few places, I apprehend, where there are not children and old people enow, to do the honest part of gleaning.'[34] Fortunately, his suggestions were not adopted, though following a judgement in the Court of Common Pleas in 1788, it was emphasized that this was a privilege granted by the farmer purely at his discretion.

For the majority of men – the labourers, small farmers and village tradesmen – work on the land was combined with the making and repairing of the tools needed for tilling the soil. A surviving census for Cardington in Bedfordshire reveals that in 1782 half of the population were agricultural labourers and their families and almost a quarter craftsmen or tradespeople. These included shoemakers, wheelwrights, carpenters, a sawyer, a butcher, a baker and five blacksmiths.[35] Twenty-four of the parish's 211 heads of household were farmers. Among the various trades that of blacksmith was of particular importance, for not only did he shoe horses, provide a rudimentary veterinary service for sick animals and repair domestic utensils, but he also made or repaired a whole range of farm implements. Rakes, spades, hoes, shovels, turnip pickers, scythes and various hooks and cutting knives were all produced for the farmers and labourers who were the main source of his income.[36]

For the rest, men would

cut brushwood or turf, from the wastes for fuel. They made hurdles to confine their sheep, and basket-work of every kind and for every purpose. They dug stone or chalk, or they puddled clay and straw to build their cottages and cattle hovels, according to the materials which their particular locality afforded: they sawed timber for the framework and boarding of barns and sheds.[37]

In areas where the land was still cultivated in unenclosed strips in the large, open, arable fields decisions on crop rotations and on the general management of the soil would be taken communally at meetings of the manorial or village courts. Parish officers, like the pinder who looked after the pound, or the common shepherd who oversaw the joint flocks of sheep, would also be appointed on these occasions. As was characteristic of pre-industrial society, some men followed more than one occupation – like Robert Day of Stony Stratford in Buckinghamshire, who is shown in trade directories of the early 1790s as a carpenter, grocer, tailor, 'Staffordshire dealer' and house agent. At Cardington at least eight of the inhabitants had dual occupations. They included a shoemaker who doubled up as a shopkeeper and a maltmaker who was also a labourer. By such efforts they could perhaps earn enough to keep themselves and their families when the income from one trade would have proved insufficient. This solution, however, earned the disapproval of Adam Smith in *The Wealth of Nations*: 'The habit of sauntering and of indolent careless application', he wrote severely, 'is naturally . . . acquired by every country workman who is obliged to change his work and his tools every half hour, and to apply his hand in twenty different ways almost every day of his life.' Specialization – division of labour – was the only way in which efficient production could be promoted.[38]

Housewives, too, had regular outside employment as dressmakers, laundresses, nurses, midwives and labourers. In areas where cottage industries flourished many women were engaged in these. At Cardington in 1782 over half of the married women had an additional occupation, most of them being lacemakers or spinners of linen and jersey.[39] Even the children played their part, helping around the home, collecting firewood, gathering rushes to be dipped into tallow to provide lighting in place of expensive candles, scaring the birds, picking stones, weeding the crops, harvesting and gleaning.

Social differences between master and man were narrowest on the small enclosed farms of the western and south-western counties. Most farmers here worked alongside their men and landless labourers were comparatively few in number. Many of the latter would, in any case, hope sooner or later to make the transition to the farming class, as was the ambition of workers in Wales until well into the nineteenth century. In the pastoral north of England, too, where resident farm servants were common, it was the custom for employer and men to eat together around one big table in the kitchen and to discuss the day's activities.

Even in East Anglia, where a more capitalistic spirit prevailed and the number of large farmers was substantial, some small men survived. They were, as William Marshall put it, the same plain men which 'farmers in general are . . . living in great measure with their servants'. He noted another class, however, who lived 'in the kitchen with their servants, but eat at a separate table; while the upper classes have their "keeping Rooms" and other commodious apartments'. Despite these careful social distinctions, though, the view sometimes presented of English agriculture as a small band of large capitalist farmers employing a vast body of landless labourers is wide of the mark in these years. As late as 1831, when farms had increased further in size and many small occupiers had fallen victim to agricultural depression after the Napoleonic wars, the proportion of labourers to land-occupiers was still only five to two.[40]

These working farmers and their servants rose early. In dairying districts, according to William Marshall, the cows would be in the yards by four o'clock in the morning during the summer months.[41] In arable Norfolk the men also dined early – at twelve o'clock – and this was a custom which Marshall commended as well adapted to the county's farming practice of undertaking 'what are called two journies a day, with the plow-teams: the men reach home by dinner-time; and having refreshed themselves and their horses, are ready to start again at one or two o'clock for the afternoon journey'. He particularly praised the efficiency of the labourers:

There is an alertness in the servants and labourers of Norfolk, which I have not observed in any other District. . . . While a boy, [the worker] is accustomed to run by the side of the horses while they trot with the harrows. – When he becomes a plowman, he is accustomed to step out at the rate of three or four miles an hour: and, if he drives an empty team, he either does it standing upright in his carriage, with a sprightliness of air, and with a seeming pride and satisfaction, or runs by the side of his horses while they are bowling away at full trot. Thus, both his body and his mind become alive: and if he go to mow, reap, or other employment, his habit of activity accompanies him; – and is obvious even in his air, his manner, and his gait.

On the contrary, a Kentish plowman, accustomed from his infancy to walk, whether at harrow, plow, or cart, about a mile-and-a-half or two miles an hour, preserves the same sluggish step, even in his holidays; and is the same slow, dull, heavy animal in everything he does.

That the Norfolk farm-labourers dispatch more work than those of other counties is an undoubted fact; and in this way, I think, it may be fully accounted for.[42]

Such skills, when combined with the experimental crop rotations and livestock breeding carried out by the larger farmers, helped to account for the county's reputation as the leading agricultural area at that time,[43] though, as Marshall himself recognized, hard work and enthusiasm brought scant financial reward to the labourers themselves.

The social standing of the farm workers was as unsatisfactory as their economic position, for however important their role in the smooth running of village society, they had little say in the way it was organized.

It was their role to defer to their 'superiors'. And although it would be incorrect to imply that a quiescent acceptance of that subordinate position was accepted by all – the occasional outbreaks of rioting over high food prices or the proposed enclosure of common land are proof to the contrary – it is clear that there was no *sustained* challenge to the general framework of power and authority.

Eighteenth-century England was a country of immense differences in wealth and influence between members of the rural community. Parson Woodforde's annual income of about £300 can be compared with the £10 per annum and his keep paid to Ben Leggatt, the parson's farm servant, gardener and general factotum. But income differentiation could be far wider even than this. At the end of the century there were around 400 families who could be described as great landlords, owning at least 5000 acres and with an average income from land of perhaps £10,000 per annum. Below them came the gentry – a total of about 4000 families[44] – who might secure between £1000 and £5000 a year. They may be compared with farmers, whose earnings ranged from £30 for a man tilling around twenty acres (part of which he owned) to £700 a year for those cultivating more than a hundred acres. Village tradesmen probably fell into the £30–£50 per annum category, while at the bottom of the scale came the labourers. Despite differences in age and skill, their total earnings (taking into account family contributions from field work and cottage industries) were unlikely to be more than between £20 and £40 a year.[45] It is a mark of their poverty, indeed, that William Marshall could quote with amazement the Statfold labourer who, when he died in 1786 at the age of seventy-three, left £100. As 'an evidence of his care and industry . . . even in delirium, he talked about his work. . . . He thought more justly, and more clearly, than any unlettered man I have met with.'[46] If Marshall's eulogies were justified, £100 appears a pathetically small reward for a life of such unremitting toil, especially when compared with the annual incomes of the major landlords.

This economic leadership of the aristocracy and gentry was reflected in their social pre-eminence. At the head of parish affairs, as of the nation's business, were the major landowners. It was they who directed proceedings in Parliament, dispensed justice as members of the magistracy and presented the clergy to their livings often enough; and, with an eye to higher rent rolls, it was they who were the prime movers in the enclosure of a village's open fields and common land. The ramifications of this latter policy will be considered in detail in the next chapter.

Nevertheless, by tradition the benefits and privileges enjoyed by the well-to-do carried with them certain obligations – though ones which did not always accord well with the more commercial spirit which some were now bringing to the management of their estates. But in most communities an attitude of old-fashioned paternalism still survived. Landlords and their agents were expected to dispense charity to the sick and the old and to promote the welfare of workers on their estates. Some, like the Earl of Winchilsea, Lord Carrington, Lord Egremont and Lord Sheffield, put forward schemes for supplying labourers with cow pastures or other forms of self-help. In this they were following the recommendations of Nathaniel Kent, a land valuer and agriculturist who was for a time bailiff to George III at Windsor. In his *Hints to Gentlemen of Landed Property*, published in 1775, Kent proposed that every cottage should have half an acre of land attached to it, so that fruit and vegetables could be grown and a pig kept. More prosperous cottagers might also have three acres of pasture land on which to keep a cow for milk and to help feed their pigs. If workers could not afford to buy a cow outright, then one should be rented to them by the land-lord. Cottages should be well maintained for 'nothing can reflect greater disgrace upon [a gentleman], than a shattered miserable hovel at his gate, unfit for human creatures to inhabit'.[47]

Elsewhere a few landlords placed such a high priority on their good relations with their tenants that they continued to under-rent their farms. This was a practice criticized by Arthur Young as likely to lead to poor tillage: 'In no part of England where rents are low is there good husbandry', he sternly declared. The area around Derby was one which earned his particular disapproval in this regard. He considered that payments there should have been at least 30s. an acre instead of the 14s. charged. But the landowners hesitated to take action:

'the world will clamour – we shall be abused at such an alehouse – and thought very hardly of at another.' – Here lies the fact. . . . If rents were raised, they would have hats off with *God bless your honour*, but twice where they now have it thrice: and on rent day, a bow 6 inches lower than common with a long scrape, is far preferable to a blunt entrance; and then it sounds very prettily in riding through their fields to hear, *How rare a landlord the squire is*; and what crowns the whole, half a dozen tenants meeting at a hedge alehouse, and nothing disrespectful to their landlord passing. This is certainly popularity; and as great minds have in every age been much flattered by possessing it, we are not to wonder that landlords find it more captivating than 5s. *per* acre *per* annum.[48]

Interestingly, too, although in most districts money rents had become customary by the late eighteenth century, remnants of the old system

of payments in cash and kind still survived. Even on the advanced
Holkham estate in Norfolk early in the nineteenth century money rents
were supplemented by a requirement for tenants to provide a quantity
of straw each year (probably for brickmaking) and the free carriage of
estate materials on a specified number of days. On the Dorfold estate
in Cheshire during the 1770s and 1780s still more varied conditions
were imposed. One farm at Acton was let for eleven years at a rent of
£32, 'the best cheese, half the fruit of the orchards, and "boon" work
at harvest'.[49]

In general, though, a more hard-headed approach prevailed, as the
landowner's interest and concern for his estate spilled over into a
passion for land improvement. There were men like the famous
Thomas Coke of Holkham who took a personal pride in agricultural
innovation, improved stock breeding and rising yields. Books of
instructions were issued to tenants and they were informed which
rotations they were required to follow.[50] Farm leases on the Holkham
estate contained covenants enjoining progressive practices on the
tenants, and Coke's methods won lavish praise from Arthur Young
in the *Annals of Agriculture* as early as 1784. At the end of the
eighteenth century Coke also began his renowned annual sheep-
shearings, which lasted until 1821, and which developed from mere
conferences between himself and his tenants into the most important
meeting of agriculturalists in the kingdom, at which hundreds of guests
were entertained. Here were placed on view the best breeds of sheep
and oxen, the finest seeds to be used in laying down meadows and new
varieties of agricultural equipment.

Coke was not alone in his enthusiasm. Indeed, well before the middle
of the eighteenth century progress in fodder cropping, particularly the
growing of turnips to feed to sheep, had been made throughout
southern England, and experiments in sheep breeding had been set in
hand. From the 1750s the newly established Society of Arts offered
premiums and prizes for agricultural improvements. Thus in 1771 a
Mr Makins of Clare, Suffolk, received the substantial sum of fifty
guineas for inventing a plough which would cut 'hollow Drains'.[51]
But it was in the final quarter of the century, at a time when the growing
population was increasing the demand for food, that the reformist
spirit became widespread. The third Earl of Egremont even converted
800 acres of his park at Petworth into a model farm and held his own
cattle show. It has been said that men such as he 'could have talked
more intelligently and with more grasp of their subject, on the best
local rotation of crops or selective breeding of cattle, than most of the

whole-time farmers of their day'.[52] The king – nicknamed Farmer George – shared in the enthusiasm, contributing to the *Annals of Agriculture* in 1787 and 1799 under the pseudonym of Ralph Robinson, which was the name of one of the Windsor shepherds.[53] Two model farms were created under his influence at Windsor, one run on the Norfolk system and the other on the Flemish.

Publicity was given to the improvers' cause by the writings of Arthur Young, William Marshall, Nathaniel Kent and others. After the traumatic loss of the American colonies, Young began to publish the *Annals of Agriculture* from 1784 so that, as he noted, 'a general attention' might be given to British farming and 'the future dependance of the state may settle more on the basis of internal resources than on such as experience has proved to be insecure'. Agricultural societies were formed with the same intention. One such, operating in the Wrexham area in the 1790s, offered premiums for the best-bred stock, for servants who had remained longest with their employers and, in order to improve the standard of local ploughing, a prize of two guineas 'and a pair of buckskin breeches' to the winner of a ploughing match. Significantly, when the semi-official Board of Agriculture was formed in 1793 it, too, saw local societies as essential to the success of its work. They would be 'Points of intercourse between the Board, which ought to be considered the fountain head of all theoretical knowledge, and the common country farmer who reads nothing'.[54]

Countless landowners also took pride in the appearance of their own houses and gardens, and properties were built or altered according to the fashionable Palladian (and later, Gothic) architectural style. Their extensive building operations created much employment for country masons and their labourers. At Worksop Manor during the 1760s, reconstructional changes after a fire were estimated to have provided work for from fifty to sixty skilled craftsmen and thirty labourers.[55] In addition to those employed on the buildings, there were men engaged in supplying and hauling stone, timber, lime, plaster, glass, lead, slate and other materials. By the 1760s slate from Westmorland was widely used in aristocratic building in the north of England, with a consequent stimulus to employment in that county.[56]

These large mansions were surrounded by landscaped parks and gardens designed by specialists like 'Capability' Brown, Humphry Repton and their imitators. Landscaping became a major preoccupation on many estates. In *Mansfield Park* Jane Austen mocks the foolish Mr Rushworth, who confides in his friends his desire to improve his grounds to match those of an acquaintance who had employed Repton.

Without such a step he considered his own house to be nothing but a 'dismal old prison'.[57]

Unfortunately, their zeal for 'improvement' led some men to disregard all wishes but their own. This applied particularly in 'close' or 'semi-close' parishes, where property ownership was concentrated in the hands of a few people, who could decide whom they would allow to live within the confines of 'their' village. In 'open' parishes, where ownership was more widely dispersed, a greater independence was possible. In Suffolk and Essex, for example, where the land had been long enclosed, yeomen farmers continued to flourish, while in the Vale of Pickering in Yorkshire William Marshall considered there was probably no part of the kingdom 'which contains so great a number of *farms*, or rather parcels of land in distinct occupation'. In the township of Pickering itself there were about 300 freeholders, and no comparable area could display such industry and economy and such 'a personal independency . . . among men in middle life'. In some places cottagers, too, had access to land; the availability of commons, in particular, led to accusations by clergy and gentry that the men who used them were idle and immoral – 'hedge breakers, pilferers, nightly trespassers . . . poultry and rabbit stealers'.[58] Squatter encroachments in forest or wasteland were similarly condemned.[59] Although the complaints may have had a germ of truth in them, one has the feeling that the greatest fault of these people was that they did not fit neatly into the desired rural hierarchy. Their position was very different from that of the inhabitants of Milton Abbas in Dorset, where in 1785 the landowner, Lord Dorchester, in the interests of beautifying his estate, had the old hamlet demolished and removed to a spot which was hidden from his eyes. Although he built a model village on the new site for his displaced tenants, they were given no say in the matter. It was forced upon them by his whim alone.

Still less enlightened was the approach of Henry Cornwall Legh, who in 1791 decided that his house, High Lea near Knutsford in Cheshire, was too close to the main road. Without ceremony he arranged for the road to be diverted, and while the work was in progress also ordered that the Red Lion Inn be demolished so that its site could be incorporated into the park and the view consequently enhanced.[60]

Most aspects of the lives of the landed classes matched the grace and ease of their home surroundings. Domestic staffs were large; aristocratic families rarely employed fewer than twenty or twenty-five servants. Even gentry households would normally keep five or six.[61] Food and drink were consumed on generous lines. At the end of the eighteenth century the French traveller Faujas de Saint-Fond described the dinner he ate in one country house. The bell rang at 4.30 p.m. and

> we all go to the dining-room where the table is usually laid for twenty-five or thirty covers. When every one is seated, the chaplain according to custom makes a short prayer and blesses the food . . . entrées, the rôti, the entremets . . . all served as in France with the same variety and abundance. If the poultry be not so juicy as in Paris, one eats here in compensation hazelhens, and above all moorfowl, delicious fish . . . at the dessert the scene changes; the cloth, the napkins and everything vanish. The mahogany table appears in all its lustre; but is soon covered with brilliant decanters, filled with the best wines: comfits, in fine porcelain or crystal vases; and fruits of different makes in elegant baskets.[62]

Farmers naturally lived far more simply than this, though on the more progressive estates, where new-style tenants were expected to pay high rents and looked forward to reaping high profits, they, too, often enjoyed a comfortable life-style, with claret and port served when they had friends to dine. According to a contemporary in the mid-1780s it was not uncommon 'for one of these . . . farmers to spend £10 or £12 at one entertainment'. In other cases, where a number of residential farm servants were employed, households were also large. On one 2000-acre arable farm near Benson in Oxfordshire in 1770 there were seventeen men and five boys all living in, with five maids to help look after them. That was above average. But at another more typical holding in the same area, comprising 300 acres, there were four men living in, together with two maids. Even a 150-acre farm at Milton in Bedfordshire had four resident male servants.[63]

A large staff of unmarried male and female servants presented the mistress of the household with considerable supervisory difficulties. In January 1779 one Norfolk farmer's wife complained in her diary that she had had to turn both the maids away 'for raking with Fellows & other misdemeaners'. Just over four years later another maid lost her place when she was discovered to be 'with child by old Richard Mayes'.[64] A fourth girl departed when she was found to have left the back door open 'for the chimney sweep and then was saucy'. Other diaries confirm that these examples were not exceptional.

Nor was catering for resident male farm servants any sinecure, as the following list of fare given to harvest men boarded at a house in Cambridgeshire indicates:

6 a.m.   1 pint of strong beer, bread and cheese.
8 a.m.   Breakfast, cold meat and beer.

11 a.m.   1 pint of strong beer, bread and cheese.
1 p.m.   Dinner, one day roast beef or mutton (pork will not do), and plain
          plum pudding; next day boiled beef or mutton, and plum pudding.
4 p.m.   1 pint of strong beer, bread and cheese.
7 p.m.   Hot hash, or hot mutton pies.
          Saturday night an addition of good seed-cake of one pound,
          covered with sugar, and a quart of strong beer poured over it.[65]

Often on the larger holdings a maid was kept almost entirely occupied in baking and brewing for the farm servants.

In addition to overseeing these domestic matters, a farmer's wife had charge of the dairy, including, in some cases, the care of calves and pigs.[66] In Dorset, where farmers subcontracted their cattle to a specialist dairyman, it was the latter's wife who made the butter and cheese and supervised the feeding of the pigs, upon which the financial success of the enterprise depended.[67]

In the evenings mistress and maids would frequently spin flax and wool to provide yarn for linen, blankets and clothing for the family. In some areas, including Westmorland, Cumberland, Lancashire and Yorkshire, this developed into commercial cloth production or the knitting of woollen stockings, caps and other items for sale. Around Kendal Arthur Young found farmers' families spinning their own wool and then taking it to market each week. 'There are about five hundred weavers employed,' he declared, 'and from a thousand to thirteen hundred spinners in town and country.'[68] An advertisement in *Wheeler's Manchester Chronicle* for 5 March 1791 confirms the close links between agriculture and domestic clothmaking:

TO BE LET

A farm situate at Royston, near Oldham . . . called the Poultry House Farm: consisting of an exceeding good farm house with room for six pair of looms, a spinning frame of 100 spindles – large and convenient Barn, Cowhouse, and outbuildings, and about fourteen acres and a quarter of meadow, arable and pasture of Lancashire measure.
N.B. The tenant of the above premises in the last year kept one horse, four cows, one calf, and plowed three acres for corn.[69]

Likewise, holdings on the edge of the Yorkshire moors resembled miniature industrial establishments; the principal chamber was filled with card stocks and spinning wheels and an adjoining smaller room was equipped with a loom. Attached to the main building there might be a clothdresser's shop and a dye house, and close at hand a tenterfield. 'The small cluster of buildings sometimes included a tiny warehouse or "takin'-in-place", to which men and women came each week to collect materials to spin and weave in their own cottages.'[70] A young fustian weaver named David Whitehead described his daily round in Rossendale as 'to milk morning and night and weave fustian the rest of the day'. As mechanization and the factory system expanded from the end of the eighteenth century, these small producers were gradually squeezed out, though the process of their decline was long and painful.

Finally there remain the agricultural labourers and village craftsmen and their families. Although the craftsman's living standards were normally above those of the farm worker, both found difficulty in coping with the higher prices of the 1770s and 1780s, especially if they were without rights to common land or had little garden ground on which to grow vegetables. The increase in the size of the labour force ahead of the demand for it added to the hardships in some areas, as the worker's bargaining position was undermined and his wages were kept low. Estimates confirm the generally worsening economic position of the labourer and suggest that whereas purchases of bread accounted for 44 per cent of total family expenditure in the 1760s, by about 1790 they accounted for a substantial 60 per cent of that expenditure.[71]

Wage rates naturally varied according to the personal skill and age of the individual worker and his proximity or otherwise to more remunerative alternative employment (see Table 1, p.33). Records for a farm at Steventon in Berkshire show that among the resident men the 'tasker' or foreman was paid £9 9s. per annum in both 1779 and 1796; the under-'tasker', £8 8s. and £9 9s. respectively; the 'fogger' (or milker), £6 in each year; and the 'best teem boy', £3 per annum on both occasions.[72] On the Scottish borders, where the shepherd was an important figure, he was reckoned to be £2 a year better off than the ordinary hind during the 1790s, while hedgers and ditchers in that area were paid wages equivalent to those of the shepherd.[73]

Incomes were supplemented, too, by the earnings of wives and children as well as by the provision of perquisites, such as milk, meat or firing. Some men were also able to purchase items of food from their employers at slightly below market rates. These transactions in kind were useful to masters, too, at a time when the supply of small coins to pay in cash was often inadequate.[74] James Wood, a well-to-do yeoman farmer of Poxwell in Dorset, was one who negotiated with his men in this way – though to counterbalance it he only paid their money wages at intervals of several weeks, which must have made budgeting difficult.

Typical of the arrangements made was that on 28 October 1781 involving a labourer named Clarke. The latter was due to receive £4 for three months' work, but from this deductions were made of 13s. for wheat purchased, 2s. 3d. for barley and 3s. 11d. for forty-seven pounds of beef, so his actual cash receipts were £3 0s. 10d. Still more unsatisfactory was the plight of a female labourer named Mrs Davis who in July 1783 was paid 9s. 6d. for nineteen days' haymaking, while her son received 8s. for four weeks' work. From their joint earnings a deduction of 14s. was made for two bushels of wheat previously purchased; money in hand was thus a mere 3s. 6d.[75]

In these circumstances it is not surprising that in 1787 the rector of Barkham, Berkshire, David Davies, should discover that when rent, fuel, clothing and other items had been taken into account, as well as food, there was a deficit in earnings in most households in his parish which could only be met by charity or poor relief. Education was neglected, since if the labourer could 'scarcely with the utmost exertions supply his family with the daily bread which is to sustain their bodies, no wonder that he should so seldom strive to procure for them that other bread, which is to nourish their souls'. Few could afford the school fees of twopence or threepence a week, for this was 'wanted for so many other purposes, that it would be missed in the family'. Shortage of milk was the reason why families drank weak tea, despite its cost, while the dearness of malt prevented them from making their own beer. 'Tea (with bread) furnishes one meal for a whole family every day, at no greater expence than about one shilling a week at an average.'[76] By this time bread, with a little bacon or cheese and vegetables, had become the staple diet of labouring families over the greater part of the Midlands and the southern and western counties.

The houses in which the labourers lived also varied considerably in quality and quantity. At Selborne Gilbert White noted in the mid-1780s that villagers lived 'comfortably in good stone or brick cottages, which are glazed and have chambers above stairs: mud buildings we have none'. Elsewhere there were model communities like Cardington, Bedfordshire, which Arthur Young described as 'one of the neatest, best built' villages he had seen: 'most of the houses and cottages are new-built, all of them tiled, and many of brick, which, with white pales and little plantations, have a most pleasing effect'.[77] But these were the exceptions. Miserable, overcrowded, single-room cottages with turfed roofs, earthen floors and unglazed windows shocked countless travellers when they ventured into the remoter districts of England and Wales in the second half of the eighteenth century.[78]

Table 1 *Weekly wage rates in England c. 1770*

	Harvest	Hay	Winter	Medium	Miles from London
	s. d.	s. d.	s. d.	s. d.	
Hatfield, Herts.	13 3	9 0	6 6	7 6	20
Houghton Regis, Beds.	15 0	11 0	7 0	8 0	37
Wanden (Wendover Dean), Bucks.	13 9	11 0	5 0	6 4	49
Hatton, Yorks.	13 0	13 0	7 0	8 5	188
Yeddingham, Yorks.	14 6	11 6	9 0	9 9	225
Danby, Yorks.	7 6	6 0	5 0	5 4	235
Morpeth, Northumb.	10 0	9 6	5 0	6 0	291
Alnwick, Northumb.	8 3	8 3	5 0	5 8	310
Garstang, Lancs.	10 0	9 0	7 0	7 6	223
Pershore, Worcs.	11 0	11 0	6 0	7 0	102
Henley, Oxon.	12 6	9 6	6 6	7 5	35
Maidenhead, Berks.	14 0	9 6	6 6	7 6	27

From Arthur Young, *A Six Months' Tour Through the North of England*, vol. 4, 2nd edn (London, 1771), pp. 292–6. Young noted that he was estimating harvest at five weeks, haytime at six weeks and winter at forty-one weeks. He also observed (p. 297) that 'fifty miles round *London* [labour] is not so dear . . . as one hundred to two hundred; from fifty to one hundred is much cheaper, and upwards of three hundred vastly lower still; but from one hundred to three hundred the price is equal to the *London* ones. . . . Within those distances are included part of two counties remarkably full of manufactures; but many reasons will hereafter prove that this is a circumstance totally without effect.' Most readers will disagree with Young's final sentence.

	Harvest	Hay	Winter	Medium	Miles from London	Rise of labour
	s. d.	s. d.	s. d.	s. d.		
Tring, Herts.	14 0	10 0	7 0	8 0	30	
Blisworth, Northants.	14 0	8 6	7 0	7 10	61	⅓ in 20 yrs
Dishley, Leics.	12 0	8 0	5 6	6 4	106	,, ,,
Alfreton, Derbys.	11 0	10 0	6 0	6 11	135	¼ in 20 yrs
Wombwell, Notts.	15 0	12 0	9 0	9 11	172	½ in 20 yrs
Swineshead, Lincs.	21 0	14 0	11 0	12 3	98	⅓ in 20 yrs
Snettisham, Norfolk	14 0	11 6	7 0	8 2	112	
Aylsham, Norfolk	12 0	8 0	7 0	7 7	120	¼ in 20 yrs
Sheffield Place, Sus.	9 0	8 0	7 0	7 3	40	
Critchill, Dorset	13 0	6 0	6 0	6 8	100	

From Arthur Young, *A Farmer's Tour Through the East of England*, vol. 4 (London, 1771), pp. 312–13.

B

Fire was a persistent threat to the wattle-and-daub, thatched dwellings, for fire-fighting equipment was virtually non-existent, and the supply of water was sadly deficient in many villages even for drinking purposes, let alone for extinguishing fires. One blaze which broke out at the small Oxfordshire parish of Stanton St John, while the villagers were in the fields, had within an hour destroyed almost all the dwellings on one side of the street. Twenty-one cottages were consumed, together with barns, stables and house contents. Their inhabitants were left with only the clothing they had on. Immediate steps were taken to launch a charitable appeal to help them, and it is an indication of their poverty that fifteen of the householders estimated the total value of the belongings they had lost at less than £10. This included furniture, clothing and garden tools.[79]

In the industrial north and Midlands, however, the living conditions of labouring families were a good deal better. Thanks to the growth of competing manufacturing industries, agricultural wages were already beginning to outstrip those in the south, save for the London area (see Table 1), while the availability of cheap fuel made it easier for cottagers to have at least one hot meal a day. Potatoes were widely eaten, sometimes boiled with a little meat. Oatcakes (or oatmeal in Scotland) were consumed on the northern borders, while barley was the normal bread corn. Indeed, in the view of Sir Frederic Eden, plentiful fuel and 'the great variety of cheap and savory soups, which the use of barley and barley-bread affords' were the principal advantages which labouring families in the north enjoyed over their southern brethren.[80] Yet, despite Eden's comments and those of others like him, labourers in the south and the Midlands were not convinced. For them, wheaten bread was a matter of status, and they ate barley or rye bread with the greatest reluctance. They had 'lost their *rye-teeth*', the men of Nottinghamshire bluntly asserted, when they were assured that rye and wheat mixed made 'an excellent species of bread'.

Prejudice against the potato was equally strong, and although by the 1780s Dorset, Devon, Cornish and Isle of Wight labourers were growing potatoes quite extensively, elsewhere in the south there was considerable resistance. In Norfolk Thomas Coke spent five years experimenting with the root and persuading his tenants to follow suit. Their unenthusiastic response was that 'perhaps it wouldn't poison the pigs'.[81] Only under the pressure of bad harvests and high prices during the French wars did some of this southern hostility to the potato break down.

The division which existed between the labourers of the north and the south of England in the matter of wages and diet applied equally to their clothing. For cheapness many workers in the rural Midlands and south bought their clothes from shops, often second-hand, or from pedlars, or else they obtained them as charitable gifts from employers and local gentry. In Sussex Lord Egremont regularly distributed clothing among the 'sober and industrious' labourers; in 1797, more than 200 suits of clothes for men and women 'of the strongest Yorkshire cloth',[82] were said to be in the process of manufacture.

In the north of England, by contrast, almost every article of dress worn by farmers, mechanics and labourers was made domestically, with the exception of shoes and hats. In Eden's view, as late as the 1790s there were 'many respectable persons . . . who never wore a bought pair of stockings, coat, nor waistcoat, in their lives: and, within these twenty years, a coat bought at a shop was considered as a mark of extravagance and pride, if the buyer were not possessed of an independent fortune'.[83]

At the end of the eighteenth century, then, England was a country in which strong regional differences persisted, in regard to both agricultural production and the way of life of its inhabitants. In the decades ahead industrialization was to intensify those distinctions. Even modes of speech – dialects – varied greatly from one part of the country to another, and strangers were regarded with suspicion. As T. S. Ashton has noted:

To the southerner Lancashire must have seemed almost as uninviting as Newfoundland and its denizens scarcely less uncouth than the Highlanders of Scotland. There were marked differences in dress between south and north, and it could not have been easy to change from a diet of wheaten bread, beef, and beer, to one of oatmeal, bacon, potatoes, and buttermilk. The northerners conversed in rough dialects that varied bewilderingly between places only a few miles apart . . . and it was not uncommon for villagers to turn out and stone a wayfarer, for no better reason than that he was a 'foreigner'.[84]

Economically the position of labouring families in the south was worsening, and many men and women who were hard-pressed to make a living in the 1780s found their plight pitiful indeed when food prices climbed sharply during the 1790s and later. It is to those difficult decades of the French wars that we now turn.

Women weeding the corn during the spring. The young woman in the foreground has a 'grub' used for extracting thistles

2 The pressures of war

The times were peculiar: the country was at war with revolutionary France, the landlords were doubling their incomes, the farmers making fortunes, and industry flourishing. What then, was to be the share of the labourer?

It would have seemed but natural that wages should have risen, if not proportionately, yet in some commensurate degree. But such was not the case. In the year 1800, the agricultural wage was still under 10s., and had only risen about 15% since 1790. . . . The farmers objected to raising wages, because of their oft-expressed fear that the labourer might become independent, and that wages, once increased, could never be reduced, should bad times supervene.[1]

I now came to the village of Eltesley – a place so deplorable as I hope to be unmatched in Britain. – Are we to be fighting for the wrong of France? Are we to preserve Holland? Are we to think of nothing but trade – and to brag of our numerous ships? When our land is desolate, our poor oppress'd, and the interior of a country threadbare to furnish a tinsel fringe.
HON. JOHN BYNG, *The Torrington Diaries*[2]

By the last decade of the eighteenth century the standard of living of most labouring families had already fallen by comparison with that of their predecessors thirty or forty years earlier.[3] Food prices were rising as population increased ahead of the means of feeding it. After 1770 Britain virtually ceased to be a grain-exporting nation and within twenty years was relying on imports for at least part of her supplies.

Unemployment and underemployment became more serious problems, despite growing recruitment into manufacturing industry and canal building. The years 1791–3 saw a particular spurt in the construction of canals; the main link from the Midlands to London – the Grand Junction Canal – was launched in 1793 and completed twelve years later. Workers of every kind were engaged on its construction, from masons to build the locks and miners to construct the tunnels to cutters and labourers to excavate the canal navigations. Some of the cutters were agricultural labourers who had seized the opportunity for adventure and higher wages which canal building offered. Others were fenmen, who were long used to the similar tasks of digging and embanking drains. As the construction gangs moved across the countryside they disturbed the slow tenor of village life; fights, robbery and occasionally murder were the companions of their migrations. There were complaints, too, from farmers about the shortage of harvest labour which resulted where canal building was under way, and early in 1793 a number unsuccessfully petitioned Parliament to prohibit farm workers from cutting canals during the harvest months.[4]

Yet despite these developments and the fact that agriculture in 1801 employed only about 35 per cent of the work force as compared with 45 per cent three decades earlier, the number of people on the land continued to grow. It was a trend which persisted into the nineteenth century. In 1831 761,348 families were reported as engaged in farming as compared with 697,353 so occupied twenty years earlier.[5] Admittedly, during the war itself opportunities to enter the armed forces or, in counties like Hampshire, to work in the expanded naval dockyards and munitions industries led to a temporary fall in population in a few rural communities between 1801 and 1811; but it was not until the second half of the nineteenth century that rural depopulation became a major force.[6]

To add to the difficulties of rising prices and underemployment, there came, in 1793, the outbreak of war with France. Disruptions of trade and an inflationary government financial policy followed, while to increase the misery of the poor there was the disastrous effect of a series of bad harvests. Between 1765 and 1794 the price of the quartern loaf (weighing 4 lb. 5½ oz.) had fluctuated between a minimum of 6d. and a maximum of 8d., according to harvest yields. After 1794 the response to grain shortage was of an entirely different order; increases of around 100 per cent occurred in a single year. In 1795, for example, over a twelve-month period, the price of the quartern loaf jumped from 7d. to 1s. 1¼d., reaching a peak of 1s. 2d. by the beginning of 1796. It then fell back, only to climb to 1s. 3¼d. in 1801 and to the still higher level of 1s. 5d. in 1812.[7] Farm records confirm the rapidity of price increases in years of dearth. Thus Peter Pownall, who farmed in the Stockport area of Cheshire, was selling wheat in April 1795 at 42s. 6d. a load; by the following June the price had reached 55s. a load and in July 65s. On the other hand, after the easing of shortages following the harvest of 1796 prices fell back to 42s. a load by October of that year and 35s. a load by August 1797. Only with the renewed scarcity of 1800–1 was the upward trend resumed, and the price reached 64s. a load in September 1801. Oat prices, too, jumped from 3s. 9d. a measure in October 1796 to 5s. five years later. To workers dependent on cash wages these violent fluctuations must have been frightening[8] (see also Table 2, p. 44).

Various attempts were made to minimize the inflationary pressures. In 1795 Parliament sought to conserve scarce supplies of wheat by proposing that bread should be made of a mixture of two-thirds wheat and one-third barley and also by laying down that only inferior quality flour should be produced (that with the bran alone extracted). Later, in December of the same year, there was a prohibition on the making of starch and hair powder, while restrictions were imposed on the use of grain for distilling. In order to increase foreign supplies of grain, import bounties were offered, a policy which was also adopted during the other crisis periods of 1800–1 and 1809–12.

Efforts were made to encourage the greater consumption of potatoes, a campaign with which the Board of Agriculture became involved soon after its formation in 1793. Not only did it promote the experimental growing of the crop but the Board also repeatedly expressed its belief that 'industrious labourers' should be supplied with low-priced seed potatoes during times of dearth. It made forecasts of the state of the crops during the crisis years of 1795 and 1801 and suggested greater use of rice. Yet despite its semi-official status and modest government financial backing, the Board had little real influence.[9]

Potato growing, particularly on waste or boggy land, was also supported by the Select Committee on Waste Lands in 1795. Instances were quoted of landowners who had successfully grown the crop on their estates, like Mr Abdy of Essex, who had grubbed up a wood, 'dunged it with Twenty Waggon Loads an Acre, and planted Potatoes'. The resultant yield of 563 bushels of potatoes per acre had been secured for an outlay of only £16 13s. 6d.[10] Certainly, there is evidence that potato eating did spread from its northern strongholds to the southern counties during the war years.[11] On the Grey family's Wrest Park estate in Bedfordshire in 1800 the steward supplied seed potatoes to the poor 'to enable them to plant their Gardens, & those who have no Gardens the Farmers will allow to plant small peices [sic] of Lands Ends &c. &c. in the Fields'.[12] By January of the following year he was informing his employers that even 'very Respectable Farmers' were forced to eat barley bread, while the price of rice had risen too high for the poor to buy it: 'in this County all the Poor Eat *Barley Bread* and I

cannot see what Bread can be procured *Coarser* or *Cheaper*'. He proposed
to cull the 'old does' in the park, so that there might be venison to
distribute to the most needy, while two months later he was buying
barrels of herrings in London for the same purpose. Each barrel contained 1200 herrings, and the scheme worked out at a modest cost of
'rather more than a half-penny' per herring.[13]

These were just some of the devices adopted during the famine years
on one estate. They were reflected in the experience of landowners
elsewhere. Even the passage of an Act in 1795 governing the killing of
partridges and delaying the opening of the shooting season from 1 to 14
September was justified on the grounds that 'the searching for, taking
and killing of partridges so early in the year as the 1st day of September,
has been found very prejudicial to the corn then growing and uncut, or
cut and not carried'.[14] Later, on 3 December 1800, the king issued a
proclamation appealing to the well-to-do to eat less so that the poor
could have more. Farmers were asked to cut bread consumption in their
households to one-third of the normal level; no one was to consume
more than a quartern loaf per week or to make any pastry; and the oat
rations of pleasure horses were to be reduced.[15]

The press joined in the campaign; *The Times*, in particular, regaled
its readers with a wealth of economical recipes during July and August
1795.[16] At provincial level *Jackson's Oxford Journal* of 25 July 1795
published a series of 'Rules' to be observed by both rich and poor in
order to achieve 'Peace and Plenty'. Among the suggestions for the
well-to-do were that they should: 'Abolish gravy soups, and second
courses. Buy no starch when wheat is dear. Destroy all useless dogs.
Give to no dog or other animal, the *smallest bit* of bread or meat.' (This
concern over the feeding of dogs was perhaps one factor, along with
financial considerations, behind the introduction of a tax on the animal
in the following year.) Charity was to be carefully distributed: 'Prefer
those poor, who keep steady to their work, and go constantly to church,
and give nothing to those who are idle, or riotous, or keep useless
dogs.'

The poor, for their part, were to avoid drink, bad company and dog-
keeping, 'for they rob your children and your neighbours. Go constantly to church and carry your wives and children with you, and God
will bless you. Be civil to your superiors, and they will be kind to you.
Be quiet and contented, and never steal or swear, or you will never
thrive.'

A number of groups and individuals clearly took the suggestions to
heart. Soup kitchens were established in many parishes and collections

organized for the provision of cheap bread and other foodstuffs for those in need. At Bampton in Oxfordshire flour was supplied at reduced rates to two local bakers, who were to provide bread for between 300 and 400 people 'whose names are specified, whom they are to supply, in the proportion of one loaf a week for each; the loaf to weigh eight pounds, for which they are to take only a shilling'.[17] Parson Woodforde contributed to a similar scheme at Weston Longeville and on 22 February 1795 recorded that 'fifty Shillings worth of bread' had been given 'at 3. in the Aft. to the Poor of Weston. . . . I weighed two of the Loaves. The Sixpenny Loaf weighed 4. Pound, 5. Ounces. The Threepenny Loaf – 2. Pounds, 2. Ounces'. Similar distributions continued for a further two months, though it is clear that the parson did *not* follow the exhortations to stint his own diet.[18]

However, sometimes when charitable arrangements were made, supplies of grain were not available to meet them. In the Cardiff area, where a Committee was formed for the purchase of cheap corn, its chairman wrote to the government in some alarm on 11 July 1795 pointing out that although £2000 had been raised, this in itself had not solved the problem: 'notwithstanding Agents have been sent out with money to different markets in Gloucestershire, Somersetshire, Wiltshire, Hampshire, and even to London itself to purchase a sufficient Quantity of grain . . . the necessary supply cannot be procured on any terms'. He appealed to the authorities to arrange for 'at least five hundred quarters of wheat to be sent to this port. And as what has been procured with great difficulty will be nearly exhausted by the end of this month, the Inhabitants of this County in general are in immediate danger of being exposed to very great distress; they trust therefore . . . a vessel will be sent without delay'.[19] A second letter written three weeks later makes it clear that although assurances had been given that grain would be forthcoming, in fact the promised consignment had been landed at Swansea, 'So that we have not in the smallest degree benefited by that supply'. The Committee estimated that there was now grain sufficient for ten more days only and they appealed for a shipment to be sent direct to Cardiff for distribution over the surrounding countryside. As Table 2 confirms, the people of Cardiff and district were not alone in their distress, for during June, July and August 1795 at least a hundred similar appeals for wheat were sent to the Privy Council from counties as far apart as Cornwall in the south-west and Durham in the north-east.[20]

Yet if the needs of the poor were not relieved by charity, there was always a danger that riots might break out, as the more desperate

attempted to seize by force what they were unable to buy. Such outbreaks had three principal motives. First, they were concerned to
pressurize those who held grain to bring it to market: farmers and
millers were particularly vulnerable to attacks of this kind. Second,
they were designed to prevent the movement of food from one part of
the country to another. This was especially true when, during the
months of greatest scarcity, the larger towns extended their catchment
areas beyond their usual limits. By the early summer of 1795, for example,
London was drawing grain not only from the Home Counties and East
Anglia, its usual sources of supply, but from Hampshire and Lincolnshire as well. So great was the movement that the mayor of Winchester
complained that his neighbourhood was being 'drained to an alarming
degree'.[21] It is significant that during the shortage of 1795–6 there were
at least fifty disturbances at centres of communication, such as coastal,
canal or river ports, or at towns in heavily populated districts which
were being used as distribution points. Third, riots might be organized
to fix a 'fair price' at which produce was to be sold. As E. P. Thompson
has noted, there was a 'deeply felt conviction that prices *ought*, in times
of dearth, to be regulated, and that the profiteer put himself outside of
society'.[22] The same principle operated when action was taken against
those suspected of giving short measure; the guilty parties were threatened – as at Northiam in Sussex – with having their property burnt if
they did not mend their ways.[23]

Alongside these developments anonymous letters and placards were
used increasingly to publicize grievances and to threaten those who
were deemed to be exploiting the misery of the poor. Up to the 1790s
anonymous letters tended to be addressed to particular individuals –
usually the rich and powerful – but during the years of scarcity these
began to be outnumbered by appeals made to fellow workers or 'the
crowd', calling upon them to take collective action. They expressed a
growing sense of corporate confidence and determination and were
usually accompanied by threats of violence or arson if the complaints
were not attended to. Sometimes it is clear that the appearance of the
appeals was effective in encouraging the authorities to 'attempt to
restrain prices, regulate the markets, to institute subsidies or activate
charities, in anticipation of riot'.[24] An example of this occurred at
Bideford in Devon during January 1801, when the mayor informed the
Home Secretary that threatening notices had been posted declaring
that if the people did not have corn 'chiper within a mounth Bideford
streets shall run with Blood'. A suggestive sketch of a man hanging
from a gallows appeared beneath the warning.[25] Although that particu-

lar threat was not implemented, by late March mob pressure in the town had been sufficient to establish an informal scale of maximum prices to be charged in the local market and in those of neighbouring communities.

Riots to prevent the movement of foodstuffs, as might be expected, were confined to the exporting areas. Thus Lancashire, which relied on other districts for perhaps three-quarters of its grain needs, experienced no anti-export riots, while Cheshire, North Wales and Cumberland, which supplied corn to the county, were all affected.[26] In the Midlands the activities of dealers from Birmingham and the Black Country were viewed with suspicion. At Burford in Oxfordshire in 1795 the people seized a load of corn as it was about to be sent out of the parish, probably to Birmingham. One of the local magistrates was alarmed that this might encourage the Birmingham people to retaliate by coming to attack the town. Similarly, a farmer's wife in Norfolk noted anxiously in her diary that loads of flour had been stopped as they were on their way to King's Lynn. On this occasion the military were called in, and after four days the consignment resumed its journey under a guard of soldiers, justices of the peace 'and a large party of farmers'.[27] As Table 2 indicates (see page 44), unrest seems to have been most acute immediately after a sudden *change* in price, rather than merely at those times when a peak price level was reached. The figures for riots in north-west England given below are chosen because, although only regional, they appear to be the most comprehensive so far collected. Attempts to produce national statistics all apparently suffer from serious undercounting.[28]

If the appearance of large crowds demanding cheap food clearly intimidated shopkeepers, farmers and property owners, it is nevertheless significant that in most of the outbreaks a residual respect for the law persisted. Despite their misery, people were anxious only to obtain unadulterated, honestly measured food, sold at a fair price in the open market. They had no broader ambitions to overturn the economic order or even to loot. When the mobs found themselves masters of the situation, they rarely turned to plunder. Instead they organized their own distribution system, selling the food they had seized at what they deemed reasonable rates and handing over the proceeds to the owners. Thus at Cambridge in July 1795 a crowd of protesters forced local butchers to sell their meat at 5d. a lb. 'and some so low as 4d.'. However, the Earl of Hardwicke, who reported the case, feared that unless the magistrates could provide protection for those attending the market, country butchers would not venture into the city and the supplies would diminish.[29]

Table 2 *Average price of wheat per quarter in England in 1795 and 1800–1, together with the number of disturbances reported in the north-west*

	Price of wheat 1795	No. of disturbances 1795	Appeals to Privy Council 1795*	Price of wheat 1800	No. of disturbances 1800	Price of wheat 1801	No. of disturbances 1801
	s. d.			s. d.		s. d.	
January	42 0	—	—	95 9	3	136 10	3
February	44 0	—	—	103 1	4	144 10	—
March	45 4	—	—	107 8	—	156 2	—†
April	62 0	—	—	113 0	—	150 6	—†
May	64 8	1	—	121 1	2	127 4	—†
June	78 0	—	9	121 6	1	129 11	—
July	84 0	6	58	136 4	—	136 11	—
August	108 0	8	37	96 2	—	124 9	—
September	79 8	3	—	107 0	4	88 10	—
October	76 8	4	—	108 7	—	77 2	—
November	83 4	—	2	119 4	—	71 7	—
December	87 8	—	1	130 0	—	74 10	—

*For 1795 appeals for wheat supplies received by the Privy Council are also included; in 1800–1 the government played a marginal role in directing the supply of grain.

†In the *south-west* of England, however, food riots were widespread during these months, beginning at Exeter on 23 March; by the end of the month 'most towns in Devon and southern Somerset' had witnessed price fixing riots. On 28 March the two counties were described as 'in a complete State of Anarchy'. Trouble in Cornwall started on 9 April with riots at St Austell, St Just and Falmouth, quickly followed by Redruth, Liskeard and Penzance. There was also a revival of unrest in Devon. By May the disturbances in the south-west appear to have subsided. These differing experiences underline the regional variations in the incidence of the riots. *See* Roger Wells, 'The revolt of the south-west, 1800–1801: a study in English popular protest', *Social History*, no. 6 (October 1977), pp. 722, 732.

SOURCES: For wheat prices in 1795, J. Stevenson, 'Food riots in England, 1792–1818', in R. Quinault and J. Stevenson (eds.), *Popular Protest and Public Order* (London, 1974), p. 52. For wheat prices in 1800–1, *Gentleman's Magazine*, vols. 70 and 71 respectively. For disturbances in the north-west, Alan Booth, 'Food riots in the north-west of England, 1790–1801', *Past and Present*, no. 77 (November 1977), p. 90. For appeals to the Privy Council, Walter Stern, 'The bread crisis in Britain, 1795–96', *Economica*, vol. 31 (May 1964), p. 171.

It is clear that in years of dearth it was industrial workers, like colliers, tinners, and weavers, and the inhabitants of market and county towns reliant on outside supplies of food, who were most likely to be involved in riots. Rural labourers rarely took part, unless another group (such as colliers or clothworkers) provided the lead. This may have been due in part to timidity, but it can be attributed more readily to the greater availability of grain in the villages. Women were particularly prominent in many of the outbreaks in country towns. Their concern for their families was, no doubt, accompanied by the knowledge that their sex would protect them from the extreme rigours of the law, should they be arrested. Thus at Aylesbury during March 1795 'a numerous mob, consisting chiefly of women, seized on all the wheat that came to market, and compelled the farmers to whom it belonged to accept of such prices as they thought proper to name'. At Carlisle a gang of women and boys paraded the streets and, despite the remonstrances of a magistrate, 'entered various houses and shops, seized all the grain, deposited it in the public hall, and then formed a committee to regulate the price at which it should be sold'. At Ipswich there was a riot over the price of butter, while at Fordingbridge, 'a certain Sarah Rogers, in company with other women started a cheap butter campaign. Sarah took some butter from Hannah Dawson "with a determination of keeping it at a reduced price"', an escapade for which she was afterwards sentenced to three months' hard labour at the Winchester Assizes. Only the age of the prisoner '(being very young) prevented the Court from passing a more severe sentence'.[30]

By the summer of 1795 resistance to the movement of foodstuffs around the country had become so severe that Parliament had to assure farmers and others that if their waggons or carts laden with corn were seized by a mob, they could obtain damages – not exceeding £100 – from the hundred of the county in which the attack took place, should all other attempts to obtain compensation fail.[31] The main emphasis was on the maintenance of a free internal food market, a policy which was continued during the later crisis years. Yet it is clear that some magistrates, concerned only with the security of their area, took a narrower, more traditionalist, view than that of the government and exerted pressure on farmers and millers not to sell wheat or flour outside their own community.[32]

Elsewhere landowners and magistrates acted to compel farmers to bring their surplus stocks to market, and in September 1800 twelve Devon landowners even threatened their tenants with the non-renewal of leases if they did not comply. There was a widespread belief among rich and poor alike that profiteering farmers and millers were withholding supplies in the hope that prices would rise still higher. And to bolster magistrates' price-cutting efforts there were the anonymous letters which, like one circulating at Buntingford and nearby Hertfordshire parishes in July 1795, warned:

we will do some Mischief if you dont lower the Brade for we cannot live . . .
We have give you a fair offer to do it before you don have your Town &
Towns set on fire . . . we will begin on the One End and Continue to the
other. Be all of one Mind we can do itt because we cannot But be killed then
& we shall die as it is.[33]

Nevertheless, the extensive literature now emerging on food riots should not lead to the assumption that violent outbreaks were common, even at the most difficult periods. True, the *threat* of violence was often present, but the vast majority of villagers and inhabitants of country towns took no part in overt disturbances during the war years.

At the same time, in order to improve marketing arrangements it was officially reaffirmed that the offences of forestalling, regrating and engrossing to raise prices artificially were illegal under the common law. Thus in April 1796 one large farmer accused of regrating at Olney, that is charged, with buying $14\frac{1}{2}$ quarters of oats at the town's market and then immediately reselling it at 6d. per quarter profit, was sentenced at Buckinghamshire Quarter Sessions to fourteen days' imprisonment and a £200 fine. *Jackson's Oxford Journal*, which reported the case, pointed out firmly that for such offences 'no respectability of character can screen the offender from severe punishment' – a policy with which it clearly agreed.[34] A trickle of other cases came before the courts, though in practice, they were probably symbolic attempts to uphold the law rather than effective deterrents.

Throughout the war years, then, there was a persistent undercurrent of unrest in many rural communities. Apart from the misery of actual hunger, there was the knowledge that wage rates were failing to keep pace with the rise in prices. In the early stages of the war farmers were reluctant to pay their labourers more in case it should prove difficult to cut rates in the future, when prices returned to more normal levels. In Herefordshire it was reported in 1805 that wages had increased little for *forty* years. At that date they amounted to a mere 6s. per week in winter and 7s. in summer, except during the harvest period, when higher rates were paid.[35] In addition, workers received a quantity of liquor (normally cider) and two dinners per week. In Wiltshire, too, winter wages had only advanced from 6s. in 1794 to 7s. or 8s. by 1805, though they then jumped to 12s. by 1814. Overall the cash wages paid to farm workers perhaps rose by 75 per cent over the war period, at a time when prices had more than doubled. And although in some areas expansion of employment in industry or in the armed forces helped to increase the bargaining power of workers – and even created seasonal labour bottlenecks – for many men in southern and midland England the situation was bleak. Wage increases were granted tardily and, as Arthur Young remarked in the critical year of 1801, 'the quantity of food which a labourer could once have bought for 5s. would now cost him 26s. 6d., supposing he had the money to pay for it'.[36] Needless to say, most workers had not. Even in 1815, when prices had already passed their peak, average weekly wages in Wiltshire would only buy the equivalent of nine loaves of bread as compared with the equivalent of fourteen loaves obtainable in 1785.[37]

The situation was aggravated by the attitude of many farmers in ending the system of 'living in'. To some extent this developed from a penny-pinching desire to keep down food bills, as well as a wish to reduce the household duties of the farmer's wife. But it was a reflection of growing prosperity and social aspirations too. Cartoonists like Gillray savagely mocked the pretensions of men who were too proud to eat with their labourers, who kept a piano in their drawing-room and who sent their daughters to a boarding school. The 'smock was rejected for the cloth coat, beer for claret and [the farmer] became absorbed in the thrills of fox-hunting'.[38] Even Parson Woodforde commented on the changing times: 'Mrs. Howlett was at Church and exhibited for the first time, a black Vail over her Face. Mem. Times must be good for Farmers when their Wives can dress in such stile.'[39]

One victim of these new circumstances was a young farm servant from Quainton in Buckinghamshire, who was suddenly set adrift from his residential post early in the winter of 1800–1. He had then to live on 4s. 6d. per week wages:

through the dearness of provisions I was obliged to live cheifly on barley bread and hog peas except when my master gave me dinner when I went out with the team . . . but it being winter and provisions dear and many servants out of place I could not extracate myself from it . . . in consequence of the dearness of provisions he would not hire me servant so long as he could have me at four shillings and sixpence per week.[40]

Needless to say, such actions could only embitter long-term labour relations. In parts of the pastoral north of England and in Scotland the concern for economy and for social differentiation also prompted farm servants, who had formerly resided in the house, to move into bothies, where they slept and ate by themselves. In the Carse of Gowrie during

the 1790s this led to men subsisting on oatmeal and milk for three
meals a day. Brose was a popular dish among them because it could be
easily prepared by pouring boiling water on to the oatmeal, adding a
little salt and then eating it with milk.[41]

Only those who, like the labourers of Northumberland, were by
tradition paid partly in cash and partly in kind escaped the worst
privations. Surviving wage agreements from Ilderton, Northumberland, give an idea of such arrangements:

Feb. 1813.   Agreed with Thos. Jobson to be hind at Ilderton from Wh[it-
sunda]y 1813 to Wh[itsunda]y 1814 – to be as spade hind or any other
employment – to have as follows:

6 Bolls of Oats ⎫   A Cow Straw – and fodder of Turnips from the
4 Do of barley ⎪   1st of Jany. once a fortnight & £4 in money – 900
2 Do of Pease ⎬   yards of drills for potatoes – a stone of such wool as I
½ Do of Wheat ⎪   have or 10/– – finds a Bondager at 1/– per day for
[A boll weighed ⎪   Howing, hay Harvest and Coals led. Spins 2 lb. of
   140 lbs.]   ⎭   Lint & brings up a Clecken of Ducks or Chickens.[42]

The reference to a 'bondager' was to the system whereby male workers
were required to provide a female labourer, whom they recruited
themselves but who worked on the land for the farmer when she was
needed. Both the bondager system and other characteristics of the
Northumberland wage agreements survived into the second half of
the nineteenth century.[43] Interestingly, too, these conditions applied
not merely to farm workers (the hinds), employed on the Ilderton
estate but also to craftsmen, including blacksmiths, carpenters and
wheelwrights.[44]

Although payment in kind had the disadvantage of reducing the
worker's freedom to spend his earnings as he thought fit, in the conditions of scarcity between 1793 and 1815 most men must have considered that a price worth paying. But the bulk of the farm labour
force lacked such benefits. It was for them that magistrates, impelled
by humanity and necessity, introduced a system of wage subsidization
from the poor rates. As early as January 1795 JPs meeting at Oxford
Quarter Sessions had agreed that labouring families required 6s. per
week exclusive of rent to maintain a man and wife, plus 1s. for each
child, 'and . . . when the utmost Industry of a Family cannot produce
the . . . Sums, it must be made up by the Overseer'. Single men would
receive nothing beyond their ordinary earnings – a fact which was later
alleged to have encouraged early marriages.[45]

A more sophisticated version of this subsidy policy was devised by

Berkshire magistrates meeting at Speenhamland the following May. This linked minimum wages to the price of bread on a sliding scale, so that when the 'Gallon Loaf of Second Flour, weighing 8 lb. 11 ozs. shall cost 1s. . . . every poor and industrious man shall have for his own support 3s. weekly, either produced by his own or his family's labour, or an allowance from the poor rates, and for the support of his wife and every other of his family, 1s. 6d.' As the price of bread increased, so the wage scale advanced pro rata.

In other cases (for example, in the rural south west – and in Sussex) the rates were used to subsidize grain and potato purchases for the poor. In 1795 Lord Sheffield reported from the latter county that in parishes around Lewes it had been agreed that 'all above 8 shillings per Bushel for wheat shall be paid out of the Poor rate', while at Breage in Cornwall, where a decision to provide cheap food had been taken in October 1800, agents were sent as far afield as Helston in the early months of 1801 in order to secure supplies.[46]

During the war and its immediate aftermath Speenhamland and its variants were to be applied in most of the counties of England and Wales. Only in the north, where alternative industrial employment helped to raise cash wages in agriculture and where payments in kind were more common, was its influence limited. By later critics the system has been accused of pauperizing the labourer and his family, and while there is truth in the accusation, given the desperate circumstances of 1795 it at least had the merit of keeping alive a growing rural proletariat. As J. D. Chambers and G. E. Mingay have written:

The Speenhamland system came into existence as a sensible expedient to meet the distress caused by a temporary dearth of corn. But in 1795 it could not be foreseen that prices would continue high for 20 years, and in the event the wage allowance was adopted as a long-term solution of the problem of inadequate wages in those rural areas in which the growth of population, and lack of alternative outlets for labour, created a pool of able-bodied men in excess of local requirements.[47]

(The final years of the Speenhamland system and its eventual overthrow will be discussed in Chapter 4, when the whole question of poor relief is examined.)

Meanwhile, if the pressures and shortages of the war years created much social unrest and led to the introduction of wage subsidization on a large scale, they had a further, still more dramatic, influence on the

structure of village society through the impetus they gave to the enclosure movement and concomitant agricultural improvement.
Although enclosure by Act of Parliament had been gaining support
from the early years of the eighteenth century and had been speeded
up by rising prices and increased demand for agricultural produce
during the 1760s and 1770s, it was during the years 1793 to 1815 that
the greatest impact was made. In those twenty-two years around 2000
separate Acts were promoted, or about 42 per cent of all parliamentary
enclosure measures. Two hundred and eleven of them appeared in
1801–2 alone and in 1801 the first General Enclosure Act was also
passed.[48]

In some counties (such as Cambridgeshire, parts of Lincolnshire and
the Midlands) enclosure meant the conversion of a village's common
land and arable open fields, with their strip system of cultivation, into
compact, individual holdings. Elsewhere, for example, in Cheshire,
Cumbria and Yorkshire, it might mean the taking in of land from the
waste in order to create additional farmsteads. But whatever the
regional pattern, the ultimate aim was the same: to raise crop yields
and to improve the quality of farm stock. The enclosure of commons
and rough hill pasture, formerly overgrown with weeds or bare through
continual overgrazing, could lead to land being ploughed up and a
suitable system of crop rotations introduced. In Hampshire there was
much paring-and-burning of the sheep downs, in preparation for their
being ploughed up for corn. In other cases, as on the heavy clay soils
of Suffolk, dairy pastures were ploughed up to make way for the growing of grain.

Certainly, food production expanded as a result of these activities.
Total corn output increased from almost 15 million quarters in 1750 to
19 million by 1800 and 25 million by 1820. There was more intensive
use of the soil, as former headlands and other common walkways were
eliminated, while economies of scale were possible on the larger, more
compact fields. Admittedly, some reorganization of field layouts had
taken place before enclosure in certain communities, but this was
inevitably a piecemeal and often inefficient process, dependent on the
good will of many different cultivators.[49]

Thanks to improvements in breeding and in the provision of fodder
crops, the weight of cattle and sheep coming to market also rose, and
many farmers took advantage of the growing demand for animal
products to add to their stock. Of north Wiltshire farmers it was said
that 'even those who are professedly dairy farmers, can seldom resist a
propensity of applying a little of their best land to the purpose of

grazing their own dry cows, and of fatting a few sheep in winter, or taking in stock sheep to winter for the down farmers'.[50] In the midland counties of Buckinghamshire, Northamptonshire, Leicestershire, Rutland and Warwickshire a considerable proportion of newly enclosed land was turned over to pasture for the fattening of livestock rather than for arable purposes.[51] In parts of east Warwickshire this led to the bringing in, from the neighbouring county of Northamptonshire, of graziers who had the necessary expertise to make a success of the venture.[52] And in this connection there is evidence that parishes where literacy rates were relatively high, and where more educated entrepreneurs were consequently able to assess market trends, were the ones which enclosed earliest. As F. M. L. Thompson points out, for the farmer the agricultural revolution was mainly 'a managerial revolution, in the sense that the new husbandry required him to manage the resources of his farm in an orderly, competent, rational, and efficient manner in order to reap the rewards of larger yields, better stock, and greater income per acre farmed, which mixed farming offered'.[53] A better education could help him to make the correct decisions.

However, if enclosure was quantitatively the most important single movement affecting land usage, because it made all other innovations possible, it was both then and later a subject of deep controversy. In 1800 Arthur Young, once its strong advocate, complained bitterly of the way in which the poor had been deprived of their rights to graze a cow or a few geese by the partitioning of common land: 'I had rather', he wrote, 'that all the commons of England were sunk in the sea, than that the poor should in future be treated on enclosing as they have generally been hitherto.'[54] Subsequently he went on to call for the provision of adequate allotments for cottagers and to describe his interview with a Mr Forster of Norwich, who had acted as a commissioner for twenty enclosures. Forster 'lamented that he had been accessory to the injuring of 2000 poor people, at the rate of twenty families per parish. . . . The poor in these parishes may say, and with truth, "Parliament may be tender of property: all I know is that I had a cow and an Act of Parliament has taken it from me"'.[55]

The Dorset dialect poet, William Barnes, made much the same point in his 'Ecologue: The Common a-took in'. In this two labourers complained that if the common land were enclosed, they would have to sell their cow and geese, since there would be nowhere for livestock to graze. They would also forfeit opportunities to cut furze and briars for firing, while the children who were too young to earn a penny by working would no longer be able to go on to the common to collect

'A bag o' cow-dung vor to burn'. The precarious independence which
their existing way of life offered would be lost. As one of the men
declared, hitherto his cow had

... run in common vor to pick
A bleäde or two o' grass, if she can vinx em, ...
An' then, bezides the cow, why we do let
Our geese run out among the emmet [ant] hills;
An' then when we do pluck em, we do get
Vor zeäle zome veathers an' zome quills;
An' in the winter we do fat em well,
An car em to the market vor to zell
To gentlevo'ks, vor we don't oft avvword
To put a goose a-top ov ouer bwoard;
But we do get our feäst, – vow we be eäble
To clap the giblets up a-top o' teäble.[56]

Even the landscape was changed by enclosure, as fences and hedges
appeared in place of the open fields and commons. Men at Tysoe in
Warwickshire looked longingly back to pre-enclosure days when they
had been free to thread their way by balk and headland to villages in
the neighbourhood and to hold their Whitsun games at the Red Horse.
Now the Red Horse itself was penned within hedges, and those wishing
to visit their neighbours had to observe the new property boundaries
and to keep to the laid-out roads instead of making their own
way.[57]

But to commercially minded observers the mixture of wage labour and
peasant proprietorship which the old system encouraged was a recipe
for idleness and shiftlessness on the part of the labouring population.
At the same time it was argued that with the fencing, draining, ditching
and more intensive cultivation of newly enclosed land extra employment would be created for the rural labour force. This could only be
to their benefit and that of the nation as a whole. John Billingsley of
Ashwick Grove, near Shepton Mallet in the Mendips, an eloquent
advocate of improved farming techniques, described in critical terms
the influence of common land on the economic and moral character of
the villagers in his native Somerset. Not only was there insufficient
winter fodder for cottagers' stock on the commons, but

The possession of a cow or two, with a hog, and a few geese, naturally exalts
the peasant, in his own conception, above his brethren in the same rank of
society. It inspires some degree of confidence in a property inadequate to his
support. In sauntering after his cattle, he acquires a habit of indolence.
Quarter, half, and occasionally whole days, are imperceptibly lost. Day-

labour becomes disgusting; the aversion increases by indulgence; and at
length the sale of a half-fed calf, or hog, furnishes the means of adding in-
temperance to idleness.[58]

Other critics pointed out that the mixing of animals on common
grazing land made care in the breeding of stock difficult and led to
cross-infections, while sheep were especially prone to liver rot on ill-
drained commons and open fields.

Yet to those cottagers who lost out by the changes enclosure meant
the end of independence. Admittedly, the heavier crops required extra
hands for harvesting and for the winter occupations of threshing and
winnowing; fresh jobs were created in hedging, ditching and fencing
the newly laid-out fields – though often, as at Tysoe, this latter task was
one for specialist workers who moved around the countryside. On the
other hand, the enclosure of newly cultivated fenlands in Lincolnshire
created a labour shortage; men were brought in from villages five or
six miles distant to weed and till the soil. The wage earner here was
always sure of employment, and so great were the pressures of harvest
that Irish labourers began to make regular visits to help out.[59] The
processing of agricultural produce – the milling of flour, the malting
of barley, the drying of hops, the making of cheese, the curing of
bacon and the tanning of leather – also expanded during these years.
Yet for the labourer faced with war-time inflation and a Speenhamland-
type system of wage subsidization these were poor compensations for
the right to keep cattle, sheep and geese on common land or, in the fen
country, to fish and to catch wildfowl on the waste and to gather fuel.
In midland parishes where enclosure was followed by the conversion of
land to pasture even the traditional right of gleaning was lost, while in
those communities employment opportunities were cut back. William
Cobbett, writing in 1806, saw it as an inexorable move towards a rural
society in which there were 'but two classes of men, *masters*, and *abject
dependants*'.

For farmers who owned their land the situation was more satisfactory,
in that they had definite claims to allotments of land when the formal
divisions were made. Unfortunately, some of the smaller men found
the costs of enclosure prohibitive at perhaps 28s. an acre (though they
might soar to £5 per acre in some areas when road charges, legal
expenses, commissioners' expenses and other items had been taken into
account). Fencing was a particularly heavy burden unless the farmer
had access to cheap timber. For this reason it is suggested that wasteland
enclosures, where there were trees which could be felled to provide the

necessary materials, were particularly profitable.[60] At Wrest Park in
Bedfordshire the Grey family steward suggested that some of the estate's
poorest wood could be used for temporary fencing, and that large
quantities of quicks could be raised from seed to provide permanent
hedges as cheaply as possible.[61] But less affluent men lacked these
advantages.

So although the total number of small owners often changed little as
an immediate result of enclosure, the *personnel* involved could alter
radically. At Napton in Warwickshire half the family dynasties which
were present in the village twenty years after enclosure had appeared
within those two decades. While in Buckinghamshire parishes enclosed
between 1780 and 1820 there was a decline in original owners of around
40 to 50 per cent. In such parishes as Little Woolstone (enclosed in
1791–5), Little Brickhill (enclosed in 1796–8) and Stoke Mandeville
(enclosed in 1797–8) the decline of original owners was over 60 per
cent.[62] Admittedly, some of those who disappeared may also have been
tenants, perhaps resident in another village, who had sold their land
allocation in order to raise capital for the more efficient running of a
rented holding. But others, who had been on the fringes of yeoman
status, were pushed down under the new regime into the ranks of wage
labourers.

Those determined to meet enclosure expenses might do so by mort-
gaging part of the land or perhaps by selling off a few acres, in the
knowledge that the increased value of the remainder would make the
project worthwhile. A more serious problem, especially in the densely
populated midland counties, was the allocation of land to the tithe-
holder as compensation – though as a result the rest was, of course,
free from tithes. Particularly unsatisfactory, though, was the policy of
obliging the rest of the owners to meet the cost of fencing the tithe-
holder's land – a practice which led to hostility towards the clergy in
the communities affected. (The vexed question of tithes is discussed in
more detail in Chapter 5.)

An added difficulty in counties such as West Sussex, Surrey and
Cumberland was the custom of enclosure commissioners carrying out
a compulsory auction sale of part of the land in order to meet the various
charges. Of sixty-eight West Sussex awards for which details still survive, twenty used sale allotments as a means of raising all or part of the
costs. The sales averaged about 15 per cent of the area enclosed. Yet in
only two parishes did all the sale allotments go to existing owners.
Those who gained most from the arrangement were tenant farmers who
wished to buy land of their own and small craftsmen and tradesmen

who had played little part in the original allocation but who were now able to gain a stake in the soil.[63]

Finally, in counties such as Wiltshire, where the common-land grazing of sheep had been an essential part of the small man's economy, the provision of a tiny fixed area in lieu was of little value.

The man with £20 worth of downland found that his rights to the down were too limited. Instead of taking an allotment of sheep down, possibly of only 20 acres in extent and situated several miles from his home, he took . . . an additional allotment of arable. Deprived of adequate means to support his sheep, he was left with insufficient dung for his arable, unless the additional ground was suitable for pasture . . . in some inclosures the problem was met by putting the small men together, and directing them to leave their down-lands uninclosed, with common rights of sheep on all land, thus, in some way, making up for their now uneconomic size and loss of stubble rights.

In many cases . . . small men disappeared.[64]

On balance the economy as a whole gained from enclosure because of the impetus it gave to greater food production, but for the casualties of the system that was small consolation. Protest was of little avail. In those days of slow and costly travel few smallholders could afford a journey to Westminster to present their case against an enclosure Bill, and fewer still were aware of the procedures necessary to effect this. Occasionally violent demonstrations against a proposal took place within the affected community itself. At Wilbarston in Northampton-shire resistance by commoners to enclosure in 1799 was so great that two troops of yeomanry had to be sent to restore order, while at Otmoor in Oxfordshire attempts at enclosure of the commons were fiercely resisted in 1801 and 1814–15, though ultimately the measure was pushed through. Yet as late as 1830 anti-enclosure feeling in Otmoor remained strong enough to lead to rioting and the throwing down of fences.[65] These were the exceptions. Most people accepted unwanted enclosures with sullen acquiescence.

For the smallholders who overcame their initial problems and were able to hang on to their land, however, a ready compensation was found in the high war-time food prices. Evidence, indeed, suggests that the number of small owners may actually have risen over these years, as larger men from time to time sold off part of their land to meet their own enclosure and other expenses:

Tenant farmers and existing owner-occupiers provided a ready market for small parcels of land at this prosperous period [Chambers and Mingay point out]. The shrinkage in the number of small owners with the fall in prices at the end of the wars, and the fall in the area occupied by them, suggests that it was not enclosure but the level of prices in years of depression, and possibly the growth of alternative occupations outside farming, which were the important determinants of survival.[66]

Elsewhere (for example, in Wales and Cheshire) war-time enclosures of the waste noticeably increased the number of smaller holdings available for sale or rent.[67]

The French wars thus had a mixed effect on agricultural fortunes, according to where one was standing on the farming ladder. For land-owners, given the opportunity of increasing both the capital value of their land and their rents by enclosure, the influences were favourable, even though in some cases family fortunes were being dissipated with even greater speed at the faro table or through extravagant living in the circle of the Prince Regent and during the London season. In Wiltshire farm rents which before enclosure might have ranged from £15 to £40 per annum rose spectacularly to between £100 and £400 after enclosure had taken place.[68] Elsewhere more modest rises were recorded; perhaps the doubling of rentals was a commoner outcome, especially in the midland counties.[69] Normally the major landowners of the parish would initiate the enclosure proposals, and they would in any case have to agree to them, since to be successful an enclosure Bill had, by custom, to be backed by those holding at least three-quarters of the acreage involved. The enthusiastic comments with which the Wrest Park steward greeted his employers' decision to enclose indicate the main reasons why estate owners took action at this time: 'I am fully convinced, that your . . . determination to expend a considerable sum of money in inclosures will not only produce double the interest it can make in the funds, but will be a permanent and substantial improve-ment to the Estate.'[70] Even the expense of building new farmhouses on the consolidated holdings could be postponed: 'as the Tenant can reside . . . in his present abode, upon having a barn, stable, & foddering hovels built upon the spot'.[71] In this way capital outlay would be kept to a minimum until the benefits of the higher rentals had been secured.

The greater interest in estate management and the increased demand for men capable of surveying and dividing up newly enclosed commons and open fields also provided a stimulus to the professions of land agent and surveyor. Earlier the duties of an enclosure commissioner had devolved upon a whole range of people, including clergymen, farmers, schoolmasters and gentlemen. Indeed, not until 1801 did Parliament adopt a standing order which prohibited a landowner or his employees from acting as a commissioner in an enclosure in which he was an interested party. Among the new breed of specialists now emerging were men like John Fellows of Foscott near Buckingham, who served as a commissioner on twenty-nine different occasions, as well as acting as a surveyor on eight further enclosures and as an umpire on three more. Fellows, by origin a petty landowner and tenant farmer, was partly responsible for fashioning the field and road patterns, and sub-sequently the farm patterns, of about 63,180 acres in his native county, or about 13 per cent of its total area. Similarly, John Davis of Bloxham, near Banbury, Oxfordshire, worked in many counties in southern England from the 1790s to the 1820s. He was engaged on a total of 113 commissions and his known area of work extended from Leicestershire in the north to Southampton in the south, and from Bedford and Maidenhead in the east to Tewkesbury and the area around Bath in the west. On one occasion at least Davis was simultaneously engaged on twenty-six different enclosures. 'With a fee of up to four guineas a day, plus certain expenses, it could prove a very rewarding profession.'[72]

By the late eighteenth century land stewardship, too, had become accepted as a specialized profession on the larger, more efficient estates. Stewards undertook regular tours of inspection of their employer's properties, examined the condition of land and buildings, heard complaints, involved themselves in negotiations over leases or the purchase and sale of land and ensured that tenants were observing their agreements. Men at the top of the profession could earn very high salaries (like the thousand pounds per annum paid to the Duke of Devonshire's agent in the 1790s), while the more perceptive of them were able to take advantage of their position to build up small estates of their own.[73] In this way both Isaac Greene of Prescot near Liverpool and the Bill family of Staffordshire rose from yeomen origins to the level of minor gentry.[74]

Only the cottagers had labourers at the bottom of the economic pile had made no advance when prosperous times ended in 1815 and prices fell. Whereas the 'rent receiver received more rent than was needed to induce him to let his land, the farmer made larger profits than were necessary to induce him to apply his capital and ability to farming . . . the labourer received less than was necessary to maintain him, the balance being made up out of the rates'.[75]

Agriculture was not, however, the only sector of the rural economy to be affected by the changes of the war years. Domestic industries were influenced by the growing industrialization in the north of England and by the blockades and disruptions of overseas trade which accompanied the hostilities. As on the land, fortunes were mixed. The Exeter serge industry collapsed during this period as a result of the loss of continental markets, while at Tiverton the poor rates soared 'entirely from the want of labour'.[76] During 1794 makers of kerseymeres in the Frome area of Somerset, who had relied on exports to France, found their market ruined by the political troubles, though here at least cloth production had revived by 1800. At neighbouring Shepton Mallet the decline proved permanent, competition from Yorkshire being a powerful factor in its industrial demise.

In the west of England there was continued resistance to the introduction of new textile machinery. As late as 1803 most Wiltshire weavers had never seen the spring loom or fly-shuttle which had been employed by Yorkshire workers from the 1760s. Yet despite the problems of labour relations and the backwardness in the introduction of machinery, producers of the finest cloths in Wiltshire prospered during the war years. Unlike the Exeter serge makers, the hostilities aided them by removing France from major competition in international markets. Since the outbreak of the war, said one clothier in 1803, 'we have had the market of the world in our hands'. Only when peace was restored, and when French competition abroad and Yorkshire competition at home intensified, did the industry run into grave difficulties.[77] But in the years just before 1815 a good weaver in Wiltshire was said to be 'scarcer than a jewel'. Elsewhere – in Gloucestershire and Yorkshire, for example – the ordering of uniform cloth for the armed forces helped to boost prosperity, and Yorkshire obtained a large share of this work.[78]

On the spinning side in both the cotton and the woollen industries production was increasingly concentrated in factories powered by water or by steam, by the beginning of the nineteenth century, though some domestic spinsters still survived. From an early stage, however, most manufacturers preferred to rely wholly on their factory output. As a Wiltshire woollen employer declared, 'work was supplied with more ease and certainty from the mills, and therefore they could not employ the poor [outworkers] on any terms'. In Suffolk, where wool was delivered to home spinners by a packman, compulsory deductions of 3d. or 4d. in the shilling were made from the sums earned. So while a poor woman would labour twelve hours to earn 6d. by spinning and reeling, 'the putter out of wool or packman by order of his master deducts 1½d. or 2d. out of the 6d.'. Since the workers could not live on 4d. a day, despite all their efforts, they were forced to supplement their income with poor relief.[79] This sad story of insecurity and exploitation was to prove characteristic of the other home trades during the nineteenth century, as the pressures of northern industrialism and mass production built up.

Meanwhile such cottage industries as pillow lace and straw plait prospered during the war. Although the former traced its origins to the sixteenth century and the latter to the seventeenth, it was during the late eighteenth century that they enjoyed their greatest success, at a time when military action and protective duties shielded them from competing Continental imports.[80] Lacemaking benefited, too, from the settlement in England of French refugees. As the *Annual Register* for 1794 recorded: 'A number of French emigrants have found employment in Buckinghamshire, Bedfordshire, and the adjacent counties, in the manufacturing of lace, and it is expected through the means of these artificers, considerable improvements will be introduced into the method of making English lace.' Trading links were established with London and other centres of fashion, and local collection networks were formed, sometimes based on a public house or village shop. A whole range of specialist workers was also recruited, such as pattern makers, bobbin manufacturers and the producers of the large straw-filled pillows on which the lace was made. In 1798 Olney in Buckinghamshire had four men employed as pillow makers, two as makers of lace patterns and one who was a bobbin manufacturer. [81]

Though the earnings of lacemakers rose during these years, their working conditions in small, overcrowded cottage rooms remained unsatisfactory. The women were particularly subject to eye and chest diseases, brought on by continued stooping over the pillow and by the strain of following the intricate patterns of the fabric they were producing. One visitor to Buckinghamshire and Northamptonshire in the mid-1780s commented on their pallor and the 'frequent sight of deformed and diseased women' in the lacemaking villages. But despite the disadvantages, to the women and girls of the south midlands and Devon, where the trade flourished, the freedom which home employment afforded was preferable to the regimentation of the factory, the restrictive routine of domestic service or the low pay and irregularity of employment of work on the land, with its exposure to all weathers. At Hanslope in Buckinghamshire in 1801 there were no fewer than 500 women and girls engaged on lacemaking out of a total population of 1275. The lace they made sold at between 6d. and two guineas a yard, according to quality, and the women themselves earned up to 25s. a week.[82] Although few communities could match this intensity of production, it does indicate the attractions which the industry exerted.

Much the same applied to straw plaiting, although here the liberty of the worker to move about as he or she plaited removed one of the physical disadvantages of lacemaking. During the war the growing demand for straw hats and the cutting off of imports of fine plaits from Leghorn gave English workers their great opportunity. The industry was concentrated around the hat-making centres of Dunstable and Luton, though plaiting in some form or other was found in most of the south midland counties.

In 1805 the industry was further protected by the levying of duties on imported plaits, and at the same time methods of production were improved by the development of the straw splitter from around 1800. Whereas straw had formerly been split with a knife in order to make the finer plaits, it now became possible to produce as many as nine equal-sized splints with the aid of the new device.

In these circumstances the plaiting work force expanded; women, children and even men were recruited. Women and children preferred plaiting to field work and in 1813 it was noted of Buckinghamshire that while lacemakers or plaiters could earn up to 30s. per week, 'it can scarce be expected they would undertake work in the field at such a rate as the farmer could afford to pay'.[83] Arthur Young similarly reported from Hertfordshire in 1804 that after about six weeks' training a girl could earn about 8s. a week at straw plait: 'The farmers complain of it, as doing mischief, for it makes the poor saucy, and no servants can be procured, or any field-work done, where this manufacture establishes itself.' Around Dunstable children began 'to pick the straw at four years old; plait at five; and at six earn from 1s. 6d. to 2s. 6d. a week. . . . Women can earn £1 1s. a week on an average.'[84] There were also criticisms of the extravagance of dress of the girls and of their alleged immorality. These sour comments were to echo through the years, for although mechanization and fashion changes began to undermine the prosperity of lace soon after the ending of the war, in the case of straw plait collapse was delayed until the final quarter of the nineteenth century.[85]

Finally, we have to consider the war's most direct influence on village life – the recruitment of large numbers of men for the armed services. In all perhaps one in every six male adults was engaged in the hostilities, either by land or sea, and there were nearly half a million under arms in 1815 alone (two-thirds of them in the army).[86] Given the high level of payments made to agricultural parishes for the support of the families of men serving in the county militia regiments, it would seem that a considerable proportion of these forces was drawn from rural districts (including Ireland).[87]

In some communities the movement away of the men created a shortage of farm labour which could only be met by the greater use of migrant workers and of women and children. More than a century later a tradition persisted on the Berkshire downs of 'petticoat' harvests during the Napoleonic wars, when the women brought in most of the grain; in Herefordshire the harvesters were Welshmen from Cardiganshire; and in Scotland the Lowland harvest was reaped by blue-bonneted girls from the Highlands.[88] Machinery, too, particularly threshing machines, came into wider use during this period. In 1802 Thomas Wigful claimed to make threshing mills which could be moved 'as easily and safely as a waggon, from barn to barn, either upon their own two pair of low wheels . . . or, more simply, under the axle of the carriage commonly called a jill', which was normally used for hauling timber. The machine could be set to work within two hours of its arrival at a barn, was worked by the power of two horses and could, with extra attachments, be applied to cutting straw, grinding, and crushing corn.[89] Although fixed threshing mills costing £100 or more were already common in the north of England and Scotland in the 1790s, the production of cheaper, portable machines, coupled with the general shortage of manpower, soon led to mechanized threshing in the south, particularly after about 1805.[90]

In recruiting the men they needed, both the army and the navy relied basically on volunteers, though in the case of the latter service these were reinforced by men brought in by the hated press gang. Sometimes those found guilty of offences by the courts were also given the option of serving in the forces instead of going to prison. But, contrary to later beliefs, there is little evidence that the majority of men had any great patriotic enthusiasm for the military life. Even the desire to defeat France, the traditional enemy, did not arouse much fervour, and support for the various constitutional associations which sprang up during the winter of 1792-3 to support king and country soon dwindled away.[91] In 1798, when fears of a French invasion led to the collection of information about the number of men aged between fifteen and sixty who were not in the armed forces and who were willing to serve as impromptu soldiers should the need arise, it is notable that many parishes deliberately left this section of the form blank, though they filled in the rest of it. Others, like the villagers of East Stratton in Hampshire, gave a grudging response: 'The above persons are Willing to be arm[d.] and Exercise[d.] Within the parish of East Stratton, but not to go out of the said parish Except the French should land in England then they are Willing to march to any part of Hampshire to meet them.'[92] At Stratfield Turgis in the same county the reply was even less enthusiastic: 'None would say he was *willing* to serve'; while at Eastrop four men were prepared to act as 'Pioneers or Labourers' – 'if paid for it'.[93] There are many similar examples.

In Cambridgeshire it was necessary to issue an address on the probability of invasion, and to warn people that a 'very mistaken notion' prevailed among some of them that their condition would not be worse if the French succeeded: 'we must look to see what they have done in other countries . . . the poor labourers of Germany could give you such horrid accounts of their tyranny and cruelty to them as would induce you' to think that they would be 'less merciful to Englishmen whom they hate and detest'.[94] This lack of zeal for the struggle is a point to which we shall return later, when the question of substitutes for the militia regiments is considered. Suffice it here to recall that in 1773 Dr Johnson had remarked of the royal navy: 'No man will be a sailor, who has contrivance enough to get himself into a jail; for, being in a ship is being in a jail, with the chance of being drowned. The man in a jail has more room, better food, and commonly better company.' And for those who were seriously wounded on active service the future was bleak. Pensions were small; not all of the injured received them; and many must have found themselves in the position of a soldier whom Dorothy Wordsworth met at Grasmere in 1800. He was aged thirty and came from Cockermouth. He had lost a leg and thigh in battle and was travelling with a donkey towards his home, though with little prospect of employment when he got there.[95] Furthermore, once a man had left his home community and joined his regiment or ship he was unlikely to have much contact with his family again until he was demobilized. The notebooks of Samuel Whitbread show that sometimes an anxious relative would inquire after a loved one to see if he was still alive or not. On 19 September 1813 a man came to Whitbread to find out about his brother, who was a private in the Coldstream Guards; after investigation, Whitbread was able to tell him that he had not 'been killed or wounded at the . . . siege of San Sebastian'.[96] To people who rarely strayed farther than the nearest market town even mere travel to Spain must have seemed a daunting adventure which most had no desire to embark upon.

Seamen were normally recruited from the coastal areas, since candidates from there were most likely to have had relevant experience of life afloat, but under pressure of war the inland counties, too, were given quotas of men to be raised for both the navy and the army. In March 1795, for example, Oxfordshire was required to raise 127 men for naval service, recruited from the various parishes or groups of parishes in the county. Bounties were offered, financed by the levying of a special rate, and parish officers who neglected their obligations could be fined.[97] Similar policies were adopted for army recruitment and even (as in 1796) for the raising of horses for the cavalry. In December of that year it was ordered that one-tenth of a county's horses be set aside to enable the king to raise a fresh cavalry force. Again in 1798 and 1803, when French invasions were feared, the contingency plans drawn up included the taking of a census of horses, waggons, carts and corn mills in the various parishes. In some cases, as in Berkshire and Hampshire, details were also taken of the stocks of grain, farm animals and hay held, as well as of available weapons. Thus Hartley Whitney in Hampshire, with a total of 132 men aged between fifteen and sixty, was able to muster ten who were armed with swords and five who possessed pistols; perhaps rather more useful were the thirty who owned billhooks or the forty-six with pickaxes.[98] Five of the men were Quakers who, as in other places, refused to take up arms of any kind.

In these contingency arrangements withdrawal routes were planned in the coastal districts for the movement of the infirm, the sick, and the women and children, should an invasion take place. In east Yorkshire, after more than eighty years, people could remember the rows of waggons which stood for weeks on end in the village streets during 1803. Each was numbered to prevent confusion and had four horses allocated to it. A surviving evacuation ticket for a family from Hornsea in Holderness in 1798 shows that the people concerned were not only allocated to a particular waggon but were told to bring with them 'a Change of Linen, and one Blanket for each Person, wrapped up in the Coverlid of your Bed, and bring with you all the Food in your possession'.[99]

Inevitably, the need for men, horses and tax revenue for the war imposed heavy burdens on agriculturalists, which counterbalanced some of the benefits they enjoyed from high food prices. Nor was it easy for parishes to raise their allotted 'volunteers', even with the aid of bounties. Many were forced to advertise in the newspapers. Thus Henley-on-Thames appealed for four volunteers for the army in December 1796 and offered a bounty 'of Fifteen Guineas, and a Crown to drink the King's Health . . . to each Volunteer'. Naval recruitment was still more unpopular – and expensive; the parish of Lower Slaughter in Gloucestershire (to quote but one example) offered a bounty of twenty guineas to raise one volunteer. In Denbigh at the beginning of April 1795 the mere rumour that more men were to be recruited for the armed forces was enough to bring a mob on to the streets. As one distressed magistrate informed the Home Secretary, they uttered 'much seditious & disagreeable Language . . . it is impossible for us to inforce the Execution of any Civil Process against so great a Body of lawless Banditti; neither will it be in our Power to carry either the Militia or Navy Acts into Force without Military Assistance'.[100] Several weeks later unrest was still reported in parts of the county.

By comparison with the discipline, hardships and dangers faced by men in the regular armed forces, the duties of those in the yeomanry and other volunteer regiments or in the county militia were a good deal less onerous. The latter were recruited by ballot from among the able-bodied men of a county and could not be called upon to serve outside the British Isles – and sometimes not even outside their own county. In theory the ballot system was a fair one; the men who were selected were able to rely upon the parish poor rates to support their families whilst they were away, something that was not available to the families of regular soldiers. But despite this theoretical fairness, it was all too easy for the 'tricks and wiles of rude and illiterate deputy-lieutenants and servile parish clerks, all intent upon doing some job in favour of some rustic friend or to the prejudice of some rustic enemy' to corrupt the system. It was also possible for men chosen through the ballot to provide substitutes, at a price, if they did not wish to take their allotment. In George Eliot's novel *Adam Bede* Adam has to spend his painfully accumulated savings to free his brother 'from going for a soldier', while at Bledington in Gloucestershire, poor unemployed men not drawn in the ballot could usually be persuaded to take money to serve in the place of those who were.[101] Interestingly enough, of forty-five men balloted at Bromley in Kent in March 1797 only one agreed to serve on his own account, and he was a labourer. Of the forty-four substitutes, twenty-one were labourers, six were grooms and four were indoor servants. One 'gentleman' who was drawn sent his forty-five-year-old butler in lieu.[102]

Military duties were clearly regarded by most people as inconvenient interruptions to the serious business of earning a living. So, ironically, those with property – and, presumably, with the most to lose if the French landed – were often the most backward in taking arms to defend it. A Norfolk farmer's daughter wrote that although some of the women in her village were quite terrified at the prospect of an invasion in the summer of 1803, her own two brothers had resolved not to leave home 'till the French come'.[103] And a man from Princes Risborough, Buckinghamshire, in the same year was so determined not to enter the militia that he offered a labourer from a parish several miles away the substantial sum of twenty-two guineas to go in his stead. He also primed the man well with ale and gave him three shillings worth of ribbons – only to find at the last moment that the proposed substitute would not go to Aylesbury to be enrolled.[104]

From time to time, as at Carlisle in the mid-1790s, men who had been listed for the ballot would gang up to seize and destroy the returns in a vain hope of evading call-up, while some of the more cautious took out an insurance policy to protect themselves against selection. In November 1796 the Berks, Bucks, Oxon. and Hants Original Militia Society Office for Providing Substitutes for the New and Old Militia offered to find a 'proper substitute' for any subscriber who would pay an annual fee of one guinea, adding carefully: 'Subscribers who are balloted must be accountable for the Bounty Money allowed by the Parish; and Persons who, at the Time of paying their Subscriptions, shall have been actually balloted, will not be entitled to the Benefits of this Society . . . No Subscriptions will be received on the Day of Drawing.'[105] Informal village organizations were also set up. At Letheringsett in Norfolk Mary Hardy, a farmer's wife, recorded in her diary on 12 December 1796 that a meeting 'of the people liable to be drawn for the militia' had been held and a subscription raised 'in favour of those that may be drawn'.[106]

In the pursuit of substitutes men were brought in from other counties. In 1796 the 600 or so privates of the Oxfordshire militia included forty-three men from Coventry, sixteen from Abingdon (then in Berkshire), thirty-three from rural Warwickshire and six each from rural Buckinghamshire and Berkshire; there were even recruits from as far away as Shropshire and Suffolk.[107] Three years later, when the number of militia privates had risen to around 1000, about one in six of them was a substitute recruited from outside Oxfordshire. Many more men were recruited from within the county, like the Adderbury weaver who acted as a substitute for a fellow weaver from the nearby parish of Bloxham.[108]

The role of the militia often seems to have been that of a surrogate police force, ready to put down internal 'riots and tumults', though militiamen might be used as escorts for French prisoners of war and as guardians of England's south-east coast against possible French invasion. They also did garrison duty in Ireland.[109]

C

Privately raised volunteers, on the other hand, had rather more freedom of action. At the turn of the century when, as he wrote, 'the country was chin-deep in the fears of invasion & every month was filled with the terrors which Bonaparte had spread in other countries', John Clare, the Northamptonshire farm labourer poet, took part in one such scheme, in the vicinity of his native Helpstone:

we had a cross-graind sort of choice left us which was to be forced to be drawn & go for nothing or take on as volunteers for a bounty of two guineas I accepted the latter & went with a neighbours son W. Clarke to Peterborough to be sworn on & prepard to join the regiment at Oundle. [T]he morning we left home our mothers parted with us as if we were going to Botany Bay & people got at their doors to bid us farewell & greet us with a Job's comfort that they doubted we should see Helpstone no more . . . when we got to Oundle the place of quartering we were drawn out into the fields & a more motley multitude of lawless fellows was never seen in Oundle before & hardly out of it there were 1300 of us . . . I was one of the shortest & therefore my station is evident I was in that mixed multitude called the batallion which they nicknamed 'bum-tools' for what reason I cannot tell . . . some took lodgings but lodgings were very expensive . . . so I was obligd to be content with the quarters alloted me which were at the Rose & Crown Inn. . . .[110]

After several weeks spent in ineffective military training, Clare was allowed to return home, to hold himself in readiness for recall should it prove necessary.

On the last time we was calld up there was a fresh bounty set on foot of a further 2 guineas to those who woud enlist for extended service as they calld it to be sent so many miles out of the country to guard barracks castles or any other urgencys that might happen five shillings of which was to be paid down & the rest to be given when they were wanted . . . I felt purposes enew for the 5 shillings & when it was offerd me I took it without further enquirey & never heard further about it.[111]

The chaotic administration he describes seems to have been typical of many volunteer forces and militia regiments. Pay and rations were particularly unsatisfactory in the latter, for the five pence a day allowed each man for food was little use in time of inflation. One Buckinghamshire militiaman, Joseph Mayett, was even forced to write home to his father to ask him to sell a coat he had left behind in order that the money might be sent on to him to buy food.[112] There were occasional mutinies among militiamen as a result of the treatment they received, though after 1800 better organization and an improved food supply reduced some of the tensions.[113]

The arrangements for the defence of the realm itself were equally haphazard. In 1807, for example, proposals were made in east Yorkshire to train all available men in the use of pikes to repel the invader – rather along the lines of the Home Guard recruited in Britain during the second world war. As the military commander of the district dryly remarked, however: 'The civilians do not feel much confidence in the advantage they may derive from the use of a pike against an enemy with firearms, perhaps a proportion of pistols carried in the girdle by Pikemen might tend to give some additional confidence.'[114]

The same attitude of make-do-and-mend, which kept military duties very much on the periphery of the average man's daily experience, was also present in a report on the defensive position of Pembrokeshire, received by the government in 1795:

To begin with the Southern district. In this division there was to *A Troop of Cavalry*, & *a Company of Infantry*, at *Pembroke*. The Troop of Cavalry has been raised, enrolled & armed by Mr. Campbell; it is perfectly established on the plan proposed & approved by the Ld. Lt. [Lord-Lieutenant] at a county meeting & is the only corps in the County that the civil power can depend upon in the case of tumults.

The Pembroke Company commanded by Capt[n.] Ackland is enrolled & officered; it consists of 76 privates – They have *no clothing* & have only 25 *stand* of arms; by their *instructions* & *attestations* they cannot be ordered more than 5 Miles from Pembroke, except in case of invasion. In short, the literal plan of Government for raising companies of Infantry for maning batteries on the coast is that upon which the Pembroke company is form'd. Now no place within 5 Miles of Pembroke exists, where such a body of men can be of use; & they can have no occasion for batteries to defend the Town of Pembroke. Capt[n.] Ackland is sensible that they cannot be of use, unless they are *cloathed & armed* & their service can *be depended* on any where *within the County* to repress tumults. This company may be rendered effective, only by authorising Capt[n.] Ackland to discharge the men of their present engagements; to enroll them all again as a company of Infantry on the same establishment as the Fisgard Volunteers, but subjecting them to the call of the Ld. Lieut. & Sheriff of the County in case of tumults. This force thus modell'd is considered sufficient for the protection of the Southern district.[115]

It will be noted that it was against internal discontent rather than a threat from an external foe that protection was principally to be provided.

It was fortunate that the much-needed reorganization of the Pembroke

men was soon carried out. For to the surprise of many it was in this
quiet corner of south Wales that a French invasion force of almost
1400 men suddenly came ashore in February 1797. It was the only
serious landing of the enemy on the British mainland during the whole
war. The unexpected arrival of the French on the coast near Fishguard
naturally aroused much alarm among the Welsh peasantry, and families
hastily moved themselves and their portable property inland. Luckily, the
threat did not prove very formidable. The French troops were poorly
led; they seem to have had little idea of the purpose of their landing; and
many of them became drunk on the large stocks of liquor they unearthed
– for the district was at that time a great centre for smuggling. Meanwhile, the local gentry were mobilizing an opposition force of militiamen and volunteers. Under the leadership of Lord Cawdor about 660
troops were gathered together, not one of whom 'had ever fired a
musket, except for amusement, yet they proceeded against the enemy
with the most cheerful alacrity', according to the *Annual Register*.[116] In
addition, some of the local farmers armed themselves with pikes and
scythes, while at St David's lead was taken from the cathedral and cast
into bullets. Lord Cawdor ranged his little army in a way calculated
to impress the enemy with an exaggerated idea of its size, and the ruse
proved successful. The demoralized Frenchmen, with their American
commander William Tate, speedily surrendered and were marched off
to Haverfordwest and imprisonment.[117] The invasion thus came to a
rapid end. But the impartial observer cannot but wonder how the small
tradesmen, farmers and labourers who made up the bulk of the militia
and volunteer regiments would have fared had serious trouble arisen.
Happily, thanks to the existence of the English Channel and the Royal
Navy, their capabilities were never put to the test against a determined
foreign enemy.

So it was that the war years passed. For some they were a period of
great change and suffering. For others, particularly landlords involved
in agricultural improvement and the more efficient farmers, they were
a time of prosperity. After 1815, the economic picture was to be
transformed yet again, as the country adjusted itself to the opportunities
and problems of peace.

Reaping wheat

Threshing

3 The post-war world

So far as the present depression in the markets of Agricultural produce is the effect of abundance from our own growth, the inconvenience arises from a cause which no legislative provision can alleviate; so far as it is the result of the increased value of our money, it is one not peculiar to the farmer, but which has been and still is experienced by many other classes of society. That result however is the more severely felt by the tenant, in consequence of its coincidence with an overstocked market, especially if he be farming with a borrowed capital and under the engagements of a lease; and it has hitherto been further aggravated by the comparative slowness with which prices generally, and particularly the price of labour, accommodate themselves to a change in the value of money.
Report from the Committee on the Depressed State of Agriculture in the United Kingdom.[1]

Some tumultuous proceedings have recently taken place throughout the county of *Kent*, arising from the outrageous conduct of agricultural mobs of the lower classes going about demolishing the threshing machines of the farmers. A body of men, amounting to upwards of 200 in number, lately assembled at the respective residences of Sir Henry Oxenden, Sir Henry Tucker Montresor, Mr. Kelcey, Mr. Holtum, and Mr. Sankey, farmers, and violently broke into their barns, where they destroyed the thrashing-machines they found in them respectively. At the adjourned meeting of the magistrates and other gentlemen of East Kent, held on the 12th of Oct. at Canterbury . . . it was resolved to offer a reward of 500 l. for the discovery of these incendiaries. The Lords of the Treasury have also offered a reward of 100 l. for the discovery and apprehension of the offenders who set fire to and burnt the barns and cornstacks belonging to the Rev. Mr. Price, of Lyminge, on the night of the 5th Oct.
Gentleman's Magazine (1830)[2]

The prosperity of landowners and farmers during the Napoleonic wars had been built on the uncertain foundations of food scarcity caused by

trade blockade and bad harvests. But by 1813, even before the Battle
of Waterloo, there were signs that the era of very high prices was at an
end. The 1813 harvest proved to be one of the most abundant in
history and, as a result, by December of that year wheat had fallen to
75s. 10d. a quarter, as compared with the unprecedented level of 155s.
per quarter secured in August 1812.[3] Both 1814 and 1815 brought
further price falls. With the prospect of peace – and thus of cheap
imports of grain from the Continent – looming ahead, agriculturalists
began to mobilize in favour of protection of the home market. They
argued that with higher rents, rates and taxes, plus the heavy cost of
farm improvements, it was no longer possible for the British producer
to show a profit if the price of wheat fell below 80s. a quarter. By
contrast, European farmers in the most favoured areas could produce
their wheat at 40s. a quarter.

Against this background petitions flooded into Parliament from
landowners and occupiers calling for a new Corn Bill. One from Devon
pointed out that the 'poor-houses were filled with agricultural labourers
deprived of their usual employment in consequence of the discourage-
ment of agriculture'.[4] To less committed observers seasonal factors
and the demobilization of men from the armed forces were more
likely to be responsible for this than a mere fall in prices. Nevertheless,
despite vehement protests from the manufacturing districts, food riots
in London and the arguments of more perceptive critics that protection
from *foreign* competition would not in itself guarantee high *domestic*
prices, the agriculturalists' claims were accepted. Given that both
Houses of Parliament were dominated by the landed interest, this was
scarcely surprising. In 1815 the new Corn Law appeared on the statute
book.

Under its provisions foreign corn could be imported and warehoused
duty-free at any time but could only be sold when the home market
price reached 80s. a quarter or, in the case of barley and oats, 40s. and
27s. per quarter respectively. Thanks to colonial preference, special lower
price limits applied to grain imported from British North America.

However, as early as 15 March 1815, when the Corn Bill was passing
through the Upper House, Lord Grenville had pointed out that
although farmers might be able to grow sufficient corn to feed the
country, 'in order to do so in an average of seasons, they must grow
too much in a plentiful season'. He wanted to know how they were to
dispose of the surplus. If there were no answer to that question, then
the object of the Bill would be defeated and farmers would become
'more distressed than they probably were at present'.[5]

Within a few months agriculturalists were to discover the truth of this comment, for to add to the domestic variations in price caused by harvest yields there were the fluctuations created by the constant switching on and off of the import tap, as prices moved above and below the cut-off level. When domestic harvests were abundant, as they were in 1815 and 1822, protection could not prevent prices from falling. This was especially the case when external factors were at work which reinforced the downward trend. Industry was depressed, thanks to necessary post-war adjustments in production and trade, and this inevitably affected consumption of agricultural produce. In addition, the decision of the government in 1819 to restore the currency to the pre-war gold standard and to end the issue of war-time paper money caused general deflation, particularly after 1821, when the scheme came into effective operation. As the Committee investigating the depressed state of agriculture in that year declared, they could not 'but ascribe a proportion of the depression of prices . . . to the measures which the restoration of our currency had rendered necessary'.[6] Country banks cut back on their lending to farmers, while some of the less prudent establishments went under – thereby adding to the general distress in rural areas.[7]

There is little doubt that the immediate post-1815 period was a difficult one for many farmers, particularly those who had purchased land at high prices under the heady influence of war prosperity and who now found themselves struggling under a heavy burden of debt. A steady trickle of owner-occupiers were unable to meet their interest payments and were forced to sell. By the mid-1830s it was widely observed that the number of farmers occupying their own holdings had fallen sharply since 1815. Sometimes they sold out to local tradesmen, who probably put in a tenant to farm the land; more often the purchaser was a neighbouring large landowner, or one of the rising new gentry. The depression thus helped to intensify the divisions in rural society between the men who owned land and the men who farmed it. The problems of the smaller men were compounded by the growing poor rates, as an increasing number of villages adopted the policy of sub-sidizing labourers' cash wages out of parish funds, using one or other variant of the Speenhamland policy. This remained a contentious issue until the passage of the Poor Law Amendment Act in 1834 introduced more rigid attitudes towards out relief (see Chapter 4).

In the meantime, as a Suffolk farmer pointed out, whereas in 1824 he had paid £121 10s. 4½d. in poor rates, ten years later the amount was more than twice this sum.[8] A few men left the land altogether because they lacked the means to pay their rates. Others, particularly those in hard-hit Suffolk who were engaged in the fattening of livestock, were so short of capital by the mid-1830s that they were unable to stock their farms from their own resources. Instead they entered into agreements with dealers who supplied the beasts and then received them back again when they were ready for market; farmer and dealer shared the profits of the venture.[9]

Village tradesmen, too, had raised their charges during the war years and continued to keep them at a high level when hostilities ended and general prices were falling. Thus a wheelwright, ploughwright, carpenter and smith of Southrop in Gloucestershire charged his cus-tomers 1s. 10d. per day to employ a man in 1793. This had jumped to 3s. by 1813 and remained there for two years. Although it was cut to 2s. 6d. in 1816, there were no further reductions up to the early 1820s.[10] Again, the cost of making a wheelbarrow went up from 6s. 6d. in 1805 to 9s. 6d. by 1810, and of mending a gate from a pre-war 6d. to 9d. Other tradesmen followed a similar pattern, to the anger of agricul-turalists. As a witness from Kent informed the Select Committee on the Depressed State of Agriculture, most of the farmers in his area had decided to make a stand on the issue, 'and the probable result will be, that they will work lower'.[11] In the long run his optimism was justified. But the high prices charged by tradesmen, coupled with the general burden of taxation, continued to be major causes of resentment among farmers for some years after the war.[12]

In their efforts to adjust to their reduced financial circumstances, a number of men economized in their living standards. As early as 1816 a Suffolk witness noted that many farmers went to market on foot instead of on horseback, while: 'Instead of dining at their clubs at their different inns, [they] . . . go home to dinner . . . Few of those who do remain to dine, drink wine, as they almost all did, until lately.' Nor did their wives and daughters now attend dancing classes or visit the milliner, while even

gentlemen of comfortable incomes (say from one to two or three thousand a year) depending on the rents and profits of land, are unable to receive their tradesmen's bills. A medical man, in great practice, instead of receiving 300 l. from the neighbouring *farmers*, as he usually does, on account of his bills, at Christmas, did not, this year, receive 20 l.[13]

Almost two decades later Robert Merry, an owner-occupier from Luckton in the North Riding of Yorkshire, claimed that farmers in his part of the world no longer went foxhunting on the scale they were used to; neither did they spend so lavishly in the market towns – to the detriment of the shopkeepers. Like their Suffolk counterparts, when they were ill they managed without a doctor.[14]

A minority of farmers and labourers reacted to the changed times by emigrating with their families, particularly to North America. According to Merry, in the North Riding there was 'not a township, or hardly a family, but what had some of the inhabitants and some of their relations gone to America'.[15] Even men with capital were going abroad in the belief that they could not 'do worse than they are doing at home, because they have been sinking so fast'.[16] The activities of emigration societies, the publication of books recounting the experiences of British settlers in America and the appearance in newspapers of letters from established emigrants all indicate the deep concern which existed in the farming community.

But the problems of English tenants were small indeed when compared with the plight of their peasant colleagues in the Highlands, where a major programme of clearances was under way. In Sutherland this was carried out principally between 1809 and 1821, under the influence of the Marquess of Stafford and his steward, James Loch. The main purpose was to turn the land over to the raising of sheep. Those tenants who refused to move voluntarily were evicted and their cottages burnt; those who protested were opposed with force and the ringleaders imprisoned.[17] Under the influence of these changes plough cultivation ceased almost entirely in the Highlands and the spade came into more general use on the small patches of land near to the coast on which the evicted people were resettled, 'mainly on land never before used for either settlement or cultivation'.[18] The new communities formed a pattern of small, scattered, coastal settlements very different from the clustered villages from which families had been moved. Although the cleared land was undoubtedly made more profitable by these developments and landlords prospered from the sale of wool, the distress caused to the Highlanders was enormous. Their whole way of life was destroyed and vast areas of the countryside were depopulated, save for the sheep and their shepherds. In the new coastal settlements, the people found the soil too thin for their crops, while seed was blown into the sea before it could sprout. Salt-blast and mildew destroyed the young shoots, and the cattle the settlers had brought with them from the emptied glens strayed back to their old pastures and were impounded until fines for trespass were paid. Some men supplemented their scanty agricultural earnings with fishing, though the coast was inhospitable and there was a shortage of safe anchorages. Others moved into kelping. But this trade, too, was controlled by the larger landlords, and their returns for the arduous tasks of cutting, gathering, drying and incinerating the seaweed were small compared with the profits earned in the trade. The fact that the kelping season lasted from April/May to August also meant that the men neglected their own small plots of land at one of the busiest times of the year. Small wonder that many chose to emigrate to Australia or Canada, or that others looked for work in Scotland's growing industrial centres.[19]

Meanwhile to those in England, like the radical journalist William Cobbett, who had condemned the war-time extravagances and pretensions of farmers, the enforced economy measures after 1815 were welcome. But of themselves they could not solve the problems faced in the countryside. This was true not only of owner-occupiers who had purchased land at inflated prices and were unable to meet their debts, but also of tenant farmers who had seen their rents more than double during the war decades. Landowners were inundated with appeals for help. On the Bolton estate near Basingstoke tenant farmers were assisted during 1815–16 by the writing off of arrears of rent and by the granting of annual rebates.[20] John Ellman, a large farmer from Glynde in Sussex, noted that his rent, which had been raised during the war from £680 per annum to £1200, was cut by a sixth in 1815 – a concession which he still retained in the early 1820s. During the crisis of 1816 rebates of 20 to 25 per cent were common.[21] Elsewhere tenancies were surrendered. In Durham and Northumberland during the spring of 1816 seventy-six farms, covering over 20,000 acres, were advertised to let, in addition to over 2250 acres which were offered for sale.[22] From Herefordshire came reports of estates taken in hand 'and ... likely to remain so, though offered to the tenants at a reduction [in rent of] from one-fourth to one-eighth'.[23]

In Cheshire even the cheesemakers were unable to pay their rents. At least one of the county's landowners approached the factors personally in an effort to get the season's produce (which was accumulating on the farms) sold to provide much-needed cash. But he was told that the warehouses were overstocked, 'not one cheese of this year' (1816) having as yet been disposed of.[24] Prices of wool, cattle and horses at the Chester fair were also reported to have fallen heavily during the year.

After 1817 less abundant harvests gave a respite to farmers and landowners, before further falls in prices in the early 1820s led to fresh appeals for help. Then, following a period of relative stability in the mid-1820s, there was another downward movement in the early and mid-1830s. Not until 1837 was a degree of security apparent for grain farmers. Nor did stock and dairy producers escape unscathed during the crises, particularly that of the early 1820s. The agent of the Harcourt Powell estate in Pembroke, for example, complained in August 1821 that stock prices were so low that oxen and heifers were selling at between 50 and 60 per cent below their previous year's level and 'for every other description of stock there was very little demand at any price'.[25] In Hampshire, too, during the dry summer of 1822 the prices of sheep and lambs plunged sharply. One farmer noted gloomily: 'No Turnips whatever at Overton Fair time & [so] the lambs there sold from 12/- to 14/- for the best, after which sheep declined still more in price.'[26] At the great Weyhill fair 100,000 sheep were offered for sale at cheap rates, but many thousands were unable to find buyers. Cobbett, who visited Weyhill at this time, noted that the horse-fair on another part of the downs was as depressed as that for sheep: 'The countenances of the farmers were descriptive of their ruinous state. . . . Met with a farmer who said he must be ruined, unless another "good war" should come! This is no uncommon notion. They saw high prices *with* war, and they thought that the war was the *cause*.'[27] For Cobbett himself, of course, excessive taxation and political malpractice were the real villains.

Nevertheless, the hardships of stock farmers were relatively short-lived, and save for the severe attacks of sheep rot at the end of the 1820s, their position began to improve from the middle of that decade. The records of one Hampshire farmer indicate that from 1827 the minimum price for ewes at Weyhill fair never fell below 20s. per animal – except in 1844, the 'Driest Summer in recollection'.[28] Admittedly, in the early 1830s there were complaints that imports of meat from Ireland were hitting some north-western stock farmers. Carcases were brought into Liverpool and then conveyed by the canal system 'into the heart of the manufacturing district'.[29] But these were minor problems at a time when overall demand for animal products was growing fast and in the north-west – unlike most other parts of the country – rents continued to rise in the post-war years. This was true of the Blundell estate in Lancashire and the Senhouse estate in Cumberland, as well as of the greater part of Cheshire.[30] As a Cheshire land agent put it in 1833, it was the condition of trade in industrial Lancashire which determined the prosperity of agriculturalists in his part of the world: 'we always find when trade is good at Manchester, cheese and the produce of the farmer sells better.'[31] And he added optimistically: 'there is no distress in our part of the country. The only class of persons that are in distress are the small farmers and those that are on bad lands.'

A very different picture emerges if the records from arable and mixed farming areas are examined. Repeated appeals for aid were received by countless landowners, and rent arrears mounted, especially on the poorer lands, just as they had in 1815–16. A statement prepared on the Duke of Grafton's farms in Northamptonshire in 1821, 'made out with a view of considering what allowances should be made to Tenants on account of the depression in price of produce and the burden of Taxes and Rates', reveals that out of a total of 125 tenants, almost one-sixth were in arrears. Some were heavily in debt, like John Gibbons of Grimscote, who farmed just over 136 acres at a rent of £252 10s. per annum. His arrears amounted to a formidable £327 16s. 3½d. He was given a rebate of 20 per cent on his rent and arrears, on the grounds that his farm was one of the dearest on the estate.[32] But it is difficult to see that this alone would have set him on the road to recovery. Some of his fellow sufferers were still less fortunate, seven of them being classed as tenants whom it was not 'desirable to retain'. Among the comments passed on these unfortunates were: 'Has bad health and no Capital', or 'Has neither Capital or Activity'. In depression years it was inevitably the marginal producer who went to the wall first. However, in 1821 almost all of the Duke of Grafton's tenants in Northampton-shire were given a rebate.

On Thomas Coke's famous Holkham estate in Norfolk, with its bias towards cereals and sheep, the situation was even more serious. During the period 1813–24 many of the tenants reverted to annual agreements as their leases ran out, since in that way rents could be more easily adjusted to changes in income. But even this could not solve their problems. Early in January 1821 Coke was himself forced to appeal to his bankers, Messrs Gurney of Norwich, for a loan because he had had to offer his tenants a few months' grace in the payment of their rent:

It is the more painful and distressing [he wrote] . . . to solicit in addition to that which I am already indebted to you the power to draw for necessary supplies, and in addition to which I shall have to borrow from four to five Thousand pounds from some quarter . . . to pay for two little intermixed Estates which I have agreed to purchase, & to pay for as soon as the Title Deeds are approved.[33]

Gurneys agreed to grant him the help he required, but by Michaelmas of that year rent arrears still stood at about £10,500. This was an increase of approximately £3000 over the previous year and had taken place despite rebates to tenants of around £1450. During the next year the arrears were cut back, but only because some of the tenants gave up their farms and realized their capital. The net result was a great turnover in farms on the Coke estate, for as one despairing tenant wrote: 'The misery and anxiety to carry on business in times like the present beggars all description.' Coke himself, like the redoubtable Cobbett, blamed 'the selfishness, folly, and extravagance of ministers' for agriculture's plight.[34]

A decade later, in the recession of the early 1830s, similar problems recurred. As the Duke of Bedford's Woburn agent pointed out, arrears were particularly severe among farmers on the heavy clays: 'The Losses they have sustained in consequence of the late Wet Season, both in the crops of corn & (what is to them still more serious) loss of Sheep from Rot, these combined with their previous want of Capital has reduced many of them I fear to a low ebb.' Two years later, in the spring of 1833, the agent was reporting not only the offer of rent rebates but 'His Grace's liberality' in writing off all arrears for his north Bedfordshire tenants. This had made a 'great impression' upon them.[35]

But, as in the early 1820s, others were less fortunate. One farmer on the Tharp estate at Chippenham in Cambridgeshire, who was in heavy rent arrear, complained that he had lost more than £1000 in the course of three years' occupancy of his holding. He was prepared to offer a further hundred pounds in order to be relieved of his lease: 'I find that unless I can be released from The Farm altogether I shall be most certainly ruined.' In this case the landlord's agent was able to persuade the man's father, also a Tharp tenant, to take over the property. But by 1836 even the offer of further rebates would not persuade the old man to continue in occupation. He said he would 'rather give up the whole of his own Farm & gave notice to that effect', wrote the agent despondently. In all, in 1836 this estate had three farms in hand, two of which the harassed agent reported he was unable to let even at sharply reduced rentals:

in consequence of their being *thrown on our own hands we are obliged* now to sow the seeds, for *any* incoming Tenant and may *eventually* unless let before Mic[haelmas] next be *obliged* to Farm it *ourselves* . . . this wd. require a capital of at least [£]5000 & a Bailiff at a salary of *£85 what we pay to our own farm Bailiff besides keeping a house for him.*

Only after several abortive attempts was the property at last let, on the understanding that the landlord would carry out a number of improvements.[36]

These lengthy negotiations make it clear why many landlords in the post-war years preferred to take the line of least resistance and to offer

tenants sufficient rebates to keep them on the estate rather than have
the problem of finding fresh occupants or of farming the land for themselves, with all the expense that this entailed. Only a few of the more
affluent were prepared to take the latter course and, if necessary, run
their property at a loss for a few years. The Earl of Pembroke was one
who did so, between 1834 and 1836, and the loss of one-tenth of the
capital of £5400 which he had laid out to stock a farm taken in hand
was considered well worth while: 'It has been good policy to hold out
and not yield to the offers of £700, 750 and 800 which were made
[for a farm previously let at £950] which would have meant all the other
tenants asking for reductions', wrote his agent.[37] It was at this time,
too, that leases gave way to annual tenancies, since farmers were unwilling to commit themselves for years ahead in view of the uncertain
conditions.

But rent reductions and rebates were not the only measures proposed
by farmers to alleviate their distress. Apart from repeated appeals for
cuts in rates and taxes, many came forward with demands for extra
protection against foreign grain imports, even though these were
patently *not* responsible for most of their problems. 'In the generation
after 1820 probably under 5 per cent of home demand was supplied
by imports', and it was precisely in the years of minimal importation –
and low domestic prices – from 1820 to 1824 and 1833 to 1836, that
the loudest complaints were heard.[38] Some of the critics claimed that
grain was 'unofficially' allowed to 'leak' out of the bonded warehouses
where it was stored. Others protested that the basis on which home
grain prices were calculated was unreliable, as it affected imports. The
returns from provincial markets were regarded as particularly suspect.
A Cornish owner-occupier declared in 1820 that the corn inspector at
Bodmin was a local barber who handed over his official duties to his
wife. She fulfilled them by going down to the market and asking one or
two people what the average price was, rather than by ascertaining it
for herself.[39] A Norfolk witness complained that millers and dealers
often did not declare the sale of the cheapest wheat because they wanted
to keep the ports open for imports. In his view, at the Yarmouth and
Norwich markets early in 1820 'scarcely one-fifth of the corn sold' was
reported.[40]

These complaints appear to have been justified to some degree.
Indeed, the inspector of corn returns for Plymouth, by trade a tavern
keeper, frankly admitted that not 'one-tenth' of the factors and dealers
in corn who were bound by law to make returns in his area actually

bothered to do so, while the government's receiver of corn returns in London, on being asked if the returns were properly compiled, bluntly replied: 'Certainly not.'[41]

Nevertheless, faulty returns clearly played no *material* role in the farmers' distress, in so far as in the years of greatest difficulty it was the abundance of the *domestic* harvest which was causing hardship; no *foreign* corn was sold. But that did not prevent an active protectionist lobby from emerging as early as 1816 to demand greater restrictions, including an extension of protection to imports of wool as well as grain. Among the most vociferous in this regard was George Webb Hall, a solicitor and farmer, who in 1819 helped to form the Central Agricultural Association, based in London. Local protectionist associations allied to this central organization were also set up, and by the end of 1819 some fifty were in existence. Webb Hall aimed his campaign at men who, like himself, were substantial farmers (often tenants) who had overextended themselves in the war years and were now suffering the consequences. As one enthusiastic disciple wrote of him:[42]

This the
    PATRIOT
True Friend of us all,
That foe to oppression, magnanimous
    HALL,
Whose *firm perseverance* has exposed to view,
The effects of that system *Legislatures* pursue.
On those poor Peasants, all
    Tattered and Torn,
Who now live in misery and quite forlorn . . .
Because of the Ships
That brought in *Foreign Grain*,
From countries where *Taxes*
    are known but by name. . . .

And when distress deepened late in 1820 the Agricultural Association and its local branches successfully pressed for an investigation into the workings of the Corn Law. But that was as far as they got. Mindful of the hostility of the manufacturing districts to the whole concept of agrarian protection, and aware of the weakness of taking action of this kind to solve problems which were essentially internal in character, the government wisely refused to extend the tariff.

An additional handicap for the protectionist movement was the division of interests among agriculturalists themselves. Stock farmers hardly looked with enthusiasm upon a plan which seemed certain to raise the price of all grains, including those for animal fodder. Perhaps even more significant was the fact that from mid-1823 grain prices rose temporarily, thereby causing farmers to lose interest in politics and agitation. However, as we shall see in Chapter 7, in the sterner protectionist battles of the 1830s and 1840s there was to be a revival both of pressure groups and of the arguments on tariff policy, until these were set aside by the repeal of the Corn Laws in 1846. In the meantime, in 1828 a new law returned to the pre-war practice of establishing, instead of the principle of a single, fixed price level, a range of prices and duties for imported grain, incorporated into an elaborately graduated sliding scale. When the average home price of wheat was below 52s. per quarter absolute protection still applied; when it was just above that price a duty of 34s. 8d. per quarter was payable. As the home price rose, so the amount of duty paid by imports fell, until when the domestic level was 73s. or more a nominal duty of one shilling only was imposed. A similar sliding scale was adopted for other grains and, as before, a system of colonial preference applied in regard to imports from British North America.

Amongst all the difficulties, however, one hopeful feature was the growing interest in land improvement by the more successful and far-sighted agriculturalists. This was especially true of men cultivating light land. In parts of Suffolk, for example, output was increased by better drainage, the introduction of a careful system of drill husbandry and the use of new crop rotations. In some cases interested landlords like Thomas Coke, encouraged their tenants to improve their methods by example and by exhortation. In February 1817 a circular letter was sent to the Holkham tenantry warning them against using weathered or stained seeds for their spring planting of barley: 'Mr Coke considers that it would be extremely hazardous to trust to damaged Barley for seed.' Coke took great care in purchasing his own seeds, and in that same month his steward arranged for twenty empty sacks to be shipped to London from the small port of Wells so that they could be returned full of hay seeds. Beans were procured from the Duke of Bedford. Coke also sent samples of seeds far and wide; in January 1817 three combs of peas were shipped by coaster from Wells to Leith in Scotland for this purpose.[43]

Elsewhere dry-soiled uplands were improved by combining new rotations of fodder crops and cereals with the folding of flocks of sheep and, in eastern England, the keeping of herds of yarded bullocks:

Dung from the livestock, powerfully assisted by a big increase in the application of bone dust fertilizer (which would have washed away on the ill-drained clays) raised yields of the crops. In turn, higher yields of the forage crops fed more stock, and these gave still more dung for still more crops. Cultivation costs were low; the working season was long. Therefore it was from this sector that a rise in output, including even that of wheat, came during the price fall. But lower unit costs than on the clays were probably not the only cause. In the later stages of the deflation, the prices of wool and malting barley (lightland, not heavyland, products) began to rise again. There was thus a positive incentive to produce them.[44]

So, if few farmers escaped entirely unscathed from the problems of the post-war agricultural recession, some, particularly stock farmers or those on light land, were relatively little affected. Many others carried on with the help of rent rebates and investment by landlords in repairs and improvements. In the course of the 1820s the Duke of Bedford's outlay on repairs grew to 25 or even 30 per cent of gross rentals, and permanent improvements accounted for nearly 10 per cent of the rentals on the Woburn estate. At Alnwick the Duke of Northumberland was spending 14 per cent of the rental on buildings and repairs, and at Savernake and Wilton in Wiltshire the figure was 12 per cent.[45]

Then from the late 1830s, as population growth once more outstripped the increase in grain output and the country became an increasingly heavy importer of corn in both good and bad years, the position began to change. Fortunately for British farmers, there were no large food surpluses which could be shipped from Europe to Britain at this time, and the North American trade was still in its infancy. So the downward trend of prices was at last arrested and confidence restored. The reduction in poor rate expenditure and proposals to reform the vexed tithe system (see Chapter 5) helped in this regard. Some men, too, combined farming with another trade or with innkeeping so as to provide a supplementary income. William Smith of Farnborough, for example, survived by linking farming with running a small pottery. His wife took in lodgers, and his daughter opened a grocery shop in which she sold some of her father's bacon.[46] For farmers such as these the simple daily round went on much as it had always done. This is confirmed by entries in farm diaries, like that of Mr Paul of Bottisham Place, Cambridgeshire, for the summer of 1833:[47]

July
1st   Sent 20 lambs to London at 1/– [per] score.
2nd   Black and White Horned Cow came off the Fen.

5th	Black & White Horn^{d.} Cow calved. Benstead began Threshg. Trefoil.
8th	Sent Forty Lamb to London. 20 to be sold by Goodbody. 20 by Moyse.
10th	Clayton and Shepherd began to hoe Sweed Turnips.
15th	Young Sow had Cornell's Boar.
18th	Old Sow piged (12).
25th	Began to mow the peas and Finished.
26th	Began reaping Wheat in Johnsons and Top Field.

Aug.

6th	Finished wheat harvest – very nice weather. Gave the men pint beer each.
9th	Yorkshire Heifer had King's Bull.
10th	Began cutting Barley.

So it goes on; daily activities – and farm celebrations – were influenced only by seasonal changes and the weather.[48] The safe ingathering of the crops was greeted almost everywhere by the holding of a 'harvest home', at which toasts were drunk and ballads sung. At Bottisham the 1833 harvest supper was held on 26 August, when the work force of nine men and three boys was regaled with 'Round Beef, vegetables, plum puddings, beer and pipes'. However, the following year Mr Paul made a contract with eight men to 'take' the harvest for £4 5s. each, 'and 2/6 for a dinner 2 Bush. Malt, 2 lb. Hops, [so that they could make their own beer,] to turn the Barley once if requisite, gave the Men . . . 1/– for Earnest'.[49] Two of the labourers elected to take a bushel of tail wheat (low-quality grain), which they could grind into flour, as part of their harvest payment rather than cash alone. This policy of purchasing food from an employer, usually on advantageous terms, continued well into the nineteenth century, though it involved a declining proportion of the farm work force. It was most common among annually hired men, like carters and shepherds, and among the Northumberland labourers, who still received their wages in both cash and kind.

Migratory harvest gangs were employed on many holdings to help at the busiest times. Some of these groups were able to synchronize their employment so as to move easily between home and host communities. During the 1830s the pattern around Rotherfield in East Sussex was first haymaking near London, then home for the corn harvest, away for a second corn harvest in the hill country around Lewes and northwards to end the season in the Kent and Surrey hop gardens.[50] Around Farnham in Surrey about half of the hop labourers migrated to assist in the corn harvest in West Sussex. The Farnham corn, meanwhile, was reaped by the men who remained behind and by the women whose husbands had left, 'who contract for the work by the acre'.[51] In Herefordshire and Worcestershire Welsh migrants were recruited, while from the 1820s Irish harvesters were of particular importance in the eastern counties. As early as 1822 Yorkshire was said to be inundated by 'swarms of Irish'. Many of these seasonal workers were poverty-stricken cottiers and small farmers from the west coast of Ireland, who were needed at home only for the planting and lifting of potatoes and who used their English earnings to pay the rent, settle their debts and meet winter expenses.[52] Needless to say, this influx of 'foreigners' and the influence it had in undermining the harvest wages of regular labourers caused much resentment in the areas it affected and led to occasional outbreaks of violence.

For farmers and landowners, therefore, the post-war years were ones of adjustment to changed circumstances and, for many, a period of hardship as well. It is now necessary to examine the position of other sectors of rural society during the same era. As we have seen, the straitened finances of agriculturalists caused them to cut back on their expenditure with local medical men and shopkeepers. Village tradesmen suffered, too, as farmers were reluctant to place orders with them or to settle the debts they had already incurred. It is significant that in the agricultural riots of both 1816 and 1830 village tradesmen took an active role. This was due partly to the fact that they were usually the most literate of the workers in villages and country towns, but the slump in agricultural business, and the difficulties this created, doubtless influenced them as well.

In the case of the agricultural labourers – the most numerous class of rural workers – the years after 1815 saw some reduction in wage levels, as basic rates fell from between 12s. and 15s. a week in 1814 to between 9s. and 10s. in 1822.[53] But still more common was the farmers' practice of cutting their permanent labour force to the bone. They relied instead on the recruitment of temporary workers, like the Irish harvesters, or on men partly supported by the Poor Law, on Speenhamland lines. During the winter months, when work was in short supply, the drop in the permanent farm labour force was particularly severe. In some Sussex parishes up to 60 per cent of the labourers were unemployed and left to pass the winter on the parish dole. In sixteen parishes in the Kentish Weald in 1823 682 men (supporting an unknown number of dependants), out of a total population of 21,719, were unemployed all the year round. And in the Blything Hundred of Suffolk there were in 1830 between 2500 and 3000 able-bodied men, of whom 1001 (with 602 wives and 2399 children) were unemployed.[54] At the same time the

fall in the number of farm servants living in, which had become obvious
during the Napoleonic wars, continued after their end. Only in the
pastoral north and west, where resident stockmen were needed, did
farm servants survive in any numbers. Even here there was a growing
tendency to lodge the servants with other annually hired men, like
carters and shepherds, or to accommodate them in separate bothies.
Cobbett, for one, complained about the change:

Why do not farmers now *feed* and *lodge* their work-people, as they did formerly?
Because they cannot keep them *upon so little* as they give them in wages. . . .
All the world knows that a number of people, boarded in the same house, and
at the same table, can, with as good food, be boarded much cheaper than
those persons divided into twos, threes, or fours, can be boarded.[55]

However, most farmers would no doubt have agreed with the Norfolk
man who frankly admitted that 'people did not like the trouble' of
having their workers living in.[56] Given such attitudes, Cobbett
considered it was not surprising that '*pauperism* and . . . *crimes* . . .
disgrace[d]' the countryside.

In many areas, too, workers were hit by the decline in cottage industries, particularly those associated with the cloth trade, which was
facing growing competition from factory-made goods even during the
war. The Duke of Grafton, in a letter to the Home Office in 1816,
attributed rioting among labourers in the Cosford area of Suffolk to
the 'total failure of the spinning of long wool, which used to afford
employment to so many thousand persons in this county'. His opinion
was endorsed by magistrates meeting at Bury St Edmunds shortly
afterwards.[57] On the other hand, in counties like Worcestershire where
domestic employment still survived the position of labouring families
was more satisfactory. In 1826 Cobbett wrote with approval of glovemaking around Worcester and observed that 'where manufacturing is
mixed with agriculture, where the wife and daughters are at the needle,
or the wheel, while the men and the boys are at plough . . . and where
the earnings come *in aid of the man's wages* . . . the misery cannot be so
great'.[58] For the same reason, he was a strong advocate of straw
plaiting as a domestic employment and did much to publicize it. It
was on account of the varied employments available to men and women
who lived in wooded districts (as well as the accessibility of firing) that
Cobbett considered them better off than their counterparts in arable
areas:

I have always observed that woodland and forest labourers are best off in the
main. The coppices give them pleasant and profitable work in winter. If

they have not so great a corn-harvest, they have a three weeks' harvest in April or May; that is to say, in the season of barking . . . which employs women and children as well as men. And then in the great article of *fuel*! They *buy* none. It is miserable work where this is to be bought, and where, as at Salisbury, the poor take by turns the making of fires at their houses to boil four or five tea-kettles. . . . At Launceston in Cornwall a man . . . told me, that the people in general could not afford to have fire in ordinary, and that he himself paid 3d. for boiling a leg of mutton at another man's fire![59]

In the north of England, where coal was cheaper and alternative employment existed in industry, the position of the labourers was far better. Wage rates were higher and the men were spared 'that hopelessness which rotted village life in the southern counties'.[60] Even in the non-industrial north of Lancashire, where agricultural labourers predominated in the working population, it was common for the men to combine field labour with quarrying, fishing, cockle gathering or canal excavation, according to the opportunities of the time and the locality.[61] As late as the 1840s there were many summer labourers who migrated from farm to farm to help with haymaking and harvest but who worked as handloom weavers for the rest of the year. And a northern labourer could always 'make his winters more tolerable' by sending sons and daughters to work in a country cotton mill. Though where youngsters were employed at an early age in this way there was a corresponding weakening of authority within the family; filial respect noticeably declined as children became independent wage earners.

A minority of men benefited from the work-creation programmes of certain of the larger farmers and landowners, who were anxious to keep their labourers contented and fully occupied. In Herefordshire during the early 1830s John Arkwright discovered that engaging 150 men on an irrigation project was 'an excellent way of finding winter work for my Neighbours'. Another Herefordshire landowner, also somewhat reluctantly engaged in job creation, noted sourly: 'I most heartily wish all our improvements were finished, as they are dreadfully Expensive, but the labouring Class must be Emp^d. Especially in the Winter Months, or they will Poach or go upon the Parish.' In Nottinghamshire the larger landowners often engaged men on road mending and land drainage when trade was slack.[62] In other cases, as on the Holkham estate, the unemployed were encouraged to migrate in search of work. In 1836 the Holkham steward noted that twenty-six young men from one parish had been sent into Northamptonshire to seek employment on the railways. Others had emigrated, and for a time Coke contributed to their expenses, paying one-third of the costs in parishes where he was sole proprietor and in proportion to his ownership where he was not.

But such efforts were of minor significance in relieving hardship, and the recurrent spells of winter unemployment, though they varied in intensity according to the state of the harvest and the inclemency of the weather, continued to cause much misery among labouring families. Some vented their frustrations by engaging in arson, an anonymous crime which yet gave the perpetrator a feeling that he was 'hitting back' at his oppressors. Others turned to the maiming of animals, the sending of threatening letters or the destruction of machinery, for only thus could they attract attention to their grievances. They had no part to play in running the community in which they lived and were excluded by poverty even from the meetings of the parish vestry. Their bitter feelings of exclusion applied both before and after the major outbreaks of 1830, a year which saw a 'perfect fury of fires' and of machine-breaking.

It was during the winter months that the anxieties of labourers were at their peak. Anything which deprived them of work at that time was likely to be regarded with hostility. Paramount in this respect were mole ploughs for drainage work and threshing machines. The latter had been introduced in many districts during the Napoleonic wars at a time when labour was scarce, but they continued in use into the post-war era, as larger farmers in particular sought to economize on wage bills. The importance of the threshing machine in this situation can best be appreciated when it is remembered that on an arable farm during the pre-machine era hand-threshing might form a quarter of the total year's work.[63] Although the true cause of the labourers' distress lay in the large increase in the rural population, coupled with the problem of absorbing servicemen returning from the war and the general dislocations of arable agriculture, threshing machines quickly became a general scapegoat. They symbolized the impersonal power of the farmer over his labourers, and older men in particular feared their speed and the injuries they could cause. To destroy them seemed, to many men, an entirely logical reaction. Unlike rick burning, it was an act not simply of revenge but of common sense.

As early as 1815 machine-breaking was reported from Suffolk; significantly, when offenders were brought to court they had little to say in their own defence beyond their difficulty 'of gaining employment, which they attributed to the use of machines'.[64] In the much more serious rioting and arson in East Anglia in the following year similar attitudes prevailed, though they were accompanied by attempts to secure higher wages and cheaper food. Nevertheless, as a contemporary observed of the Suffolk parish of Clare, it was the threshing machine which the poor hated 'beyond all things'.[65] In this area machines were burned quite openly during daylight hours. Eventually the unrest was put down with military help, and seven men involved in rioting at Ely, Littleport and Downham Market were hanged.

This firm reaction by the authorities did not end the discontent: it merely drove it temporarily underground. Early in 1822, however, at a time when farmers were again in financial difficulty and anxious to keep wage bills at a low level, machine-breaking returned to East Anglia. On 6 March the rector of Banham in Norfolk wrote nervously to the Home Office to describe the problems he and his fellow magistrates were encountering:

The Machine Breakers were very busy in the adjoining hundreds all Saturday, they finished . . . between 10 & 11 o Clock at night by [bringing] a Machine into the market place of Wymondham and then demolishing it. Sunday was a day of rest. They made two parties on Monday, one going to the East of Wymondham the other to the West and broke a considerable number that day, finishing about 8 oC in the evening or rather later. On Monday I consulted with my Brother Magistrate Mr. Wright . . . and we sent round to the different Parishes in the Hundred calling a meeting of all persons having a horse and capable of attending to assemble at 9 oClock on the following morning wh. they readily did, and we swore in about 250 respectable people as Special Constables – finding the 16th Dragoons had not arrived I sent to Col. Wray . . . who joined. The Rioters finding that these preparations were made went into some of the adjoining Hundreds, all but one small party, we sent to the Castle at Norwich, being identified as having been very active in breaking machines the night before, and also in forcing men away from their Labour, & compelling them to join the disturbances.[66]

Although these riots, too, were suppressed with military help, they seem to have had a residual effect. Thus occupiers at Wingfield in Suffolk abjured the use of threshing machines 'on a penalty of £5', and a number of other parishes followed suit. Sir B. Bunbury, Bart, even sent a circular letter to his tenants, encouraging them not to use these implements. In the autumn of that year labourers were still going round the Suffolk villages to check whether threshing machines were in use. They dismantled the only one they found, 'breaking nothing and dispersing with three cheers'.[67]

Such outbursts indicated the frustration felt by ill-paid and ill-fed men and women for whom the future seemed to offer little hope of improvement. They were forerunners of the still larger uprisings which were to take place in the southern and south midland counties during the latter half of 1830.

The winter of 1829 was a particularly harsh one; the harvest was not gathered in until 'the snow was already on the barn in early October'.[68] In the opinion of one Hampshire farmer it was the severest winter he ever remembered, 'hard Frost, with a great Quantity of Snow on the Ground, from the middle of Dec[embe]r to the middle of Feby'.[69] The labourers must have faced the spring of 1830 with the memory of cold, hunger and unemployment clear in their minds and the conviction that they were not prepared to endure another season like it. 'Fear of the winter' was the reason given, together with low wages, for riots at Mardon in Kent later that year.

The men's forebodings were doubtless increased by the fact that the summer of 1830 was wet and cold and the harvest unimpressive. In addition, on a broader front there were rumours of revolutionary turmoil in France and demands for political reform in this country. William Cobbett was also blamed for inciting disaffection through the columns of his *Political Register* and his lectures. As one Member of Parliament complained in December 1830, when the arson and rioting were already under way, Cobbett had declared that the poor had been 'never so much as talked of, much less resolved on, until the labourers rose, and the fires began to blaze'.[70] When a Sussex man under sentence of death for arson, claimed that he 'never should of thought of douing aney sutch thing if Mr. Cobet had never given aney lactures', Cobbett was charged with publishing a libel with intent to incite labourers to acts of violence. He was brought to trial in July 1831 but conducted his own defence with such spirit that the jury failed to agree on a verdict. After this the government decided to drop the case.[71]

Indeed, despite the accusations levelled at Cobbett and his supporters, the 1830 riots were clearly not the work of one man or of any small group of leaders. They marked the accumulated bitterness of the southern labourer at the hardships of his life over many years. Not even the influence of Continental revolution and British political crisis provided the actual spark, though they added to the explosive atmosphere. As Hobsbawm and Rudé have written:

In North and East Kent it may have been Irish labourers and threshing machines, in the Weald the cut in poor relief, elsewhere in the country other local factors may have revived action here and there . . . Small sparks which would have produced little except a few burned ricks or broken machines turned into a conflagration when fanned by the double wind of another winter like the last, and politics.[72]

The first move came at Lower Hardres near Canterbury on 28 August 1830, when a threshing machine was destroyed. But as in the earlier outbursts, machine-breaking was only one aspect of the discontent. Arson, the sending of threatening letters signed by the legendary 'Captain Swing', meetings to demand increases in wages, attacks on justices of the peace and parish overseers, opposition to the Poor Law system and demands for gifts of money and provisions all played their part, too. Rioting even occurred in villages where there were no threshing machines. Often the determining factor seems to have been the size of the population. A large village rioted, while a smaller one with the same grievances but less power remained passive.[73] Parishes in which nonconformity was strong or where markets and fairs provided a centre for communications were more likely to protest than those without these attributes. If they had a history of local disputes, perhaps over enclosure matters or over the administration of charities, this, too, would increase the propensity to riot. Occasionally, as with the hand papermakers of Buckinghamshire, industrial workers under threat from new machinery also joined in.

But it must be remembered that the impact of the disturbances was extremely variable, so that while Kent, Hampshire and Wiltshire were heavily involved, only about one Oxfordshire parish in ten was affected. The picture in Buckinghamshire and Bedfordshire was equally patchy, while there was no response from the north of England, where the problems of low wages, unemployment and poor relief were less severe. In an area of general unrest the movement might spread by sheer contagion – as in the Kinwardstone hundred of Wiltshire, where twelve out of seventeen parishes were involved, comprising 80 per cent of the population, or in the Blackmoor Vale in Dorset.[74] In Hampshire threats of arson were written on bridges and barns, sometimes smeared with blood. But it was machine-breaking which provided the underlying theme of the disturbances from late August, when the first appliances were destroyed in East Kent, into early December, when they were broken in Essex, Worcestershire, Buckinghamshire and Warwickshire.[75]

The outbreaks naturally aroused alarm among the propertied classes. Letters flooded in to the Home Office, and Sir Robert Peel felt constrained to warn the lord-lieutenant of Kent against offering overgenerous rewards for the discovery of the malefactors: 'If thousands are to be offered as a reward to accomplices not actually setting fire to the premises, are we quite sure that there is not cunning and wickedness enough to plan the fire with a view to the reward?'[76] Metropolitan police officers were dispatched to the affected areas to assist in tracking down those responsible. And where prisoners were taken Sir Robert recommended 'great exertion in encouraging them to inform against their accomplices by an offer of Pardon. . . . I shall be perfectly prepared to sanction this offer – whenever, after full consideration by the Mag[istrate]s. it shall be deemed necessary or expedient to make it'.[77]

A Hampshire farmer wrote of the 'large Mobs assembled to the terror of the Country, and broke nearly all the Threshing Machines, a vast deal of Agricultural Property consumed by Fire',[78] while on the Hampshire/Berkshire border, Miss Mitford, a clergyman's daughter, recorded the events and the rumours which disturbed her own small community:

we tasted of fear, the bitterest cup that an imaginative woman can taste, in all its agonizing varieties. . . . Oh the horror of those fires – breaking forth night after night, sudden, yet expected, always seeming nearer than they actually were, and always said to have been more mischievous to life and property than they actually had been!

She wrote of the men's

day-light marches on the high road, regular and orderly as those of an army, or their midnight visits to lonely houses, lawless and terrific as the descent of pirates. . . . Nor were the preparations for defence, however necessary, less shocking than the apprehensions of attack. The hourly visits of bustling parish officers, bristling with importance (for our village, though in the centre of the insurgents, continued uncontaminated . . . and was, therefore, quite a rallying point for loyal men and true;) the swearing in of whole regiments of petty constables; the stationary watchmen, who every hour, to prove their vigilance, sent in some poor wretch, beggar or match-seller, or rambling child, under the denomination of suspicious persons; the mounted patrol, whose deep 'all's well,' which ought to have been consolatory, was about the most alarming of all alarming sounds; the soldiers, transported from place to place in carts the better to catch the rogues, whose local knowledge gave them great advantage in a dispersal; the grave processions of magistrates and gentlemen on horseback; and, above all, the nightly collecting of arms and armed men within our own dwelling, kept up a continual sense of nervous inquietude.[79]

In some cases farmers voluntarily broke up their own machines rather than face the fury of the mob; in others there is evidence that smaller men, angered at the refusal of their more prosperous neighbours to give employment to threshers during the winter months, joined with the labourers in demanding the destruction of the machines. Elsewhere they urged the men on, 'with a view of obtaining a reduction of the rents and tithes'.[80] This was the case in south-east Norfolk, where farmers offered higher wages to their workers on condition that their own tithes were reduced.[81] Filled with resentment against the tithe system, they were unscrupulously using the labourers to fight their battles for them. For this reason, too, attacks by Swing rioters on parsons were common – though they were frequently also inspired by dislike of the clergy's role in Poor Law administration or in the exercise of their authority as magistrates.

At Otmoor in Oxfordshire disturbances were linked with anti-enclosure riots, while at Crowmarsh in the same county one of the first victims was a large farmer who was about to make an attempt (the last of many) to promote an enclosure Act for the neighbouring parish of Benson. At Newton Tony in Wiltshire a farmer tried to save his thresh-ing machine by bargaining with his assailants: 'If you will disperse and go to work and protect our property when others come to destroy it, I will give you beer and money and anything else in reason.' But his price was apparently not high enough. The rioters forced their way into his barn and within five minutes his threshing machine was in ruins.[82] A variety of motives thus lay behind the unrest; specific issues gave particular bitterness to uprisings in certain localities, though resentment at low wages and the indignities of unemployment was common to most.

In the end peace was restored with the aid of the military and of special constables. But there was a clear determination among the ruling classes that the events of that fateful year should never be repeated. Afraid that local magistrates might not be stringent enough in their judgements, the government appointed special commissions to try prisoners in some of the most seriously affected counties. The ones selected were Hampshire, Wiltshire, Berkshire, Dorset and Bucking-hamshire. Elsewhere the ordinary judicial machinery was allowed to carry out its work at assizes and quarter sessions. In all 1976 prisoners were tried by ninety courts sitting in thirty-four counties. Of these nineteen men were hanged (all but three of them for arson), 481 were transported to Australia (including some whose only offence had been the writing of anonymous 'Swing' letters), and over 600 more were imprisoned in this country.[83]

To families left behind even the sentence of transportation was like one of death, for they had little hope of seeing their loved ones again. W. H. Hudson has described how more than seventy years later the memory of those bitter events lingered on among villagers on the

Salisbury Plain. When the men came out of the court house on their way to jail or to the convict transport ships to Australia they filed past their weeping womenfolk waiting outside. Few ever saw the men again, though many a wife and her children waited and hoped through the long years. While the cases were being heard 'there was money in plenty subscribed to hire witnesses for the prosecution. . . . The smell of blood-money brought out a number of scoundrels who for a few pounds were only too ready to swear away the life of any man, and it was notorious that numbers of poor fellows were condemned in this way.'[84]

Some of the ringleaders did manage to escape capture – perhaps like a man from Filkins in Oxfordshire who was concealed in a heap of straw on a local farm. But even they had to leave their home districts and to remain away for many years.[85]

From the government's point of view the repression served its purpose, since despite sporadic outbreaks of arson and rioting, there were no major upsurges of discontent among the rural workers until the agricultural trade union movement got under way in the early 1870s. Indeed, it is interesting to observe that those East Anglian parishes like Littleport, Wisbech, Ely and Upwell, which had been most harshly treated after the 1816 revolt, took little part in that of 1830. Five of the men hanged in 1816 had come from Littleport.[86]

To those labourers who did escape punishment in 1830 the riots brought some benefits, in that wages were raised in the wake of the disturbances in many villages and had not been reduced to their pre-1831 level by several years later. A Sussex farmer frankly admitted in 1836 that if it had not been for the riots 'wages would have been lower at this time than they are. At that time there was a considerable rise of wages, and they never have reduced themselves in proportion to the fall in the price of wheat.' A colleague from Buckinghamshire agreed, pointing out that there were 'several instances of landlords requesting their tenants not to reduce the price of labour. I do think those burnings and those riotings had the effect to keep up the price a little.'[87] In other cases the use of threshing machines was abandoned. A land agent from the home counties declared that they were 'generally exploded now; it is considered that where they are kept they may expect a visit'. To a colleague from Wiltshire there was scarcely one threshing machine in use in his district where once there had been a hundred.[88]

Nevertheless, for many the gains proved insubstantial and short-lived. Even those who obtained wage rises in the aftermath of 1830 were not always able to retain them. On the Salisbury Plain pay was initially increased by a shilling a week, but once employers' anxieties had subsided and the men showed themselves more submissive than before, the extra shilling was cut off. Wages returned to what they had been: 'seven shillings a week for a hard-working seasoned labourer, with a family to keep, and from four to six shillings for young unmarried men and for women, even for those who did as much work in the field as any man'. But, as W. H. Hudson significantly adds, 'there were no more risings'.[89] Only the secret vengeance of rick fires was resorted to by the more desperate, while a few determined men moved away in search of better paid employment elsewhere.

Countless households, too, were dependent on the vagaries and anxieties of the Poor Law for at least part of their income. For them the 1830 riots brought a deterioration of relief conditions rather than an amelioration, following the implementation of the 1834 Poor Law Amendment Act. It is to an examination of their position and to the growth of the Poor Law system generally that we must now move.

Labouring family c. *1830*

4 The relief of the poor

ELOPED. From Piddington in the County of Oxford, John Holmes, Black-smith, a Native of St. Mary's Parish at Reading, in the County of Berks, leaving his wife chargeable to the Parish of Piddington aforesaid. – Any Person who will apprehend the said John Holmes, and bring him to the Overseers of Piddington, aforesaid, shall receive ONE GUINEA Reward, and all reasonable Charges, by applying to JOHN SHAW, Overseer of the Poor. – The said John Holmes is a stout made young Man, about twenty Years of Age; long thick black Hair, dark Eyes, is of a swarthy Complexion, about five Feet 8 inches High. – Had on, when he went away, a Blue Coat, light Waistcoat, Nankeen Breeches, White Stockings, Shoes tied with Strings, an old round Hat, and a White tie Handkerchief round his Neck.
Jackson's Oxford Journal (1796)[1]

By the combined operation of increased thrift and somewhat diminished consumption on the part of the Labourer, and an increased rate of wages on the part of his employer, the painful effect which must inevitably result from scarcity, will be rendered tolerable. But this will not take place, if the natural order of things is disturbed, and if an attempt is made by a resort to the Poor rate, to persuade the Labourer that increased providence and caution are unnecessary on his part, and the Farmer that the rate of wages must not necessarily be adjusted to have a reference to an increased cost in the means of subsistence.
Letter from the Poor Law Commission to Thame Union, Oxfordshire (1838)[2]

The problem of rural poverty persistently engaged the mind and con-science of English society from the reign of George III to that of Victoria. Although the scale of the problem varied over time, according to seasonal factors and the size of harvest yields – or, from a longer-term point of view, the growth of population and the changes in the nation's agricultural and industrial structure – it never disappeared. Not until the 1860s, when greater affluence among farmers enabled them

D

to pay better wages and when the increased mobility of labourers encouraged them to do so, was noticeable progress made.[3] Even then there were many black spots. It is against this background that the Poor Law system has to be considered.

In the 1770s the relief available to those in need either took the form of charity (a subject considered in the next chapter) or it stemmed from laws passed under Elizabeth I in 1598 and 1601. Although these were amended over the intervening years, notably by the Act of Settlement of 1662 and by legislation passed in the 1690s, the basic provision remained that each year every community must appoint overseers of the poor whose task it was to collect a rate from the occupiers of property within their area and to use the money to give 'necessary relief' to those of its 'deserving' inhabitants who were unable to support themselves. During times of war they had the further duty of aiding the families of militiamen who were away on active service. In some cases a parish poorhouse or workhouse provided shelter for the needy, while justices of the peace were expected to supervise the work of the parish officials, approve the rates and order relief to districts affected by famine or other disasters. The following extracts from the overseers' account book for Sibford Gower, Oxfordshire, in October 1774 give an idea of the kind of aid bestowed and the degree of interest taken in the welfare of the villagers assisted:[4]

	£	s.	d.
Paid Ann Kings House room		9	0
To Ann King since 2nd May at different times	1	19	0
Bought for Do a kettle & cup		4	3
Nursing Do 6 weeks & washing		3	6
Susannah Treadwell & Ann King Chimney pole, fire rack and links		1	9
Fuel for Do		6	8
Wm. Young's Lodging & washing		4	2
2 New Shirts & Making & Other mended for Wm. Young		8	3
Jane Bevins a pettycoat & mending pattens		2	7½
Gave Do being out of Place			6

However, under the terms of the 1662 Act each pauper could only obtain help from the parish in which he or she could claim a 'settlement', and until the second half of the nineteenth century one of the most vexed questions involving poor relief was the issue of where the unit of responsibility for a particular individual lay. Thus under legislation passed in 1691 it was possible to gain settlement not merely by birth or, in the case of a woman, by marriage, but also by living in a tenement of a yearly value of £10; by paying parish rates; by serving a year in a public office or charge; by completing an indentured apprenticeship; or by obtaining an annual hiring.[5] (In practice this latter provision was often evaded by employers engaging their servants for a few days less than a year, and in at least one south Norfolk parish a farmer who neglected this precaution could be fined £50 for each settlement allowed, under the terms of his lease.)[6] In the nineteenth century the issue was the subject of further controversy, and paupers were moved across parish boundaries like pawns in a game of chess: as late as 1849 13,867 removal orders were issued by justices of the peace in England and Wales, covering perhaps 40,000 paupers, or nearly 4 per cent of all those relieved.[7]

Resort to litigation to resolve settlement disputes was adopted in the more extreme cases, and in 1780 a small Westmorland community spent £44 in legal charges in order to rid itself of one pauper. This was equivalent to supporting the person concerned for almost nine years at the current relief rate of 2s. per week, but the parish overseers doubtless considered it a matter of principle, which they felt obliged to uphold.[8] Similarly, at Mollington on the Oxfordshire–Warwickshire border Sir Frederic Eden observed in 1795:

The Poor's Rates in this neighbourhood vary from 2s. to 4s. in the pound. The difference in the several parishes . . . arises, in a great measure, from the facility or difficulty of obtaining settlements: in several parishes, a fine is imposed on a parishioner, who settles a new comer by hiring, or otherwise; so that a servant is very seldom hired for a year. Those parishes which have for a long time been in the habits of using these precautions, are now very lightly burthened with Poor . . . while other parishes, not politic enough to observe these rules, are generally burthened with an influx of poor neighbours.[9]

Because Mollington had taken the necessary precautions its inhabitants were reluctant to discuss their financial position with Eden 'from an apprehension, that a discovery of the smallness of the taxes, in their parish, might oblige them to contribute towards easing the heavy burthens of the neighbouring parishes'. Elsewhere communities safeguarded themselves by demanding from any labourer who came to work in them a certificate recognizing his chargeability to his parish of settlement.

But it was in cases involving the settlement by birth of illegitimate children that the selfish attitude of villagers was seen most clearly. It became of immediate concern to officials to send away the expectant mothers of such children, since if they delayed, the child would become their responsibility when it was born. So there appear entries in the overseers' accounts like that at Eynsham in Oxfordshire on 20 January 1788: 'To a Woman big with Child to help her on the Road 1s. 0d.'[10] While at Wool in Dorset the accounts for 1833 have the following entries:[11]

20 July	Relieved a travelling woman and her two children	1. 0d.
22 July	The above woman being in the family way, having	
	refused to leave the parish gave her to leave	2. 0d.
	Paid Christopher Brown for conveying her to the next	
	parish	1s. 0d.

Often the removal of the women was carried out with considerable harshness, so that in 1814 a girl who was being sent from Bedwellty to Haverfordwest in Pembrokeshire gave birth to her child on the way.[12] Her case was not unique.

The Bastardy Act of 1733 provided one way out of the dilemma. Under this Act a pregnant woman had only to charge a man on oath before a magistrate with having got her with child to enable the magistrate 'to apprehend and imprison the man', unless he gave security to indemnify the parish from all expense. However, another clause of the Act authorized his release from penalty if he would agree to marry her. This meant that a pregnant unmarried woman would often be encouraged by parish officers to name as the putative father a man from a neighbouring village. Arrangements would then be put in hand to secure a marriage and, with it, the woman's settlement in her husband's community. Parson Woodforde officiated at one such forced marriage in Norfolk in January 1787:

Rode to Ringland this Morning and married one Robert Astick and Elizabeth Howlett by Licence . . . the Man being in Custody, the Woman being with Child by him. The Man was a long time before he could be prevailed on to marry her when in the Church Yard; and at the Altar behaved very unbecoming. It is a cruel thing that any Person should be compelled by Law to marry. I recd. of the Officers for marrying them 0.10.6.[13]

At Sawston in Cambridgeshire three years later the overseers spent the substantial sum of £7 12s. 8d. on what was apparently another 'forced' wedding.[14]

An equally strong determination to avoid the burial expenses of strangers prevailed in other communities. In 1773 a coroner's inquest at Shipton-under-Wychwood, held on a woman and her child who had been found dead on the road, established that both had died from

starvation and that shortly before their death they had been turned out
of a nearby village by the overseers, so that their funeral expenses might
fall elsewhere.[15] It was to prevent cases like this that legislation in 1795
restricted removal to those fit to travel.

The Bastardy Act of 1733 had effected one significant change in the
relief system. Another was to grow out of legislation passed a decade
earlier, which permitted parishes to establish workhouses and to refuse
relief to those who would not enter them. This measure also authorized
overseers to enter into contracts for the maintenance and employment
of the poor. Normally that meant that for a fixed payment from the
parish the contractor would assume all responsibility for workhouse
relief and would retain any profits derived from the employment of the
paupers. From 1756 this legislation was further extended by local Acts
permitting groups of parishes to join together in incorporations in
order to establish a common workhouse for the whole unit. The policy
was widely adopted in East Anglia, and by 1776 eight incorporations
had been set up in the two counties of Norfolk and Suffolk alone.
Each had a workhouse capable of accommodating between 150 and
350 persons, who were engaged in making fishing nets and ropes or
corn sacks and plough lines, according to local demand.[16] The idea was
to balance 'the interests of the poor in a humane system of relief with
those of the ratepayers in an economical administration'.[17] At the
Rollesby House of Industry opened by the East and West Flegg
Incorporation in Norfolk in 1777 the reformers' intentions were carefully inscribed over the entrance:

For the Instruction of Youth
The Encouragement of Industry
The Relief of Want
The Support of Old Age
And the Comfort of
Infirmity and Pain.[18]

But in practice the problems of administration, the difficulty of providing suitable employment for the inmates and the high cost of the
enterprise led to a weakening of resolve by the nineteenth century, and
in many cases there was a growing resort to the payment of small sums
of out-relief to the needy. Nevertheless, the incorporations, as administrative units, lasted well into the nineteenth century; by 1834 a quarter
of Norfolk parishes were covered by them.[19]
Outside East Anglia the vast majority of poorhouses served individ-

ual parishes only, and while some were fairly comfortable, despite their rigid rules and regulations, many more resembled the sad picture drawn by the Suffolk poet George Crabbe of Aldeburgh in 1783:

Theirs is yon house that holds the parish-poor,
Whose walls of mud scarce bear the broken door;
There, where the putrid vapours, flagging, play,
And the dull wheel hums doleful through the day; –
There children dwell who know no parents' care;
Parents, who know no children's love, dwell there!
Heartbroken matrons on their joyless bed,
Forsaken wives, and mothers never wed;
Dejected widows with unheeded tears;
And crippled age with more than childhood fears;
The lame, the blind, and, far the happiest they!
The moping idiot and the madman gay.

Faced with conditions like these, public opinion began to swing round towards a policy of giving more widespread *outdoor* relief, particularly to those who were thrown out of employment by economic depression or whose earnings were insufficient for their support. Their attitude was reinforced by the sharp rise in population which occurred in England during the second half of the eighteenth century and which rendered the old methods of relief inadequate, especially when they were accompanied from the early 1790s by bad harvests at home and the inflationary effects of war with France. In 1782 an Act sponsored by the MP Thomas Gilbert had allowed parishes to restrict their workhouse to the aged, sick and handicapped, so that it became a refuge for the infirm rather than a place of punishment for the able-bodied unemployed. This latter group were to be found work and their earnings were to be subsidized out of the poor rate if they proved insufficient for their maintenance. As under the earlier incorporations, groups of parishes could join together into unions to operate the new measure. However, because its terms were permissive only a minority of communities elected to adopt it. By 1830 they numbered less than 1000 of the 15,000 parishes in England and Wales. Nevertheless, Gilbert's Act was important, in that it explicitly authorized the assistance of the able-bodied from the rates and the payment of out-relief to them.

From 1795 this policy, humane in intent if not always in execution, was to be taken further under the Speenhamland system and its variants. As we saw in Chapter 2, under the scale of allowances introduced, the income deemed necessary to support a man and his family was regulated by the price of bread. If his normal income did not match that minimum need, then he would receive a supplement from the poor rates. Not all parishes adopted a bread scale, however. Some provided subsidized food, as was the case at Newton Vallence in Hampshire, where each labourer, whether young or old, with or without children was permitted to buy flour at 8s. a bushel; all extra costs were met from the poor rates: 'A man with this allowance is supposed to be capable of maintaining a wife and 2 children, and paying his rent from his earnings: when the family exceeds that number, a proportionate allowance is made.'[20] The policy was reinforced by the Parochial Relief Act of 1800, which allowed (but did not compel) overseers to give up to a third of total relief in cereal substitutes.[21]

Soup kitchens were another form of aid, though one not always appreciated by the poor they were designed to assist. According to a Yorkshire vicar, the soup was 'either shamefully wasted, or given to the pigs'.[22] And at Newent in Gloucestershire, where a soup kitchen was opened twice a week early in 1800, it was decided 'out of respect to the opinions, tastes, judgements and even prejudices of others . . . on the day of sale above mentioned' to sell 'other articles of Food, such as Rice, Potatoes, and white Herrings', at reduced prices.[23]

Far more common was the payment of child allowances, especially to large families. By 1832 82 per cent of the sample parishes reporting to the Royal Commission on the Poor Laws from Sussex gave such payments; in Buckinghamshire, 71 per cent did so; in Suffolk, 74 per cent; and in Warwickshire, 60 per cent.[24] Elsewhere, for example in Kent, parishes organized community farms and workshops for the employment of paupers or provided allotments where they could cultivate vegteables.[25] In at least one Warwickshire village a communal bakehouse was built in 1795, and arrangements were made for a rota of persons to buy flour and serve bread to the needy at below cost price.[26] Such were the devices adopted to deal with the severe problems of poverty and hunger during the war years and in the period of agricultural depression which followed.

The apprenticeship of pauper children, as provided under the 1598 and 1601 Acts, was a further method used by overseers to ease relief burdens; apart from its possible long-term value in giving a child appropriate training, it was a convenient way of moving the youngsters concerned outside parish boundaries, thereby enabling them to gain a 'settlement' in a fresh community. In the north of England this could involve sending the children to be 'apprenticed' in the new cotton mills. In other cases the youngsters might be set to a trade or put to a farmer. At Tysoe in Warwickshire great care was taken over this, and a small boy m'ght be 'escorted many miles', so that he could enter an appropriate workshop.[27] But there was always a danger that, like Oliver Twist, these solitary young apprentices would be ill-treated. A Devon girl engaged by a local farmer at about the age of eight in 1810 later recalled the beatings she had endured from her mistress. Twenty-five years later she still had marks upon her from the blows she had received as a girl.[28] Happily, most youngsters were more fortunate than she, but for the unlucky ones that was small consolation. Even the 1802 Health and Morals of Apprentices Act, which was specifically designed to regulate the hours and working conditions of pauper children in the textile mills, proved a dead letter for want of an effective enforcement agency. Young apprentices in the factories, as elsewhere, remained virtually without defence against systematic exploitation.

But if pauper children received little protection from the law, their elders at least were rather better placed from 1796, when a special complaints procedure was introduced for them. If relief were for any reason withheld by parish officers, an aggrieved applicant had the right to present his case to local magistrates, and it is clear that a number did so. For example, the minute book of the magistrates for the three hundreds of Aylesbury shows that on 29 November 1800 William Brookes of Princes Risborough complained that he had applied 'to the overseers for work, or to give him relief, wch, they refused'. In this case the parish officers were ordered 'to employ him, or give him 5s. p. week'. There were many similar encounters.[29]

The work provided by parishes for paupers like Brookes was inevitably limited in scope. It might take the form of setting them to repair the roads or of sending them from one ratepayer to another, on the so-called 'roundsman' system, until they found someone willing to engage them, at a wage subsidised by the parish. This system was in use in some communities by the 1780s, and it is significant that as early as 1794 the chairman of the Oxford Quarter Sessions was deploring 'the Custom too commonly practised in most Parishes of making the Poor go, what is called, *the Rounds*, at Wages inadequate to the common Wants and Necessaries of Life'. He called unsuccessfully for the adoption of 'some better Mode of employing the Poor, during the Winter months'.[30]

Not surprisingly, the workers concerned had little interest in the tasks they undertook as 'roundsmen', since they were given relief whether they performed well or not. Occasionally, especially in the early nineteenth century, unemployed labourers were even put up for

auction – a procedure redolent of the slave market and utterly demoralizing for those concerned. Although basically designed to discourage
applications for relief from the able-bodied, the aged, too, might be
subjected to this indignity in some parishes. At Dolgelley in Wales
they were regularly let out 'in a sort of Dutch auction' at the annual
vestry 'to those who would take them for the least amount'. In 1822
this same vestry also declared that no relief should be given at all if
there were 'a clock or any useless furniture in the house'. Only when
that had been sold did the applicant become eligible for aid from the
parish.[31]

A variation on the theme of relief to the able-bodied was the use of
the 'labour rate' system, whereby each ratepayer agreed to employ a
certain number of men according to his poor-rate assessment. If he had
no need of the workers, he could pay to the parish the equivalent value
of their wages. Although of dubious legality until temporarily authorized by an Act of Parliament in 1831, this method at least had the merit
of providing a man with a regular employer and of permitting the
latter to choose which workers he would engage. As early as 1824 the
Select Committee on Labourers' Wages was enthusiastically claiming
that 'much good' had been effected by the adoption of this approach.[32]

Originally Speenhamland and its alternatives had been introduced to
deal with the pressures of the war years, when the parish poor-rate
expenditure soared,[33] but it was a policy which continued in many
parishes into the post-war era as well. Indeed, one writer has argued
that in 1814 *per capita* relief payments in real terms (taking into account
wartime inflation) were probably no greater in most counties than
they had been in 1792. Only in the period of economic (particularly
agricultural) depression after 1815 did the outlay begin to rise sharply,
reaching its absolute peak in 1817–19.[34] In those crisis years national
expenditure on poor relief reached almost £8 million per annum, or
between 12s. and 13s. per head of the population, as compared with
less than £2 million spent in 1783–5 and £5.7 million in 1815–16.
Machine-breaking and arson among the labourers in these years underlined the tensions caused by poverty and unemployment, particularly
in East Anglia. Men no longer regarded the receipt of poor relief as a
disgrace. As the Duke of Bedford's Woburn agent wrote in 1816, once,
they 'would shudder and lament at the Idea of taking Parochial relief',
but now they accepted it as the only way to stay alive.[35]

So it was in conditions of high poor-rate expenditure, and following
the investigations of a Select Committee on the Poor Laws, that in 1819
a new Act allowed parishes to set up select vestries to control relief

payments more rigidly. Salaried assistant overseers could be appointed to supplement the work of existing unpaid officers, and the vestries were to be elected by the most substantial ratepayers, using a system of plural voting, since it was argued that the well-to-do had the greatest personal interest in cutting expenditure. By 1828 nearly 3000 parishes in England and Wales had taken advantage of the Act, but the zeal with which they pursued reform varied widely. Of the select vestry at Thame in Oxfordshire it was reported in the mid-1830s:

they have expended Six thousand pounds in one year for the Relief of the Poor – and . . . their average expenditure for the last three years is upwards of £5,000. At the time of my visiting this Parish they had 127 able bodied men out of employ, very many of whom I discovered loitering about and playing with halfpence at the old game of pitch and hustle upon the Roads, where they professedly were at work.[36]

Although as trade revived in the early 1820s there was a slight fall in national poor relief expenditure, in rural areas it remained high throughout the decade. In some country districts, indeed, new relief plans were still being formulated at a time when other communities were trying to prune their payments. Cambridgeshire, for example, did not draw up a county-wide bread scale until 1821, while in the Chelmsford division of Essex the bread-scale system first made its appearance in that year.[37] Only in the north of England, where alternative employment was available in the growing industrial towns and in the mining industry and where the annual hiring of farm workers was more common, did parish relief prove less significant. The 'roundsman' system was, in any case, not appropriate to pastoral communities, where labour requirements remained fairly constant throughout the year. In Westmorland an inhabitant of Barbon township observed in 1832: ' "Roundsmen" is [a term] not understood.' But in the southern counties, with chronic unemployment and underemployment and consequent low wages, reliance on relief in one form of another was prevalent. As one writer has recently observed 'the overwhelming majority of rural parishes in south-eastern England gave family allowances after the war'.[38]

In an attempt to reduce the burden of surplus labour, parish-sponsored emigration was adopted in some counties. Kent and Sussex were both involved in this during the post-war years, as was Oxfordshire. But given the scale of the problem, the movement of a few hundred people could do little more than scratch its surface. More significant was the voluntary migration of people from some of the leading Speenhamland counties during the period 1801–31. Two counties – Wiltshire and Berkshire – both had a high rate of estimated natural increase and a very heavy loss through emigration to other areas. Buckinghamshire, Dorset, Huntingdon and Oxfordshire also seem to have lost between a quarter and a third of their total natural increase through migration during the three decades.[39]

Meanwhile, to a growing number of critics the relief system had become a costly way of perpetuating pauperism. There were demands by some for the abolition of *all* forms of parish aid. The MP J. C. Curwen, when calling in 1816 for the appointment of a Select Committee to investigate the Poor Laws, did so in a speech 'notably tinged with abolitionism and rancor against the poor'.[40] But abolition was no answer in a society already torn by internal dissensions and disorders. The other possibility was to restrict the terms on which relief was given. This might be done through the adoption of well regulated select vestries, with strict scales of allowance, or by taking firm action to discourage applicants. At Tysoe the Easter vestry meeting of 1818

unanimously agreed that all men and boys who are out of employ shall walk from the Coal Barn as far as the Red Lion Inn in Middle Tysoe, or stand in the gateway near the Barn the full space of ten hours on each day from the above date till Michaelmas next, and also it is agreed that if any person enter any house during the ten hours he or she shall receive no pay from the Parish.[41]

The discomfort and boredom which such a policy represented are easy to imagine. The auctioning of paupers mentioned above, was another aspect of this approach, while in Nottinghamshire still more rigorous experiments were made in cutting back relief payments and imposing the labour test without exception on applicants. At the centre here was the deterrent workhouse, which would be 'looked to with dread by [the] labouring class, and the reproach for being an inmate of it extend downwards from Father to Son'.[42] In that way, it was felt, men would be encouraged to seek work for themselves.

Elsewhere the 'roundsman' system itself was brought to an end in an attempt to restore normal employer–worker relationships. By 1832 only three counties (Oxfordshire, Northamptonshire and Warwickshire) out of fourteen especially affected by the Speenhamland system admitted to the Royal Commission on the Poor Laws that they still had 'roundsmen' employed in more than 20 per cent of their sample parishes, though several more admitted to the less demoralizing labour-rate method.[43]

The difficulties which the relief system could create for the worker are made very clear in the reminiscences of Joseph Mayett of Buckinghamshire. After he had been demobilized from the armed forces Mayett returned to his home parish of Quainton in 1815 and managed to obtain employment. But

at Michaelmas my master declined business and I was out of work and I being a Single man and at that time the King wanted Soldiers So the parish would not imploy me but I was determined not to go for a soldier again. So I set up to gather old raggs and sell a few things such as tapes laces thred and cotton &c. at which I done pretty well at first and still enjoyed my liberty.

Then: '18th of Dec. I married one of the young women that had recently joined the Church.' After this he was able to obtain work.[44] His experience was matched by reports from East Anglia and from Northamptonshire, where it was declared in the early 1830s that thanks to the scale system, farmers were encouraged to employ married men rather than single, since the wages of the former were subsidized by the parish:

in many villages, particularly in the southern district, they will not employ the single men at all; in others they pay them a much lower rate of wages for the same work, in the hope of driving them to seek work out of the parish. Instead of this, they marry directly, knowing that if they cannot maintain themselves, the parish must do it for them, and that the farmers will be more ready to give work to men likely to become burthensome, than to those who are not. The usual remark they make is, 'Well, I'll go and get a wife, and then you must do something for me.'[45]

In Wales, too, by the early nineteenth century parish relief was rarely paid to single able-bodied men in regular employment, though married labourers with more than three children were almost universally aided.[46] By such methods it was possible to discriminate between the 'deserving' applicant, who would receive favourable treatment, and the 'undeserving' or the 'roughs', who were given short shrift. The outwardly deferential were more likely to benefit than the defiant or the over-independent, so that in this way poor relief could be made an instrument for social control.

Nevertheless, by the mid-1830s the whole relief system was coming under strong attack, as public opinion swung against an arrangement which seemed designed to promote pauperism and to ruin the rate-payer. The tenor of the argument changed from the late eighteenth century's humanitarian concern for the poor to a preoccupation with the difficulties of those who were supporting them through the rates. As one contemporary sourly put it: 'The common ties of Master and Servant have been destroyed . . . and the only relative situations left are those of pauper and rate payer.'[47]

Nor was this all. Where pauperism was particularly heavy the propertied classes feared the insubordination of many of those relieved. A stronger discipline than mere benevolence seemed necessary to restore good order. In the north Devon parish of North Molton there were complaints that the parish vestry

was in continual alarm at the threats and depredations of the labourers and yielded to their threatening demands. Nearly the whole of the labouring population was during [the] winter [of 1835] entirely supported by the parish & their conduct & character were such as to make them the terror of the Neighbourhood.[48]

At Swallowfield in Berkshire a magistrate who had been active in promoting a select vestry in 1829 later claimed that he had been so afraid of arson that 'for the first time, [I] insured my farming stock'.[49]

Yet, though it was the effect of relief on able-bodied recipients which aroused the concern of contemporaries, it must be remembered that the majority of those aided – perhaps 70 per cent of them – were the elderly, the sick and the very young, to whom most of the criticisms did not directly apply.[50] But to those mesmerized by the vision of innumerable able-bodied men living on 'the parish', the need for reform was paramount. During the summer and autumn of 1830 their fears were reinforced when the labourers in the southern and south midland counties of England embarked on their campaign of arson and machine-breaking in an attempt to secure wage increases and the destruction of the threshing machines which they blamed for winter unemployment. They also showed their hatred of the poor-relief system by singling out parish overseers for attack in many areas. Indeed, in the view of several witnesses, including the incumbent of Kidlington in Oxford-shire, the 'Swing' riots had been sparked off by 'the mal-administration of the Poor Laws'.[51]

Often it seemed that the worst riots had taken place in those areas where poor-relief payments were at their highest. And it was with this in mind that the government appointed the 1832 Royal Commission on the Poor Laws. It followed similar examinations by Select Committees in 1817 and 1831. Evidence was collected from 3000 parishes, or about one in five of the total, but with a bias towards the agricultural rather than the industrial areas. Although it is alleged, with some truth, that the investigators were seeking abuses in order to justify reform, there is little doubt that the cases they reported upon were genuine. Unfortunately, their failure to recognize the true reasons for unemployment was later to cause much hardship. Moral weaknesses were pinpointed instead of such factors as population pressure, agricultural and industrial change and the problems of sickness and old age. These were the things which created pauperism, not the relief system itself or the innate laziness of the population.

The Commission's main recommendations were published in 1834. It called for the establishment of a central board to administer the Poor Law system throughout the country. At local level out-relief, save for medical attention, was to be ended for all able-bodied people. Instead they would be given indoor relief only; that is, the 'workhouse test' would be applied. Within the workhouses paupers were to be classified and separated according to age and sex; husbands, wives and children were all to be divided from one another. The prime objective was to discourage the able-bodied from seeking relief of any kind by making their position more uncomfortable, or 'less eligible', than that of any independent labourer.

The government hastened to act on the recommendations, and later in the same year the Poor Law Amendment Act was passed. In addition to covering the points mentioned above, it provided for groups of two or three dozen parishes to join together to form unions, with one workhouse to each union.[52] Administration within the union was to be controlled by a board of guardians, who would include all the local justices of the peace, plus members elected from among the ratepayers and property owners of the constituent parishes. In the event over three-quarters of the guardians in rural unions proved to be farmers, and as late as 1860 Sir John Walsham, the government's Poor Law inspector for East Anglia, could describe country boards as 'chiefly an association of farmers'.[53] Responsibility for the initial examination of claims for aid and for the distribution of relief was to be in the hands of paid relieving officers.

Within the unions, however, each parish continued to bear the cost of relieving its own poor, and this retention of such a small unit as the basis of relief proved a great weakness. Apart from its financial shortcomings, it led, as in the late eighteenth century, to repeated wrangles between communities over which of them was responsible for the 'settlement' of a particular pauper. Under the new Act conditions had been changed, so that it was no longer possible to gain settlement by annual hiring or by holding parish office, while an illegitimate child now normally took its mother's settlement. Nevertheless, disputes continued, even taking place within a single union. Thus the parishes of Bix and Henley within the Henley Union in Oxfordshire argued for five months over who was responsible for one miserable applicant. Eventually it was resolved that the Henley overseer should arrange for the man's removal to Bix and for the recovery of the amount 'due for his support'. But clearly the issue had aroused much ill feeling.[54]

Where landownership was concentrated in the hands of a few men who were also the principal ratepayers in a parish, cottages might be demolished in order to keep down the number of those who could claim a settlement. In this way rate expenditure, too, would be kept to a low level. One writer attributed the shortage of labourers' cottages in many Lincolnshire villages in the mid nineteenth century to the uneven distribution of the population:

the cause invariably assigned is the unwillingness of the parishes and pro-prietors to rebuild old houses or erect new ones in consequence of the 'Law of Settlement'. They wish to keep down the population in their respective parishes with a view of having less poor rate to pay.... In the neighbourhood of Kirton-in-Lindsey there is . . . the same lack of cottages, the owners neither building nor repairing them, because they would be obliged to support the families which might settle there. Consequently this town [Winterton], having many small freehold estates, is crowded with the poor from other parishes who hire dwellings here and go two or three miles to work.[55]

That was not, of course, a new problem. Under the old regime, too, the owners of 'close' or estate villages had sought to restrict population in an attempt to minimize their rate burden. But in 1846 the tendency was encouraged by a new Poor Removal Act, which conferred irre-movability upon any family who had continuously inhabited a parish for five years. Ironically, the Act had been designed to help the poor by clarifying the settlement issue, but in practice it encouraged 'close' parish landlords to force out those poor people who were likely to become chargeable. The burden on neighbouring 'open' parishes, where landownership was widely spread, became correspondingly greater, as they found themselves responsible for labouring families who had hitherto lived within their boundaries but had not been settled there. In Norfolk the lowest parish poor rate in 1847 was a mere ½d. in the pound, while the highest was 12s. 4d.; in 1861, the respective figures were ¾d. and 6s. 5¾d.[56] One Norfolk landlord even bought land in adjacent parishes for the sole purpose of housing his labourers outside his own community.[57] Over the years attempts were made to ease the position, but it was not until the 1865 Union Chargeability Act was passed, extending responsibility for relief to the whole union, that most of these problems were solved.

In the meantime, once the 1834 Act had been passed assistant commissioners were appointed by the central authorities in London to organize the parishes into their respective unions. In all over 15,000 parishes were to be combined into some 600 Poor Law unions. In drawing the boundaries for these the approach of the individual commissioners varied. Normally, when they reached the market town which was to act as the centre for a proposed union they would call a meeting of landowners and occupiers of land to persuade them of the value of the reforms. The method then adopted would depend to some degree on the nature of landownership and of existing Poor Law practice in the district. In Northamptonshire, where there were numerous peers and great landowners, the assistant commissioner had to give weight to the views of the larger magnates, 'and Poor Law unions in this area were therefore designed to accommodate the structure of land ownership and to reflect the related systems of social and political deference to the gentry'.[58] Likewise in Buckinghamshire, when assistant commissioner W. J. Gilbert was taxed by the Poor Law authorities with extravagance because he had hired carriages to travel in, he responded sharply by blaming the state of the county's roads and the inadequacy of the gigs offered for hire: 'I am certainly careless about my own convenience as to how I travel but I much doubt whether a nobleman's porter would not desire an arrival in such a vehicle to walk into the kitchen instead of the Parlour.' Making a good impression on a nobleman's household was obviously deemed an essential part of Gilbert's duties – at least in his own estimation.[59]

By contrast, in Norfolk, which was a county with fewer major landowners, the interests of the smaller landed gentry had to be considered: 'but . . . this [was] of only secondary importance. [The] first priority was to take account of the institutional restrictions which the local relief administration of the old Poor Law imposed upon them'. Before 1834 Norfolk had one-third of its parishes either in incorporations or in unions under Gilbert's Act. The assistant commissioners had to gain the consent of two-thirds of the guardians or directors of each union or incorporation before these could be dissolved and new Poor Law unions created.[60] The geographical problems presented by the earlier bodies also meant that one-third of Norfolk's rural unions had no central market town, but instead had to establish their workhouses and the place of meeting for their guardians in a village.

Occasionally there were clashes between the assistant commissioners over 'border' communities. When Edward Gulson undertook the unionization of some Berkshire parishes he was angered to find that his colleague Gilbert had already appropriated them for Buckinghamshire unions. Gulson even wrote to the Poor Law Commission in London to complain of Gilbert's determination to 'pursue his own course'. But these were only minor and perhaps inevitable difficulties.[61] By May 1837 most of the administrative work in the rural southern and south midland counties had been completed. Normally a workhouse had also to be constructed, though in some instances the old parish poorhouses were taken over or, as in East Anglia, the workhouses of the incorporations or Gilbert unions could be adapted for the new purpose. Among the many Poor Law unions building anew, however, was that at Witney in Oxfordshire, and it was from there that one of the guardians wrote to *Jackson's Oxford Journal* in 1835 to inform possible inmates of what lay in store for them:

First, I find upon entering, your own clothing will be exchanged for the workhouse dress, the men in plain grey cloth, the women in a check bed gown, over their other garments. Their own clothes to be cleaned and returned when they can maintain themselves. The men are then passed to their wards, and the women to theirs, and the children to other wards, according to age, sex, and other circumstances. Your food, according to its kind will be . . . served up by weight and measure, all sitting down in large dining rooms, one of which will be a Chapel to those of the Church of England. Dissenters will be allowed to go out to their own place of worship upon condition of immediate return.

No pauper will be allowed to go out without leave, and that but upon a particular occasion.

FOOD. Breakfast – Bread and gruel. Dinner – Meat and potatoes, three days, the other days soup. Supper – Bread and cheese or broth. No tea or beer allowed, except to the sick. Children will have their hair shorn close, be kept clean and educated.[62]

He failed to mention that strict silence had to be observed during meals or to describe the tasks which the paupers were expected to carry out, such as stone breaking, oakum picking, gardening and household work for the women and girls, though he did point out that opposition was pointless, for it had all been planned 'under the authority of Parliament . . . [and] the only resistance you or I could possibly offer is to strive to maintain our own independence'.

It is perhaps not surprising in these circumstances that in Suffolk the

workhouse and the gaol were both regarded as prisons; the workhouse
was considered the more uncomfortable of the two. The chaplain of
Bury St Edmunds gaol claimed that 'the *inducement of having more to eat*
led many of the inmates of Union Houses to commit offences', so that
they could be sent to prison.[63] And in those parts of Norfolk where
new workhouses were required, watchmen had to be employed to
prevent people from tearing the structures down before they could be
completed.[64]

The prime purpose of the Poor Law reform movement was, of
course, to reduce expenditure by discouraging appeals for aid. If that
were to be achieved, relief conditions had to be made unpleasant and
the concept of 'less eligibility' kept well to the fore. At Kendal workhouse the paupers were engaged in weaving canvas on handlooms, and
this won the approval of the assistant commissioner:

The most boorish agricultural labourer may learn it in a few days, and
cannot either by awkwardness or design injure the Material, or Machinery
. . . it is applicable to all ages and both Sexes from 14 to 60 . . . [and] the
Confinement and Monotony of the process render it highly undesirable
and irksome, to all Classes of Paupers.[65]

Nevertheless, in the initial stages of unionization the authorities felt
the need to proceed with caution in order to avoid provoking violent
resistance. The frightening memories of 1830 were still clear in many
minds, and it was realized that the poor looked upon the new developments with much suspicion. They particularly resented the interfering
investigations of the relieving officers and the policy of paying relief
partly in cash and partly in bread, instead of primarily in cash, as had
been the custom prior to 1834. Although opposition to the changes in
rural areas never reached the level of that in the industrial north, serious
outbursts did occur. In the Milton union in Kent, where a policy was
adopted of giving relief in the form of tickets redeemable for goods
rather than cash, riots were so severe in the spring of 1835 that special
constables had to be sworn in and metropolitan policemen sent down
from London. Within a short time twenty arrests were made, some of
them in near riot conditions, and when the prisoners were taken to
Canterbury gaol the yeomanry escorting them were stoned. Likewise
in the Amersham union in Buckinghamshire the closure of Chesham
workhouse in May 1835 and the removal of its inmates to the central
workhouse at Amersham led to disturbances. A large crowd massed in
front of the workhouse gates and refused to allow them to be opened
to let through the cart carrying the Chesham paupers to their new

destination. A magistrate present read the Riot Act and the crowd temporarily fell back, permitting the cart, accompanied by this single magistrate, to start on its journey. The distance to the village of Chesham Bois was only short, but the road was uphill all the way. The crowd followed closely behind as the cart wound its slow way along, and one by one the paupers were removed from it, until at Chesham Bois it was empty. The mob then turned on the magistrate, pelting him with stones and generally assaulting him. He managed to escape by hiding in a hedge, while his attackers, having achieved their objective, dispersed. The paupers, meanwhile, had returned to Chesham workhouse. The next day police arrived from London, and on the day following that the yeomanry were called in. Arrests were made and soon after the paupers were removed, under guard and without incident, to Amersham workhouse.[66]

Rumour played a part in these disturbances – as in north Devon, where relieving officers were assaulted and driven from villages, while relief in money was demanded and relief in kind rejected. Bakers were attacked in the hope that they would refuse to supply the union with goods for distribution as relief. But one of the causes of this unrest was said to be the universal belief among the labouring people that the new law meant death either in the workhouse or through the distribution of poisoned bread. 'Some of the paupers', an assistant commissioner commented, 'actually believed that if they touched the bread they would drop down dead.'[67] In Norfolk there were vicious attacks on relieving officers; one man was left for dead after having his throat cut and his head battered in by a man to whom he had refused assistance. A fortnight before this, in late May 1836, another relieving officer from the Swaffham union was stabbed.[68] Yet the outbursts were essentially sporadic, and despite the fears of those in authority, they were quickly put down – often by a few magistrates and policemen acting on their own. There was no sustained or planned campaign to halt the unionization process. As a historian of the anti-Poor Law movement has put it:

A sort of panic born of wild rumours seems to have swept across whole districts resulting here and there in brief periods of rioting. These were, with few exceptions, both sudden and unplanned. Only in East Suffolk was there a long period of rising discontent and lawlessness before the major outbreak; elsewhere the riots took place within three months or less of the formation of the Union.[69]

In Wales resistance proved more persistent. The 1834 Act was so unpopular there that it was difficult to find men prepared to act as guardians. In general only the poorest farmers were elected – the majority of them quite illiterate – and some had to be paid surreptitiously for their services. In west Wales many were of the same class as the paupers whom they relieved, and often they were elected on the sole understanding that they would refuse to build a workhouse. Some, like the guardians of Tregaron union, had to be pressed repeatedly before they would agree to erect one, while Lampeter, despite all efforts by the Poor Law Commission, was still without one in 1843.[70] By the late 1830s seven Welsh unions had no workhouse; at Narbeth the building was burnt down in 1839 before it could be completed. The guardians, for their part, offered stubborn resistance to all of the Commission's proposals. They particularly resented the payment of salaries to relieving and medical officers, for often these officials were better off than they were themselves. William Day, the assistant commissioner for Wales, had to intervene on several occasions to veto a reduction in officers' salaries. In other instances guardians were reluctant to commit people to the workhouse because they lived better there than the smaller independent farmers did. Two-thirds of the ratepayers in the principality were said to be 'barely removed from pauperism'.[71] And when the so-called Rebecca Riots broke out in Pembrokeshire, Carmarthenshire and Cardiganshire in 1842–3, ostensibly in opposition to the erection of new toll gates, it was widely believed that hatred of the Poor Law was a powerful underlying cause. Certainly, the legislation was frequently discussed at secret protest meetings, and memorials were sent to the queen and the Home Secretary asking for it to be changed. But in the long run the Poor Law was only one of many grievances nurtured by small farmers in impoverished west Wales; as an alien English intrusion, it provided a convenient scapegoat for other difficulties.[72]

Against this uneasy background, therefore, Poor Law guardians throughout England and Wales hesitated to implement the 1834 Act in full. Although relief to supplement wages had been explicitly frowned upon by the Poor Law commissioners in London, this practice continued in the mid-1830s, as in the Henley Union, where in May 1836 the board decided to allow a labourer, his wife and eight children an allowance of two gallons of bread, even though the man was 'in full work'. On 8 September 1835 the same guardians had approved a resolution calling upon the overseers and surveyors 'of every Parish within the Union . . . [to] seek out for, and give employment to their own Poor who need it, rather than make it necessary for the Board, to order them into the Workhouse'. According to the principles of 1834, such people should have been referred for indoor relief.[73]

In east Lancashire the wages of handloom weavers, hit by the growth of the factories, continued to be subsidized. Assistant commissioner Alfred Power admitted that

the outdoor relief system could not be abolished overnight in the weaving districts of Lancashire, and had merely advised the select committee of [1838] that any future relief should be given in provisions rather than in money. Thus the willingness of the new Poor Law officials to ignore the letter of the law and to relieve handloom weavers with tools, food, and subsidized wages seems, in short, to have continued for as long as the weavers remained a serious social problem.[74]

On rather different grounds, the assistant commissioner for Kent and East Sussex was pained to discover that labourers on out-relief were still able to enjoy themselves. At Uckfield when they were 'supposed to be starving, they were dancing at 2s. 6d. a-head', while elsewhere labourers' balls were given and 'one pauper in receipt of out-relief actually gave a ball'.[75] To encourage such pauper junketings was quite against official policy. Again, in October 1842 assistant commissioner Hawley reported that at the two workhouses in Kendal the guardians had refused to conform to Poor Law regulations, notably in regard to 'classification':

The married Paupers whether able or infirm are all allowed to sleep together and this objectionable practice is defended by the Guardians as a principle applicable to the administration of rewards & punishments! for on a pauper in *one* of the Workhouses committing any specific offence he is immediately separated from his wife and sent off to the other . . . in both Houses the able bodied women are paid in proportion to the amount of the proceeds of their labour, their weekly gratuities . . . averaging about three halfpence. This is paid to them during their residence in the workhouse, and the clandestine conveyance of tea, coffee, and other forbidden articles into the workhouse is the necessary result of the practice.

Nonetheless, he advised caution in dealing with the guardians, whom he described as 'composed of such factions and inflammable materials' that a 'conciliatory policy' was essential to end the 'abuses'.[76] The guardians, for their part, put up a stout resistance to Poor Law directives before they were eventually forced to give way.

Gradually, therefore, pressure was exerted from London on recalcitrant boards, and a flurry of letters, orders, circulars and assistant commissioners descended on those who refused to mend their ways. Out-relief to the able-bodied remained an especial difficulty. With indoor assistance the order of the day, reformers had believed that employers would find it cheaper to engage labourers rather than 'pay for expensive indoor relief in the workhouse, while the labourers themselves would prefer independent labour to the deterrent conditions in the workhouse'.[77] But those aims were never achieved, despite the issuing in 1844 of an Outdoor Relief Prohibitory Order by the Poor Law Commission and its adoption by almost five-sixths of the unions, including virtually all of those in rural areas. Some guardians argued that on humanitarian grounds it was wrong to split up families by sending them to a workhouse, if a little outdoor relief would keep them together. Others discovered that on a *per capita* basis out-relief was cheaper than maintenance in a workhouse, even at the low standard of living which its inmates enjoyed. The outdoor pauper could be fobbed off with a shilling or so and a loaf and left to make the best of things. In 1860 paupers in the eastern counties were only costing 1s. 9d. a week if relieved outside the workhouse but 3s. 5½d. a week if taken inside.[78] And in the quarter ending Christmas 1837 it cost (excluding establishment expenses) £1 6s. 2d. to maintain an indoor pauper in the Chipping Norton union in Oxfordshire, but only 16s. 4d. per head for those on out-relief; in the Banbury union the respective figures were £1 1s. 5d. and 19s. 1d.[79]

So there began to be a 'bending' of the regulations, especially on the pretext of illness or to cover 'sudden and urgent necessity', a vague expression in the Poor Law regulations which permitted out-relief to the able-bodied and which was never clearly defined. Allowances on account of sickness were given indiscriminately by half the unions in East Anglia, and another fifth gave freely to those with large families.[80] As Sir John Walsham observed of this area in 1856, despite the issuing of prohibitory orders: 'the tendency everywhere is to substitute outdoor for in-door relief whenever the guardians may legally do so'.[81] In Wales, too, out-relief remained dominant, while in 1847 certain unions in England, such as those for Crediton in Devon and Boston in Lincolnshire, obtained special powers to offer out-relief in return for the performance of certain specified tasks, usually on workhouse premises. Permission was given because of the 'great distress' prevailing among the labouring people, 'in consequence of the failure of the potato crop & the high price of provisions', and the fact that the respective workhouses were already full.[82]

Another variant adopted in the counties of Essex, Suffolk, Norfolk,

Cambridgeshire, Hertfordshire and Bedfordshire was the 'ticket' system, which bore a great similarity to the old 'roundsman' idea. Under it an unemployed man who applied for relief received a ticket from the relieving officer. This he had to take round to employers in the parish, who either gave him work or signed a statement saying that they could not employ him. Only when that had been done would the guardians offer relief. Unfortunately, the policy encouraged farmers to offer low-wage jobs which the men could not refuse, and in an area already noted for its surplus labour (save at harvest time) and its depressed wages, the ticket system reinforced an already unsatisfactory situation. For this reason it was very unpopular among the men. It also permitted guardians to postpone giving relief to a worker for a period of up to a week from the time his last wages had been paid – yet another example of the principle of 'less eligibility' in operation.[83]

So whatever the intentions of the 1834 Poor Law Amendment Act may have been, in practice outdoor relief continued to flourish. In 1850 of 1,000,000 people aided, only 110,000 of them were inmates of a workhouse; in 1860 the respective figures were 860,000 and 125,000. Even in Norfolk, where the Poor Law Commission had initially managed to reduce the proportion of the able-bodied on out-relief – to only 64 per cent of all adult able-bodied paupers in 1843 – by the 1850s the percentage had jumped to 82.1 and remained high in succeeding decades.[84] The position in nine specimen counties during the 1840s is given in Table 3. Except for Norfolk, and to a smaller extent Sussex (a formerly notorious Speenhamland county), none managed to register fewer than three-quarters of its able-bodied paupers on out-relief, while at least a quarter of all paupers were able-bodied. Clearly, in such circumstances indoor relief was seen as a possible device for dealing with the recalcitrant or the 'undeserving' able-bodied, but it was not used as a broad deterrent in the manner envisaged by those who had framed the Poor Law Amendment Act.

One alternative to the provision of out-relief was, of course, to assist 'surplus' labourers to emigrate, along lines recommended by the 1834 Poor Law Report itself. Between 1835 and 1837, 6403 people from twenty counties in southern England were helped by their parishes to emigrate, mainly to Canada. Nearly two-thirds of them came from East Anglia. But the scheme then ran into difficulties, as landowners and farmers realized that they were losing some of their best workers permanently. From the late 1830s the pace of emigration slackened. In all, between 1834 and 1853 about 24,000 people were assisted to move, Australia being the most popular destination in the later stages.[85] From

Table 3 *Paupers relieved during quarters ending 25 March in each year 1840–5 in specimen counties, distinguishing between former Speenhamland and non-Speenhamland areas*

	1840	1841	1842	1843	1844	1845
SPEENHAMLAND COUNTIES*						
Buckinghamshire						
Total paupers	15,884	18,624	18,475	18,458	19,479	20,588
Proportion of paupers who were able-bodied	27·4%	29·6%	27·6%	30·7%	31·9%	31·6%
Proportion of able-bodied paupers on out-relief	87·1%	83·5%	82·8%	78·0%	73·7%	77·1%
Dorset						
Total paupers	19,416	21,549	21,305	22,591	22,248	23,910
Proportion of paupers who were able-bodied	22·6%	24·7%	24·4%	26·6%	26·2%	26·7%
Proportion of able-bodied paupers on out-relief	87·9%	86·9%	85·5%	85·3%	86·0%	87·0%
Norfolk						
Total paupers	31,076	33,034	34,876	37,666	41,255	42,161
Proportion of paupers were were able-bodied	20·1%	20·7%	22·1%	24·1%	25·3%	25·2%
Proportion of able-bodies paupers on out-relief	75·5%	72·4%	67·8%	64·0%	66·2%	66·9%
Oxfordshire						
Total paupers	14,880	16,360	16,478	19,043	19,245	22,046
Proportion of paupers who were able-bodied	25·0%	26·3%	26·2%	29·4%	29·8%	30·0%
Proportion of able-bodied paupers on out-relief	85·3%	80·4%	80·0%	80·5%	79·8%	81·8%

	1840	1841	1842	1843	1844	1845
Sussex						
Total paupers	26,149	29,257	29,494	31,223	29,619	31,027
Proportion of paupers who were able-bodied	22·3%	24·6%	23·6%	26·1%	26·0%	26·3%
Proportion of able-bodied paupers on out-relief	72·2%	71·6%	73·5%	70·7%	73·9%	74·5%
Wiltshire						
Total paupers	30,009	30,003	35,827	36,735	36,250	36,296
Proportion of paupers who were able-bodied	26·1%	26·1%	30·4%	29·6%	29·4%	29·3%
Proportion of able-bodied paupers on out-relief	83·2%	78·4%	80·6%	75·8%	75·2%	76·5%
Yorkshire, North Riding						
Total paupers	11,929	12,692	14,327	14,742	14,962	13,754
Proportion of paupers who were able-bodied	19·9%	20·8%	28·6%	29·5%	29·5%	26·5%
Proportion of able-bodied paupers on out-relief	91·6%	90·1%	74·8%	79·8%	76·5%	79·3%
NON-SPEENHAMLAND COUNTIES						
Cumberland						
Total paupers	11,925	11,634	11,999	11,227	11,357	11,108
Proportion of paupers who were able-bodied	25·3%	24·6%	26·2%	27·1%	27·0%	26·4%
Proportion of able-bodied paupers on out-relief	83·5%	82·3%	82·4%	75·0%	73·7%	78·4%

	1840	1841	1842	1843	1844	1845
Westmorland						
Total paupers	4745	5112	6115	7270	6223	5331
Proportion of paupers who were able-bodied	27·2%	26·2%	30·8%	36·9%	30·5%	29·9%
Proportion of able-bodied paupers on out-relief	79·6%	84·1%	77·1%	78·6%	83·1%	83·1%

*The Speenhamland counties are defined by M. Blaug, 'The myth of the old Poor Law', in M. W. Flinn and T. C. Smout (eds.), *Essays in Social History* (Oxford 1974), p. 145.

SOURCES: *Annual Reports* of the Poor Law Commission.

the mid-1850s the impact of the scheme was negligible, though it remained in existence to 1870. But by then opportunities for railway building and industrial employment in England had helped to reduce the attractions of overseas settlement for redundant rural workers.

In bringing about these *internal* population movements individual initiative was the principal factor. Nevertheless, a small attempt was made by the Poor Law Commission between 1835 and 1837 to encourage migration to the northern industrial areas; 4323 people were removed under its auspices during that period. The scheme came to an end with the industrial recession of the later 1830s, but even before then a number of the rural migrants had found adjustment to life in a manufacturing town too much for them. Nearly half of the total migrants came from Suffolk, and two out of every five of them had returned home before August 1837, that is, before the real onset of the depression.[86] Clearly those prepared to move of their own volition were more likely to make a success of the venture than those who moved under Poor Law guidance.

It now remains to consider the position of the 'legitimate' recipients of out-relief – the old, the genuinely sick and the disabled. To them, too, the unsympathetic 'less eligibility' policy of 1834 was applied, despite the Poor Law Commission's original, more humane, intentions. Often it took the form of extremely low levels of relief. In the Bicester Union, Oxfordshire, during 1837 2s. per week in cash and a loaf was the relief given to elderly men and women living alone, even when they were paying a weekly rent of 1s. or 1s. 6d. Without help from friends and neighbours they must have starved.

A further problem was that when old people received their meagre out-relief the union would normally require their grown-up children to contribute something towards it. If they refused to do so, they could be brought before the magistrates and compelled to pay; the effect of such a measure on family relationships is only too easy to imagine. The nature of this peremptory approach can be gauged from an entry in the Bicester minute book during October 1848:

The Clerk was directed to write to the three sons of Joseph Hinks of Weston on the Green to inform them that their Father and Mother had become chargeable . . . that the Board had been informed that they were of sufficient ability to contribute towards their support – and unless they did so – an order would be applied for, to compel them to do so.

(As in the eighteenth century, a similarly firm line was taken with men who absconded, leaving their wives and children chargeable; a warrant for their arrest was speedily issued.)[87] And for those old people who were unable to subsist on out-relief there was always the dread of ending their days in the 'house' itself, with its rigid and unsympathetic daily routine. As early as 1842 the Poor Law commissioners had told the unions that workhouse uniform was not compulsory for old people, as long as their own clothes were removed, but few took advantage of the concession. As one man recalled:

The poor old folk are as plainly branded by their dress and in many cases more ashamed of it than a felon would be. . . . Even if they have decent clothes on entering . . . they are only permitted to wear parochial clothing and must walk about the streets labelled as paupers. I have known many refuse to avail themselves of the monthly holiday because they were ashamed to be seen so dressed.[88]

Although most would have been better off, in terms of food, on indoor relief, they preferred the freedom of their own homes and familiar surroundings to the regimentation of a system which, as at Forehoe in Norfolk, kept the old men from the workhouse garden 'because their gardening prowess had produced a more luxurious diet which was not sanctioned by the official workhouse dietary'.[89] Occasionally, as with the Andover workhouse in Hampshire, this official insensitivity slid over into outright brutality, and inmates were harshly treated and half-starved. The disclosure of conditions at Andover in 1845–6 led to a reorganization of the central Poor Law administration and the appointment in 1847 of a new Poor Law Board to replace the former Poor Law Commission.[90]

Despite their fears, however, most old people in receipt of relief – like their younger brethren – did *not* enter a workhouse. It was cheaper to keep them outside.

Apart from providing aid in cash and kind to the needy, the Poor Law unions had the duty of supplying medical relief and, if necessary, pauper burials. Such help had also been a feature of the pre-1834 regime, and contracts had regularly been concluded between parishes and local doctors. In 1783 Wateringbury parish in Kent agreed with John Hosmer, surgeon, that he should 'take the poor of the said parish and find them with proper medicines and attendance for the sum of six pounds six shillings for the year . . . but he . . . is to be paid over and above for all midwifery cases, fractures and inoculation [against smallpox]. He is also not to attend any parishioners but those within four miles of Wateringbury.'[91] At Eynsham in Oxfordshire not only were medical services provided, but arrangements were also made for villagers to be treated at the Radcliffe Infirmary in Oxford. In June 1787 3s. was spent in hiring a cart to take a sick woman to the Infirmary, plus a further 16s. 2d. to fit her out with 'Linen, Stockings &c' for her stay. The parish had disbursed £3 3s. in the previous March on 'Infirmary money', and this was a regular entry in the overseers' accounts. Almost four years later, in an attempt to combat smallpox, a campaign of mass inoculation was embarked upon; £20 18s. 6d. was paid to a Dr Lankshear 'for Inoculating 159 poor Persons' and £6 11s. 6d. expended in relief 'to divers poor Families whilst the Inoculation of the Small Pox was carrying on'. J. Pimm was allowed, 'for his trouble in visiting the Poor under Inoculation', £1 1s. od.[92] Should an illness prove fatal, the parish would also finance the funeral.

After 1834 these various duties were taken over by the unions, and district medical officers were appointed within each of them. Needless to say, as with most union operations, economy was the order of the day. Many guardians even called for tenders for their posts in the early days, and the lowest figure offered was the one that was accepted. From 1842, however, such undignified procedures were ended, as medical men were put on a salary. But a serious remaining problem was that under most contracts doctors were expected to provide medicines out of their salaries. Only in midwifery cases and for mending broken bones was extra cash available. Given that contracts might be as low as

£10 per annum – that sum being paid in the Boston union in 1847 to a doctor with responsibility for 430 people – practitioners were encouraged to provide the cheapest medicaments possible. In this respect some paupers probably fared worse under the post-1834 system than they had done earlier.[93] Not until 1865 did the Poor Law Board in London issue a circular encouraging guardians to hold stocks of cod-liver oil, quinine and other 'expensive medicines' upon which doctors and patients could draw, but as it was a permissive measure, not all unions took advantage of it.

On the other hand, from the start 'prescriptions' of meat, bread, wine or beer could be paid for out of the rates, and so it became common for medical officers to order mutton or beer for anything from fever and tuberculosis to ovarian diseases. Free vaccination against smallpox, replacing the earlier inoculation method, was also provided in some unions from an early stage, even before it received governmental blessing in 1840. At Bicester in October 1835 district medical officers were asked to 'vaccinate every person in their respective parishes that may require it', and the comparatively generous fee of 1s. 6d. was to be paid in each case. But many parents, suspicious of the quality of the vaccine used, objected to these initiatives, and up to the 1870s the vaccination policy was limited in application. The clerk to the Crediton union summed up the typical response when he observed in 1847: 'There has been a less number of Children vaccinated in this year than in any preceding one, because the small pox has not shewn itself and people will not have their Children vaccinated unless they are in immediate fear of the small pox.'[94]

Another weakness was that the medical districts were often too large to be covered by one doctor. In Northumberland the Haltwistle union had two districts comprising 108 square miles, while in Westmorland the Shapwest district covered 98 square miles; the distance from the surgeon's residence in one direction was nine miles. Likewise the Banbury union in Oxfordshire, which contained fifty-one parishes (in pre-1834 days attended by fourteen or fifteen doctors), in 1836 entrusted its entire area to three men. One of them held a district of thirty-three parishes, fifteen miles in width. Speedy attendance upon the sick was impossible, especially as doctors were only supposed to take on a case when they had been duly authorized by the relevant relieving officer. Some of the patients died unvisited, and in 1838 it was decided to rearrange the union into eight districts, each with its own medical officer.[95] Not until 1842 was a General Medical Order issued which stipulated that the maximum area for medical districts was to be 15,000

acres, with a population not exceeding 15,000. Special permission had
to be obtained from the Poor Law Commission by unions which were
unable to conform.[96]

Without Poor Law medical aid many sick people would have been
unable to afford any treatment beyond that provided by family care
and home-brewed herbal remedies. But the weaknesses of the system
seriously undermined the value of the help that was given. Charles
Kingsley, rector of Eversley in Hampshire, pointed out in 1854 that
people from his parish were forced to walk four or five miles over a
'moor and two fords' in order to seek help from their medical officer,[97]
while a Kent clergyman claimed that doctors paid more attention to
patients they received through friendly societies and medical clubs
(see Chapter 5) than to those acquired through the Poor Law. They
took a greater interest in club patients because there was rivalry between
them 'from the patient having a choice and being able in the subsequent
year to change his medical adviser. . . . I consider the class of medicine
given to paupers generally unsatisfactory, and the mode in which it is
dispensed to them objectionable.'[98] In addition, as with other aspects of
poor relief, not all who applied for aid received it; or if treatment were
offered, it might take the form of a loan, which the recipient was
expected to repay. Medical loan tickets were widely issued in Northamptonshire, Warwickshire, Devon, Cornwall, Essex and Cambridgeshire, and there was much subsequent hardship for families trying to pay
off a debt which they had been unable to avoid.[99] Every encouragement
was given to poor people to join friendly societies or clubs which would
provide appropriate help when they were ill, but many simply lacked
the means to do so. The self-help approach was commended by the
Poor Law Commission in a letter to the Chipping Norton guardians in
March 1837:

Medical relief, like all other relief, should be afforded at the expence of the
Ratepayers only to such persons as are wholly unable to provide for themselves. The Comrs. [look] forward to the period when the Gns., acting on this
principle, shall remove from the mind of the Labourers, the too generally
prevailing impression, that they must always be dependent on the parish for
Medl. attendance & to the institution of Medical Clubs as powerful auxiliaries
to this end, and to the total freedom of the Labourers from a state of pauperism.[100]

Once established, the basic philosophy of the poor relief system,
formulated in the 1830s and 1840s, persisted almost to the end of the
century. The stigma of pauperism was inculcated from an early stage,

and only those who could manage in no other way resorted to Poor Law assistance. So while the 1834 Act may have fostered self-dependence – it boosted friendly society membership, for example – it failed to recognize the genuine needs of the poor. Old people, in particular, were victims of its insensitive approach, while children, too, were drawn into the money-making process at an early age as a result of its provisions. Once the 'family allowance' aid of the old Poor Law was withdrawn, and that reform at least was widely implemented, the children of low-wage families were forced to make a contribution to household income as soon as they were able. As a witness from Framlingham in Suffolk declared: 'The New Poor Law had a visible effect on education, in making children used as earners at an earlier age.'[101] Some observers commented favourably on this development, like a farmer from Over Norton in Oxfordshire, who declared in 1836: 'The whole agricultural population must improve, for the parents are now anxious to make every child work as soon as possible for the common fund of the family; by this means they are brought up in habits of industry early, and the union between the several members of a family is strengthened.' He also claimed to detect an improvement in the character of his adult workers: 'they are more civil, more attentive, they come in better time in the morning, they are more obedient, in short they are anxious now to keep their places, and before they did not care about it, for they could always fall back upon the parish'.[102] Another farmer from Malseyhampton in the Cirencester union agreed:

We had some families which received relief on account of the number of their children. . . . All this is now discontinued. Now they exert themselves, and by the wife and children's earnings receive more weekly than before . . . I have men working for me now who used to be always grumbling and insubordinate, and good for very little as labourers; now they are contented and trustworthy, and go whistling to their work as happy as birds.[103]

Doubtless, in their inmost thoughts the labourers were anything but as 'happy as birds'. But in their outward relations they had clearly concluded that discretion was the better part of valour when it came to accepting the new regime.

So while certain critics could, with Benjamin Disraeli, condemn the 1834 Act as a national disgrace, which announced 'to the world that in England poverty is a crime', most people – rate payers and poor men alike – came to tolerate the system which it introduced. Its principles were to accord well with the self-help views which flourished in the middle years of the nineteenth century, and the fact that it also initially

Table 4 *Expenditure per head on the relief and maintenance of the poor with reference to the population in 1831*

	SPEENHAMLAND COUNTIES										NON-SPEENHAMLAND COUNTIES			
	Buckingham-shire		Norfolk		Oxfordshire		Sussex		Wiltshire		Cumberland		Westmor-land	
	s.	d.	s.	d.	s.	d.	s.	d.	s.	d.	s.	d.	s.	d.
1834	16	11	15	9	15	10	18	1	14	6	5	1	8	1
1835	14	6	14	0	14	0	15	6	13	5	4	7	7	3
1836	10	2	11	10	10	2	11	10	11	1	4	1	6	7
1837	8	8	9	1	18	9	8	7	8	9	3	10	5	10
1838	8	5	8	7	8	5	8	10	9	5	3	10	5	6
1839	9	2	9	10	9	4	10	5	10	9	3	9	5	4
1840	9	11	9	3	9	10	10	7	11	1	4	4	6	0
Decrease in expenditure per head, comparing 1840 with 1834	7	0	6	6	6	0	7	6	3	5	0	9	2	1
Decrease in *aggregate* expenditure, comparing 1840 with 1834	42%		41%		38%		41%		26%		14%		23%	

SOURCE: Seventh *Annual Report* of the Poor Law Commission, PP 1841, vol. 11, p. 13.

achieved one of its principal objectives by reducing poor rates – thanks partly to its firm policies and partly to wider employment opportunities outside agriculture – helped to make it palatable to the better off. In the decade following 1834 poor rates fell nationally from the £7 million or so expended in 1831 to between £4.5 million and £5 million per annum, and for twenty years after that expenditure fluctuated between £5 million and £6 million a year.[104] The position in seven rural counties is given in Table 4. To reformers the reductions secured in former 'extravagant' Speenhamland areas like Sussex, Buckinghamshire and Oxfordshire were no doubt especially welcome.

As for the farm labourers themselves, many left the land for employment elsewhere. From a peak of over 2,000,000 people engaged in British agriculture in 1851, the number of those so occupied began a prolonged and inexorable decline; almost the whole of the loss represented wage earners. In 1851 agriculture was still the most important British industry in terms of employment; in 1871 there were more people in domestic service than in agriculture, and more in commerce and finance (excluding transport) than there were in either.[105] In bringing that situation about the 1834 Poor Law Amendment Act and the unimaginative social policies which it ushered in played a partial, though not decisive, role.

E

The 'Fool Plough'. This was part of the celebrations held on Plough Monday, which was the Monday following 6 January. On this day boys and young men would dress up and would drag an old plough through the streets, asking for money or other gifts. If they did not receive them, they might plough up the lawn or ground in front of the house of a reluctant giver

5 Village institutions

'It is certainly a remarkable circumstance,' H.M.I. the Reverend F. C. Cook declared with enthusiasm in 1846, 'that on entering a country village, the most striking, and frequently most ornamental building next to the church, should be the schoolhouse for the children of the poor.'[1]

To every class we have a school assign'd,
Rules for all ranks and food for every mind. . . .
GEORGE CRABBE, in *The Borough* (1810)[2]

The education of the majority of children in rural England during the late eighteenth and early nineteenth centuries was a haphazard affair, dependent for its existence upon the ebb and flow of local circumstances and upon the degree of interest taken in day-school provision by village clergy and squires or, more rarely, by parents themselves. The clergy had a particularly important role to play at a time when religion and education were still thought to be inextricably linked, and many clerics felt it their duty to inaugurate, and even to finance, a village school. Those unable to do so often experienced a sense of failure, like the Oxfordshire vicar who in 1854 admitted pathetically to his bishop that his 'great want' was a day school: 'I am shorn of my strength entirely for want of one. I could make use of the school for giving lectures at night and otherwise instructing my poor ignorant congregation.'[3]

Alongside the day schools, by the last decades of the eighteenth century the new Sunday schools had emerged, which sought to give moral guidance and a modicum of instruction on the Sabbath to their pupils, thereby fitting them to read the Bible and, in the case of those attached to the Church of England, the catechism as well. Unlike those in the larger industrial towns, few village Sunday schools embarked on any more ambitious plan of instruction than this. By 1818 such rural counties as Northamptonshire, Wiltshire, Buckinghamshire and Dorset had attracted a respectable level of Sunday-school support; well over 7 per cent of the total population in all four counties was enrolled in the schools, which put them at the top of a list of county rankings in that year.[4]

In these early days the initiative for establishing Sunday schools might be taken by interested lay people rather than the clergy, and Nonconformists were particularly active in this regard. And while it is true that much of the financial support for them came from wealthier members of the rural community, since no fees were charged, a sprinkling of poorer men contributed – like William Grummitt, a Lincolnshire labourer and Methodist who opened a free Sunday school in 1812 at the village of Normanby. Later, because of the large number of pupils, he took over a barn, and when he died while mowing in a field in 1823 an obituary paid tribute to his zeal: 'his expanding heart considered as his family to be trained up for heaven, the whole rising youth not only of his own but neighbouring villages'.[5] To him the Sunday school was a means of serving the joint ideals of education and religious worship, and he was not alone in that approach.

In addition to these broader parish schools, there were private-enterprise establishments which could vary from satisfactory day schools run by efficient teachers for their own profit to small 'dame' classes organized by those who were too old or too inefficient to earn their bread in any other way. In these, young children were taught, with varying degrees of efficiency to read and sew and, in a few cases, to write and do simple arithmetic. Typical was the school conducted at Ardley in Oxfordshire, where the incumbent reported in 1808 that 'a poor woman' received 'a few small children, while their parents [were] employed in Husbandry'. It was no doubt with this kind of institution in mind that the Rev. John Allen, an inspector of schools, wrote in 1840 of

those [schools] kept by widows and others, who are compelled by necessity to seek some employment . . . without any real feelings of interest in their work . . . the room commonly used as a living room, and filled with a very unwholesome atmosphere; the mistress, apparently, one whose kindly feelings had been long since frozen up, and who was regarded with terror by several rows of children, more than half of whom were, in many cases, without any means whatever of employing their time.

He did admit, however, that there were examples of a better type, kept by persons fond of children and of 'cleanly, orderly habits'. These, he considered, could not 'altogether fail of attaining some of the highest ends of education as regards the formation of character'.[6] As late as 1851 a third of all children attending school in England were private day pupils, many of them doubtless attending institutions of 'dame'-class calibre.[7]

Elsewhere there were small endowments bequeathed by earlier generations which permitted the setting up of a free school, though often the sums involved (£4 to £6 per annum) were far too limited to secure the services of efficient teachers. Charity schools were also established under the influence of the Society for the Promotion of Christian Knowledge, which had been formed in 1698. As its name suggests, its prime purpose was to encourage the growth of religious feeling among the children of the poor by instructing them 'in reading the Bible and the catechism'. The Bible formed the chief reading book in the schools and was the basis of all exercises. In some cases it was explicitly laid down that the master was not to teach from any books which were not approved by the parish clergyman.[8]

The hours of attendance were long, particularly in the eighteenth century. At Thornton-on-the-Moors in Cheshire new rules drawn up in 1791 required master and scholars

to meet in the school at 7 o'clock in the morning from Lady-day to Michaelmas and remain there till 11, and return at one, and remain until 4: that they break up at Christmas for a fortnight, at Easter for nine days commencing with the eve of Good Friday; and at Whitsuntide for one week, commencing on the eve of Whitsunday, and no longer.[9]

Normally the timetable would be modified when the harvest was in progress, so that the children could help in the fields, while the need to conserve lighting and heating led some schools to open later during the winter months.[10]

In a number of villages, prior to the passage of the 1834 Poor Law Amendment Act, it was the custom for overseers to pay the school fees of some of the poorer children out of the rates and to provide apprenticeship premiums for them. After 1834, however, a less generous spirit prevailed. An inspector of schools in 1850 found that in country districts many boards of guardians even refused outdoor relief to parents who sent their children to school. Not until 1855 did a new Act formally authorize guardians to pay for the education of the children of outdoor paupers, and even then, because it was a permissive measure, most ignored it.[11]

However, still more unsatisfactory was the fact that a substantial

minority of parishes at the beginning of the nineteenth century were
without schools of any kind. In Oxfordshire over a quarter of the two
hundred or so rural parishes making returns to the Bishop of Oxford
in 1808 had no weekday provision, and many were without Sunday
schools either.[12] In 1818 the Select Committee appointed to inquire
into the 'Education of the Lower Orders' concluded that 'a very great
deficiency exists in the means of educating the Poor, wherever the
population is thin and scattered over country districts'.[13] The problem
was further aggravated by the fact that family poverty often prevented
children from attending the schools which were available. Either parents
could not pay the fees of a penny or twopence per week or they required
the youngsters' help around the farm or the workshop. In the 1780s
Joseph Mayett of Quainton remembered being 'deprived of a Liberal
Education for instead of being sent to School I was set to Lace making
to provide something towards a livelihood'. Mayett's father was a
labourer, earning 6s. a week in winter and 9s. in summer, and he found
it impossible to support a family of seven children without his son's
assistance. Joseph's mother, like some other parents, gave the boy a
little instruction in reading, but as her own skills in this were limited,
it was a case of the blind leading the blind.[14]

So it was against this background, with many children left to pick up
an education as best they could, that two voluntary school societies
came into existence. These were the National Society, which was
associated with the Church of England, and the British and Foreign
School Society, which although ostensibly unsectarian, enjoyed much
support from Nonconformists. Each was designed to prepare the
labouring classes for a life of honest, self-dependent toil and an acceptance of the social order as it then existed, and each employed older
pupils as monitors to help with the teaching. In 1812 the first annual
report of the National Society defined its 'sole object' as being

to communicate to the poor generally, by the means of a summary mode of
education, lately brought into practice, such knowledge and habits, as are
sufficient to guide them through life, in their proper stations, especially to
teach the doctrines of Religion, according to the principles of the Established
Church, and to train them to the performance of their religious duties by early
discipline.

This approach was echoed more than forty years later by a speaker
at a conference of Oxfordshire schoolmasters, when he told his audience
that once they had 'manufactured a steady, honest, God-fearing,
Church-going population', they had done their duties as teachers.[15]

Thanks to the support received by the National Society from clergy and gentry, Church of England schools rapidly outnumbered those of their British and Foreign rivals and, indeed, those established by other denominations, like the Wesleyans or the Roman Catholics. By the late 1850s they outstripped the British and Foreign schools in the ratio of about seventeen to one, to the annoyance of some of the more committed Nonconformists.[16] In the great majority of villages it was a choice of 'church' school or none at all, and often 'church' school meant 'church' Sunday school as well. In the mid-1860s five boys were suspended from Ermington National School in Devon 'for attending the Dissenting Meeting House instead of attending Sunday School'. In the following year the pupils were told that 'all who persisted in attending the Methodist Sunday School could not be permitted to attend this school'. Happily, in other parishes a more generous spirit prevailed. At Bardney, Lincolnshire, in 1851 co-operation was such that the Sunday scholars would attend the Wesleyan chapel one week and the parish church the next, while at Torksey and Mareham-le-Fen in the same county Wesleyan and church Sunday scholars held their anniversary celebrations together.[17]

From 1833 the day-school building programme was boosted by the provision of annual government grants to elementary education. The initial payment of £20,000 was handed over to the two major voluntary societies to enable them to increase their accommodation, and it was followed in 1839 by the appointment of the first inspectors of schools, who had the task of investigating conditions at local level. In 1846, as the weaknesses of the monitorial system had become clear, the government sought to promote the training of teachers by further grants and by the introduction of a form of apprenticeship, or pupil-teachership, for would-be entrants to the profession.[18]

Thanks to these initiatives, standards began to improve, though there were still those who doubted the value of the mass education that the voluntary societies were seeking to provide and believed that too much schooling would cause discontent. Among the smaller farmers, in particular, there was resentment at what they saw as efforts to raise labourers' children above their station by giving them an education. Maps and geography lessons were frowned upon by men in East Anglia, since they might lead later to the migration of workers and a consequent 'diminution of the reserve of labour which was useful to the farmers during harvest'. The well-to-do also had reservations, believing that 'the cultivation of the intellect unfits for manual labour'. As one inspector of schools complained in 1845, there were fears 'that education may destroy the present relations between master and servant and substitute no better. That instead of a plodding, hard working peasantry, who do their labour much as the animals they tend, we shall have an effeminate class of persons, averse to rough work, conceited and insubordinate.'[19] Just over a decade later Bishop Wilberforce of Oxford was expressing a similar opinion when he declared that there was 'perhaps, too much outcry against children being taken from School early to work on farms', adding frankly that they 'did not want everybody to be learned men, or to make everybody unfit for following the plough, or else the rest of us would have nothing to eat'.[20]

But to other observers, concerned at the growth of theft and arson in country districts, particularly during the troubled 1830s, education began to be seen as a much-needed instrument for social discipline and an essential moral framework to counterbalance the weaknesses of working-class family life. As the secretary of the newly established Education Department put it in 1841: 'The teacher of the peasant's child occupies, as it were, the father's place, in the performance of duties from which the father is separated by his daily toil, and unhappily at present by his want of knowledge and skill.'[21] Six years later T. B. Macaulay, MP for Edinburgh, echoed this view when he declared that with the 'rural population growing up with as little civilization, as little enlightenment, as the inhabitants of New Guinea . . . there is at every period a risk of a *jacquerie*'. It was the schoolmaster who was to be entrusted with the 'mind of the rising generation, on whom the prosperity and future eminence' of the nation depended.[22] But the *Edinburgh Review* expressed this view most starkly when it declared in 1839: 'We must build more schools or more prisons.'

Nevertheless, despite the advance made in school building and in the provision of teacher training facilities during the 1840s, the quality of instruction in many villages left much to be desired even in the middle of the nineteenth century. Accommodation was often poor, as HMI Allen pointed out in 1845. Of fifteen schools he had visited recently in Radnorshire, only three were provided with suitable buildings. Converted cottages or, as in Radnor, portions of the church were used for school-keeping purposes. In one village, Allen noted with obvious disapproval, the 'font (containing bits of candles, slates, and fragments of books) was in that portion which had been set apart for the school'.[23] The curriculum, too, was normally limited to the 'three r's', plus religious instruction and needlework for the girls.

Another serious obstacle to progress was the shortage of properly qualified teachers. In the mid-1840s HMI Watkins commented sadly that of 495 teachers whom he had met during the previous year, 'I cannot think that above two-thirds are tolerably qualified for their many and important duties, and I must further express my belief that one-third are insufficient, neither intended by nature nor fitted by art for the situation in which they are placed.'[24] The schoolmaster of Barmby Moor in Yorkshire during the 1830s and 1840s was a hunchback, who probably taught because he was unfit for manual labour. 'When the vicar offered to teach him fractions, decimals and land surveying, he said "he thought he had as much knowledge as his head would carry". He used to punish children by putting the thumb in a noose suspended from the ceiling at a height which forced them to stand on tip toe.'[25] At Stoke Orchard in Gloucestershire the school was run by an illiterate labourer who had been given the job because he had been 'forced to give up his work by old age and the crippling effects of rheumatism'.[26]

To HMI Mitchell, writing despondently of Norfolk in 1850, it seemed that there was a 'lamentable state of un-education' in the county, 'arising from defect of funds, consequent bad teachers, and deficiency of books and maps &c., which the teachers would not, however, know how to use, even if they had them'. Shortly afterwards he also complained of the unreasonableness of school managers in expecting their masters and mistresses to perform a whole range of extra-curricular duties: 'To the labours of the school are superadded a night school, a Sunday school, a clothing fund, an organ, a choir, a collection of subscriptions, &c., &c., for a salary of £30 or £40 a year.'[27]

The situation was aggravated by the fact that many masters, in their anxiety to eke out an inadequate salary, would of their own free will undertake a variety of outside tasks. As late as 1850 there were several parish masters in Devon who united their office with shopkeeping, shoemaking, postmastering or acting as parish clerks, while the *Post Office Directory* for 1847 records that William Webster of Chinnor, Oxfordshire, combined teaching with land surveying and beer retailing; his fellow head at Burton Latimer, Northamptonshire, advertised land-surveying skills alongside a grocery business.[28] It was all too easy for these commercial activities to take precedence over the humdrum business of teaching in the village school.

One of the greatest obstacles to educational advance in country districts, however, was the employment of children on the land, since this led to great irregularity of attendance and a very brief school life. Only in the north of England, where adult wage rates were rather higher, was a greater value placed on education, while in pastoral districts, where the need for child labour was limited, the problem was also less severe. But in most counties children over the age of seven or eight would be absent intermittently for casual field work during the spring, summer and early autumn, and at the age of about ten they normally left school for good. Bird scaring, weeding, potato and turnip setting and picking, bean setting, haymaking and harvest were but a few of the tasks on which they were engaged. 'Many children absent "pulling turnips"', wrote HMI Watkins at Market Weighton in East Yorkshire during 1844. At Fridaythorpe in the same area children away 'pulling turnips' led to a 'general want of activity in the school business'. Three years later, at Sutton on Derwent, he discovered 'half the first class at present at work in the fields' when he visited the school in May.[29] In other cases children stayed away because they had no clothes or boots to wear to school, or else their parents could not afford the school fees. This was especially true after the passage of the 1834 Poor Law Amendment Act ended child allowances from the poor rate as well as the occasional payment of school fees for the most needy children.

In Wales youngsters suffered the additional handicap of knowing little English, since that was the normal medium of instruction in the schools. As a report on education in Carmarthen, Glamorgan and Pembroke put it in 1847: 'No specific attempt is made to teach English. The children are left to pick it up as they best can . . . Hence, children are constantly found, who can read whole chapters with comparative fluency, and give the Welsh for single words, yet have not the remotest idea of what they have been reading about.'[30]

In areas where cottage industries flourished these could also adversely affect school attendance and literacy. In 1840 Bedfordshire and Hertfordshire had the lowest male literacy rates in the whole country, while twenty-five years later, at a time when just over 31 per cent of all women and 21 per cent of all men marrying in England and Wales signed the marriage register with a mark only, the percentages of those unable to sign in Bedfordshire were 44 and 35 respectively.[31] It is significant that Bedfordshire and Hertfordshire were both counties where straw plaiting flourished, and boys as well as girls were engaged upon it.

But if elementary education over the period 1770 to 1850 left a good deal to be desired in country districts, the schooling provided for the better-off members of rural society was hardly satisfactory. In 1861 the *English Journal of Education* observed: 'No one who has the least acquaintance with National schools under government inspection would hesitate to prefer the instruction there given to the miserable and pretentious smattering of knowledge promised in the advertisements of private academies for the middle classes.' A more recent critic has commented, 'the condition of our public or higher schools was worse between 1750 and 1840 than at any time since King Alfred'.[32] Harsh discipline and unimaginative concentration on the classics remained features of many of the public schools, despite the work of reforming headmasters like Samuel Butler (1774–1839) of Shrewsbury or Thomas Arnold (1795–1842) of Rugby.

For Arnold education had a dual basis – religion and a liberal culture. But despite his efforts to mould life at Rugby in accordance with his philosophy, excesses lingered on. Even in the 1830s such practices as tossing fellow pupils in blankets and roasting small boys before an open fire were not unknown, as readers of *Tom Brown's Schooldays* will recall.[33] At Westminster School conditions were far worse, however. The future HMI John Allen, who left the peace of a rural Pembrokeshire rectory for Westminster in 1824, later recalled this period as the unhappiest of his life. Bullying and cruelty were endemic, and on more than one occasion he was compelled 'for expressing horror at some pictures which were forced on his attention . . . to toast bread at the fire with his naked hands; and when he was supplied with a fork to save his fingers, this was savagely broken over his back. Once he was roasted before the fire, so that he fell ill'. On another occasion he almost died when a pewter pot was hurled at his head.[34]

Although the smaller private establishments were without the refinements of cruelty which characterized the public schools, from an educational point of view they had serious deficiencies. Many were run by clergymen who had found the rewards of the Church inadequate to their needs. Others were owned by men who in education and background were little better than the notorious Mr Squeers in *Nicholas Nickleby*, or else they offered a sternly spartan regime, like that endured by the Brontë sisters at the Clergy Daughters' School at Cowan Bridge in the 1820s. Newspaper columns abounded with private school advertisements – like that for the Academy at Wantage in Berkshire run by a Mr Jennings, where 'young Gentlemen' were boarded and educated by the headmaster and three assistants on the following terms:

Board, English, Writing, Arithmetick, and Merchants Accompts. Sixteen
    Guineas per Annum.
Ditto, with Latin and Greek, Eighteen Guineas per Annum.
Ditto, with French, Twenty Guineas per Annum.
Dancing, Drawing, Musick, and Military Exercise on the usual Terms.[35]

In *Tom Brown's Schooldays* Thomas Hughes (1822–96), the son of a comfortably off Berkshire family, recounted what was substantially his own experience at Twyford School in Hampshire. Here the headmaster and his assistant merely came into the classes when lessons had been prepared. The real work of the school was carried on by two poorly educated ushers, whose one object in life was to ram Latin and Greek into their charges. To make their task as easy as possible they encouraged tale-bearing among the pupils. They also favoured the 'biggest boys, who alone could have given them much trouble; whereby those young gentlemen became most abominable tyrants, oppressing the little boys in all the small mean ways which prevail in private schools'.[36]

Yet despite the weaknesses of middle-class education in the years before 1850, it attracted a growing number of pupils. The more substantial farmers, for example, were anxious that their children should not mix with the offspring of their labourers. Some employed governesses for the younger children, and sent the older ones to the private schools and academies which were growing up in most market towns; in the case of the boys, an increasing number also attended grammar and even boarding schools.[37] At the beginning of the nineteenth century Hannah More mocked the pretensions of Somerset farmers who sent their daughters to be educated at fashionable boarding schools: 'Of knowledge they had just enough to laugh at their parents' rustic manners and vulgar language, and to despise and ridicule every girl not as vainly dressed as themselves. . . . They spent the morning in bed, the noon in dressing, the evening at the harpsichord, and the night in reading novels'.[38] But the rapid expansion in middle-class education during the nineteenth century, particularly after the coming of the railways eased transport problems, showed that parents were not discouraged by sour comments such as these.

By the 1850s, then, elementary education had come to be seen as one way of exercising moral guidance and social discipline over the labouring classes. But it was not the only instrument to hand. Charity, too, by rewarding the worthy and ignoring the backslider, could perform a similar function. This was carefully stressed by the Grey family's steward in Bedfordshire, when he wrote to his employers in 1809 advising that 'no drunkards or woodstealers' should be allowed to partake of the annual charity beef distributed by the estate: 'In Short . . . it should be given to objects of charity only.' In the previous year he had expressed satisfaction that his mistress intended only to 'distribute *occasional* charity'. He considered that benefactions at stated periods did little good, since they were 'peremptorily claimed, instead of being gratefully received'.[39] Some years later Joseph Arch, the agricultural trade union leader (1826–1919), recalled the difficulty he experienced in his home parish of Barford, Warwickshire, in getting his share of the village charity coals because he was a man of independent views, unwilling to submit to his social superiors.[40]

Happily, in other communities a more generous spirit prevailed. The diaries of Parson Woodforde reveal countless examples of philanthropy, as on 4 January 1783, when he sent a shilling to 'poor old Joe Adcocks Wife who very lately fell down and broke her Thigh'. On 28 December 1787 he gave sixpence to 'a poor Sailor with one Arm'. Meals, too, were regularly sent out to the sick and aged from the parsonage kitchen, apparently without regard to their attitudes and opinions.

Over half a century later another cleric, William Risley of Deddington, Oxfordshire, recorded in his diary similar acts of charity. In the autumn of 1843, for example, he bestowed on one girl a Bible and prayer book, while his wife gave her a gown and bonnet, 'on her going to service'. Later he wrote to Twinings to 'order a quantity of tea' to be given away to the poor and made arrangements for his bull, 'which had been up feeding for some time to be killed & distributed' among needy parishoners. He also organized a clothing club both at Deddington and at the nearby hamlet of Hempton.[41] Still greater zeal was displayed by Charles Kingsley when he became incumbent of Eversley in Hampshire during the same decade. A coal club, a shoe club, a loan fund, a maternal society, a lending library and a singing class to improve the church music were but a few of the ventures he set in hand. He also addressed cottage meetings in the outlying districts during the winter months and held adult evening classes at the rectory on three nights each week.[42] Evening instruction was popular among a number of the clergy, for it provided a means of combining moral instruction with the teaching of the 'three r's' to those who had left school before they could master these basic skills.

Elsewhere, as newspaper reports confirm, help in the form of food, clothing and coals would be given at Christmas or New Year by clergy, squires and the larger farmers. *Jackson's Oxford Journal* for 5 January 1793 provides a typical example; the Duke of Marlborough donated

Seven Fat Oxen, with a proportionable Quantity of Bread ... to the Poor of Woodstock and the neighbouring Villages; and to One Hundred and Thirty Poor Families Ten Shillings each in Fuel. Her Grace the Duchess of Marlborough to these Donations added a liberal Portion of Ale to drink his

Majesty's Health: Her Grace was likewise pleased, on New Year's Day, to order Plenty of Bread and Cheese for One Hundred and Sixty-Six Labourers and poor People employed in the Park, with Ale also to drink the King's Health.

Forty-two years later the same newspaper was describing the generosity of the squire of Stratton Audley in providing a Christmas feast for the old people of the parish; the guests were 'in a high state of happiness – full of gratitude and quite uproarious in praise of their generous patron, who is almost idolized in the village and neighbourhood for his bland and gentlemanly manners'.[43] This report indicates the attitude of humble gratitude expected from those who benefited from casual philanthropy and the ephemeral character of much of the help bestowed.

In other cases there were endowments for the apprenticeship of poor children to a trade or the provision of land for allotment purposes. Sometimes plots were set aside for cultivation by the poor when the parish was enclosed, or the incumbent would allocate a part of his glebe for the same purpose. Nevertheless, throughout the period attitudes toward these allocations were equivocal. Larger farmers were often reluctant for their men to hold land, fearing that this would encourage them to stay away from work at the busy seasons in order to plant or harvest their own crops. But the fears were largely groundless. Women and children would normally gather the produce of allotment gardens, for their menfolk could not afford to miss the opportunity of earning higher wages at harvest and seed-setting times.

It was the clergy who probably put most pressure on landlords to grant allotments. In south Lindsey it was only after a lengthy campaign by the curate of Swaby that the reluctant agents of the Ancaster estate granted five acres to the parish 'to keep him quiet', while the Rev. W. M. Pierce saw to it that 'almost every poor man in his parishes has an allotment of land'. In defiance of the wishes of the farmers he let three acres of his glebe at Fulletby to labourers and helped to provide them with tools.[44] But it was from the 1830s, following the labourers' revolt of 1830 and the implementation of the Poor Law Amendment Act of 1834, that allotment gardens enjoyed their greatest vogue. In this development the Labourer's Friend Society was particularly active.

The Society was formed in 1831 and enjoyed much influential support, including the patronage of the king and queen. Its avowed aim was to give labouring people access to land where they had been deprived of this by enclosure.[45] In a report issued two years later its organizers argued persuasively that if labourers had a small plot of their own, they would gain in self-respect and would have a means of family support without resort to the Poor Law.[46] Accounts were given of parishes in which successful experiments had been made, like Byfield in Northamptonshire, where in 1828 the rector had let out a twenty-five acre field for 'spade cultivation to the poor but industrious labourers, in half acres and quarter acres'. Within four years the project had proved its worth, and some men were selling crops to the value of £8 from their holdings. Others kept the produce to feed themselves and their families through the winter and also to help support a pig.[47]

Unfortunately, the 'social control' aspect of allotments was also prominent in many communities, and those who were allowed to rent land were expected to attend church regularly and to conform in other respects. A clause included in the rules of the Rugby Poor's Friend Society, drawn up in 1830, stipulated that 'if any occupier be detected in any act of dishonesty, or being a drunkard, or frequenter of public-houses, shall (after having been reproved) still persist in such a habit, he shall not be allowed to continue to rent his allotment after the end of the year.'[48] And Mrs Mary Ann Gilbert of Eastbourne, who experimented with allotment provision in Sussex during the 1830s and 1840s, issued her tenants with cards on which were printed injunctions about 'Thrift and the value of Ready Money'. A tenancy could be forfeited if it were proved that hay, straw and manure had been left to waste on the roadside. Competition among the tenants was encouraged, as the following notice indicates: 'One penny, three half pence, and twopence per ear will be given in 1843 by Mrs. Gilbert for the greatest number of ears of wheat from one grain, the plant being produced complete at the next Battel Horticultural Show.'[49]

The value of giving labourers a stake in the soil was underlined in 1843 by the Select Committee on Allotments. Two years later a new General Enclosure Act empowered commissioners to set aside land for allotment or recreational purposes when they were making their allocations. Unfortunately, it had little effect. In Norfolk there were complaints that much of the land apportioned was unsuitable for the purpose or was too far from the cottages. Out of 6000 acres enclosed in the county after 1845, the poor received only 132½ acres for allotments and 49¼ acres as recreation ground.[50] Other counties fared little better and, as before, it was primarily through the initiative of private landowners or clergymen that allotment gardens became available.[51]

As for the benefits which land cultivation could bestow, these were summarized by John Earley, a Witney blanket manufacturer, in 1840:

it is one of the best means of emptying the beer-shops; . . . it saves many

evils, and brings up the children to industry by the example set by the
parents; it gives the poor man a feeling of respectful independence . . .
independence of the poor's rates. The allotment system will not only give a
man bread, but also cheese with it; [he] knows an instance of a man who was a
pauper with a large family, but who had rented a piece of land, and witness
never goes into his house but he sees a flitch of bacon on the rack.

Friendly societies, however, were even more popular than charity and
allotments as a means of encouraging a spirit of self-dependence among
labouring families. Many agricultural societies offered prizes to men
and women who had been long-term members of these clubs, while
landowners, clergy and even farmers regularly subscribed to village
and county societies in order to boost their funds and thus to make
them more attractive to labourers and artisans. Weekly contributions
to such bodies were deemed to encourage thrift and prudence, while
through the sickness and funeral benefits offered they provided a means
of support for families without resort to the Poor Law. It was in these
circumstances that the Rev. Joseph Townsend, rector of Pewsey in
Wiltshire, wrote as early as 1786: 'The system of Friendly Societies
should be pushed as far as it will go.'[52] By the end of the century his
words had clearly been taken to heart. In 1801 Somerset had 123
enrolled friendly societies; Devon, 156; Gloucestershire, 111; Norfolk,
203; Wiltshire, 30; and Warwickshire, 188. Significantly, however, it
was the industrial areas of Lancashire and the West Riding of Yorkshire, with 820 and 330 societies respectively, which dominated the
movement. Some of these were doubtless clandestine trade unions,
outlawed by the Combination Acts of 1799–1800.[53] Nevertheless, it
was the more highly paid workers who could best afford weekly club
subscriptions, and this fact helps to explain the larger membership in
the northern counties. In 1803 perhaps 16 per cent of Lancashire's
population were friendly society members, as opposed to 5 per cent of
those in Norfolk and Suffolk and 6 per cent of those in Wiltshire.

Most of the societies exercised a firm moral influence over their
members. Hilton Friendly Society in Dorset excluded any person who
was known to be 'a profane swearer, drunkard, sabbath breaker, thief
or otherwise notoriously wicked', while a Kingston Deverill society in
Wiltshire prescribed the substantial fine of half a crown if a member
challenged one of his fellows or 'maliciously' stamped his feet.[54] At
Nether Stowey in Dorset rules drawn up in 1797 made the following
provisions:

For striking a member . . . sixpence – for fighting on Club nyte with – he
having struck the first blow . . . six pence – for returning the blow . . . one

penny – for being out after sunset while receiving sick pay . . . five pence – for returning to town while the Club was at church . . . six pence – for playing shove half-penny during service . . . sixpence – fined eightpence for four oaths and four pence for two oaths, and four pence for not keeping silence when called upon.

Twelve years later came the addition: 'That £2 os. od. be paid for the funeral expenses of a wife, but no member to bury more than *one wife* at the expence of the Club.'[55] This latter was a point of some significance, for labouring people had a particular dread of being buried 'on the parish', even though many of them were destined to be so. As Martha More observed of labourers' wives in Somerset during the 1790s, despite their desperate poverty they declared 'with as much fury as they dared to exhibit before us . . . they would rather relinquish the comforts and blessings of assistance at their lying in, to enrich the stock and procure a handsome funeral'.[56] They had a pathetic desire to leave the world with dignity and independence, and not to be shuffled off with the grudging attentions of the parish vestry and the Poor Law.

More constructively, a number of clubs also appointed a physician to care for sick members. The Hampshire Friendly Society, for example, paid its doctors 1s. per head 'for each member in their respective districts', soon after its formation in 1825. By 1833 this had been raised to 3s., and surgeons were required to 'administer such medicines and other professional necessaries as may be required during the continuance of the Disorder'.[57] No benefits were to be allowed for illnesses 'brought on by fighting or the Venereal disease', however, the latter being a major killer in the nineteenth century.

The Hampshire Society, which had branches throughout the county, offered endowments for children, too, which became payable when they were ready to take up an apprenticeship.[58]

Although these organizations were already numerous by the beginning of the nineteenth century, they received a boost with the passage of the 1834 Poor Law Amendment Act. Faced with the deterrent approach of that legislation, tradesmen, craftsmen and labourers resolved ever more firmly to assist one another in times of sickness, accident or death rather than call upon the Poor Law union for aid. As one of them declared: 'We must look out for ourselves, and provide for a day of sickness and old age, now that there is no parish to look to.' In these circumstances the number of societies in rural areas rose sharply towards the middle of the century. By 1855 there were 565 of them operating in Somerset; 651 in Gloucestershire; 271 in Wiltshire; and 785 in Devon. In addition, the larger national bodies like the

Manchester Unity of Oddfellows, were beginning to recruit in country districts. In 1845 the Oddfellows had forty branches in Devon, twenty-one in Westmorland and fifteen apiece in Oxfordshire and Hampshire, to name but four counties, while in the same year the Ancient Order of Foresters could claim three branches in Hampshire and six in Westmorland.[59] In the long run this expansion of the more secure national bodies was to be in the long-term interest of society members, even if it meant some severing of members' ties with the local community. And, of course, certain of the district societies did survive. The Hampshire Friendly Society, for one, is still in existence after more than 150 years.

Besides their benefit functions, these village clubs also served an important social function. At their meetings, often held in a public house, members could discuss problems of common interest, while a society's annual feast day was often the major event in a village's year. Then members, dressed in their best clothes and wearing ribbons and rosettes in the club colours, would march to church, preceded by banners and a local band. There they would attend a service and then walk in procession to their club meeting place, where a substantial dinner would be awaiting them. Outside on the streets there would be all the fun of the fair, with jugglers, cheap-jack salesmen and plenty of entertainment booths. A vivid picture of the feasting enjoyed by members is provided by the Dorset poet William Barnes:

An' there they meade sich stunnen clatters
Wi' knives an' forks, an' pleates an' platters;
An' waiters ran, an' beer did pass
Vrom tap to jug, vrom jug to glass:
An' when they took away the dishes
They drink'd good healthes, an' wish'd good wishes,
To all the gre't vo'k o' the land,
An' all good things vo'k took in hand;

Once the meal was over and the toasts had ended, it was time to continue the club walk or to visit the dance which would be held to round off proceedings. Youths 'with peonies in their button-holes, without invitation, seized . . . maids all dressed in white and frisked and bobbed them round as merry as lambkins'.[60] The old country dances were enjoyed as the young people romped to the gay tunes of 'four hand reels', played on the fiddle or on the drums and brass of the village band. Songs and traditional ballads would ring out as men and women rejoiced in the welcome break from their laborious daily round. And although some of the clergy frowned upon the drunkenness which from time to time characterized the feast-day celebrations, most accepted it as an inevitable accompaniment of the functioning of the friendly societies they wished to foster.

Friendly society festivities were, by tradition, held on Whit Monday. But there were other junketings associated with particular dates throughout the year – like May Day, when the children paraded the village with their garlands, headed by a May Queen and begging for pennies. St Valentine's day was another occasion when boys and girls would chant traditional rhymes and ask for pennies and sweetmeats. In Norfolk Parson Woodforde's diary shows him to have been a regular contributor to the youngsters' celebrations in his parish on 14 February. Far less respectable were other popular recreations, like bull and badger baiting and cock fighting. This latter was a sport which attracted all classes, and in the eighteenth century contests were often organized in the village churchyards, especially at festival times, while inter-village or even inter-county fights were common. These larger contests would last for days. In May 1771 a 'Cock Match' was advertised in the press between the 'Gentlemen of Gloucestershire and Herefordshire'. It was to take place at the Spread Eagle Inn in Gloucester, and the contestants were 'to shew and weigh 31 Cocks on each Side in the Main, for Four Guineas a Battle, and Forty Guineas the odd Battle; and Twenty for Byes, for Two Guineas a Battle. To weigh on Monday the 20th of May, and fight the 3 following Days'.[61] In the same year Parson Woodforde noted a two-day cock fight between Somerset and Wiltshire at Ansford, which ended in a victory for Somerset: 'I believe my Brother John won a good deal of money at it.'[62] Sometimes the teams of cocks would battle on until only one bird remained alive; and it was a matter for regret that cock fighting was not finally made illegal until 1849. Compared with such barbarous amusements, village cricket, quoits and football matches seemed very tame and respectable.

These sporting events had little real connection with organized religion, even though the excuse for their occurrence was occasionally a religious festival. But, as we have seen, in the case of both elementary education and the organization of charities and friendly societies such religious links did exist, particularly with the Church of England. It is to this aspect of village life that we must now turn.

Although in the England of George III religion no longer played the central role in the life of the people that it had in the middle of the previous century, it remained a powerful influence on their day-to-day existence. It encouraged those burdened with the cares of this world to look for reward in the next and to accept their daily hardships with resignation. It gave consolation to many and, among the more devout, could form the subject of deep and anxious meditation. The Baptist farmer Philip Whitaker, of Bratton in Wiltshire, devoted much of his spare time to theological matters and engaged in soul-searching debates with the local minister during the latter years of the eighteenth century. In 1786, when he was only twenty, Whitaker started to enter in a large vellum-bound book the 'Texts preached from at Bratton'.[63] Likewise at a small Hampshire parish, where the Church of England curate became a convert to the Baptist Church in about 1809, his sermons were so inspirational that people flocked to attend the services and evening lectures he held. At harvest time they even carried a Bible to the fields with them, and 'while resting during the heat of noon one would read it aloud to the rest'.[64]

But among most country people this zeal and sense of mission had been lost, particularly within the Established Church. Often men were appointed to livings by the Crown or by powerful lay patrons who paid more attention to their political views than to their religious suitability. In other cases livings were in the gift of private landowners, who might present them to a younger son or brother in order to provide him with a career.[65] The Press frequently included advertisements of preferments offered for sale, as on 16 March 1793, when *Jackson's Oxford Journal* reported the proposed auction of the rectory of Meoles, 'desirably situate within Twenty Miles of Liverpool, in a sporting and beautiful Part of Lancashire, of the net annual value of Five Hundred and Twenty Two Pounds; subject to the life of the present Incumbent, aged upwards of Eighty Three Years, and very Infirm'. Given such businesslike arrangements, it is difficult to see how spiritual considerations could enter very deeply into the negotiations. The mention of sport is also significant, for this was the era of the hunting parson – men like Jane Austen's eldest brother, James, who kept a pack of harriers whilst a young curate. Or the Rev. Bute Crawley in *Vanity Fair*, of whom it was said:

there was not a fight within twenty miles at which he was not present, nor a race, nor a coursing match, nor a regatta, nor a ball, nor an election, nor a visitation dinner, nor indeed a good dinner in the whole county, but he found means to attend it. . . . He rode to hounds in a pepper-and-salt frock, and was one of the best fishermen in the county.[66]

Such men as he paid more attention to the quality of their horses and the success of their hounds than to the execution of their religious duties.

A further handicap was that more than half the parishes of the country lacked a resident incumbent. Indeed, in Wales during the eighteenth century some of the bishops themselves were non-resident. Benjamin Hoadley, bishop of Bangor from 1715 to 1721 never set foot in his diocese, while Richard Watson, bishop of Llandaff from 1782 to 1816, lived chiefly on his private estate in Westmorland, where he was heavily engaged in agricultural improvement. In 1827 in England and Wales as a whole 6120 incumbents out of 10,533 benefices did not reside within their parishes. Some held sinecures; many more were pluralists, who left their parochial work to ill-paid curates, though there was a substantial group of men who, thanks to the low value of their livings, had to serve several parishes in order to make a living. Among them was James Hakewell, who during the 1780s and 1790s simultaneously held five Oxfordshire livings (two rectories and three vicarages) and secured an income of only £117 from four of them in the mid-1780s. In the nation as a whole it was estimated early in the nineteenth century that over one-third of all benefices were worth £150 per annum or less.[67]

The financial plight of the curates was, however, a good deal worse than this. When Samuel Horsley became bishop of St David's in 1788 he had the greatest difficulty in getting their miserable stipends raised from £7 to £15 a year.[68] James Marshall, curate of Ireby in Cumberland from 1777 to 1842, never secured more than £50 per annum, and at times, in order to eke out a living, he kept a couple of work horses. With these he 'practised carting coals from Bolton Collieries to Keswick, filling the carts and conducting them to market himself'. Another Cumbrian curate, whose stipend was a mere £28 a year, supplemented his income by farming the fishery of Buttermere lake and by hiring himself out to help with the sheep clippings. He would 'keep the whole gathering in a roar of laughter with his stories and anecdotes'.[69] More commonly, though, hard-up clerics combined their religious duties with teaching at a private or grammar school or perhaps instructing a few pupils in their own homes.[70]

Against these examples must be set a small group of major pluralists who were extremely prosperous. They included Robert Barnard, whose two livings at Witney in Oxfordshire and Lighthorne in Warwickshire yielded the very comfortable sum of £1170 in 1825. Still more affluent was Richard Pretyman, who secured an income of over £4000 per annum up to his death in 1866. In 1819 he was instituted to the rectory of Middleton Stoney, the value of which amounted to £436 per annum; through his father, the bishop of Lincoln, he was appointed warden of the Mere Hospital at £1200, canon of Lincoln at £1665, and precentor at £335.[71] In addition, he was rector of Walgrave in Northamptonshire at about £1000 per annum and rector of Wroughton at £510.

But by the middle of the nineteenth century a new reformist spirit in the Church was bringing such undesirable practices to an end. The Plurality Act of 1838 had prohibited the holding of more than two livings and had laid down a maximum of ten miles as the distance that might lie between them; it had also limited their joint maximum value to £1000. This was extended by an Act of 1850, which made unlawful the taking and holding of any two benefices, 'except in the case of two Benefices the Churches of which are within three miles of one another by the nearest road, and the annual value of one of which does not exceed £100'.[72] Those like Pretyman, who already held more than one benefice, were allowed to retain them for the rest of their lives.

Of course, even in the early days there was a substantial proportion of men who carried out their religious duties conscientiously, despite the temptations to do otherwise. The note books and accounts of the Rev. David Davies, rector of Barkham from 1782 to 1819 and author of a well-known book on eighteenth-century labouring life, bear witness to his concern for the welfare of his flock and his efforts to provide charitable help to the needy not only from his own resources but from those of his friends as well. Among the twenty-three families whom he aided with charity bread on St Thomas's Day in 1782 were people like John Hill, described as 'an old man almost worn out', and Widow Warner, who lived with a deformed daughter on a weekly income of 2s. – which was itself apparently provided by Davies. But many other clerics, with lower standards, took little interest in either the economic or the spiritual lives of their parishioners. Bishop Blomfield's son aptly summarized the changes which had taken place in clerical attitudes between 1810 and 1860 when he wrote:

The most obvious difference is the low standard of character and duties which then prevailed among clergymen, compared to what is now generally expected of them. Fifty years ago, a decent and regular performance of Divine Service on Sundays was almost all that anyone looked for in a clergyman; if this was found, most people were satisfied. The clergyman might be non-resident, a sportsman, a farmer neglectful of study, a violent politician, a bon-vivant, or a courtier; but if he performed in person, or by deputy, that which now usurped the name of his 'duty', that was enough.[73]

A few clergymen were particularly culpable, like the rector of Bray-brooke in Northamptonshire, who in 1799 was charged before the Peterborough consistory court with habitual drunkenness and neglect of duty. According to the farmer who brought the case, he had several times been so drunk that he 'was not able to sit on Horseback or to walk and have several times fallen from off [his] Horse . . . [and] been carried or led Home drunk to [the] said Rectory House and other Places'. On Ash Wednesday and Good Friday in 1798 he had flatly refused to conduct divine service. The court found him guilty, declaring he was to be punished according to 'the Exigency of the Law' and was to pay all the costs of the suit.[74]

By the 1840s, however, such neglect was becoming unusual. The new breed of clergy which was now emerging was determined to end the decades of abuse. They included men like William Andrew, incumbent of Ketteringham in Norfolk, whose enthusiasm for the cause was such that he read nothing but the Bible or books concerned with the understanding of the Bible:

He had no interests outside his parish, no hobbies but gardening, and in these years he had twinges of conscience about gardening. If he went out for an afternoon's walk he took a bundle of tracts in his pocket and distributed them to travellers along the Norwich to Wymondham road. If he found that riders or drivers hurried their horses to avoid his offerings, he would cut a cleft in a long stick, fix a tract in the cleft, and hold it high in the road for the horseman to snatch as he galloped by.[75]

His religious zeal led to clashes with the squire, Sir John Boileau, who objected to his attempts to dominate the social and spiritual life of the parish. As Boileau firmly declared: 'I will rule this parish and the minister shall be subservient to me.' Although Andrew put up a strong fight against such authoritarianism, in the end the squire triumphed.[76]

Nevertheless, even with the improvements which were taking place in regard to plurality of livings and non-residence, other causes of estrangement between an incumbent and his parishioners remained. Among the most acute were those connected with enclosure, with the clergy's role as magistrates and, above all, with the payment of tithes. Discontent over enclosure related often enough to the generous size of the allocations made to clerics to extinguish tithe payments when new property boundaries were established. The fact that the costs of fencing this land had to be met by the other parties to the enclosure also caused some murmuring. At the same time, thanks to these arrangements, the disparities in the incomes of clergy themselves increased. Some clerics grew to be important landowners as a result of the allowances they received, and the more substantial rectories acquired several hundred acres. Vicarages and curacies, on the other hand, had to be content with the much lower equivalents that the small tithes were considered worth. In all, rectories received almost twice the amount of land 'given to vicarages and perpetual curacies, although they figured in roughly the same number of awards'.[77] As Eric Evans points out: 'After enclosure, in many areas of England, a much sharper line of division could be drawn between the privileged and the non-privileged clergy.'[78]

It was from the ranks of the privileged also that clerical magistrates were drawn. On a national basis the clergy's share in the magistracy rose from about 11 per cent in 1761 to almost 22 per cent in 1831, though as Table 5 shows, in counties in which enclosure had led to a substantial distribution of land in lieu of tithes, their contribution was still more important.[79]

Table 5 *Proportion of all magistrates who were clergymen in selected counties, 1761 and 1831*

County	1761 %	1831 %
Lincolnshire	15	47
Cambridgeshire	18	45
Bedfordshire	6·5	41
Northamptonshire	14·5	39·5
Warwickshire	9	36
Somerset	7·5	35

SOURCE: Eric J. Evans, 'Some reasons for the growth of English rural anti-clericalism, *c*. 1750–*c*. 1830', *Past and Present*, no. 66 (1975), p. 104.

This increasing role was partly due to the fact that in some country areas the clergy were the only men qualified by education and property for appointment. Unfortunately, although many of them dispensed their duties with efficiency and dedication, those very qualities served to isolate them from the poorer members of their flock. Too often they seemed to be administering rich men's justice – especially in cases involving the game laws or petty theft – rather than acting as mediators between rich and poor. And it was on these grounds that a minority of them refused to serve. One such, Charles Jerram, rector of Witney from 1834 to 1853, noted that although earlier service on the Surrey

Bench had enabled him to attack social evils connected with public-house administration, Sunday observance and the Poor Laws, this had been more than counterbalanced by the alienation from his parishioners which had taken place. There was a lack of trust between them, and the parishioners, 'looking for a constantly sympathetic friend in their minister, found themselves frequently aggrieved'.[80] He refused to repeat the experiment in Oxfordshire.

Despite these undoubted difficulties, however, it was the tithe issue which aroused the greatest ill feeling between parson and people. The issue grew to particular prominence in the later eighteenth century, when farming fortunes began to revive and when agricultural improvements were increasing yields. The cultivation of new crops, such as turnips or potatoes, was a further cause of dispute, as farmers resisted paying tithe on non-traditional crops. Indeed, tithe owners' attempts to collect their dues on potatoes brought them into conflict with agricultural labourers who were growing the crop on their allotments. In some cases, as we have seen, tithes had been extinguished by land allocations at the time of parish enclosures; in others, tithing rights were held by lay impropriators, who were as determined as their clerical counterparts to collect their legal dues. But in most villages the clergy were the principal recipients and, as such, the focus of discontent for those forced to pay. Tithes in kind, though less common than cash payments, were particularly resented. As a Buckinghamshire farmer declared with more sentiment than grammar: 'There is many unpleasant things . . . in taking the Tithes in kind after the Farmer have done his best for his Crop to have the tenth taken by the Rector or the Layman as taking the Tithes is the greatest evil in the country.'[81] And a correspondent to the *Monthly Magazine* in 1798 sourly observed: 'Very few clergymen in England who take tithes in kind retain the good opinion of their parishioners, and therefore have but little prospect of ministering to their religious improvement.'

Farmers who objected to the system did all they could to make collection difficult. In Hampshire during the 1790s one man gave notice to the tithe owner that his turnip crop was ready. The clergyman accordingly sent his team and servants at the appointed time, when the farmer 'drew ten turnips, and desired the other to take one of them, saying he should not draw any more that day, but would let him know when he did'.[82]

Those incumbents anxious to avoid such skirmishes, accepted money compositions instead, as the vicar of St Mary's, Lichfield, reluctantly agreed to do in 1773:

As the gathering in kind of wooll and Lamb, of Calf and Milk and seperating & distinguishing of land agisted or depastured by unprofitable cattle would be attended with endless trouble, as well as continual Quarrels with the persons from whom due, the Vicar in lieu thereof takes a Composition of one shilling and sixpence an acre for all land depastured or grazed without exception.[83]

However, even this approach could give rise to trouble. At Motcombe in Dorset during the early 1770s there was much annoyance when the parson rode round the parish calculating the payments due to him for agisted beasts or for the garden produce of the poorer villagers: 'The vicar could be seen gazing over gates and peering into the dusty recesses of barns to discover the hidden sack of apples or the pound bag of clover seed, each tithed at 3d.' During the year ending Lady Day 1774 these efforts brought him just over £100.[84] But parishioners bitterly resented such prying, and where non-Anglicans were involved their objections were also reinforced by religious sentiment. There were cases, as at Wallingford, where an aggrieved cleric had to take a determined non-payer to court. Here Stephen Green, a Quaker, refused to hand over to the rector the tiny tithe payment of 3s. 8d. in both 1809 and 1811, until ordered to do so by the magistrates.[85] Small wonder that another clergyman should note with resignation in 1828: 'I do really think I don't get much more than a fourth part of my dues & if I collected the tithes in kind the land occupiers would harass me to death.'[86]

During the agricultural depression which followed the French wars criticisms of the tithe system intensified. They reached a peak in the mid-1830s, at a time of falling grain prices and of renewed cries of distress from farmers. After several unsuccessful attempts, with Tithe Commutation Bills introduced each year from 1833 to 1836, legislation reached the statute book in the latter year. Its main purpose was to eliminate both the vagaries of tithing in kind and the disputes which took place over valuations when money compositions were accepted, though in the debate in the Commons more than one speaker also expressed the hope that it would encourage capital expenditure on the land, particularly the clearing of previously neglected wastes.[87] Under the new measure payments in cash only were to be accepted, calculated on the basis of the prices of the three principal arable crops, wheat barley and oats. Tithe commissioners and their assistants were appointed to oversee the implementation of the new system from 1 October 1838. If the parties were unable to agree voluntarily to the new arrangement, compulsory awards would be made, based upon the average value of tithes taken in the seven years from Christmas 1829 to Christmas 1835. Tenant farmers benefited from the provisions, in so far as the burden of tithe payments was officially transferred from them to the landowners.[88] Tenants could no longer be cited in tithe suits by aggrieved incumbents. Although the Tithe Commutation Act of 1836 could not make payments palatable, at least it removed some of the main grievances which had clouded relations between clerics and their parishioners over the years.

The Church of England, then, faced many difficulties in the late eighteenth and early nineteenth centuries. Some of them, like plurality, tithes and non-residence, were, as we have seen, to persist into the 1830s and beyond. Others were to be tackled by reformist clergymen of the day, of whom the greatest was undoubtedly John Wesley (1703–91). Wesley was ordained a deacon of the Church of England in 1725 and from the beginning wrestled hard within himself to achieve his own private 'holiness'. He laid much stress on the redeeming power of Christ; salvation by faith rather than good works was his message. He taught his followers to look for reward in the world to come, after they had endured the trials and tribulations of their earthly existence. From the start singing played an important part in Methodist worship and thereby gave great emotional uplift to men and women who had little enough cause to rejoice in their daily lives. Many were so deeply affected by Wesley's sermons and those of his followers that they displayed their feelings by 'outcries, convulsions, visions, trances'. Yet despite this emotionalism, overall discipline was strict. It was Wesley's practice 'to refuse the Methodist ticket to any woman who wore "either ruffles or a high-crowned cap". The particularities of the Quakers were not to be emulated, but the neat plainness of their attire was.'[89]

For a long time Wesley sought to work within the Church of England, and in this he had the initial support of certain of the leading members of that Church – like Bishop Ross of Exeter, who urged in a speech in the House of Lords that toleration should be extended to the dissenters and the fullest legal security given to them for the free exercise of their worship.[90] Wesley himself spoke with appreciation of Ross's tolerant attitude. But the differences grew stronger and a major breach between the Wesleyans and the Anglicans came in 1784, when the former began to ordain their own ministers. Soon local Methodist societies, with their class leaders, circuit networks, and ministers appeared over much of England. Lay preachers helped to fill the gaps in the ministry and from the start played a vital role in the life of the Wesleyan connection. Despite hampering doctrinal differences, notably with the Calvinists, enrolled membership in the British Isles rose from 43,380 in 1780 to 71,668 by 1790, including 294 ministers at the latter date.[91] It was, however, in the following decade that Methodists finally emerged as a major religious body. Most of these early members were of humble background, and women were prominent among them. Thus of 161 members in rural communities (that is, excluding Bedford and Luton) within the Bedford St Paul's circuit in 1794, 111 were women; and of the 107 people for whom occupations were given, the biggest single grouping (thirty-nine) were lacemakers. Labourers came second, with eighteen members, and farmers third, with ten. The rest covered a wide variety of occupations, including village craftsmen, school teachers, hat makers, shopkeepers, dealers, higlers and one 'gentleman'.[92] A similar prominence has been observed among women in parts of Lincolnshire, where many acted as Sunday-school teachers and missionary collectors in connection with the Primitive Methodists.[93]

Early Methodism was a missionary faith. If a Wesleyan went to a village where his Church was unknown, he sought to establish a local society. John Furz, one of Wesley's preachers, in telling the story of his life mentioned that the vicar of his home parish of Wilton near Salisbury, preaching against this new departure, declared: 'For there is springing up amongst us a . . . religion called Methodism; it is like the plague. They that have it infect whole families.'[94] In George Eliot's novel *Adam Bede* Dinah Morris, the niece of a local farmer, carried her enthusiasm with her when she went to visit her relatives, even preaching upon the village green:

The villagers had pressed nearer to her, and there was no longer anything but grave attention to all faces. . . . At last it seemed as if, in her yearning desire to reclaim the lost sheep, she could not be satisfied by addressing her hearers as a body. She appealed first to one and then to another, beseeching them with tears to turn to God while there was yet time.[95]

Until the Wesleyans could afford to build their own chapels they often met in barns and cottages or out-of-doors. This was especially true of the Primitive Methodists, for whom the 'most distinctive of the means of grace was the camp meeting'. It had been the determination of Bourne and Clowes, the founders of the connexion, to hold camp meetings which had led to their expulsion from the Wesleyans:

The camp meeting, usually held on a Sunday in summer, began in the morning; a wagon was drawn into a country lane, with one or more ministers and several local preachers present. There was singing, prayer, a sermon, an exhortation, then a break for dinner. In the afternoon a procession went round the village singing hymns, returning to hear short sermons from the preachers. At a camp meeting at Tetford [in Lincolnshire] in June 1837, eight preachers spoke for ten minutes each; they alternated with more hymns and prayers – at one point two or three praying parties formed and prayed out loud simultaneously. Ending at five the meeting was followed by a love-feast in the evening. . . . Lovefeasts were as popular in Primitive Methodism as in other branches of Methodism . . . they featured the quasi-sacramental breaking of bread in common and the drinking of water from a common loving-cup, but the chief events were the spiritual testimonies offered by members.[96]

Whatever the virtues of Methodism, however, from the end of the eighteenth century its appearance within a parish was regarded with hostility by most Church of England clergymen, who feared it would undermine their own influence. At the small Norfolk parish of Lether-ingsett a farmer's wife noted in her diary during April 1795 that the rector had 'kicked up a dust with the Methodists' at his evening service – though this did not influence her own religious practice, which consisted of attending both parish church and Methodist meeting on the Sabbath.[97] More than half a century later the incumbent of Goring, Oxfordshire, blamed dissent for engendering 'a bitter and party spirit among the people' and thereby hampering his ministry, while at Chipping Norton in the same county a colleague complained that there was a 'positive premium on Dissent in the fact of the chief employers of the people being Dissenters and almost openly preferring those of their own denomination'.[98] But among their flocks the lines were usually less rigidly drawn, and many people attended both church and chapel as the fancy took them.

In general, Anglicanism proved strongest in the smaller parishes especially in those where landownership was concentrated in the hands of one or two men who were active supporters of the church. In such a 'close' parish, the squire could exclude dissenters from his estate simply by refusing to let farms or cottages to them. In the mid-1840s the agent of the Ancaster estate in Lindsey noted of one applicant for a farm that he 'would be a very good tenant but there is one objection to him being a Dissenter'. At Torksey in the same area the curate, troubled by the advances being made by Primitive Methodists in the parish, appealed to the principal landowner, Lord Brownlow, to buy up the few cottages not already in his hands, since some of them were being used by the Primitive Methodists as places of worship and Sunday school. 'It would facilitate materially the getting rid of that sect,' he declared, 'and by that means the putting an end to the only existing Sunday school.'[99] Occasionally matters worked the other way. At South Reston, Lincoln shire, the chief resident owner became a Wesleyan local preacher and 'threw his influence against the Church'. Nevertheless, it is significant that in 1851 in Kent and Lincolnshire – two counties where dissent had considerable support – less than one in five *estate* villages had a Nonconformist place of worship.[100] In that year almost 40 per cent of the whole church-going population of Lincolnshire were Methodists, as was appropriate for the county of Wesley's birth.

It was in the larger 'open' parishes, particularly those in which there was rural industry, that Methodism flourished, for there the influence of squire and parson was more restricted. However, such parishes also tended to be less disciplined; more drunkenness and disorder were found than in their carefully controlled 'close' counterparts, and this perhaps militated against Methodist success. In 1854 one Oxfordshire incumbent considered that 'indifference and gross drunkenness are greater impediments here than any sectarian opposition', and he was not alone in reaching that conclusion. Nevertheless, in Cornwall, Wales, Bedfordshire and parts of the Midlands Nonconformists outnumbered Anglicans. In Wales feelings ran particularly high for here not only had there been decades of neglect by the Church but the landowners, who were mainly English, were usually Anglican in sympathy and were opposed by the mass of the population, the small peasant farmers and labourers, who emphasized their Welshness by attending chapel. Nonconformity and political radicalism both grew apace in Wales during the years 1815–70, and as early as 1844 the *Quarterly Review* was commenting on the 'wide-spread alienation from the doctrines and disciplines of the Established Church' which had become 'so prominent a feature in many districts of the country'.

In scattered parishes, like those of the mid-Kent Weald, where families might live miles from their parish church, dissent also flourished. The people occasionally attended church, but regular worship there, especially during the winter, was out of the question. In these circumstances a small dissenting chapel, perhaps held in a local cottage, was a natural alternative.[101] Elsewhere, in isolated forest settlements established by squatters in Wychwood in Oxfordshire and the Forest of Blean in Kent, more eccentric messianic sects grew up alongside Methodism. In the early nineteenth century Dunkirk, a remote community in the Forest of Blean, became for a time the centre of a sect led by the mentally disturbed John Nichols Tom, the self-styled Sir William Courtenay, who claimed to be the Messiah. His mission ended tragically in 1838 when, following a series of riots and impostures, Tom and seven followers were killed by the Kentish militia in the battle of Bossenden Wood. The dire poverty and brutality which these events revealed shocked the local gentry and clergy – and, indeed, Parliament itself. In an attempt to 'civilize the inhabitants an Anglican church and school were built about 1840, and in the following year Dunkirk was formed into a separate parish'.[102] It wa almost as if a mission had been started in some far-off foreign clime rather than in Kent.

Happily, such excesses were rare. In most cases it was the Wesleyans and the Primitive Methodists who succeeded when the Anglicans failed. The Baptists, too, claimed their adherents, though in general there was a decline during these years in the position of 'old dissent'.[103] Nevertheless, at Eversley Charles Kingsley found the Baptists his most formidable religious opponents in the 1840s; they had obtained a hold on the congregation, thanks to the neglect and dishonesty of the previous rector. Kingsley found the altar cloth moth-eaten; local farmers were pasturing their sheep in the churchyard; and heavy arrears of poor rates and the curate's salary awaited payment.[104] Bratton in Wiltshire, where some of the leading farmers and trades-people became Baptists, was another parish where this sect became, for a time, the dominant religious group in the village. In 1777 there were about twenty members of the Baptist Church in the parish; by 1822, the number had jumped to 117, and it continued to grow slowly until it reached over 160 by the 1860s.[105]

Roman Catholics, by contrast, were little represented in country districts, save where the local squire was himself a Catholic. Towards the end of the eighteenth century one writer even claimed that all rural Catholics below gentry level were 'servants or the children of servants, who have married from those families, and who chuse to remain round the old mansion, from the conveniency of prayers, and because they hope to receive favour and assistance from their former masters'. This was an exaggeration, though it does seem that Catholic landlords selected co-religionist tenants for their farms – a choice perhaps not altogether surprising when it is remembered that it was only in the period 1778–1829 that anti-Catholic legislation in Great Britain was at last dismantled.[106] Most Catholics doubtless sought to congregate in an uncertain and sometimes hostile world.

On a social plane, Protestant nonconformity was also important in offering labouring men and women the opportunity to run their own affairs and thereby to acquire self-confidence and administrative expertise. Many local preachers and class leaders among the Primitive Methodists, for example, were agricultural labourers,[107] though among the Wesleyans they were rather less prominent, as farmers, craftsmen and shopkeepers predominated here.[108] But even these groups were unlikely to take a leading role in the Anglican Church. In addition, the more independent villagers valued their freedom from the firmly hierarchical structure of the Church of England. Joseph Arch was one who became a dissenter for this reason in about 1840, when he was only fourteen. As he later wrote:

I never took Communion in the parish church in my life. When I was seven years old I saw something which prevented me once for all. . . . First, up walked the squire to the communion rails; the farmers went up next; then up went the tradesmen, the shopkeepers, the wheelwright, and the black-smith; and then, the very last of all, went the poor agricultural labourers in their smock frocks. They walked up by themselves; nobody else knelt with them; it was as if they were unclean . . . I said to myself, 'If that's what goes on – never for me!'[109]

Arch later became a local preacher with the Primitive Methodists.

Yet despite the great upsurge of Methodism in the late eighteenth century and the revival of the Church of England in the early nine-teenth, it must not be forgotten that many of the old ways also persisted – such as the belief in witchcraft and in the efficacy of the local 'wise man' or 'white witch' in combating unfavourable influences. As a writer on Lincolnshire put it at the end of the nineteenth century, during these years 'the old and simple heathendom still lay untouched . . . hidden, beneath successive varnishes of superstition, religion, and civilization'.[110] It found expression in legends and stories of 'boggarts' and evil spirits, and in the attempt to propitiate hostile forces by smear-ing blood on the door-sill to 'skeer awa'ay th' horrors', or placing bread and salt on the flat stones found along the side of the road in order to get a good harvest.[111] In Yorkshire the Rev. J. C. Atkinson commented on the cottagers' practice of keeping a 'witch-wood', cut from an appropriate part of the rowan tree, as a permanent charm against evil influences. Special rituals were practiced by buttermakers, too, if the butter would not form, since this was believed to be the result of malign intervention.[112]

It is against this background that a recent writer has gone so far as to state that 'paganism was dominant . . . in popular religion . . . the village poor considered themselves to be Christians, but . . . "the stronger influence on the individual in his everyday life" was pagan not Christian'.[113] That is too sweeping a judgement, for many followed these superstitious practices more from a desire to be 'on the safe side' than because they believed absolutely in their power. Nevertheless, there can be little doubt of the influence exerted by superstition on day-to-day living. It persisted in country districts until the end of the nineteenth century.

Far more alarming, especially in the earlier years, was the readiness of villagers to blame one of their neighbours for the natural misfortunes of their existence, such as illness or the loss of farm livestock. Many old people, suspected of possessing the 'evil eye', had their lives made miserable by allegations of witchcraft. At Mears Ashby in Northampton-shire a woman was 'ducked' as late as 1785 because it was believed she was a witch. If she floated, it was argued, she must be guilty. But this unfortunate instantly sank, and her life was with difficulty saved: 'On which the cry was No witch! No witch! and the woman met with pity.' But a predecessor at Tring in Hertfordshire thirty-four years earlier had been less fortunate. She and her husband were both stripped naked by an infuriated mob, 'their thumbs [were] tied to their toes' and they were then dragged two miles to a muddy stream, where they were thrown into the water. They were also beaten with sticks and the old woman died as a result of her experiences, though her husband survived.[114] Eventually one of her tormentors was hanged for murder.

By the nineteenth century these expressions of mob anger against supposed witches had disappeared, but belief in their powers and influence proved more persistent. In Norfolk a woman admitted wounding a neighbour with a knife during September 1846 and 'professed herself ready to suffer any penalty which petty sessions might impose, because she had cured herself of pains and aches by drawing blood' from the neighbour, whom she believed to be a witch.[115] It was thought that if a suspected witch could be made to bleed by her victim, her powers would be destroyed.

Even religious services themselves might be used as vehicles for superstitious practices. In Lincolnshire the purpose of church atten-dance at Christmas was often less to celebrate the birth of the Saviour than, in pagan fashion, to commemorate the dying year and to prepare for the new.[116] In other cases confirmation was considered to be a cure for rheumatism, and there are accounts of old people trying to be con-

F

firmed more than once for this reason.[117] On a lighter note, such
festive events as the visits of mummers at Christmas also had their
heathen side, for when the actors came in

from the wintry dark in their masks and queer disguises, they were somehow
fearfully transformed. Something of alien significance clung about them as
they went through the words and actions of their age-old death-and-resur-
rection play, with its hero who died and rose again, as the seed dies in the
ground and springs up afresh as the living corn.[118]

Mumming was thus a symbol of the earth's eternal fertility rather than
a mere Yuletide celebration.

However, while such beliefs might be excused among poor and
uneducated men and women living in remote rural areas, it is dis-
concerting to discover that even Anglican clergymen were not proof
against them. The Rev. William Ettrick, vicar of Affpuddle and Toner's
Puddle in Dorset, began to blame an old woman named Susan Wood-
rowe for the evils that befell him. Mr Ettrick had engaged Susan
to work in his garden at the end of February 1804 and shortly afterwards his horse, 'a hard and healthy and not very old creature', became
ill. Despite all efforts, it died the following September. Later Ettrick
remembered that before it began to ail Susan had asked for some hair
from its tail. This, he was now convinced, she had used to cause the
horse's death. Then in June 1804 the vicar's fourth child, a son, was
born, and Susan assisted at the birth. Almost immediately the child
began to sicken and the anxious father suspected the old woman of
being the cause of the trouble. He thought he noticed that the baby
became worse if she approached. Even when she passed by the outside
of the house, unseen by those within, the child would shriek and
almost spring out of his father's arms. On 14 November Ettrick noted
that the baby had been eased 'by my application of a phylactery inscribed with sacred words in the original character & tied round its
Body, after wh. we have had a sudden & entire Peace. . . . I was once
incredulous about the power of Witchcraft, but have no doubts
remaining.' Unfortunately the respite proved short-lived. On 1
December the 'poor tormented Infant', who

had an entire freedom since my application of the means – Untill Susan . . . has
come again for some Days to wash &c. we have reasons very strong and
many to ascribe to this ill looking & worse tempered wretch, the sufferings
of this Child, the Curse upon the Horse &c. She has often dropped expressions
that excite great suspicion . . . but never once offered the bare civility of
wishing the child better.

Eventually, on 4 January 1805, the vicar decided to dismiss her. After this his fears seem to have subsided, though as late as 11 September 1805 he was recording in his diary:

Bees – have but one stock now left and those we are taking on – they have dwindled away unaccountably, Susan having had hands upon them last yr. They have not swarmed once this yr. tho' some were very heavy and two have declin'd and gone, leaving empty combs. Keep no more Bees.[119]

If the Rev. William Ettrick could allow his anxiety over witchcraft to gain so great a hold, how much easier must it have been for his unlettered fellow villagers to fall into the same trap? There was much in their lives that was uncertain and threatening. Belief in magic and in the power of omens was one way of emphasizing their helplessness in the face of a malign fate. It is significant that omens presaging death were particularly widespread at a time when medical treatment was in its infancy and mortality rates high. In some areas even to leave a body unburied over Sunday was a sign that there would be another death in the parish before long, while the small natural accidents of life, like overturning a loaf of bread as it was taken out of the oven, had the same ominous meaning.[120] With unexpected dangers threatening on every side, it was only prudent, in the eyes of most people, to take steps to propitiate evil spirits, wherever they were found.[121] In such circumstances superstitious rituals inevitably flourished.

West Berks Association
FOR THE PROSECUTION OF FELONS.

SIX
POUNDS
REWARD.

Whereas

During the Night of Monday, December the 21st, 1835, some person or persons stole

Seven Turkies

From a Fowl House at *Anville Farm*, near Hungerford, the property of Mr. WILLIAM CURNICK.

Whoever will discover the Offender or Offenders, shall on Conviction receive the Reward of £1 from Mr. Curnick, and £5 from the West Berks Association.

MATTHEWS and HULBERT,

Hungerford, Dec. 23rd, 1835.   Solicitors to the Association.

HALL AND MARSH, PRINTERS AND BOOKBINDERS, IMPERIAL PRESS, SPEENHAMLAND.

As the advertisement indicates, protective associations were common in the days before professional rural police forces were in full operation

The 'Swing' riots of 1830

6 Crime and punishment

To steal fruit ready gathered was a felony; to gather the fruit and steal it was only a trespass. If you were seen stealing goods from a shop, you could be transported, but if you stole them without being seen, you could be hanged. . . . Special rewards were offered to stimulate capture and prosecution, in the hope that such incentives would supply the place of an organized police force. In general the law-breaker, whether vagrant or bandit, whether victim or culprit, reaped the advantages of that inefficiency of government which had helped to produce him. There was, however, one significant exception. . . . In 1770 Parliament passed the first of a series of Game Laws which became fiercer and fiercer in the generation that followed. The statistics show that in the next generation the Game Laws were carried out much more thoroughly than any others; the convictions for poaching assumed a larger and larger share of the volume of crime. The explanation is obvious. The Justices were specially interested in enforcing these laws, and they had a police for this purpose in their gamekeepers.[1]

The sources of crime in rural districts are chiefly the four following: beer-shops, the game laws, the tramp system, and the arrangements of cottages and lodging-houses . . . To steal game is not regarded as a sin among the villagers; and thus the precipice of crime is sloped to an inclined plane. From poaching the youthful delinquent proceeds to petty larceny, from this to some greater offence.
REV. H. WORSLEY, *Juvenile Depravity* (1849)[2]

Although crime in rural England during the late eighteenth and early nineteenth centuries never assumed the threatening proportions that it did in the towns, it remained a cause for unease. Offences against property were especially deplored, for property was regarded as 'the measure of all things'. During the course of the eighteenth century the number of capital statutes was increased from around fifty to about two hundred and most of the new penalties related to attacks on

property. By the early nineteenth century the British Parliament had
established 'one of the bloodiest criminal codes in Europe'.[3] Yet
despite their commitment to the death penalty, country gentlemen
were unable to rest secure. Justice Christian of Ely wrote in 1819 in
favour of the retention of capital punishment for housebreakers but
at the same time, had to guard his own property with dogs, firearms,
bells and lights. He even took a brace of double-barrelled pistols to
bed with him when he retired for the night.[4]

Clearly, the suppression of crime was beyond the capacity of the
existing law-enforcement agencies – parish constables, private prosecuting societies and magistrates. Yet paradoxically, many still clung
to those traditional methods because of the opportunity they gave for
the exercise of discretion by the injured party. This latter could, as a
recent writer has pointed out, 'decide . . . upon the severity of the
prosecution, either by enforcing the letter of the law, or reducing the
charge. He could even pardon the offence completely by not going to
court.'[5] To the seemingly penitent, or those with powerful friends,
mercy could be shown, while to those regarded as 'undesirables' a
harsher face would be turned. Even offenders unfortunate enough to
be brought before the assizes could still hope to escape the ultimate
penalty:

Roughly half of those condemned to death during the eighteenth century
did not go to the gallows, but were transported to the colonies or imprisoned. . . . The grounds for mercy were ostensibly that the offence was
minor, or that the convict was of good character, or that the crime he had
committed was not common enough in that county to require an exemplary
hanging. The judges also used the pardon when necessary to meet the
requests of local gentry or to propitiate popular feelings of justice. The bench
could ultimately decide whom to recommend for mercy and whom to leave to
hang, but they were not usually willing to antagonize a body of respectable
feeling.[6]

Not until the middle of the nineteenth century, when professional
police forces became general, did certain of the anomalies disappear
and some of the tensions begin to relax. Though by the 1830s there
were already signs that the era of draconian punishments was coming
to an end. Thirty years later the number of statutory capital offences
had dwindled from over two hundred at the beginning of the century
to virtually no more than two – murder and treason.

Even more than in urban England, crimes in the countryside were
committed from a mixture of motives and took many different forms.

As we have seen, arson and machine-breaking might be resorted to by men made desperate by poverty and unemployment, or they might be used merely to pay off old scores. Incendiarism – a capital offence until 1837 – was a traditional form of protest, together with poaching, the maiming of animals, sheep stealing, the sending of threatening letters and, of course, rioting. When parishes in East Anglia became involved in an outbreak of incendiarism during 1843 and 1844 it is significant that they were primarily ones affected by severe or moderate unemployment and correspondingly low wages. Many of the men were forced to rely on parish relief – often combined with the 'ticket' system, which required them to go round from farmer to farmer seeking work – while the earnings of those in employment were a mere 7s. to 9s. per week. There were 'idle gangs of young and sullen labourers' ripe for trouble. Complaints were made, too, that employers held back wages when the weather was bad or when work was short, and that they dismissed men at a moment's notice.[7] Such lack of sympathy and trust between master and man inevitably poisoned relations, and it is notable that a high proportion of those subsequently accused of arson were workers who had recently left their employer or had been threatened with dismissal. Again when James Caird visited Huntingdonshire and Cambridgeshire during the early months of 1851 he commented on the 'incendiary fires' which were 'of almost nightly occurrence' in the area. Here, too, the labourers' discontent at low wages was the reason suggested for this desperate position. As Caird wrote: 'A man might as well expose his life to the risk of a shot from a Tipperary assassin, as live, like a Cambridgeshire farmer, in constant apprehension of incendiarism.'[8] Similar anxieties had been experienced by the victims of earlier attacks in 1815–17, 1822, 1825, 1829–33 and 1835–7, though in the last period at least only those connected with the implementation of the new Poor Law had had particular grounds for fear.[9]

At the beginning of the century magistrates and the victims of arson sought to counter outbreaks by the traditional method of offering rewards for the discovery of the culprits, or, if the government agreed, by combining these with the gift of a free pardon to accomplices who would help to secure a conviction. Home Office records abound with pleas from nervous magistrates that an offer of a pardon should be included in an advertisement of rewards. In some cases if a public official or public property were involved, an official award might be proffered, too.[10] Occasionally these initiatives were supplemented by a third, namely the calling in of a Bow Street Runner from London (or after 1829 a metropolitan policeman) to help with investigations. During the late eighteenth and early nineteenth centuries Bow Street constables operated as detectives all over the country and made up much of their earnings from the special fees they secured on these occasions.

An outbreak of stack fires at Alford in Lincolnshire during 1821 provides an example of an occasion when all three approaches were used. One of the magistrates wrote to the Home Secretary in much alarm, pointing out that one hundred guineas in rewards would be offered for the discovery and conviction of the perpetrators and asking that a pardon be offered to accomplices. In addition, an officer from Bow Street was applied for. Although this request was granted, the officer's arrival did not bring success, and after a fortnight he gave up the case. The day on which he left a further fire broke out, though it was 'suppressed before it had gained much ground'. As the magistrate anxiously observed, every precaution had to be taken, 'both by public & private Watch', in order to check the outrages.[11]

Incendiarism, as an instrument of vengeance or intimidation, was one of the most feared rural crimes. Other offences, such as sheep stealing, poaching and petty theft might be sparked off by hunger rather than revenge or a desire to defy a social superior, while there were some crimes, like smuggling, which were regarded as legitimate reactions to oppressive legislation. Even the most respectable members of society winked at the activities of smugglers during the French wars, and many, like the Norfolk parson James Woodforde, took advantage of their services. Early in March 1794 Woodforde had '2 Tubbs of Geneva brought . . . this Evening by Moonshine, 4. Gallons each Tub'. And on 13 December in the same year he was: 'Busy all the Morning almost in bottling two tubs of Gin, that came by Moonshine this Morn' very early.' In his case the goods were supplied by a local blacksmith, but often whole communities were implicated. When Charles Kingsley moved to the rectory at Eversley in 1844 he discovered that most of the older men in the district 'had smuggled in their time or connived at it, though they now limited their activities to poaching'.[12] At Morwenstow in Cornwall the vicar complained despairingly that his parishioners were 'a mixed multitude of smugglers, wreckers, and dissenters of various hue'. This was something of an exaggeration, for by the 1840s and 1850s smuggling was on the decline even in Cornwall, and 'wrecking' took the form of stripping wrecks which had been driven on the rocks rather than luring vessels to their doom, as had earlier been the case. Nevertheless, the vicar had great difficulty in curbing the predatory instincts of his flock.[13]

Despite the policing efforts of the customs and excise men, backed up from time to time by the military, it was only when import duties were reduced that the smuggler's trade was undermined. In 1784, when the import duty on tea was lowered from 119 per cent to 12.5 per cent, the amount entered for home consumption within a year increased from under 5 million pounds to nearly 16.5 million pounds. 'It had quite suddenly become unprofitable to smuggle tea, which immediately began to flow through the ordinary legal channels of trade in increasing volume.'[14] The same was true of other smuggled goods, particularly imported spirits during the nineteenth century. As *The Times* reported in September 1818, if duties were halved on hollands (gin) and brandy, so that the former could be retailed at about 15s. and the latter at 18s. per gallon, 'the temptation to purchase smuggled spirits would be done away, and all the host of expenses of riding-officers, revenue cutters . . . would be saved, and the dis- agreeable service of patrolling troops on the coast become unnecessary'. When the duties were eventually cut the accuracy of the newspaper's predictions was confirmed.

Another crime widely tolerated by the well-to-do was duelling, despite the fact that it was a capital offence. Down to the middle of the nineteenth century jurors regarded a fair duel with such leniency that acquittals were the rule rather than the exception. In March 1829 even the Prime Minister, the Duke of Wellington, had such an encounter with the Earl of Winchilsea over the latter's opposition to his plans for Catholic emancipation. And in Wales a dispute between two rural magistrates at Tenby petty sessions in March 1839 led to a conflict in which one of the participants was shot in the groin, a wound which seriously imperilled his life. This was possibly the last event of its kind to be fought in the principality, and it was a sad commentary on the calibre of Welsh magistrates, whose duty it was to uphold the law,[15] that it should have been carried out by two of their number.

Confidence tricksters were found in all ranks of society – from the dishonest gentlemen horse dealers portrayed in R. S. Surtees' amusing novel, *Mr. Sponge's Sporting Tour* to their no less ingenious, if more humbly connected, brethren who preyed on unsuspecting farmers at local fairs and markets. John Fielding was particularly anxious to advise the latter in his *Farmer's Guide Through Fairs and Markets*, published in 1775:

it is hoped . . . that all farmers, husbandmen, and other persons, will on their going to a fair, with any property about them, resolve to observe the following rules, *viz*.

1st.   To put up at such public houses as are known to be most reputable, or, for want of room there, at such other houses, where their neighbours or intimate acquaintance usually resort to.

2d.   Never to disclose in public company, (where too often in *the corner* sits a silent spectator and hearer) that they *have more money than wit*, but as much as possible to confine all knowledge of what their pockets contain, to themselves.

3d.   When they go into a fair or market, with money in their pockets, to have some friend or companion with them, from whom they should never seperate till their business is done; after which let them go back to their quarters, drink a chearful glass, and return home in good time, or stay where they are all night.[16]

Farmers also had to beware when they rode back with the proceeds of their market dealings, for in the late eighteenth century robbery by highwaymen and footpads was still quite common, especially near London, though even the provinces did not escape unscathed. In the Chester area, indeed, so feared were attacks on the mail that it was almost impossible to recruit post boys, and those appointed were quite likely to throw up the job at a moment's notice. According to the Surveyor to the General Post Office, in August 1796 no less than forty different boys had been employed during the previous weeks to ride with the mail from Chester to Woodside Ferry and Warrington, which 'shews the aversion of the Boys'.[17] So desperate had the situation become that 'little Boys under the age prescribed by Act of Parliament almost naked [had] been sent with those Mails, & deserting them [had] under my directions to the Deputies been apprehended & sent to Bridewell'. Despite repeated pleas from the Post Office and complaints from the general public, it was not until December 1801 that the Treasury at last authorized the appointment of armed guards.[18] Mail coaches, too, were held up from time to time. Even the presence of guards was not sufficient protection, for the robbers placed obstructions in the path of the coach, such as felled trees or harrows and ploughs, and when the vehicle shuddered to a halt they made their move.[19]

As late as the mid-1830s there were angry comments about the insecurity of the roads, as well as of pilfering from cargoes transported by canal and the new railways. A commercial traveller who operated in the south of England claimed that it was on rare occasons only that he travelled after dark: 'Occasionally in a moonlight night I may; but it would be contrary to prudence for any person who travels about the country with much money in his pocket to be out after dusk.' Another witness, a straw-hat maker from London, confirmed the dangers and said that he had himself been fired on near Harpenden while on his way to Luton market to purchase straw. A third traveller maintained that farmers in northern towns commonly waited for hours 'to make up parties for their return home after dark from the markets, rather than risk the journey alone'.[20] Migratory gangs were held responsible for some of the depredations. In the Droitwich division of Worcestershire magistrates blamed 'strangers' for a whole catalogue of offences, ranging from burglaries to horse and cattle stealing: 'the burglars are supposed to come from Birmingham; the horse-stealers still farther off . . . the cottager's dwelling is in the daytime frequently broken into by trampers and others in the guise of seafaring men, whilst the in-mates are at labour in the field'. Elsewhere, as in the St Thomas's Poor Law union area of Devon, it was gipsies who were the 'greatest pest'. They robbed farmers of anything 'from their horses to their potatoe-fields, and every species of property that cannot be locked, is daringly [taken] by these night marauders'.[21] It will be seen that these offences were not 'class' crimes, but often involved the poor in stealing from the poor. Eventually such disclosures were to lead to the establishment of a professional rural police force.

In the meantime, however, it was the traditional method of harsh punishments that was applied to combat most forms of lawlessness. One of the earliest of the draconian penalties which reached the statute book in the eighteenth century was a measure passed in 1722, known as the Waltham Black Act. It was originally designed to deal with the attacks of deer poachers operating, in disguise, around Waltham Chase. But the Act extended the death penalty to people who appeared armed and disguised in other forests, parks and enclosed grounds, or who unlawfully hunted deer, maimed cattle, cut down trees, set fire to farm buildings and stacks, shot at people or were guilty of extortion. At its broadest it provided capital punishment for a vast range of offences, and although originally designed to last for three years, it was regularly renewed for the rest of the century. Cases under the Act continued almost until its repeal in 1827. In 1814 an Essex labourer, William Potter, was executed for cutting down the orchard of a neighbouring miller. He was one of the unfortunates who did not benefit from a gesture of mercy from his superiors, for despite the presentation of a petition against the sentence by the committing magistrate, among others, a reprieve was refused. Potter, like most labouring men, was not 'acquainted with the terms of the Black Act', save when he encountered its all-embracing powers through bitter personal experience.[22] His case also demonstrates the vagaries of the punishment system, since he was called upon to pay the ultimate penalty for an offence which to many must have appeared comparatively trivial.

However, it was over the matter of game (not merely deer stealing, an issue with which the Black Act had been concerned, but also the poaching of small game) that the greatest ill-feeling and friction arose between rich and poor in rural society. It is to this emotive question that we must now turn.

For the landed classes of England hunting, shooting and fishing were *the* major leisure activities. As one Devon lady wrote of a male relative: 'He is as great a Nimrod as ever, he does nothing but hunt now, he goes out every day. They are very extraordinary hares for they breed after they are killed, for . . . if he kills a brace by night it is generally two by the morning.'[23] To a Victorian enthusiast sport was essential if a gentleman were to remain in the country: 'his personal residence is retained upon his acres by a combination of country pursuits and pleasures. . . . The game, the kennel, and stable, the decoy and the river, afford to the rich man recreation for every leisure hour.'[24]

Among such sportsmen mass slaughter was the order of the day. At the end of the eighteenth century Thomas Coke, of Holkham, the most celebrated exponent of shooting birds in flight, on one occasion shot forty brace of birds with ninety-three shots in eight hours. Each bird was shot singly.[25] But the popularity of shooting – and the size of the bags – increased dramatically in the early nineteenth century, when Joseph Manton, the most famous English gunmaker, perfected the flint-lock to give an efficient gun which was light and easy to handle. A three-day shooting party of eight guns at Ashridge in Hertfordshire during 1823 killed 1088 head of game, while in November 1845 2517 pheasants were killed in five days at another noble seat – an achievement which drew hostile comment from the Press.[26]

With this expansion came a need to increase the total head of game available. On many estates the interest in preservation was reflected in the formation of a separate game department, with a correspondingly heavy cash outlay. At Longleat expenditure on pheasants rose from £264 in 1790 to about £400 in 1810 and £2555 by 1856. At Belvoir the £90 a year spent on game in the early 1790s had risen to £500 by 1800.[27] The number of keepers was increased, too, and during the hunting season armies of watchers were recruited from among the local labourers to keep a look-out for poachers. In the view of at least one steward, however, this was detrimental to good order and discipline among an estate's work force. He claimed that it so unhinged and unsettled the men 'that the steady & good part of them say the Extra Money they get, does no good either to themselves or their families, for it is for the most part spent at the Alehouse . . . no Amount of Money can restore a Man to quiet habits who once gets out at Night to look after game.' And he added darkly: 'they begin as watchers & finish as poachers.'[28] But such critical views were mere cries in the wilderness when balanced against a landowner's enthusiasm for his coverts.

With an increase in estate outgoings there came naturally a desire on the part of landlords to protect their investments. It was in these circumstances that the bitter clashes between preservers and poachers took place. At the same time the anger of farmers was aroused as they saw their crops attacked by a growing number of animals and birds which they had no authority to kill. Often they were even prevented from trimming hedges which might act as cover for pheasants. On the Holkham estate tenants were expected to preserve pheasants and partridges 'as much as possible'. To this end they were to 'bush the stubbles after Harvest . . . do not disturb your hedge rows in the spring months and breeding season. . . . It is also requested that you will give your corn weeders and mowers strict charge to preserve all Pheasants and Partridges Eggs & Nests – also young Hares'. It was perhaps not surprising that early in 1819 one Holkham tenant, whose land adjoined the coverts, should complain of his poor crops: 'off 10 acres of Barley I had only 7 Loads, and I may safely say one third of that had no ear'.[29] Some of the more embittered men would tread on clutches of partridges' or pheasants' eggs out of spite, and many poached discreetly and allowed their labourers to do so. One Yorkshire farmer was found to have 1500 hare skins in his house.[30]

Meanwhile, in a landowner-dominated House of Commons, amendments to the Game Laws were keeping pace with the new enthusiasm for preservation. In the first sixty years of the eighteenth century there were only six Acts directed against the ordinary poaching of small game. In the next fifty-six years thirty-three such Acts reached the statute book. And to add to the tension there was the fact that until 1831 the right to shoot game was a privilege annexed to a particular social position. Under an Act of 1671 the killing of game was prohibited to all save owners of land worth £100 a year, lessees of land worth £150 a year, the eldest sons of esquires or of persons of higher degree and the owners of franchises. But the legislation had many anomalies.

The eldest son of an esquire without the necessary property qualification was not debarred from shooting, though his father was. And the exception in the 1671 Act permitting gamekeepers to kill led to qualified men 'engaging' their unqualified relatives and friends as ostensible keepers. Among the gamekeepers listed in Hampshire in the summer of 1798 were two clergymen and at least one younger son of a 'qualified' landowner. One of the clergymen, the Rev. William Heathcote, must have been especially enthusiastic, for he is shown as 'keeper' on two separate estates.[31] Likewise the Minute Book of St Katherine's Chapter, Canterbury, shows that the dean and chapter appointed clergymen to be gamekeepers on their estates in the late eighteenth century; at Hadleigh, Suffolk, the Rev. Thomas Drake was so selected in 1788 'during our pleasure'.[32] On Wiltshire manors in the late eighteenth century perhaps one-fifth of the approximately 250 gamekeepers employed were of this honorary variety.[33]

A further restriction was introduced in 1784, when a new tax on hunting was imposed. Anyone wishing to hunt game had to take out a certificate on which he paid a stamp duty of two guineas. Failure to comply could lead to a fine of £20 or three months' imprisonment.[34] Imposition of the maximum fine was not compulsory, but it meant that magistrates anxious to punish a man whom they suspected of being a commercial poacher could bring the full weight of the law to bear upon him. The fine was equivalent to almost two years' wages for a labourer, and even with ill-gotten gains from the illegal sale of game few working men could have afforded such a heavy sum.

More controversial still was the fact that owners of only a few acres of land were not permitted to kill the game which their own fields supported, though a qualified neighbour could come in to do so. If he entered uninvited, the owner's only recourse was an action for trespass – a remedy which most smaller men hesitated to use against the rich and powerful.

The sale of game was prohibited, too, and an unqualified person found in possession could face a fine of £5 per head or three months' imprisonment.[35] Yet, no middle- or upper-class dinner was complete without a game course, and ironically most of this was obtained through illegal purchase from London poulterers, who had themselves purchased the game from poachers or dishonest gamekeepers.[36] William Taplin, writing in the early 1770s, claimed to know of a waggoner who had bought as many as twenty-one hares at a time from a gamekeeper in Hampshire. He paid half a crown apiece for them and then disposed of them at 3s. 6d. each to a London poulterer.

So it was that landowners, through their parliamentary power, began the long battle to eliminate the poacher by repressive legislation. Because poachers, faced with a growing army of gamekeepers, began to operate increasingly at night, an Act of 1770 laid down that anyone convicted of poaching between sunset and sunrise was to be punished with up to six months' imprisonment. For a second offence the punishment was doubled, and a whipping was added. Although this measure was replaced three years later by another giving the option of paying a fine (ranging between £10 and £50, depending on the number of prior convictions) or of serving a term of imprisonment, the depredations continued. The net effect, indeed, was to encourage poachers to work in gangs in order to avoid arrest. In Norwich they grew so bold that they would warn keepers of their plans: 'if you choose to begin an engagement we are prepared.'[37] Poachers and gamekeepers were killed and injured in the resultant skirmishes. In 1781 two keepers were shot by an eleven-man gang raiding the Duke of Cumberland's covers, though when they ran out of ammunition they were taken prisoner by the Duke's servants, who were armed with cutlasses.

Gangs like these became the terror of the countryside and the focus of game preservers' anger. So in 1800, at a time when high food prices made many poor people desperate, a fresh Act was passed under which two or more persons found poaching together were to be punished with hard labour. For a second offence they were to be imprisoned and whipped or, alternatively, made to serve in the army or navy. But once again, the harsher punishments called forth defiance from the poachers. Some landowners responded by taking advantage of an Act of 1722 which gave an informer the choice of either proceeding normally against an offender before a JP or suing for his portion of the fine 'by action of debt' in a court of record. If he selected the latter procedure and was successful in his suit, he was entitled to recover not only his half of the fine but also double the costs of the prosecution. The defendant thus became liable for a heavy penalty, and if he could not pay it, this could land him in a debtors' prison for an indefinite period. This was a mode of proceeding advocated, for example, by the steward at Wrest Park, Bedfordshire, in June 1800, when he wrote to inform his employer, Lady Lucas, of the arrest of a shoemaker named Thomas Crouch, who had been caught poaching a hare on a Sunday. The normal penalty for this was three months' imprisonment or a fine – but one of the local magistrates had recommended that a civil suit be brought against Crouch:

the Expense of which He being unable to Pay, He must be sent to Goal and may be kept there a *year* or *two* Or untill your Ladyship may please to Release Him.

This sort of Punishment *in these times*, may be deem'd too *Harsh & Strong* ... at the same time something must be done to deter these Idle fellowes from such illegal ... practices, or all the Game will be kill'd both *here and at Harrold*. – I must beg therefore to request that your Ladyship will be so good as to say which way you would have me proceed; that is, to make him pay £10, or £20 or go to Goal for 3 months – or to bring an Action against him which may keep him in Goal for a very Long time or as it were for *Life*. Mr Alston [the magistrate] is [a] great Stickler about Game, On that account would recommend *strong measures* against Crouch, who I make no doubt has kill'd much Game in *his Woods* which join to Harrold woods. ... It is a well known fact, and no uncommon thing, for these Gangs of Poachers to make a subscription purse to pay the penalty in case they are detected – one of Crouch's acquaintances is just now come out of Goal for Snaring at Lord St. John, about 5 miles from Harrold.[38]

It was against this uneasy background that in 1803 Parliament passed the infamous Ellenborough Act, under the provisions of which anyone who offered armed resistance to lawful arrest (which included arrest by a keeper) could be hanged as a felon. For a time the new measure seemed to have an effect, but in the misery of the post-war agricultural depression men were ready to risk the gallows rather than see their families starve. In some cases, where gangs were especially well organized, the Bow Street Runners were called in to help catch offenders. *Jackson's Oxford Journal* of 3 February 1816 described one such group in the neighbourhood of Downham, Norfolk, 'whose numbers and daring proceedings, so terrified the people around, that the civil authorities were not very forward to act against such desperadoes. They acted with impunity for many months past, and got so bold as apparently to defy the constables, gamekeepers, &c.' Three local landowners eventually wrote to London for police help, and two officers were duly dispatched to the scene of the trouble. One of them infiltrated the gang, attending their suppers, poaching excursions and so on. In this way he discovered the men's plans, and within a fortnight he and his colleague were ready to pounce. Ten of the gang were arrested, most being taken 'in their beds', and were committed for trial.

Not all counter-attacks were as successful, however, and so in 1817 even unarmed poaching by night was made punishable by transportation for seven years; anyone who returned within that time was to be transported for life. In the poacher's eyes transportation was only a little less terrible than the gallows; faced with the terrors of transportation and of a parting from wife and children, men gathered together with even greater determination in order to avoid arrest. 'There is hardly now a jail-delivery in which some gamekeeper has not murdered a poacher,' wrote Sydney Smith, 'or some poacher a gamekeeper.'[39] Parish constables, too, were attacked if they proved overdiligent in seeking out poachers. In the late 1820s the constable of Downham Market was murdered when he pursued the 'lawless banditti of poachers . . . who . . . infested' the area, and at Hilgay, also in East Anglia, another man was murdered by a poaching gang.[40] Needless to say, most constables turned a conveniently blind eye to the poachers' activities.

Landowners, for their part, responded by establishing joint prosecution societies and calling for the full weight of the law to be enforced against those caught. Typical of this approach was an indictment for night poaching heard at Hampshire Spring Assizes in 1818. Two men were accused of seeking to kill game on the Titchfield estate of Henry P. Delme. On Mr Delme's behalf it was observed:

Offences of this nature, notwithstanding the endeavours of the Legislature to check them, are now become so *frequent* and still *growing to such an alarming extent* that unless the full measure of Punishment authorized by the Statute is imposed in *the present* and *other similar cases* the most serious consequences must result. The Gentlemen of the neighbourhood have found it necessary, and formed a resolution, to prosecute them in the most effectual way seeing by experience the evils to which they lead.[41]

The punishment demanded was transportation.

However, it was at the Lent Assizes at Winchester three years later that an event occurred which shocked even the hardened public opinion of the day. Of sixteen prisoners tried and sentenced to death on this occasion, only two were executed. One had helped to kill a gamekeeper employed by a major Hampshire landowner, and the other had shot at a keeper employed by Lord Palmerston, then Secretary at War. They were executed despite the fact that the jurors had recommended both young men to mercy. The judge observed that it was necessary that the extreme sentence of the law should be applied in these cases to deter others, since '*resistance to gamekeepers was now arrived at an alarming height*, and many lives had been lost'. As the radical journalist William Cobbett declared, the impression was thus created that 'it was necessary to put these two *men to death*' to deter others from resisting gamekeepers.[42]

As public opinion began to turn against the extreme penalties of the game laws, so a slight softening of the legal attitude towards poachers became apparent. At the same time there was pressure to abolish the qualifications which restricted the killing of game to a privileged few, to legalize its sale and purchase and to declare it the property of the owner on whose land it was found. In 1827 came the repeal of the Black Act, which had been little applied in the immediate pre-repeal period. The same year also saw the prohibition of mantraps and spring guns, though this measure was induced more by anxiety about the number of innocent victims maimed, especially children, than by concern for the injuries sustained by poachers. The following year a new Night Poaching Act was passed. As Lord Wharncliffe admitted in Parliament, it had largely been called forth by the great difficulty of getting convictions under existing legislation: 'Juries were unwilling to subject a man to be transported merely because he was found armed, when he had not killed any game; and thus, from the severity of the punishment, the offender escaped conviction.'[43]

Under the new measure anyone found poaching at night would face a sentence of three months' imprisonment with hard labour, and at the end of that term he had to find a surety for himself of £10, plus two sureties of £5 each. If he could not obtain these, he had to serve a further six months in gaol. For a second offence the penalty was doubled and for a third the offender could be transported for seven years, as before. An armed offender who put up resistance to arrest could still be transported for seven years, even if this were his first offence and if he had not actually taken any game but was merely searching for it.

Three years later, at a time when one-seventh of the criminal convictions in the country were for offences against the game laws, further reforms were introduced. The archaic qualifications for shooting game were at last abolished; its sale and purchase were legalized; and those who were discovered to be in unlawful daytime pursuit of game could be fined a maximum of £2 or, if they were in a gang of five or more persons, the penalty was increased to £5 per head. For killing game without a certificate the penalty was a maximum of £5. Those who were unable to pay the fine could be sentenced to a term of imprisonment, with or without hard labour; for fines below £5 this was for a maximum of two months. Despite the protests of at least one MP, however, these penalties could be imposed by a single magistrate sitting alone.

Although the 1831 legislation had eliminated some of the main causes of bitterness in rural areas over the game laws, others remained. Farmers continued to resent the damage caused to their crops by preserved animals and birds and their own inability to kill the offenders if landowners reserved the right to shoot over their tenants' holdings. In addition, the old conflicts between poachers and keepers continued. As John Bright told the Commons early in 1845, during the period 1833-43 'there were no less than forty-two gamekeepers killed . . . in twenty-five of these cases a direct verdict of wilful murder was returned.'[44] During 1844 alone there were at least nineteen more serious encounters between poachers and gamekeepers, in which thirty-one people were 'grievously, and some of them desperately, wounded', and two gamekeepers were murdered. Bright went on to give examples of the cases – such as the battle near Salisbury involving five gamekeepers and five poachers, in which two gamekeepers were taken to the infirmary, one with both his arms broken, and two poachers were carried home and believed 'not likely to recover'. Nor was this the sole cause for concern. In Buckinghamshire, to quote but one county, it was estimated that the damage occasioned by game 'amounted to at least one-fourth' of the county's crops. A number of other speakers pointed to the great increase in game-law cases in recent years, and although supporters like the Hon. Grantley Fitzhardinge Berkeley stoutly defended field sports as a source of amusement and recreation for the landed classes, it was eventually agreed to appoint a Select Committee to examine the issue.

The Committee's findings substantiated many of Bright's allegations. One of the witnesses, Samuel M. Phillipps, an Under-Secretary of State for the Home Department, confirmed the increase in the number of game convictions – from 2424 in 1839 to 4270 in 1844. In such counties as Berkshire, Hertfordshire, Oxfordshire and Wiltshire these offences made up about a quarter of total male summary convictions in 1843; in Bedfordshire and Buckinghamshire they comprised almost one-third and in Rutland, more than two-fifths. Elsewhere their impact was less dramatic (see Table 6) but it is significant that in certain of the Home Counties, where easy access to London provided a ready market for the sale of illicit game, convictions were particularly high. Phillipps also revealed that between May 1844 and March 1845 the Home Office had required forty discharges from prison and fourteen commutations of sentence as a result of illegal sentences being imposed under the game laws. 'In some cases too great a penalty has been imposed. For instance, under the trespass clause in the Game Act, where 40s. is the maximum penalty, £3 have been imposed. In other cases the

Table 6 *Game law convictions in specimen rural counties in relation to total male summary convictions, 1839–43*

County	Total male summary convictions					Percentage of game law to total male summary convictions					Proportion of game law convictions to 100,000 of male population				
	1839	1840	1841	1842	1843	1839	1840	1841	1842	1843	1839	1840	1841	1842	1843
Bedfordshire	184	206	232	296	366	28·3	24·8	28·9	24·7	36·1	102	99	128	138	246
Berkshire	624	572	538	531	466	13·6	13·1	14·7	19·0	24·4	108	94	99	125	139
Buckinghamshire	363	379	407	511	559	24·5	26·1	30·7	26·1	31·8	118	130	163	174	230
Cambridgeshire	431	408	449	487	595	6·5	3·7	8·5	10·5	9·2	35	19	47	62	66
Cornwall	298	266	240	296	325	0·6	2·3	3·3	2·4	1·2	1	4	5	4	2
Cumberland	228	245	229	269	283	2·6	4·5	2·2	5·6	4·6	7	13	6	17	15
Dorset	275	347	377	392	400	13·1	11·2	9·8	13·5	16·3	44	47	44	63	76
Hampshire	1149	1299	1135	1311	1418	12·3	11·6	12·5	12·0	11·8	84	87	81	89	93
Hertfordshire	487	583	541	613	534	21·6	19·6	20·3	19·6	24·7	138	148	142	153	167
Norfolk	1030	1091	1289	1424	1369	6·7	8·9	8·6	10·3	12·9	35	49	56	73	88
Somerset	1477	1663	1549	1911	2126	4·6	3·5	3·5	2·8	2·8	33	28	26	26	28
Suffolk	842	760	614	737	922	17·6	20·4	22·2	19·0	21·3	97	101	88	90	125
Westmorland	64	108	90	131	135	17·2	6·5	6·7	9·9	14·8	39	25	21	46	70
Wiltshire	585	856	684	841	847	21·0	13·0	18·6	20·5	26·4	97	87	99	133	172
England	42,683	47,429	47,022	53,998	56,428	5·6	5·3	6·0	6·6	7·5	34	35	39	48	54
Wales	597	533	607	786	933	6·3	6·5	6·9	7·3	8·3	9	8	9	13	17

SOURCE: *Select Committee on the Game Laws*, PP 1846, vol. 9, pt 1, p. 265.

imprisonment has been too long with reference to the penalty.'[45]
Phillips considered

Transportation for killing a hare or setting a snare a third time at night . . .
a most unjustifiable punishment. I think in all cases where the punishment
is transportation under the Night Poaching Act, the trial ought to be, not
at the quarter sessions [where they were under the jurisdiction of the magi-
stracy] but before a judge of assize. The administration of justice should be
free from the least suspicion.

Despite the evidence gathered by the Committee and Bright's
demand that all special protection for game should be ended, nothing
was done. Indeed, the Committee's own report accepted the principle
of protection on the grounds that this was consistent with the general
concept of property rights.[46] It also declared that landlords had on the
whole treated their tenants fairly and had given compensation when
just claims were made. Although landlord–tenant relations in this
regard varied considerably, there is evidence that some payments were
made. For example, Mr Pusey, MP, allowed a rebate of £916 for damage
done by game on 389 acres during the summer of 1844.[47]

The only legislation to result from the investigations of 1845–6 was,
therefore, an insignificant measure of 1848 permitting tenant farmers
to kill hares without taking out a certificate, provided their landlord
agreed. And in the excitement which surrounded the repeal of the
Corn Laws, Bright – and the general public – lost interest in the
game question. The privileges of the preservers continued un-
diminished.

As far as poaching offences were concerned, although the more
serious cases like assaults on gamekeepers did decline, the overall
total continued to mount. By 1870 there were 10,580 game-law prosecutions in England and Wales. The increase was due partly to legislative
changes in the second half of the nineteenth century, particularly the
1862 Poaching Prevention Act, and partly to improvements in policing.
But there is no doubt that many men echoed the views of the agricultural trade-union leader Joseph Arch:

The plain truth is, we labourers do not believe hares and rabbits belong to
any individual, not any more than thrushes and blackbirds do. . . . To see
hares and rabbits running across his path is a very great temptation to many
a man who has a family to feed . . . and so he may kill a hare or a rabbit when
it passes his way, because his wages are inadequate to meet the demands on
them, or from dire necessity, or just because he likes jugged hare as well as
anybody else.[48]

Critics might point, with some justification, to the fact that habitual poaching often led to more serious offences. But to the average villager concerned with killing an occasional rabbit, hare or pheasant it was merely taking a share in the bounty of the countryside to which he had every moral right.

To a few men, however, poaching was a good deal more important than this. For them it became an accepted way of supplementing their income. During the 1850s, for example, it was claimed that in the Beccles area of Suffolk, where herring fishing occupied the men in the autumn, 'if this is unsuccessful, many of them take to poaching, for . . . they are dependent upon its success for their maintenance during the winter'.[49] Others prided themselves on their skill with gun and net, and it became hard for them to lie in bed at night 'when the wind [was] just strong enough to make the Scots pines sound like the sea, and there [was] barely light for a fox to observe the prey it [had] caught by scent and sound, or the gamekeeper to see the rabbits that [came] bounding out of the blackness into the poacher's long net'.[50] Some, like the Leicestershire poacher, James Hawker, always wore a long covert coat, which came down over the legs and contained secret pockets in which hares and pheasants could be hidden. Hawker usually walked with a limp, not through any physical handicap but because he carried a sawn-off rifle down his trouser leg.[51] On these nefarious excursions a well trained dog, usually a lurcher or cross-bred greyhound, was an essential companion, whose function was to warn of keepers, to drive hares into the nets and to 'pull down injured deer'.[52]

The taking of game was one major cause of law breaking in rural areas, but petty theft was still more prevalent. Indeed, in the nation at large during 1838 (to quote but one year) almost two-thirds of all convictions were accounted for by simple larceny.[53] It was largely to combat this that the various voluntary prosecuting societies were formed by the propertied classes. By the late 1830s there were over 500 of these bodies in existence – like the Aldermaston Association for the Prosecution of Felons, established in 1800 to cover Aldermaston itself and the neighbouring communities of Wasing and Padworth. According to its published rules, it was formed to prevent 'Robberies, Burglaries, Felonies, and Thefts, from being committed in these several Parishes', and for the purpose of

defraying the Expences of Advertising, Apprehending and Prosecuting all such persons, who may be found guilty thereof; and the more effectually to secure the Property of the Subscribers to this Association, the under-mentioned Rewards independent of what are allowed by Act of Parliament, will be paid for the apprehending [of] any Person guilty of the following Offences, upon Conviction.

There then came a list of possible payments, so that for the conviction of a burglar, a housebreaker, a highway robber, an arsonist or anyone discovered stealing or maiming a horse the sum proposed was £5 5s. For sheep and cattle stealing or the receiving of stolen goods the amount was £2 2s., while half that sum was proffered in respect of the theft of pigs or poultry. For unmasking thefts of garden produce, firewood, farming implements and similar items the reward was 10s. 6d. Most of the associations followed a similar reward pattern.[54]

But even when the criminal had been identified, the problem of apprehending him still remained. The parish constable, chosen from among a parish's rate payers and reluctantly holding office for a year, was rarely prepared to endanger his own safety. So often it was left to the aggrieved person himself to arrange an arrest as best he could and then to hand over the prisoner to the constable to be confined in the local lock-up until he could be brought before a magistrate. The following extracts from the constable's book for Midgham, Berkshire, in 1771–2 indicate the tasks undertaken and the constable's charges (met from the rates) for carrying out these duties:[55]

To expences going with Phillips and Swain to the justices	3s. 0d.
To expences having Norris before the justice and to a bill of John Marshalls	5s. 8d.
To expences for Man that was found dead in the Road bear and victals for the jurymen	10s. 0d.
The Parson and Clarke	3s. 6d.
For carrying the Man to Church	8s. 0d.

In prosecuting offenders, the members of protective associations, like that at Aldermaston, would normally be able to depend on the backing of their organization. The minute book of the East Hendred Association for the Protection of Property indicates the way that this operated. Thus on 24 March 1814: 'John Hudson having detected John Goddard in stealing poles and Fences belonging to Robert Hudson a Member of this Association Ordered that the said John Hudson be paid One Pound out of the Stock of this Association. Provided he appears and gives Evidence at the same in a legal way.' While on 15 October 1819 came the entry: 'Ordered that John Hatter, George Stolen, John Lewis and William Simons, Laborers, all of this Parish for an assault on William Kent, be prosecuted at the Expence of this Association.'[56]

Arrest and conviction for an offence were, in these circumstances, something of a lottery. As we have seen, much the same could be said of the sentences imposed – one man was pardoned while another was hanged. At Oxford Quarter Sessions in March 1776 a woman who was convicted of housebreaking was sentenced to twelve months' imprisonment and a branding; a man charged with a similar offence received a sentence of six-months' imprisonment and a branding; and a second woman guilty of housebreaking merely received a whipping.[57] Yet three years later a former pig dealer and sievemaker from a nearby village, who had broken in and stolen two silver buckles, was hanged. He had earlier been imprisoned for 'cutting down young Timber' and was described as a 'most notorious Poacher'.[58] These antecedents were apparently enough to ensure that he paid the maximum penalty. Burglary (providing there was no violence to persons) ceased to be a capital offence in 1837, while the use of branding was virtually ended by an Act of 1779. The judicial whipping of women ceased in 1820.

To a growing band of reformers, however, it was the persistent anomalies in the use of the death penalty which were most in need of attention. In May 1823 Sir James Mackintosh stressed this in the Commons, when he unsuccessfully pressed for a new approach:

if a foreigner were to form his estimate of the people of England from a consideration of their penal code, he would undoubtedly conclude that they were a nation of barbarians . . . what other opinion could a humane foreigner form of us, when he found, that in our criminal law there were two hundred offences against which the punishment of death was denounced, upon twenty of which only, that punishment was ever inflicted – that we were savage in our threats, and yet were feeble in our execution of punishments. . . . Many small delinquencies were raised to the rank of capital crimes, and the same vengeance was denounced by the law against the offender who destroyed a tree, or cut down a twig, as was denounced against the wretch who committed a parricide. Laws of undue severity were also unduly executed; and the consequence was, that when a hundred individuals escaped, and one fell under the vengeance of the law, the fate of the individual who so fell was considered as an act of arbitrary rigour, instead of being considered as a sacrifice required by justice . . . what was the lesson to be derived from a consideration of the criminal law of England? Why, that the man who cut down a twig, or injured a cherry-tree, or stole a sheep . . . was as black a criminal as he who murdered his father, or betrayed the interests of his country to a foreign enemy.[59]

Despite his protests, horse, sheep and cattle stealing remained capital offences until 1832, while for twenty years after that date they could be punished by transportation.[60] Yet as Sir James's comments underlined, in practice the fate of men convicted for such offences differed widely. Of 288 persons found guilty of sheep stealing during the three years 1823–5 inclusive, only four were executed; 148 were transported for life; thirty-two were transported for fourteen years and eleven for seven years. At the other extreme, ten people were imprisoned for six months or less. Likewise with horse stealing – ostensibly another capital offence – only thirteen of the 493 persons convicted between 1823 and 1825 were hanged. Of the remainder 233 were transported for life; thirty-eight were transported for fourteen years and nineteen for seven years; and eleven escaped with six months' imprisonment or less.[61] It is significant that when William Ewart, MP, supported the repeal of capital punishment for these offences in 1832 he did so by pointing out 'that an unduly severe punishment must be an extremely uncertain punishment'. The death penalty, once inflicted

was beyond recall. Hence it was, that prosecutors trembled at the punishment, that Juries hesitated, that Judges paused, and that guilt escaped unpunished, or rather rewarded with impunity . . . in the year 1831, there were sentenced to death for sheep-stealing in England and Wales, 162 persons – executed one; sentenced to death for horse-stealing, 125 – executed none. . . .[62]

Lord Althorp made the same point: 'To have capital punishments multiplied on our Statute-books, for crimes for which the punishment was seldom or never enforced, was, in his opinion, highly objectionable.'[63] It was against this background of changing public attitudes, therefore, that repeal came in 1832.

Alongside the reforms in sentencing policy came significant alterations in policing, too, as disillusionment with the old methods grew apace. As we have seen, the existing parish constables were of little use, since the most industrious and energetic rate payers normally sought to avoid serving altogether or, if this proved impossible, they frequently engaged inefficient substitutes instead.[64] Those constables who were farmers were said to be 'deterred from interfering with old offenders, or with beer-houses, or other resorts of the dissolute, by an apprehension of injury to themselves or property'.[65] Elsewhere men might refuse to serve beyond the borders of their own parish. One magistrate from the East Riding of Yorkshire complained that he had known 'instances in which the constable [had] been sent for to quell a riot or disturbance, and he [had] returned for answer that he could not come himself, *but that he sent his staff by the bearer*.[66] In 1842 a final attempt was made to improve the efficiency of parish constables by enacting that every rate payer between the ages of twenty-five and fifty-five would be liable to serve. But, like its predecessors, it proved unsuccessful.

Many of the constable's duties were, of course, scarcely 'police' ones. They included relief items more appropriate to the overseers' accounts and such miscellaneous matters as arranging payments for the killing of vermin or ensuring that the fencing of common land was maintained, and the stinting of animals properly observed. The preparation of tax returns and militia lists also formed part of his responsibility. This range of activities is shown in the constable's accounts for Cuddesdon, Oxfordshire, during 1781:[67]

Pd. for making the Assessments for the Land & Window Tax	3s. 0d.
Pd. for making Ditto for the House Tax	1s. 6d.
Pd. for my Return of Ale Houses	2s. 0d.
Pd. to an old Soldier	1s. 0d.
Pd. Mr. Kings for letting the Water out of the Road	2s. 6d.
Pd. for 24 Dozen of Sparrows	6s. 0d.

Given the ineffective role of the parish constable as an agent for law enforcement, therefore, magistrates had to fall back on the enrolment of special constables to cope with serious disturbances. But these, too, were often of little value. Indeed, prior to 1831 even the method to be adopted for their recruitment was unclear, and after that date there was no guarantee that men called out would agree to serve. In August 1843, during the Rebecca Riots, only six of nearly 200 men summoned to Carmarthen to act as special constables actually appeared, and three of them refused to be sworn. Their excuse was that their homes and possessions would be destroyed by the rioters if they agreed to serve. Although they thereby rendered themselves liable to heavy fines, the Home Office deemed it prudent not to enforce the penalties.[68]

When special constables failed, justices had little choice but to call upon the Home Secretary for military assistance in maintaining order. They had a pathetic faith in the law-enforcement capabilities of even a small body of soldiers, as Home Office records make clear.

In the meantime, discontent at the lack of effective policing was growing in country districts, spurred on by the creation of the metropolitan police force in 1829. Some communities, of their own accord, began to recruit paid policemen, often bringing down a London man for the job. Beckenham in Kent was a case in point. Two trained policemen were engaged in the mid-1830s and, according to one of the land-owners responsible for the move, the effect on the crime rate was dramatic. In addition, vagrants were rarely seen: 'You do not see a beggar publicly. They may get into the grounds under the pretext of selling tapes and things of that kind. I have not been asked for relief by a vagrant in the village of Beckenham for the last twelve months.'[69] Equal satisfaction was expressed at Wymondham in Norfolk, where three policemen had been obtained from the metropolitan force: 'Before the introduction of a police . . . not only was the town itself exposed to constant disturbance and depredation, but farmers in the neighbouring villages were often robbed of their poultry, sheep, and other farm produce, which could easily then be carried without observation into the town at night, and be disposed of in various ways.'[70] (See Appendix 3 for examples of police recruitment in Oxfordshire.)

It was in the light of evidence of this kind, presented before the Royal Commission on a Constabulary Force between 1836 and 1839, that the first county constabularies were set up under the County Police Act passed in the latter year. The measure was permissive, however, and only about half of the counties in England elected to take advantage of it. The others no doubt feared the cost involved, or perhaps a rather lower level of local crime proved the decisive factor. Some of the larger rate payers may also have remained committed to the discretionary powers bestowed by the old system, whereby an injured party could choose to prosecute or to excuse an offender as he thought fit, without outsiders becoming involved. With the recruitment of professional policemen that became more difficult.

Nevertheless, those counties which did adopt the legislation were well satisfied with the result. In the early 1850s Mr J. Beadel, a large farmer from Essex, one of the first counties to implement the Act, claimed that crime had been much diminished as a result:

horse-stealing was very prevalent, and now it is very rare. There used to be a great many more incendiary fires than there are at present. . . . I think a great deal may be attributed to that, as compared with the old constabulary . . . the police is a preventive force, whereas the old constabulary did not wish to prevent crime; their profit was in the commission of crime; they were paid for serving summonses and conveying prisoners to gaol, and they had no object in preventing crime.[71]

A magistrate from Gloucestershire, another 'policed' county, agreed: 'the amount of undetected crime has decreased about 15 per cent. the ast five years. For the last two or three years we have not had a single case of sheep-stealing or cattle-stealing.'

So it was that in 1856 a new County and Borough Police Act at last made professional rural constabularies compulsory throughout the country. As a result of this measure, the English countryside became more secure, while in market towns the duties of the police also extended to such matters as the enforcement of paving, lighting and sanitation regulations. The diary of a Basingstoke police constable for 1853–4 shows him taking action to prosecute a man who had 'emptyed his Hog sistern into the Street', contrary to the Paving Act, and seizing a flute, a box and some books under a distress warrant from a man who had let off a firework in the market place on 6 November and had refused to pay the resultant fine. The fine and costs amounted to £2 3s. and the warrant of distress to 1s. 6d. He also gave refuge at the police station to people who were found destitute – like the '1st Class boy from her Majesty's ship Ilustrious', who had slept 'in the station' on 14 November 1854.[72]

Despite the importance of the duties which policemen undertook, however, they were long regarded with a wary eye by country people, who saw them as representatives of an alien, potentially repressive, force. Joseph Arch, for example, in complaining about the operation of the 1862 Poaching Prevention Act, saw the police as 'so many Jacks-in-the-Box . . . set free to spring out on the labourer, from the hedge, or the ditch, or the copse, or the field'.[73] In game-law cases, especially, they were condemned as mere lackeys of the preservers, despite the efforts of many of them to maintain impartiality.

Finally, for those wrongdoers who were captured and sentenced to terms of imprisonment the condition of the gaols in which they were to spend their time were also of material concern. Almost up to the end of the eighteenth century the total number of people in prison at any one period was small. Thanks to the various alternative punishments, ranging from the pillory and whipping to transportation and hanging, prisoners consisted of debtors, those awaiting trial for felony, those awaiting trial or sentenced to terms of hard labour for misdemeanours (including vagrancy) and those committed as a consequence of their failure to find sureties. In 1779 no fewer than 130 of the gaols and houses of correction had under ten inmates of all classes.[74] In that year John Howard estimated that the total average number in prison was only 4375, of whom nearly half were debtors. In view of the conditions that he found in many gaols, this was fortunate. Thus at

Clare in Suffolk, where, significantly, no justices had visited the prison for many years, the thatched building was ruinous: 'Each prisoner pays a penny a day for straw, etc. Keeper a weaver: salary, £13 13s. 4d. . . . At my first visit in 1779, the three prisoners, though they were women, had each a heavy chain, and the two impressed men had chains and logs.'[75] However, one of the worst abuses discovered by Howard – apart from lack of hygiene – was the practice of allowing gaolers to 'farm' the prison and to sell to the inmates all foodstuffs beyond a small quantity of bread and water. The plight of those imprisoned for debt in such circumstances was pitiable, for few obtained the fourpence a day from their creditors to which they were entitled under an Act of George II.[76] Even when men were found innocent by the courts in criminal cases they could be returned to prison because they had not paid their fees to the gaoler.[77]

As a result of Howard's disclosures, two Acts were passed in 1774, twelve months after he began work. The first set free all prisoners detained on account of non-payment of fees and authorized the use of county rates to pay a salary to the gaoler. The second prescribed minimum standards of cleanliness in the prisons – though, as Howard's later visits were to show, this had little practical effect. Nevertheless, during the 1780s a number of progressive counties did seek to eliminate the squalor and indiscriminate association of prisoners which characterized the old gaols. In Sussex, county prisons were built at Horsham in 1775 and at Petworth in 1781. Each adopted the new system of cellular construction, separate confinement and the continuous employment of the prisoners. But these measures were applied with such vigour that the prisons became 'a terror to the local criminal population'. Likewise at Fisherton Anger prison near Salisbury the justices had, by 1784, given the gaoler a fixed salary, prohibited him from trafficking with the prisoners, stopped the sale of drink in the gaol, excluded all visitors except by order of the magistrates and built a row of solitary cells. But so greatly did prisoners fear solitary confinement that it was alleged that a man sentenced to a year's imprisonment petitioned to be hanged rather than endure it.[78] By 1800 some forty-six gaols had been built on the cellular system.[79]

In the new century the problems of accommodation intensified, particularly with the rapid increase in crime during the desperate years which followed the ending of the French wars. Despite the efforts of Howard and his successors, conditions in most prisons in the 1810s and early 1820s were as unsatisfactory as they had been forty years earlier when he began his campaign. At Maidstone county

gaol the journal of William Cutbush, gaoler from 1809 to 1819, gives
an idea of the chaotic day-to-day routine. Cutbush, a smith by trade,
had been employed on construction work at the prison before he
became its gaoler:

1817

December 18th	Thursday. In the night, Bradley in the lower hospital (with the itch) pulled the flue down and attempted to get out. White and McIntosh behaved very bad, ironed them all and put them into the dungeons. Mr. Brooke and Mr. Douce visited and ordered them to be closely confined.
December 19th	Friday. Prayers. Collis tore his blankets and behaved very ill. Put him in the other dungeon. . . .
December 23rd	Tuesday. The men in the dungeons behaved very well and promised to behave well in future. Took them all up out of the dungeons. . . .

1818

January 20th	Tuesday. The prisoners of the Common side hursled Morrison, a prisoner, who came in late last night and took two handkerchiefs away from him. Searched and found them both and found out that [five names] were concerned in it. Ironed them all.[80]

At Ilchester gaol in Somerset conditions were still worse. Here two
men imprisoned for debt died in January 1822, and it was established
at the inquest that the rooms in which they had been held had been
repeatedly flooded. There had been 'six floods within the last eight
weeks', and there was no room 'in which deceased could sit with a
fire, that was not six inches deep in water'. The coroner also complained
that three fellow prisoners had been forced to sleep in the same room
as one of the corpses: 'The Jury were very indignant and remonstrated
against the practice.' As a result of the complaints made, a special
Commission of Inquiry was appointed to visit Ilchester in February.
It confirmed the unsatisfactory conditions. The 'lower or poorer
debtors' had nothing to live on 'beyond the county allowance of
bread and water', though for the better off, supplies of eggs, milk,
bacon and other items were available for purchase. The accommodation
was seriously substandard and the conduct of the governor deplorable.
Not only had he neglected his duties and used 'oaths and other improper language', but he had behaved with great cruelty, 'applying a
blister to the head of Thomas Gardner, by way of punishment, nor can
we refrain from expressing our astonishment that any medical man

should have lent himself to such a purpose'. On another occasion a young woman with a baby at the breast had been placed in solitary confinement for four days, two of them without a fire, during severe winter weather because she had quarrelled with a fellow prisoner. During the whole of her confinement she had been provided only with bread and cold water in a bucket. These and other cases were debated in Parliament, and as a result of the Commission's findings, and of general disquiet at conditions at the gaol, the governor was dismissed. He was subsequently tried and found guilty of applying the blister to Gardner's head and was fined £50. Much-needed rebuilding work was also carried out at the prison, but clearly, given conditions such as these, broader national reforms were needed.[81]

So it was that in 1823 the Home Secretary, Robert Peel, sponsored a new Gaol Act, which for the first time 'made it peremptorily the duty of the Justices to organize their prisons on a prescribed plan, and to furnish quarterly reports to the Home Secretary upon every department of their prison administration'. They were required to provide sufficient, secure and sanitary accommodation for all prisoners; to transform the gaoler or master from an independent profit maker into a salaried servant of the local authority; to subject all criminals to a reformatory regimen; and to ensure the 'systematic inspection of every part of the prison by visiting justices'.[82] The prisoners were to be protected against irons and chains and tyrannical punishments by requiring the use of these to be notified to the visiting justices. In addition, the Act moved away from the tentative experiments with a 'separate system' of confinement applied at Horsham, Petworth and a few of the other gaols towards the 'classification' of prisoners into five different groups, which were each to associate in productive labour. Instruction was to be given in reading and writing, while plentiful supplies of religious tracts were to be made available, so as to promote repentance and reform among the prisoners.

Unfortunately, although the 1823 Act had aimed to improve conditions, it soon became a subject for heated debate. There were allegations that the unchecked opportunities for meetings between prisoners in a common workroom, or even on the tread-wheel, were giving rise to that mutual 'contamination' which had excited reformers in the 1780s. No distinction was made between a crime committed by a hardened offender and one committed by a youth tempted for the first time. A Sussex JP pointed out the difficulties which could arise when a labourer was committed for stealing something as insignificant as an egg. Often, thanks to his prison experience, he would leave gaol 'much worse than when committed'. This man was also opposed to offenders being committed for trial at a 'remote' quarter sessions or assizes for minor offences rather than being dealt with summarily:

I will take the Case of [a] Man who was committed for stealing Two Pounds of Meat; on the Score of his having been Three Weeks in Prison previous to the Trial [at the assizes] the Judge only sentenced him to Two Days further imprisonment, he had therefore only Two Days of the really salutary discipline of the Prison, though he cost the County as much as if he had been committed for Three Weeks to hard Labour.[83]

The inappropriateness of prison for the theft of such a small item as two pounds of meat did not seem to occur to him.

By the mid-1830s, however, a compromise between the 'separate system' and 'classification' had been worked out. This was the 'silent system', whereby prisoners were not allowed to talk, even when they worked together or were on the tread-wheel. But it proved impossible to prevent 'improper' communication from taking place, through hand signals or when the warders were not watching. So demands for a revival of the 'separate system' grew, particularly after a new Prisons Act of 1839 gave approval to separate confinement, despite its allegedly harmful effect on the mental condition of some of the prisoners. Reading gaol was one of the pioneers of the new approach. Here inmates were required to spend an hour or two a day in their solitary cells grinding flour with single-handed mills. The rest of the time was spent on 'lessons', in which the Bible was the principal vehicle of instruction. In the view of the chaplain, the Rev. John Field, if a man were given nothing to do but to read the Bible, or be taught to read it, he would co-operate, if only to save himself from going mad. Yet, despite the relative physical comfort of this regime, it was said that criminals were 'driven from Berkshire to Buckinghamshire' by dread of the 'Read, Read, Reading Gaol', as it was nicknamed.[84] Most prisoners feared solitary confinement more than any other punishment. In the view of the keeper of the Marlborough house of correction, nothing would be more likely to discourage inmates from the commission of further crimes than to place 'all of them in separate solitary Cells . . . and in order that Solitude might be more fully felt, no kind of Labour should be given them'.[85]

By 1859 prison inspectors were reporting that in the southern and western district 'so universal . . . is the testimony in favour of the Separate System in the English prisons . . . that there remain only two county prisons in which it has not been adopted, either wholly or in part'. These two backsliders were about to remedy their deficiency.[86]

By the mid nineteenth century, therefore, prisons were more hygienic than they had been when Howard began his work; the supply of food was generally adequate in quantity; and much of the old physical barbarism had been eliminated from punishments. But to countrymen reared in open spaces and used to the fresh air the rigid discipline, close confinement and isolation of the 'separate system' were objects of deep fear and hatred. For many, prison proved an embittering experience. As a young Norfolk poacher, who was imprisoned in Norwich gaol during the 1860s, angrily recalled, he made a vow to be 'as bad as they had painted him.' And he added: 'It is not the Punishment that hurt you, it is the dark looks and jeers of other People that hurt wen they know that you have been there.'[87]

G

Many mid-century landowners took a pride in owning prize farm livestock. This portrays a scene at Wiseton in 1844

7 Politics and protectionism: 1830s–1850s

At election time he supported, and always carried, Whig candidates: and in return he had been appointed lord lieutenant of the county by one Whig minister; and had received the Garter from another. But these things were matters of course to a Duke of Omnium. He was born to be a lord lieutenant and a Knight of the Garter.

ANTHONY TROLLOPE, *Framley Parsonage*[1]

Although no sector of rural society was immune to the pressures of early nineteenth-century agricultural and industrial change, the position of the landed interest altered less than most. In the south-west and the west of England, it was the gentry who predominated; in the north, the large territorial magnates. These were the people with power, and few members of the 'dependent classes' were prepared seriously to challenge the leadership they offered. Even in 1867 Walter Bagehot could describe English society as 'deferential', and despite the effects of the Reform Act of 1832, Parliament remained the preserve of the landowner into mid-Victorian times. Of course, not all villages were squire-dominated. In some places the land of a parish was owned by a number of proprietors, none of whom held absolute sway, either through birth or because of the size of his estate. And in parts of the north of England, where the farming population lived in isolated and scattered hamlets rather than large villages, the power of the nobility and gentry was likely to be even more circumscribed. In parish affairs the bigger farmers would take the lead.[2]

Nevertheless, in political matters the dominance of the landed classes was clear. Although there were exceptions, most landlords considered it their right to direct tenants how they should vote on polling day. Thus on the Holkham estate in Norfolk the steward circularized the tenantry at the time of the 1817 election, advising them of the candidate favoured by Thomas Coke. He suggested that the farmers should make arrangements to convey electors to the polling station and should ensure that they cast their vote for the appropriate candidate; *'all the wavering & uncertain voters'* were to be brought to the poll as early as possible:

never lose sight of them from the time of leaving their homes until they are polled. . . . The *Staunch* Voters should follow the uncertain ones. It will be desirable that as many of Mr. Coke's principal Tenants & other friends should attend the nomination as can make it convenient, but Mr. Coke particularly wishes the Votes of such Gentlemen, to be reserved until all those of the description I have before mentioned have been polled.

You will please to use every honourable means to procure Votes.

Perseverance generally gains the battle, & do not forget that both your worthy Landlord, and your own honor is at stake in this contest.

I trust to your discretion in not making an improper use of this letter, by making the contents known to any person who would take advantage of the intelligence it contains. Much *very much* depends upon your activity and prudence in support of the cause we are engaged in.[3]

Thomas Coke himself was MP for Norfolk from 1776 to 1806 and again from 1807 to 1832, but, as this letter shows, his political efforts were not confined to his own cause.

In other instances during the pre-reform era landlords relied on the ownership of 'rotten' or proprietary boroughs to give them power to nominate MPs, and such places often changed hands for very high prices. Gatton in Surrey, with a population of only 135, was a case in point. In 1830 it was sold for £180,000, although there were a mere six houses within the boundaries of the parliamentary borough itself.[4] Elsewhere a magnate might win control of a 'corporation borough', in which the corporators constituted the sole electorate. Corporators often welcomed a rich patron who could aid their town or themselves, and once established, he was likely to maintain his ascendancy. Prior to the passage of the Municipal Corporations Act of 1835 corporations were normally self-electing, and it was possible for a patron to increase his influence until the corporators consisted mainly of members of his family, his tenants and his servants. Marlborough in Wiltshire provided one example of this. Here the Marquess of Ailesbury was patron, and the corporation usually consisted of his steward, butler, footmen and other dependants. At the time of the 1832 Reform Bill one of his agents was acting as mayor.[5] Likewise at Banbury, where the Earl of Guilford exerted the predominant interest, leading townspeople were angered by their inability to vote and by the sight of the earl maintaining his influence through a number of non-resident corporators chosen from among his family and friends. Their partisanship also damaged the respect in which the corporators were held when discharging their duties as magistrates. In February 1831 a petition from Banbury, pressing for reform, attributed the 'spirit of turbulence and disrespect' among the lower orders of the town to the magistrates' reputation for partisanship and their consequent lack of authority. Significantly, after the fifth earl's death in 1827 control of the town's affairs passed to a radical, nonconformist and largely Unitarian group in the general elections of 1831 and 1832 and in the first election for a reformed municipal corporation in 1835. This group provided the leadership of Banbury society until about 1860.[6]

The venality of corporations in some of the smaller boroughs was notorious. 'Everyone has heard', the *Morning Chronicle* announced in July 1830, 'of what Camelford cost the Marquess of Cleveland till the arrangement with the Marquess of Hertford. The Members who were returned for the marquess paid the voters in £1 notes enclosed in a deal box marked "China" '.[7] Not surprisingly, the excesses of pre-Reform Act electioneering helped to drive many a landed family into debt.

Other observers echoed the complaints – like the Norfolk petitioners who, under the influence of William Cobbett, and to the anger of many MPs, in 1823 blamed the calamities of 'this now unhappy country . . . to the predominance of certain particular families, who, since the passing of the Septennial act, have, by degrees, appropriated to themselves a large part of the property and revenue of the whole nation'.[8] A county meeting in Hampshire during March of the same year approved demands for reform of the tithe system and the House of Commons as well as cuts in government expenditure, particularly of the 'immense standing Army in time of Peace – unnecessary or overpaid Places – and last, though not least, an enormous Civil List'.[9] These latter comments were a reference to the widespread system of patronage and nepotism in operation. In 1818 Sir Bellingham Graham, a Yorkshire baronet, was receiving pensions from four different offices, for each of which he had been declared unfit. While the Whigs, although deploring in opposition 'the malign influence of the landed gentry at Westminster', did not hesitate to follow suit when they came to office in 1830. Lord Grey, as Prime Minister, provided his three sons-in-law and two brothers-in-law with posts and bestowed upon his elderly but impoverished friend Thomas Creevey the sinecure appointment of Treasurer of the Ordnance, worth £1200 a year, with free quarters in the Tower.[10]

William Cobbett, in laying the blame for agricultural depression on the effects of the government's monetary policy and its failure to reduce taxes, repeatedly called on farmers to support parliamentary reform to effect necessary changes. He began his tours of the country-side in earnest in 1822, being determined, as he wrote in September of that year, to place himself 'in the midst of the great fairs of the west, in order before the winter campaign begins, that I may see as many farmers as possible, and that they may hear my opinions, and I theirs'.[11] The Whigs, too, sought to exploit rural dissatisfaction for their own ends during the 1820s by advocating parliamentary reform and con-demning electoral corruption. In April 1822 Lord John Russell pointed out that there were 140 boroughs returning members to Parliament which had populations of less than 5000 each, 100 of them having less than 3000 inhabitants: 'By these 140 boroughs, 280 members are returned to parliament.' This represented more than half the total members of the lower House, and the system which prevailed in most of these places, 'and particularly in the Cornish boroughs', was notori-ous: 'I could . . . read a number of letters clearly showing many instances in which the return of members to this House, was procured by money only; by bribery the most direct.'[12]

Despite spasmodic rural support for the reformers' position, how-ever, it was the underrepresented and rapidly growing industrial towns which made the major impact in securing political change. Many landed families, indeed, shared the Duke of Wellington's repugnance for reform. As the clergyman member of one Oxfordshire family wrote, in premature triumph after the defeat of an early Reform measure in 1831: 'Hurrah for . . . the Majority against the . . . bill on Friday last. Mr. Blackguard reform is thrown out of the House of Lords, I hope for ever.'[13] In Staffordshire the Tory landowner Ralph Sneyd was so filled with horror at the Reform Bill crisis of 1831 that there 'entered his mind even the terrible thought of going into exile abroad, where property and person would be safe'.[14] To the second Earl of Malmesbury, parliamentary reform in England was 'the twin sister' of 'Revolution in France and the Netherlands'.[15]

Nevertheless, there is some evidence that in the months immediately before the passing of the Reform Act certain ultra-Tory opponents of the measure altered their stance as a result of the 1830 'Swing' riots and indications that some of the smaller farmers, hit by rent and tithe payments, were supporting the labourers' demands. In other cases larger farmers refused to act as special constables because they were dissatisfied with the governmental system. As one reformer put it, the unrepresentative character of the Commons ensured that 'the manufacturing artisan enrols his name in affiliated societies, instead of subscribing to petitions, [and] that the agriculturist winks at, if he does not encourage, the outrages of his labourers'.[16]

Against this background the Earl of Winchilsea solemnly warned the Lords on 4 November 1830 that if 'moderate Reform did not take place', the best institutions of the country would be destroyed: 'Their Lordships . . . would neglect the duties they owed to their country, the confidence of which in the wisdom of Parliament had been much shaken, if they did not take some measures to win back the respect and confidence of the people.'[17] However, in his case, as in that of other ultra-Tories, anger over Wellington's granting of Catholic emancipation in 1829 was largely responsible for the adoption of an anti-Wellington line over the franchise question, too.[18]

To supporters of reform the eventual passage of the Bill in 1832 was the occasion for much celebration. The sour comments of a Bedfordshire lady show that in her small community: 'All the mob of Potton made a great riot to celebrate the passing of the reform bill, and paraded the town with the most hideous yells, accompanying a triumphal car in the shape of a waggon covered with fresh boughs and bearing flags . . . I do not suppose that any of them understood what they were so noisy about.'[19]

But in the long run the hopes of supporters of the new measure were to be dashed. Admittedly, there was a widening of the franchise and forty-two new borough constituencies were created; however, of the more than 140 new seats established sixty-two were given to English counties. Rotten boroughs disappeared, though Professor Gash has listed some seventy 'proprietary' borough seats which remained under patronage after 1832. As he points out, 'it was still possible . . . to buy a seat in the House of Commons.'[20]

Violence and drunkenness at elections were yet more difficult to eliminate, even though their scale began to diminish. On the Isle of Wight, for example, contests in the post-reform era were fiercely fought; meetings were disrupted and candidates were pelted with eggs. At the small town of Newport during the 1835 election the Tory candidate was pursued by 300 rioters, while attacks on Tory supporters were common. In a contest in 1851 an election agent for the Conservative candidate was so badly beaten up by a mob in Ryde that although he managed to escape into a house, he died from his injuries shortly afterwards. Small wonder that after such a tragic event special constables were sworn in for the 1852 campaign.[21] 'Cooping' of voters (the abduction of the supporters of an opponent until the election was over) was another device employed by the ruthless and determined. And in two-member constituencies in Yorkshire people seeking a quiet life were said to split their votes, choosing one candidate from each side. This upset the tallies of the election agents, and often led to such peace-seeking voters being booed as 'mugwumps'.[22]

Electoral corruption also persisted, since the Reform Act had neither imposed a maximum for official expenses nor laid down any effective measures against bribery. In the proprietary borough of Malton Earl Fitzwilliam made regular payments to the town's charities and improvement schemes after 1832, and in 1837 his agent suggested that he should make 'an unsolicited contribution' of £100 to the Methodists, who were seeking to liquidate the debt on their chapel, so as to 'rivet this large body to your interest'. A year earlier Henry Martin, land agent and, when necessary, electoral agent for the Earl of Durham, had reported that in the northern division of the county there was 'a very large number of 40s. Freeholders who [were] ready to sell themselves in the event of an election, chiefly Pitmen and labourers'. He inquired whether they should be enlisted in the estate's political cause.[23]

But these were relatively modest commitments. In other cases demands were so great that candidates withdrew from the electoral race because of the expense. The £14,000 needed for the south Durham contest in 1841 was, in the view of Lord Harry Vane, 'scandalously preposterous' – almost enough to cause his retirement from active politics. Even 'legitimate' expenses could verge on the corrupt. Philip Pusey's outlay of £12,237 18s. 8d. for his unsuccessful candidature in Berkshire in 1832 included such items as £6 4s. paid to a Mr Heath for 'Journey to Cheltenham for Captain Magaghan to poll' and £82 11s. spent in the Abingdon district on 'Flagmen, Messengers and Conductors'. At Wallingford, where Pusey's agent 'took an express Journey . . . on the second day of the Election to bring up voters', it was proposed that he should receive £10 10s. for his trouble.[24]

It is also clear that when payments were not forthcoming, those anticipating them felt cheated. This applied in 1852 at Wallingford, where the local Poor Law relieving officer had taken an active role in promoting the successful candidate and expected a payment of £80 to £100 for so doing. Wallingford had a long history of electoral corruption. After the 1826 election £3000 was allegedly spent in this way by the Whigs, through a shoemaker named Gill. When the poll was over, Gill enveloped in a leathern apron up to his chin, and bending under the weight of numerous bags of gold coin, took his nocturnal rounds. Pursuant to previous arrangement, the outer door of the house of the 'immaculate' voter was in most instances left open, and here, at the threshold, without question asked or answer given, a packet of twenty sovereigns was deposited.[25]

The practice was repeated at succeeding contests, until the passage of the 1832 Reform Act caused the bribers to proceed more circumspectly. But that did not assuage the anger of the relieving officer in 1852, when his hopes were disappointed:

I certainly think there is something like ingratitude shown by the party towards one who worked hard suffered much & was acknowledged by all to have rendered material service at the expense of offending many friends & incurring much displeasure. As to the awkwardness of the affair I can see but little without you have all formed a different opinion of me to what was expressed at the time, & are afraid to trust me now . . . if such be the case I consider I ought to know the reason of the change & if not I am at a loss to know why I am the only one that is left unremunerated. I feel convinced a way could *easily* be made to satisfy me. . . . The long time and the evasive answers I have received leaves me to think that what several of my friends warned me of is too true that a man may work himself almost to death & be called a good fellow &c during the time but as soon as tis over he may go to the Devil for what the Party care but the time will come (if life is spared) when a Vote might be wanted . . . but [I] shall pause before I render service to any party as ingratitude & opprobrium appear to be the reward.[26]

Unfortunately, the correspondence does not indicate whether his persistence won the day. But in such circumstances it is small wonder that one observer could claim in 1852 that bribery was 'perhaps in fuller action . . . than ever before', or that eight years later Lord Monson should observe bitterly after heavy expenditure at Reigate: 'It appears that however Reform may extend the franchise it is not likely to extend the choice of members to any class that is not able to bear the bleeding by their constituents.'[27] Even the Corrupt Practices Act of 1854, curtailing polling at county elections to one day and placing restrictions on the conveyance of voters to the poll, did not solve the problem.

Not surprisingly, in this situation the number of MPs under aristocratic influence showed little decline between 1831 and 1865, though to keep their seats in the post-reform era landowners and their nominees had to pay more attention than hitherto to middle-class views. On the Duke of Bedford's Woburn estate in 1833 even the preparation of lists of tenant farmers' rent arrears, etc., was postponed from the autumn of the previous year because of the 'delicacy in working up these things in the face of an *Election*'.[28] Concern not to offend voters' sensibilities was to be still more evident during the 1840s, when protectionism absorbed the attention of farmers. Those county candidates who neglected to take agriculturalists' views into account suffered at the polls.

However, in many rural constituencies landowners closed ranks in order to maintain their collective control, for if they agreed on a candidate, voters had little opportunity of exercising their franchises. Contests were disliked by the county magnates because of the bad feelings they engendered as well as their cost. As the contemporary writer William Howitt put it, when an election came 'to the county Hall, it [came] often as a hurricane, and frequently [shook] it to the foundations, leaving in its track debts and mortgages, shyness between neighbours, and rancour among friends'.[29] As late as 1847 there were no contests in nearly three-fifths of the constituencies; as Professor Gash has succinctly observed: 'the composition of the House of Commons in the age of Peel was decided almost as much by the elections that were not contested as by those that were'.[30]

Carmarthenshire provided one example of this closing of ranks by the landed classes. Prior to reform influence in the county had been disputed by two magnates, Lord Dynevor and Earl Cawdor; the former broadly supported the Tories and the latter the Whigs. But the reform agitation raised doubts in Cawdor's mind as to his old allegiance, so when the general election of 1837 was held he transferred his support to George Rice Trevor, the nominee of Lord Dynevor. Thereupon Cawdor's agent wrote a letter to his tenants firmly informing them: 'I shall depend upon you to plump for Colonel Trevor at the coming election, who is the only candidate supported by your noble landlord, and I have no doubt that you will do so. Your well-wisher, R. B. Williams.'[31] In addition, a sub-agent was instructed to interview four tenants who were suspected of supporting the other side and who were in arrears with their rent. The interview took place on the first day of the poll, and they were told that as they were 'so independent and so very ungrateful for the indulgence and favour shown to them by their landlord', the agent would expect to receive their rents immediately and would then see 'what further is to be done in the matter'.[32]

But that was too blatant even for the standards of the 1830s, and Cawdor was attacked both in the Press and in a petition to Parliament, which drew attention to this interference by a peer in the election of a Member of the lower House. However, when the matter was debated in June 1838 Cawdor's action was defended by his friend Sir James Graham, Member for the Pembroke boroughs. He argued strongly 'that landlords might appropriately guide the judgement of their tenants', and interestingly enough, although Lord John Russell drew attention to Cawdor's change of allegiance and noted mockingly that the tenants were 'wandering about in search of information as to which way their landlord was going to vote', he did not press the matter further.[33] Thereafter the gentry arranged things among themselves. What David Williams calls the 'Holy Alliance' between Cawdor and Dynevor was now complete, so that when in 1842 the sitting member for Carmarthenshire died they were able to arrange for the return of a Tory member without a contest.[34] In this way the working of democracy could be thwarted.

Cawdor was not alone in seeking to influence the way his tenants voted, and in many respects the changes in the franchise introduced by the Reform Act strengthened rather than weakened the hold of the large landowners over the county constituencies. Alongside the old forty-shilling freeholders were new categories of leaseholders and copyholders and, most important, of tenant farmers paying an annual rent of £50, who were enfranchised as a result of a clause inserted in the Bill on the initiative of the ultra-Tory Marquess of Chandos. Given the conditions of open voting, when everyone knew the way a man used his franchise, it was easy for the landlord or his agent to put pressure on an occupier to vote in the way desired. Failure to comply might lead to eviction from a holding, and in view of the keen competition which existed for farms on good estates under generous landlords, few sitting tenants were willing to risk losing their livelihood for party-political considerations.[35] Furthermore, although open coercion was frowned upon, it was accepted that a landlord had a legitimate influence over his tenants in the interests of a well run and harmonious estate. This doctrine was clearly expressed by the Whig landlord Sir Charles Monck, of Belsay Castle, Northumberland, in a letter to his north Lincolnshire tenants in 1852:

Nothing is more agreeable to the Constitution, and to all ancient usages of the Kingdom, or more advantageous to true liberty, than that landlords should endeavour by all fair means to lead their tenants. The Queen leads the Nation, and landlords in a similar manner lead their tenants. . . . I expect of my tenants that they shall not engage their votes before they have communicated with me and come to know my wishes. . . . If it shall after that appear that my wishes and yours are in contrarity there then ought to be the fullest explanation and consideration between us . . . I promise you that to the opinion of the majority I will submit. But . . . if I am bound to set an example of submission to the majority, the minority must be bound to follow that example, that the estate might not be divided, but act with its full weight for the benefit of all.[36]

Monck went on to emphasize his good relations with his tenants, despite their holding farms at will, and ended by giving his reasons for supporting his chosen candidate in the coming poll. The tenants duly consulted with one another and then announced that they were ready to concur with his wishes and to 'plump' for his selection. Similarly in south Lincolnshire, where there were forty-four parishes owned by a single proprietor at the time of the 1841 election, thirty-two of them cast their votes in the same way. This included *all* the voters in the parish, both freeholders and tenants.

Some landlords even expected their tenants to follow them when they changed sides, as Cawdor did in Carmarthenshire. Among them was Lord Willoughby de Eresby, who until 1839 had exerted no direct influence over the politics of his tenants at Grimsthorpe, Lincolnshire. In that year he asked them to support the Whig candidate and in 1841 to vote for the two Tory candidates, Trollope and Turnor. A few tenants plumped for Trollope, but most split between the two men, as their landlord had requested. There were no voters for the Liberal candidate on the estate in that year.[37] Again, on the Monson estate the tenants voted Conservative in 1835 and 1841 under the Tory fifth lord, and then swung over automatically to the other party when he was succeeded by a Whig.[38]

Yet it would be wrong to see this compliance with the landlord's wishes as inspired merely by farmers' fears of the repercussions if they voted the 'wrong' way. Occasionally, particularly in Wales, evictions did take place over political issues, but most landlords were unwilling to remove an active, improving farmer merely on account of his political views. This was especially true during periods of agricultural depression, when some tenants adopted an almost abusive tone in their demands for rent reductions or landlord-financed improvements. In such conditions political considerations alone would be unlikely to decide a tenant's fate. On many estates farms remained in the same families for generations, and landlords were reluctant to take 'a precipitate action that might provoke the indignation of the farming community or the malice of political opponents'.[39] In Lindsey, Lincolnshire, as late as the 1840s it was said that tenants were 'never changed unless they die, or become unfortunate in business, or without there is gross neglect',[40] while of landlord–tenant relations generally in Britain a report in the previous decade had declared: 'So much of the feudal system yet remains among the higher ranks of society . . . that it would be considered discreditable to turn off an old tenant from an estate, unless misconduct, or absolute necessity, compelled a change.[41]

Some landlords prided themselves on allowing their tenants freedom to vote as they wished. Dr John Lee of Hartwell, Buckinghamshire, was so fearful of influencing the political opinions of his tenants that he kept his own preferences a closely guarded secret until nomination day.[42] And at Danby in Yorkshire in the late 1840s the agent of Lord Downe told the tenants of his lordship's desire that they should vote in accordance with their own inclinations, though in the view of the incumbent the majority of the electorate, whether freeholders or tenants, continued to support the Conservatives.[43] Most landowners did not go as far as this, but a substantial minority was clearly in favour of non-interference.

So if eviction from a holding remained a possibility for over-independent tenant farmers, the great majority was aware that it was a threat which was seldom implemented. More common as a reason for tenants following their landlord's lead was their belief that the aristocracy and gentry were the natural leaders of rural society, whose duty it was to protect all sections of the agricultural interest. It is clear that on estates where political influence was regularly exercised tenants were genuinely reluctant to promise their votes without discovering their landlord's wishes. In other cases, as the Select Committee on Parliamentary and Municipal Elections delicately observed in the late 1860s, the inducement to vote with the landlord might 'frequently proceed rather from the hope of future advantages to be conferred than from the fear of injuries to be inflicted'.[44] Viscount Palmerston, for one, attributed his defeat in Hampshire in 1835 partly to the fact that tenant farmers, hard hit by agricultural depression, were 'in arrear and looking for abatements, [and so] . . . more than usually dependent on the landlords'.[45]

Often, though, loyalty alone was the decisive factor. In the 1850s the Earl of Yarborough was able to persuade his Lincolnshire tenants to vote for his chosen candidate not so much because of deference but on account of

the large sums which he subscribed to all kinds of local cause and charity. He was, too, a prominent freemason, being Grand Master of the Province from 1849. But his best political investment was the Brocklesby Hunt, whose

country extended over most of northern Lindsey above a line from Gainsborough to Louth, and which gave some social cohesion to that vast
neighbourhood. As Member for North Lincolnshire Yarborough had
consolidated the family interest, not only through local patronage but also
by devoting himself to major public undertakings – the passing of the
General Inclosure Act of 1845, the creation of the port of Gainsborough,
and above all the building of the Manchester, Sheffield, and Lincolnshire
Railway.

He was thus able to draw on a feeling of local loyalty that resembled a kind
of patriotism in miniature. . . .[46]

Political activists, for their part, recognized this special relationship.
It was always a matter of conventional courtesy to seek the permission
of the landlord before canvassing his tenants, whether he was a member of the same political party as the canvasser or not. And in some
counties, including Herefordshire, it was considered improper to
canvass tenants on behalf of a political party or candidate to which the
landlord was known to be opposed. The protest of a member of the
Grosvenor family against Mr Gladstone's canvassing in the 1841
election expressed the customary view on electioneering etiquette: 'I
did think', said the wounded patrician, 'that interference between a
landlord with whose opinions you were acquainted and his tenants
was not justifiable according to those laws of delicacy and propriety
which I consider binding in such cases.'[47]

In these political arrangements the labourers and village tradesmen had
little part to play, save where they lived in their own cottages and were
enfranchised under the forty-shilling freeholder category. Joseph
Arch, who in the 1870s was to lead the first national trade union for
agricultural workers, was one rural labourer who voted under this
provision. He began his political work in the Liberal interest, in
opposition to the Tory landlords in his home parish of Barford,
Warwickshire, during the 1860s. But such men as he were exceptions.
Many of those eligible to vote did not bother to register on the electoral roll. Thus in the Northleach polling district of East Gloucestershire in 1863 there were at least 102 men who were not registered,
although they were perfectly well qualified. If they had been included,
the electorate in the district would have been 15 or 20 per cent larger
– big enough to influence its overall political complexion.[48] But the
more cautious men recognized that to be overactive in the wrong
political cause could be damaging. The diaries of the Rev. William C.
Risley, vicar of Deddington and a Tory party supporter, show that in

May 1838 he sent for John Flint, the schoolmaster at the nearby parish of Adderbury, and

reprimanded him severely for mixing himself up with the disorderly & disaffected in the Parish . . . & attending certain Meetings connected with Politics & party spirit on the subject of the new Poor Law, & advocating a petition for the repeal of the same . . . he expressed his sorrow & promised to conduct himself differently & properly for the future.

This did not prevent Risley from giving him 'another lecture as to his recent & future conduct' just over a week later, presumably to ensure that the lesson had been well learnt.[49] Persistent defiance in such cases could lead to loss of employment.[50]

So in most parishes it was only through riot and arson, as in 1830, that the small tradesman or labourer, the despised 'Hodge' or 'chaw-bacon', could normally make an impact on rural affairs. But in 1833 to a small group of labourers in the Dorset parish of Tolpuddle there appeared a third alternative – trade unionism. During the early 1830s urban workers were forming combinations: why should their country cousins not follow suit?

Tolpuddle's pioneering efforts in rural trade unionism stemmed from events during the previous year, when George Loveless, later to be one of the leaders, and a few fellow villagers met local farmers to agree on higher wage rates. These were designed to bring payments into line with those offered elsewhere in Dorset, where 10s. a week was customary. But the employers failed to keep their side of the bargain. Instead wages in the Tolpuddle area were cut from 9s. to 7s. a week, with the threat of a further reduction to 6s. Despite fresh meetings with farmers and magistrates, the men were unable to change their employers' decision.

By this time – mid-1833 – George Loveless had emerged as a man of considerable resource and determination. He had also become aware of trade-union developments elsewhere and to this end had obtained details of the Leeds Flax Dressers' Trade Union from his brother, who was a flax dresser in the small Dorset town of Bridport. But the major development was the formation of the London-based Grand National Consolidated Trades Union by the cotton manufacturer and socialist reformer Robert Owen, who aimed to create a union of all the trades. It was with that organization that Loveless made contact during October 1833.[51] Shortly afterwards a meeting was held in the cottage of Thomas Standfield, Loveless's brother-in-law and a future unionist. About forty labourers attended, together with two delegates from the

Grand National itself. After the meeting it was decided to form an independent trade society at Tolpuddle, with an elected committee. It was intended that ultimately this would affiliate with the Grand National. In the meantime, in order to guard the society from spies, a special password was agreed upon, and to induce loyalty to the movement an initiation ceremony for members was held on 9 December. As with other friendly societies at that time, strict rules were drawn up governing the moral conduct of members and opposing violence. The main aim was to secure solidarity and the promise of a withdrawal of labour should the wages of members be further reduced. Such broader objectives as obtaining higher pay and better working conditions were not included in the rules.

News of these events began to reach the ears of James Frampton, a magistrate of Moreton House near Tolpuddle, who had been active in suppressing the 'Swing' riots three years earlier. It must be remembered that although trade unionism had been legalized by the repeal of the Combination Acts in 1824–5, it was still regarded with suspicion by those in authority, who considered it a possible cloak for revolutionary action. In any event, by the end of January 1834 Frampton's alarm – and that of other magistrates – had become sufficiently strong for him to employ 'trusty persons to endeavour to obtain information respecting the unlawful combinations which [were believed] to be forming among the labourers'. He also wrote on behalf of himself and his fellow magistrates to inform the Home Secretary, Lord Melbourne, of developments.[52] Melbourne expressed approval of Frampton's efforts to track down the culprits, and eventually the magistrate managed to find two labourers who had taken part in the December initiation ceremony and were prepared to give evidence about it. After consultation with the Home Office it was decided that although trade unionism as such was legal, the administering of secret oaths was not. It was on those grounds that the Tolpuddle labourers were to be proceeded against.

No warning was given of these moves until Saturday, 22 February, when a notice was posted around the village warning that 'designing Persons' had been inducing labourers to enter into illegal societies to which they bound themselves by 'unlawful oaths'. All such members were liable to transportation for seven years.[53] Two days after this George Loveless and five of his fellow union leaders were arrested and taken to Dorchester gaol. Frampton wrote to Lord Melbourne to inform him of the steps taken, and on 3 March the Home Secretary replied, advising that the case be proceeded with as speedily as possible.

However, he was opposed to the issuing of public proclamations or the offering of rewards for information on the subject of trade unionism since 'such an act would give publicity to a state of things in Dorset, which, as far as [I am] aware, has not yet spread in any other county'.[54] In his letter Melbourne also requested copies of the depositions against the men and such details of the society's organization and meetings as Frampton could furnish so that the government could prepare the indictment.

About a fortnight later the six men were brought before the assizes in Dorchester. Loveless, belatedly appreciating the seriousness of their position, forwarded a short written defence in which he firmly disavowed any intention of breaking the law or causing injury: 'we were uniting together to preserve ourselves, our wives, and our children from utter degradation and starvation'.[55] His efforts availed the men nothing, and on 19 March they were found guilty of administering illegal oaths – under an Act passed in 1797 to combat naval mutinies! Each was sentenced to the maximum term of seven years' transportation.

The severity of the punishments and the way the law had been stretched to deal with the case aroused anger in trade union and radical circles, and petitions began to pour in to Parliament appealing for the sentences to be remitted. Even those who had no love for trade unionism felt constrained to oppose the severity of the punishments. *The Times*, for example, considered the 'real gravamen' of the men's guilt was 'their forming a dangerous Union, to force up, by various means of intimidation and restraint, the rates of labourers wages. . . . The crime which called for punishment was not proved – the crime brought home to the prisoners did not justify the sentences.' Likewise the Tory *Standard*, although agreeing that the law as now promulgated should be upheld in the future, nevertheless advised that 'those who have sinned in ignorance' should have 'the benefit of that ignorance; let the six poor Dorsetshire fellows be restored to their cottages'.[56]

The matter was also debated in Parliament itself. On 26 March the MP for Oxford presented a petition signed by more than 1500 of his constituents. At the same time he drew attention to the probability of the men's ignorance of their violation of the law and the severity of their sentences. The petitioners pointed out that friendly societies frequently administered secret oaths to their members and were presumably equally liable to punishment. There was also objection to the fact that 'men professing so much morality' – for two of the prisoners, George Loveless and his brother James, were Methodist local preachers

– should be 'consigned to associate, for a period of seven years, with others who were transported for crimes of the most infamous and disgusting complexion'.[57] Similarly on 30 April the MP for Colchester, Daniel Harvey, drew attention to the fact that among the rules of the society had been the requirement that 'no immoral songs or toasts should be allowed . . . . Was not this a proof that the conduct of these people did not merit condemnation?' He pointed out that farmers and landowners had established agricultural associations, and asked why the labourers should not be free to form unions.[58]

The protests were without avail, however, and the men were speedily dispatched to penal colonies in Australia. But that did not end the agitation for their release. In London a special 'Dorchester Committee' was formed and further petitions and demonstrations were organized, particularly by trade unionists and radical politicians. Slowly, as the opposition showed no signs of fading away, the government began to alter its stance. Thanks in part to the actions of a more sympathetic Home Secretary, Lord John Russell, by the spring of 1836 a free pardon and passage back to England had been secured for all six of the men – thought it was three more years before the last of them, James Hammett, actually returned to this country.[59]

Although the men's actions were thus belatedly vindicated, the misery and suffering which they and their families had endured were perhaps a sufficient deterrent to prevent other labourers from following their example. Certain it is that despite the emergence of trade unionism among skilled urban workers by the middle of the nineteenth century, in country districts it was not until the 1860s and 1870s that trade combinations again made an effective appearance.[60]

If rural labourers played little part in the growth of trade unionism during these early years, the same is true of their role in the other great working-class political agitation of the 1830s and 1840s, Chartism. Only among displaced and discontented country cloth workers, hit by northern industrialism and technological change, did the Chartist programme of political reform, and particularly of universal suffrage, prove attractive. In Somerset and Wiltshire the movement centred on Bath and the smaller decaying textile towns like Trowbridge and Bradford-on-Avon. In rural Wales it merged with the anti-Poor Law movement and the Rebecca Riots, and in Gloucestershire there was unrest around the small town of Wotton-under-Edge, where by July 1839, according to local JPs, there had been a Chartist society in existence for 'several months'.[61]

Something of the alarm which Chartist demonstrations and political activities aroused in the few rural areas they did affect is evident from a letter written by a Trowbridge resident to a friend in Stroud on 1 May 1839. Trowbridge had had a Chartist association as early as June 1838 and by November of that year was claiming a membership of 550, most of them cloth workers.[62] A meeting held in the town on 19 November was attended by about 3000 people. After a torchlight parade through the streets speeches were made, and events terminated with a 'discharge of firearms and much shouting'.[63] Many of those present wore green scarves or ribbons (green being a republican colour). In the months that followed other meetings were held, and it was against this background that the letter of 1 May was written:

We are in a dreadful state here with those infernal Chartists – they collect every night by hundreds in the Market place, they have already broken several windows, set fire to Ingram's Hay Rick – also burnt a Barn with a lot of corn and two large hay ricks of a Farmer in the neighborhood – tonight we expect a regular Row. Vincent is coming & the Troop [of soldiers] at Bradford will be in readiness at a moment's call. For this last fortnight business has been at a complete standstill. In some of their windows they have got a large bowl full of bullets and marked over 'Tory pills' so you can see the state we are in. Have you a brace of pistols you could lend me until this row is over? for I have not a single weapon in my house, but a stick, which I have been already obliged to use. I should say there is at least 300 Muskets in the Town and five times as many ball cartridges.[64]

Confirmation of the arming of the Chartists was received by the Home Office from other quarters. Yet despite rioting in the town during late April and early May, the arrival of military reinforcements and the arrest of some of the local leaders brought the situation under control by the end of June.

In other towns the opposition was still less determined. At Wotton-under-Edge in July 1839 even local JPs had to admit that although disorder had been anticipated, a meeting held in the middle of that month had 'passed off peaceably'. But perhaps Charles Napier, the general commanding the northern district, pinpointed the most characteristic magisterial approach when he noted that JPs in every community 'will tell . . . the same story, that their town or village is the "focus of Chartism" whereas it is only the focus of their own fears'.[65] As the historian of Somerset and Wiltshire Chartism has written:

During its ten years of activity [1838 to 1848] Chartism gained hardly any hold in the rural areas. . . . It is true that there were some groups in Wiltshire villages, but it can usually be proved or inferred that, as at Bromham or

Hilperton, industrial workers were settled in them. . . . The failure of the rural population hereabouts to adhere to Chartism lay rather in the cleavage between town and country, and the deep suspicion of the urban mob felt by countrymen. . . . Where Chartism was present in these counties, cloth was usually being manufactured. A technological revolution was in progress in the cloth trade, and, partly in consequence of it, the manufacture of cloth in the West of England was being concentrated into fewer centres and within those centres into fewer business units. These developments cannot have failed to cause economic distress to some workers, and, since Chartism was a protest against distress, it may be concluded that the movement penetrated the two Avon valleys in consequence of these economic upheavals.[66]

Even the establishment in 1846 of the Chartists' National Land Company, as an expression of the movement's 'back-to-the-land' philosophy, found little response in country districts. The aim was to establish a network of self-sufficient smallholdings which would be cultivated by spade husbandry; each was to be allocated among the Company's subscribers by means of a ballot. Perhaps their knowledge of rural conditions made labourers suspicious of the rosy picture painted of life on the land in their own cottage and smallholding, 'where a man need ask no employer for wages and no landlord for a roof'.[67] But whatever the reason, it was only in such industrial villages as those around Leicester and Loughborough, which were hit by a decline in the domestic hosiery trade, that substantial support was shown. At a meeting held on the banks of the Soar during the summer of 1847 hundreds of stockingers sang the 'Chartist hymn': 'there were speeches, and the Land Plan was explained amid "breathless attention"'.[68]

In view of the Company's clouded legal position and its ultimate failure, it was perhaps fortunate for the labourers that they took little part in its affairs. For during the three years of its effective existence perhaps 250 of its 70,000 members were actually settled on allotments.[69] All the rest, who had each subscribed towards £1 6s. shares in the Company, lost their money when the enterprise foundered.

As for the Chartist leaders themselves, most adopted a dismissive tone towards country people. To one of them, Henry Vincent, the Gloucestershire villages were 'steeped in ignorance, beer and superstition'.[70] With such an attitude he was unlikely to win much support.

Political agitation among the working classes of rural England thus offered little real threat to the established order in village society. Paradoxically, it was from the farmers – and on the issue of protectionism – that the most serious challenge was to emerge. As we saw in Chapter 3, belief in agricultural protection was strong among countless landowners and occupiers in the post-Napoleonic era. Even those who demanded a reduction in taxation or poor rates in order to help them out of their financial difficulties clung to the view that control of foreign food imports was essential if prosperity were to be restored. They held to that faith even when falling prices and the development of more effective competition at home showed that for less efficient agriculturalists import control was of little value. During the 1830s, and particularly after the formation of the Anti-Corn Law League in 1838, Tory Party leaders made it their business to win the votes of farmers by pledging to retain protection at a time when Whigs and Radicals seemed to be flirting with the idea of repeal.

One of the prime movers behind this Tory policy was the Marquess of Chandos who, as early as October 1832, addressed meetings in his native Buckinghamshire at which he affirmed his support for protection. 'So long as I have a voice in the country I will say no to free trade in corn,' he declared firmly. 'All men, who would not see the ruin of the agriculturist, must unite in saying that the cause has a right to protection; the farmer to remuneration.'[71] Chandos was active in the formation of the Buckinghamshire Agricultural Association in 1833, seeing this as a forum for the discussion and dissemination of Conservative views. It combined ploughing matches and the offering of rewards to industrious farm servants with meetings at which speeches were made against the continuance of the unpopular malt tax and in favour of protection.[72] Other associations on similar lines appeared elsewhere, including the Hinckford Agricultural and Conservative Club and the Saffron Walden Agricultural Society, founded in Essex in 1833. Existing agricultural societies, like the Kesteven Agricultural Association formed in Lincolnshire in 1826, also turned to political issues in the early 1830s. In these circumstances Tory candidates in county seats and rural boroughs laid great stress on the problems of agriculture in their addresses at the general election of 1835. The strategy proved successful, for they gained a hundred seats. And the pattern of loss of rural seats by the Whigs and of gains by the Tories was repeated in the 1837 election. By 1841 of 144 English county seats the Whigs held only twenty; in 1832 their tally had been 102.[73] The Whigs' failure to take account of the anxieties of the rural electorate was a powerful (though not the sole) factor in their defeats, especially at a time when the activities of the Anti-Corn Law League were adding to farmers' worries.

The League owed its existence to the support of the industrial towns, where a policy which promoted cheap imported food and possibly a wider overseas market for manufactured goods proved attractive both to industrialists and to their workers, who had been hit by the economic recession of 1838–42. But in the early days League supporters hoped to detach farmers from the protectionist cause by emphasizing that it was the *landowner*, not the occupier, who gained from import restrictions. In 1839 lecturers were dispatched to agricultural districts in the south-west and East Anglia but despite their claims of support, there is little evidence that they achieved any real success. Only in pastoral areas, like Wales and the dairying counties of Cheshire and Lancashire, was interest shown, as livestock farmers saw the benefits that would accrue from cheap imported animal feed. In the case of the two latter counties there was also concern to ensure the prosperity of the industrial towns which provided their chief markets. In Wales, where there was already anti-landlord feeling among some tenant farmers, the Anti-Corn Law movement did much to wean other men from 'their semi-feudal loyalty to the older families by proving that the interests of landowners and of their Welsh tenants conflicted even in agricultural matters'.[74]

In the arable counties, however, opposition to League ideas was fierce. At a meeting at Saxmundham in Suffolk during the spring of 1840 one delegate, James Acland, was attacked by a mob of about 300 and was only saved from serious injury by the intervention of the police and friendly members of the audience. Similarly at Woodbridge he was assaulted when he returned to his inn after addressing a meeting in the market-place on market day. Nevertheless, these attacks did not blunt his enthusiasm, and by the middle of May he was appealing to the men of east Suffolk to realize that the 'BREAD TAX inflicts starvation upon you. Its repeal will emancipate you from want, from ignorance and from slavery.' He called on farm labourers to support the reformist cause: 'You have too long been kept in ignorance . . . Your condition is worse than that of the Slave, the Pauper, or the Convict, . . . and your employers and paymasters would break my head because I seek to instruct your minds as to your condition, its cause, and the means for its improvement.'[75]

Despite such appeals, rural workers took little part in the Anti-Corn Law agitation, even though, like other wage earners, they would have benefited from cheaper food. In some cases employers exerted pressure on them to sign pro-protectionist petitions. Joseph Arch claimed that his father was deprived of employment for eighteen weeks during one winter because he had refused to sign for 'a small loaf and a dear one'.[76] But few pro-League demonstrations were organized in country districts. In June 1845 one such was held at Upavon in Wiltshire, attended by over 1000 people, at which speeches were made in favour of repeal of the Corn Laws. The chairman pointed out that thanks to protection, agricultural labourers and their families did not get enough to eat. One man claimed that his children 'would jump across the house if they saw a couple of potatoes, and quarrel which should have them. . . . When he came home at night, and found them crying for food and he had none to give them, it almost drove him mad.'[77] The chairman warned that masters might threaten League supporters with dismissal, 'and thus they keep you in fear; and you will never be better as long [as] you are kept down in this way'. At the close of the meeting cheers were given for the League and for repeal. But isolated events like these did not constitute convincing overall support.

On the other side of the coin, farmers reacted by mobilizing more determinedly in favour of protection. At the 1841 general election the Conservatives' commitment to protection assured them of victory in the county constituencies and thus, ultimately, in the country as a whole. Among the constituencies where the protectionist influence was seen most clearly was the southern division of Lincolnshire, where prior to 1841 there had been two Whig MPs. But when the Conservatives threw doubts upon the Whig commitment to protectionism hostility mounted until both of them decided to retire before the poll was held; in their place two protectionist Conservatives were returned. In the north of England even the representatives of some of the great Whig county families failed at the polls. Lord Morpeth and Lord Milton were defeated in west Yorkshire and Lord Howick in north Northumberland.[78]

Yet within a year of this victory, Sir Robert Peel had begun to dismantle those very import duties which, despite all alarms and excursions, had remained intact during more than a decade of Whig administrations. The Prime Minister hoped, by reducing the general level of duties, to increase trade and thereby replenish the government's overall tax revenue. At the same time he sought to cut the high prices of consumer imports in an attempt to placate the industrial areas. There was also the argument that if Britain were to increase her exports of manufactures, she must open up her home market to the foreigner, while there is evidence that Peel himself appreciated that protection alone could not aid the inefficient farmer: only better agricultural methods could do that. In advocating a revised Corn Law Peel saw no inconsistency with his earlier statements on protection. As prime minister he regarded it as his duty to look beyond the narrow interests of landlords and farmers to those of the country at large.

In Parliament the announcement of the proposed tariff revisions was at first accepted quietly by a wide section of the Tory Party and by certain of the major landowners, but among farmers a very different spirit prevailed. Linconshire was especially resentful of the proposed changes; as one report put it, the county was 'in a flame'. In Essex, too, disappointment at the attitude of county members was clearly expressed. As one farmer critic put it: 'They were looked up to as the protectors and defenders of agriculture. . . . Were their banners not emblazoned with the words "The Farmers' Friend"?' Yet they had taken no action to oppose the Corn Bill: 'I do consider that it was in the power of those gentlemen to have made much a stand on the duty to be imposed . . . as would have compelled Sir Robert Peel to leave his high station, and enter into a compromise.'[79] Pressed by angry electors, a number of county Members now adopted a more critical stance, but despite this the Corn Law of 1842 went ahead. Thanks to the backing of Whigs and radicals, a later measure also permitted the import of foreign livestock (previously prohibited) upon the payment of a nominal duty.

To protectionist farmers the first session of Peel's Conservative government was a grievous disappointment, and they did not hesitate to express their anger to the county Members. Nevertheless, they hoped that by the end of the session the worst was over. They soon found that their hopes were to be dashed, for in February 1843 the Colonial Secretary announced that negotiations were under way to reduce still further the duties on Canadian wheat imports. Although this was merely an extension of the existing colonial preference system, it caused great bitterness among erstwhile Conservative rural voters. Many would doubtless have agreed with the Leicestershire tenant who charged Peel with a 'gross breach of faith'.

Nor were their views lost on county MPs. A number of them speedily bowed to constituency pressure and pledged themselves to oppose the Canadian Corn Bill.[80] At the same time farmers showed themselves ready to publicize their grievances. As one of them declared: 'the stream of our fortunes is careering away in an impetuous torrent towards the open gulf of Free Trade; we must stem it quickly . . . or we are lost! We must stem it by our unaided efforts, as we have been deserted by our natural leaders.'[81] Yet despite their endeavours, government support again proved sufficient to secure the Bill's passage.

Agriculturalists now responded by forming fresh protectionist organizations of their own. The Essex Agricultural Protection Society, for example, was set up in December 1843 under the influence of a local tenant farmer and land valuer, and was rapidly imitated in other counties. Inspired by these activities, an 'aristocratic' protectionist society also emerged in February 1844, meeting at the London home of the Duke of Richmond.[82] Shortly afterwards the two groups, aristocrats and farmers, met to co-ordinate policy and to form themselves into a central society to oppose Corn Law changes. By March 1844 this Anti-League, as it became known, boasted nearly a hundred associated organizations in England.

Then late in 1845, in the face of massive potato crop failure in Ireland, Peel decided to suspend the Corn Laws. He realized that, once suspended, they would not be reimposed, but he was already convinced that only improved 'high' farming techniques would bring prosperity to British agriculture. To this end he proposed an immediate reduction of duties on imported grass and clover seeds as well as animal feed and the offer of a government loan of £2 million to encourage drainage schemes. Although too small in itself to achieve very much, the drainage loan was a psychological move designed to popularize 'high' farming.[83] Reforms were also introduced to reduce the rate burden on the land.

Needless to say, these moves did not disarm Peel's critics. As repeal came nearer, pro-protection forces mobilized themselves in a last desperate effort to prevent change. A number of local societies even became involved in the registration of county voters in an attempt to secure political backing for their cause. In some cases associations also decided to exert open pressure on MPs. The Cambridgeshire society passed a resolution pledging electoral loyalty only to those prepared to support protection. While at a by-election in Nottinghamshire South during February 1846 protectionists helped to elect a candidate opposed to the government's policy.[84] Likewise in Northamptonshire and the West Riding of Yorkshire several of the Whig gentry firmly informed the pro-repeal Earl Fitzwilliam that they placed the maintenance of protection before their party loyalties and traditions. In fact, as Lord Clarendon put it to Fitzwilliam, thanks to the events of 1846 'the landed gentry were in a state of rabies, they thought themselves both plundered and betrayed, and nothing could have satisfied them but retracing our steps'.[85] Another pro-reform landowner, Earl Spencer, was obliged to resign from the Northamptonshire Farming and Grazing Society in order to prevent its dissolution; earlier a vengeful Tory farmer had stolen into one of the Earl's barns in order maliciously to feed the wrong food to a prize cow.[86]

It was in these bitter circumstances that Lord George Bentinck, Member for King's Lynn, emerged in February 1846 as the spokesman for the protectionist wing of the Conservative Party, with Benjamin Disraeli as his lieutenant.[87] Yet, as with the earlier tariff reform measures, the tide of repeal could not be checked. Indeed, from a broader national view, it was important that it should not be.

However, with the passage of the Bill to end protective duties, on corn, save for a nominal registration payment of 1s. per quarter, farmers' disillusionment with the Peelites was absolute. Only a few of the more perceptive saw that the mere retention of import duties had not assured prosperity in the past and could not do so in the future. And it was perhaps appropriate that the collapse of protectionist hopes should coincide with the insolvency of the Marquess of Chandos (now the second Duke of Buckingham and Chandos) who had done so much to promote the cause in the 1830s. The duke had spent heavily on rebuilding his estate at Stowe and on his various political campaigns, and in 1848 he went bankrupt, with debts of £1.5 million, of which around £950,000 had been incurred between 1839 and 1845.[88]

The changes in the Corn Law were scheduled to come into full operation in 1849, and during the winter of 1849–50 meetings were held in rural areas up and down the country at which demands were made for a return to protection. Tenant farmers again resolved to put forward their own candidates at the polls. In 1849 men in the strongly protectionist North Hampshire constituency, for example, expressed their disappointment and anger by nominating a candidate at a by-election in opposition to the choice of the county's Tory leaders. The attitude of these dissidents was summed up by a large tenant farmer from Tufton near Whitchurch, when he declared that men such as he 'must now look to themselves; they have heretofore looked to those above them, but they have deceived them. . . . The farmers of Hampshire will not submit to take the nominee of the gentlemen of the county without even being consulted in the matter.' Yet although the farmers' candidate polled well, territorial influence remained strong enough for the 'official' candidate to be returned.[89] In the 1852 general election, however, there were greater successes. In Cambridgeshire the county Farmers' Association put forward and helped to elect a protectionist candidate, and in Berkshire farmers forced out Philip Pusey, one of the most distinguished agriculturalists of the day. Pusey had publicly announced his rejection of protectionism in the previous year, and so the Berkshire Protection Association put up a candidate, who was successful.[90] Although protectionists did not capture a majority of seats, they emerged as the largest party in Parliament after the 1852 election.

In these early days, too, landlords were assailed by tenants demanding reductions in rent. From Enstone in Oxfordshire in 1852 a tenant farmer wrote to the dean and chapter of Christ Church, his landlords, asking that a 15 per cent rebate, introduced in 1850, should be continued 'as long as this confounded free trade system is persevered in, and things are at present so dreadfully depressed. . . . I see nothing but ruin can be the fate of Farmers under it.' He quoted cases of neighbours who had been faced with financial disaster: 'a farm . . . adjoining mine was . . . let at Michs. 1848 for a term of years but the tenant had lost all his money & it came into the hands of the owner at the end of two years.'[91] Another Christ Church tenant, protesting at the amount of the fine he had been called upon to pay for the renewal of his lease at Thrupp in Northamptonshire, echoed the complaints: 'corn is not at this time worth one half of what it was when your Surveyor made his valuation in 1847 and the scarcity of money at this time renders the situation of every Farmer most seriously distressing'.[92] On the Duke of Bedford's Woburn estate rebates were also allowed, ranging from 12.5 to 15 per cent in most cases during the early months of 1850. Stock losses added to the difficulties of some farmers, and in one case half a tenant's total rent arrears were written off by the duke in an effort to help him to re-establish himself.[93] By the end of 1850 it had been decided that those tenants whose rents had been fixed prior to the Corn Law changes of 1843 would no longer have to pay the cash sum then agreed. In future they would pay one-third of the rent at a fixed amount and the remaining two-thirds would vary according to the average price of wheat over the preceding four years. For newer tenants corn rents, changing annually in accordance with price fluctuations, were to operate.[94] In these circumstances gross rentals on the Bedford estate fell from £36,932 in 1850 to £34,816 a year later and to £33,359 by 1853. Not until 1854 was the upward movement resumed.[95]

Yet despite the fears and uncertainties which characterized the early 1850s, and the temporary transformation of one wing of the Conservative Party into what was virtually a protectionist party, the dislocations proved short-lived. For one thing, in spite of the growing importance of imports, there were no large surpluses of grain available in Europe which could swamp the British home market, while the North American trade was in its infancy. Imports had contributed around 7.5 per cent of total wheat consumption in 1843–6; this rose to 19.5 per cent in 1847–8 and to 26.6 per cent in 1849–59. The trend was generally upwards thereafter.[96]

By the middle of 1852, therefore, agricultural prices had begun to rise once more, and with the onset of the Crimean War they moved still higher. Although there were some fluctuations, this marked the beginning of a period of general advance and prosperity for British agriculture:

The next twenty years saw steady wheat prices and rising meat prices as an accelerated population growth concentrated in the towns guaranteed an expanding urban market for agricultural products. Secondly, the extension of the railways to all parts of the island provided opportunities for even the most remote farmer to reach these markets easily and cheaply. Thirdly, by adopting increasingly sophisticated agricultural improvements, farmers became more efficient. They learned more about fertilizers and natural manures such as guano. They also benefited from the development of new mass-production methods that, for example, cheapened the cost of drain-pipes. Many farmers adopted the comprehensive system popularly known as high farming which was based on heavy capital improvements (such as new farm buildings and drainage) and on the extensive use of new feeds, fertilizers and implements. . . . As in the past, rural prosperity dampened discontent: farmers lost interest in political agitation.[97]

Meanwhile Peel himself, although a committed advocate of 'high' farming, justified repeal on the broader basis that it was to the advantage of the country as a whole. As he told his Tamworth constituents in 1847, it had 'tended to fortify the established institutions of this country, to inspire confidence in the equity and benevolence of the legislature, to maintain the just authority of an hereditary nobility, and to discourage the desire for democratic change in the Constitution of the House of Commons'.[98] In other words, it had been a strategic retreat, designed to keep intact the main strongholds of aristocratic power and a limited constitution. A number of the larger proprietors (especially the Whigs), including Earl Fitzwilliam and the Earl of Radnor, agreed with his pro-repeal views, but the country gentlemen and farmers, especially in the arable eastern counties, regarded protection as essential to their prosperity. They were concerned purely with their own short-term and narrow interests. Only in the 1850s, when Peel himself was dead, did their attitude change, as English agriculture moved into its 'golden age' and their fears of financial disaster were set aside for almost three decades. Nevertheless, the repeal of the Corn Laws was a clear sign of the declining political and economic power of the landed interest and of the emergence of urban industrialism and commerce as major forces. Although during the age of Palmerston that loss of influence was disguised, from the late 1860s and beyond it was to manifest itself with a growing and unmistakable clarity.

Boy returning from an errand with insufficient change, c. 1856. The bare cottage interior was typical of labouring homes at this date

8 *The rural community in the mid nineteenth century*

Early Victorian England was the home of earnest and practical men. . . . Evangelical piety often went hand in hand with practical intelligence, and a sense of being ever in the eye of the Lord often prompted a mastery of things, the better to serve the Master of all men. This cast of mind is usually and rightly associated . . . with the counting house and the professions. But it was also communicated to that other England, of meadow and stream, of parsonage and country house, where by 1840 it had gained an ascendancy . . . a fundamental seriousness that nurtured responsibility and self-discipline, and a zest for the labours of the intellect as well as for those of private and public affairs. . . . Fresh winds were blowing in upper-class society, and they blew most powerfully in the decades of the forties and fifties.[1]

The injurious effects of insufficient and unsuitable cottage accommodation for the agricultural labourers . . . are to be seen not only in the wretchedness of their mode of living, but in many other phases of their physical, social and moral condition. . . . The vast majority of the evils inseparable from the constant attendance on ale-houses and beer-shops are also in a great measure traceable to the comfortless condition of the labourers' dwellings.
Morning Chronicle (1850)[2]

By the middle of the nineteenth century rural society was different, in many respects, from the country communities of eighty years earlier. Thanks to the effects of enclosure and the agricultural depression which followed the Napoleonic wars, the tripartite system of land cultivation had become more firmly established; and landlords, farmers and labourers each played their separate roles within the community. Over much of England and Wales landownership had become concentrated in the hands of a few people. In 1873 it was estimated that 18,546,000 acres, or about half of the total area of the country, were owned by a mere 4217 people, each of whom possessed 1000 acres or more. In some counties the role of these very large owners was particularly prominent;

over one-third of the cultivated areas of Cheshire, Wiltshire, Dorset, Nottingham, Northumberland and Rutland was occupied by estates which, in aggregate, totalled 10,000 acres, and in Northumberland and Rutland half the land was so occupied.[3]

Admittedly, neither the small owner nor the smaller tenant had altogether disappeared. In 1851 it was reported that 91,698 farmers in England and Wales, or about 40 per cent of the whole, employed no agricultural labourers, relying solely on their own efforts and those of their family. Fifty years later owner-occupiers still held perhaps 10 to 12 per cent of the cultivated area, and in certain districts, like south Lancashire with its dairy farms, the fenlands of Lincolnshire and parts of Westmorland, their contribution was important.[4] A return of land distribution for 1870 showed that between a half and three-quarters of all holdings in the Lincolnshire fens were of twenty acres or less. Not all were owner-occupied but many were, and men often borrowed money to start their farming operations and then built up their properties bit by bit.[5]

Westmorland, too, had numerous small proprietors, or 'statesmen' as they were known, holding farms worth between £10 and £50 a year, either freehold or by customary tenure from the lord of the manor. In the middle of the century there were said to be almost 7000 of them in Cumbria as a whole, as well as a large class of small farmers who were not proprietors. Thus in 1851 at the township of Crook, among the Westmorland fells, there were six men who classed themselves as 'landed proprietors' and a further eighteen who were farmers, out of a total population of 139.[6] At nearby Kentmere there were twenty-two farmers in a population of 193; their holdings ranged from one man with five acres and a second with ten to others with substantial farms of 300 and 500 acres respectively.[7]

Another variation on the theme was found in sheep-rearing districts, like those in Northumberland, where the population was scattered and the flocks wandered over vast areas. In one far-flung community – the township of Grey's Forest, on the edge of the Cheviots – the population of forty-four was divided among six hamlets. Twelve of the twenty-two males living in the township were shepherds, and two more worked as agricultural labourers. And, of course, as in all sheep-rearing districts, when tending their animals the men were dependent on the skill and energy of their dogs, without whose aid 'the best selected flock would be but a profitless concern'.[8]

A further variation was provided by the forest areas, like Wychwood in Oxfordshire, where settlement patterns were less ordered and freeholders more numerous than in communities devoted to traditional farming. With employment on the land strictly limited in a forest region, by-employments were widely followed by men and women anxious to supplement their earnings. In the case of Wychwood this led to the growth of the glove industry, which was centred on Woodstock.[9]

Nevertheless, places like these were the exception rather than the rule. In much of southern and central England, and especially in 'close' parishes where land ownership was concentrated in the hands of one or two substantial proprietors only, society was clearly stratified. In Norfolk and Leicestershire, for example, between a third and a half of all villages fell into the 'close' category; in Bedfordshire about one-quarter did so, and in South Lindsey, Lincolnshire, as much as 59 per cent of the land was in 'close' parishes – though this included only 44 per cent of the population, since such communities tended to have fewer inhabitants than their 'open' neighbours.[10]

At the head of affairs as in earlier decades, were the major landowners – the nobility and gentry – followed by the parsons, the substantial farmers, the rural craftsmen, the shopkeepers and the smallholders. At the bottom of the scale came the agricultural labourers and their families, together with those with minor specialist skills, like mole catchers, thatchers or hedgers and ditchers, and the new categories of railway workers. Among the women domestic service provided the most common employment, though, as in the late eighteenth century, in areas where cottage industries survived or where rural factories had been established these employed substantial numbers of women. Table 7 indicates some of these occupational differences, including, as it does, two basically arable parishes in Suffolk and one in Northumberland, two in Buckinghamshire, where there was also a heavy representation of women engaged in cottage industries, and two predominantly pastoral communities in Westmorland with by-employments in slate quarrying and bobbin turning.

Despite the battles over protectionism which were discussed in the last chapter and which led to a worsening of relations between some landowners and their tenant farmers during the 1840s, in practice the social leadership of the landlord was rarely challenged. For their part, he and members of his family expected to dispense charity and patronage to those who lived on or near their estates; in the case of non-resident owners the local agent or the clergyman would be deputed to give help on their behalf. Even such comparatively humble appointments as those of mail guard, letter carrier or Post Office messenger

H

Table 7 *Occupations in certain selected communities at the 1851 census**

	Wyverstone (Suffolk)	Denham (Suffolk)	Branxton (Northumberland)	Mursley (Bucks)	Kentmere (Westmorland)	Crook (Westmorland)	Little Horwood (Bucks)
Total population	329	318	284	553	193	278	339
Male occupations							
Clergymen	1	1	1	1	1	1	1
Landed proprietors	—	—	—	—	—	6	1
Farmers and smallholders	14	12	4	15	22	18	21
Farmers' sons	1	6	2	6	8	1	8
Farm servants and agric. labourers	77	63	39	121	17	16	101
Shepherds	1	1	3	3	2	—	—
Farm bailiffs	1	1	—	—	—	—	—
Slate gatherers and quarrymen	—	—	—	—	3	3	—
Drystone wallers	—	—	—	—	—	1	—
Blacksmiths and apprentices	4	2	2	2	1	—	2
Wheelwrights and apprentices	—	—	—	2	—	—	—
Carpenters and apprentices	3	1	2	6	—	2	3
Tailors and apprentices	1	—	1	1	—	—	—
Shoemakers and apprentices	6	2	7	4	—	2	—
Masons and apprentices	—	—	4	—	—	1	—
Sawyers and apprentices	—	—	—	1	—	3	—
Bakers	—	—	—	1	—	1	—
Millers and apprentices	1	1	—	—	—	—	—
Plumbers, etc.	—	—	—	—	—	1	1
Bobbin turners and borers	—	—	—	—	—	14	—
Butchers	1	—	—	4	—	—	—
Grocers	1	—	3	—	—	—	—
Victuallers and innkeepers	1	1	1	1	1	—	2
Railway workers	—	—	1	4	—	—	—
Teachers	—	—	—	—	—	10	—
Worsted manufacturers	—	—	—	—	—	—	—
Annuitants and others of independent means	—	—	—	—	1	2	1
Others†	3	2	5	29	—	3	5
Total occupations	114	93	74	201	56	82	146

Female occupations

Landed proprietors	—	—	—	1	—	—	—
Farmers and smallholders	—	2	—	—	—	1	1
Agric. labourers and farm servants‡	16	—	31	—	—	—	—
Shopkeepers	—	—	—	3	—	1	—
Domestic servants	—	15	22	18	8	9	9
Dairy maids	3	1	—	—	1	—	2
Plaiters	—	—	—	48	—	—	9
Lacemakers	—	—	—	51	—	17	65
Worsted spinners	—	—	—	—	—	1	2
Dressmakers	2	4	4	6	—	1	1
Laundresses and washerwomen	—	1	—	5	—	—	1
Shoebinders	2	1	—	2	—	—	—
Teachers	1	1	—	—	—	—	1
Annuitants and others of independent means	1	2	—	3	—	3	3
Others†	—	2	—	10	—	—	3
Total occupations	25	28	57	147	9	33	96

*Those classed as paupers are excluded; housewives are only included where a specific additional occupation is shown in the census returns.

†'Others' include gamekeepers, male servants, male plaiters at Mursley, nurses, etc.

‡The large number of part-time women land workers is not recorded.

SOURCES: 1851 Census returns at the Public Record Office: Wyverstone, HO 107.1975; Denham, HO 107.1796; Branxton, HO 107.2422; Mursley and Little Horwood, HO 107.1722; Kentmere and Crook, HO 107.2441.

might well only be filled by the authorities after consultation with the major landowner of the area. Post Office records show the considerable patronage exercised by the Earl of Leicester in Norfolk during the early 1850s, while in May 1853 a messenger who was to work between Henley-on-Thames and Hambledon in Oxfordshire was nominated by a local magnate, Lord Camoys. In October of the same year Sir Thomas Fremantle, a Buckinghamshire landowner and MP, nominated a messenger for the Winslow-to-Mursley route, near to his family seat.[11] There are countless similar examples, In fact, in the early 1830s the secretary to the Post Office complained that 'scarcely a day' passed without recommendations being received from patrons wishing to further the interests of their protégés.[12] The rates of pay offered for these appointments, although above the basic wages of many agricultural labourers, were hardly generous at around 12s. to 15s. per week; yet in an uncertain world, with unemployment an ever-present threat, government service represented financial security, so even such poorly paid positions as those of letter carrier were eagerly sought after, though they might yield as little as £4 or £5 per annum.[13] Small wonder that Professor Gash has written of patronage in this period as 'primarily a question of the lower reaches of the government service. . . . Every vacancy in the civil service . . . was sought after with drab and pathetic tenacity by a host of aspirants.'[14]

Positions as porters or plate layers on the railways were also often filled through the exercise of patronage, perhaps by directors who were major landowners as well. One supplicant, William Bullock of Steventon (then in Berkshire), 'humbly' petitioned to be appointed porter in 1842. He produced a supporting statement from fellow villagers claiming that he was 'a sober, honest, industrious person' suitable to be a candidate for that office. At this time country porters earned about 16s. to 18s. a week – plus any tips they might secure.[15]

The words 'sober, honest, industrious' had, however, a wider significance than that of a mere phrase in a job application. For if one characteristic of the early Victorian countryside was the clearer drawing of class boundaries, another was the growing emphasis placed by authority on the need for reliability and sobriety on the part of workers. Agricultural societies offered prizes to men who had remained longest with a single employer; the factory method of fining those who had broken a farm's rules and regulations was introduced on a few of the more commercial undertakings; and, above all, there was a glorification of the 'work ethic'. The need to encourage efficient diligent labourers provided a continuing theme for speeches at agricultural meetings during the 1850s and 1860s.[16]

Under this moral influence the well-to-do looked with a new sense of responsibility upon their own social and economic duties. Admittedly, not all of them displayed these virtuous traits: men like the seventh Earl of Cardigan or Squire Osbaldeston still indulged their extravagant whims. But it is significant that in 1848 the sixty-two-year-old Osbaldeston was forced to sell his Yorkshire estates in order to pay debts incurred in hunting, horse racing, gambling and other activities. As he wrote ruefully: 'On a fair calculation I have lost nearly £200,000 by betting and keeping racehorses during a period of 45 years; and £100,000 through the misdeeds of agents, etc.'[17] Already men such as he were something of an anachronism in the England of Victoria – survivors from the heady and reckless days of the regency.

Far more characteristic of the new era were improving landlords like Earl Fitzwilliam and the Duke of Bedford. It was during the 1840s that the Woburn estate grew to a new maximum and that, thanks to a burgeoning income from urban rentals, debts which topped £500,000 in 1839 had been eliminated by the mid 1850s.[18] During these years increased attention was paid by the estate not merely to better methods of tilling the soil but also to the building of cottages and the establishment of self-help schemes among villagers to replace the distribution of largesse. From the time he succeeded to the estate in 1839 until his death in 1861, the seventh Duke of Bedford was to finance the building of 374 cottages on his estate in Bedfordshire and 288 on that in Devon. As he himself wrote: 'To improve the dwellings of the labouring class, and afford them the means of greater cleanliness, health and comfort, in their own homes . . . are among the first duties and ought to be among the truest pleasures, of every landlord.'[19]

In September 1850 the Woburn agent listed three principal reasons for not building any more one-bedroomed cottages on the estate:

1st   Old people are better with a Lodger both for Company & safety, and there are many middle aged single women who have no friends or home: these want lodgings & they cannot be so well as with an old Couple whom they may assist. . . .

2nd   Suppose a Man is left a Widower, he wants a female to take care of his house & himself, & it is of more consequence that whoever takes care of him, shd. be in the House at Night than in day time. . . .

3rd   There are few who have families grown up & gone away, who have not some orphan grandchild or nephew or niece to whom they are ready to offer a home, if they cannot afford to maintain them altogether.[20]

A similarly enlightened spirit informed the activities of Charles Higgins, squire of Turvey, also in Bedfordshire. Between 1849 and 1851 he built forty-eight cottages as well as shops, and in the spring of 1847 he financed the building of a national school in the village. In the 1830s he had obtained medical qualifications in London and during these mid-century years he treated the destitute sick in the surrounding villages, keeping a stock of medicines at his home.[21] Higgins 'organized, and took under his own personal charge, [the parish] Benefit Clubs, – taught in the village school three times on every Sunday, opening it always in person, – visited from house to house'.[22] Such a high degree of personal commitment as this was, admittedly, rare. More typical was the paternalistic approach of men like Sir John Boileau of Ketteringham. His views were well summarized in a speech which he made to his tenants at a dinner held for them in February 1854. In it he emphasized

the comfort of living in Ketteringham, where they had a comfortable church – good school for the children – decent cottages and gardens at moderate rents or low ones – sure of being attended to if sick or find a friend if in want of one – and no man well-behaved out of employment at fair wages. Therefore they ought to be zealous, diligent, respectful workmen for their employers and kind to each other . . . obliged to punish for the thefts committed this year, and they might be sure while desirous to encourage the good I must and would bring really bad conduct to punishment. Mr. Beck now in charge of the estate, a kind good man, but the rules for cottagers for not taking in lodgers etc. must be carefully kept by him.[23]

To his credit, Boileau was a firm opponent of the use of child labour and refused to employ boys under twelve; even then he would only take them if they had remained at school until that age. He also attended cottagers' weddings. On one occasion in 1853, despite worries over the ill health of his wife, he made it his business to go to the wedding of two of the villagers and gave them a hot pie and some beer for the marriage feast. While the service was in progress he sent one of his ervants to put an American clock in their cottage as a gift.

Even more than in earlier decades efforts were made during these years to strengthen the links between a landlord and his tenant farmers. Now that the days of independent yeomen were disappearing, occupiers began to take a pride in the estate to which they belonged:

When young Queen Victoria, one fine July day in 1841, visited Woburn, 150 mounted tenantry were drawn up on either side of the park entrance to receive her (the best mounted near the gate), and they escorted her to the

Abbey, falling in rank two by two behind the carriage. The rent audit was a pleasant occasion on which there was a dinner for the tenants, sometimes of venison.[24]

Significantly, in 1848, when a tenant farmer on the estate was found to have 'made free with materials both old & new, belonging to the Duke', including timber, lead and door hinges, he was firmly told by the Woburn agent that until the expiry of his tenancy agreement he would not be permitted 'to be present with the other Tenants at the Half Yearly Audit Dinners, nor can I hold any intercourse with you except on matters strictly relating to the occupation of, & quitting the Farms'.[25] Clearly, until he left the estate in the autumn of 1850 he was to be treated as a pariah – excluded from the social ambience of Woburn with all that that meant.

This nurturing of links between villagers and squire meant that while he and his relations continued to live their private lives, sheltered from the public gaze, the villagers translated events in his family history into communal celebrations. A wedding, the birth and coming of age of an heir, even a betrothal, called forth festivities in which the whole parish would share. When a death occurred in a gentry family the whole village would be expected to attend the funeral, and 'householders drew their blinds to show their respect'.[26] At Ketteringham the coming of age of the heir in 1848 was the cause of a great parish gathering, and the gates of the park were thrown open to all. On the following day an invitation to dinner was issued to the tenant farmers. Later, as bands played, celebratory guns were fired, and church bells rang, a feast was held for the cottagers and labourers. There were two long tables, loaded with plum pudding, roast beef and vegetables. Two days after that games for children and adults were organized; the more venturesome climbed a soapy mast for a shoulder of mutton, ran sack races and raced blindfold with wheelbarrows.[27] Most estate owners followed this pattern when they arranged parish junketings.

As in the eighteenth century, the larger mansions also exerted a powerful influence over local employment. Indeed, in the mid-Victorian years domestic staffs tended to be bigger than they had been a century earlier. Lord Shaftesbury once described Woburn as 'not a palace, a house; it is a town, a municipal borough, a city'. On a more modest scale households like that at Shrubland Hall in Suffolk employed a staff of over 100 – in the case of Shrubland the number was actually 173. This was made up of seventeen indoor servants, sixteen in the stables, sixteen keepers and night men, four warreners, ten employed in the parks, forty gardeners, three lodge keepers, two blacksmiths, seven carpenters, three painters, two engineers, thirty-eight men on the home farm, nine engaged in the brick kilns, four bricklayers and two wheelwrights.[28]

In their efforts to regulate the attitudes and behaviour of the labouring classes, however, the bigger landlords were not alone. A similar concern was shared by the new generation of clergy, too. The proposals listed by the curate of South Stoke in Oxfordshire in January 1852 indicate the main areas of clerical interest. In this case the curate was appealing – with little success – for financial help from the dean and chapter of Christ Church, who were major landowners in the village, to enable him to launch his projects. The first requirement was a better school, the next, a parochial library:

A Library would I believe be hailed with delight by all. The younger portion of my flock – including young men of the age of 27 – I find most anxious for instruction as their regular attendances [at evening classes] on four nights in every week sufficiently proves.

The establishment of a Sick Benefit Club is universally allowed to be most beneficial to the character of the poor, if conducted on sound principles; & I am the more desirous of forming one, in as much as there is a Club in the neighbouring Parish to which some few belong, but as its meetings are held in a Public House, it proves in every way an evil & not a blessing. As regards the next object, that of Clothing Clubs, there is, I must state, one at present for women, which however only admits 20 members as there are not Funds from which to increase the monthly payments of a larger number. The present addition being made by the sole liberality of the vicar.... This Club I desire to increase Fourfold. – My last & not a less important object is the establishment of a Clothing Club for boys & one for Girls, which in a former Parish I found most beneficial.

He estimated the annual subscriptions needed for the most urgent proposals would be £44, made up of £24 for the weekly and Sunday school, £12 for the clothing club and £4 each for a clothing club for boys and for girls. 'A Donation of £5 would be all that is at present necessary for starting a Library, whilst as regards the Sick Benefit Club, my plans are not sufficiently matured to enable me to state what this would require but I hope no very large sum.'[29] To the curate's disgust, Christ Church eventually sent the meagre sum of £5 to enable him to open the library. Given this response it was perhaps not surprising that in November 1853 he should upbraid the dean and chapter, and their Nonconformist principal tenant, a farmer, for the poor state of the cottages they owned, claiming that he had lately been called upon to inspect different properties

and those belonging to Christ Church are notoriously the worst. The privies, if such they can be called, are a disgrace to the 19th century, & though your Tenant has been made aware of it, he does nothing. One indeed is left as a public nuisance & eyesore. Imagine an aged man & his wife compelled to hang up pieces of old sacking on hurdle or other stakes to screen them from public observation. Such is their Garden House – the property of Christ Church. Any one would say that the pigs in Mr. King's [the tenant's] yard are better off. . . . At Woodcote there are 5 cottages in Mr. K's hands with no Garden House at all & 3 more with only the pretence, being totally unfit. There are other owners of property who I am thankful to say do not imitate Christ Church, but in almost every instance where there is a nuisance it can be traced to Christ Church through their Tenant.[30]

Nevertheless, profligate landlords like Squire Osbaldeston and neglectful institutional owners of property like Christ Church were not the sole (or even the worst) offenders as regards cottage accommodation. Particularly in 'open' parishes, where houses were owned by tradespeople and widows for speculative purposes or as a means of supplementing a small income, conditions were often deplorable, and owners often lacked either the means or the will to carry out repairs and improvements. In 1864 Dr Hunter, reporting to the Medical Officer of the Privy Council, condemned the 'miserable hovels, neglected cabbage gardens' which characterized such communities, whose inhabitants sought work 'many miles from home'.[31] In his view 'open' villages were used as 'dumps' for undesirable residents from estates, for 'should a man lose his honesty, or a woman her virtue, both are ejected from the close parish, and of course take up their abode in the next open one.' He did not mention, however, that some families *preferred* the greater social freedom bestowed by open parishes, despite their physical disadvantages, or that law-abiding Nonconformists might be excluded from an estate village on religious grounds. In 1852 it was stated that not a single dissenter resided in the Cambridgeshire parish of West Wratting, and elsewhere informal religious tests of prospective tenants were common[32] (see also Chapter 5).

Among the 'open' villages to come under Dr Hunter's critical eye was Harbury in Warwickshire. Here lime burners and plate layers from the railway vied with agricultural labourers for the cottages:

Lodgers occasionally swarmed here, and rents were rather high. Water was scarce, and many of the houses rotting. Rents were about £4 [per annum]. In

the decennium 1851–61, although there was a slight increase of population
no less than 67 more cots were destroyed than were built . . . here, in 1864, I
visited families of 4 adults with three children, of 2 adults with 6, of 2 adults
with 4, each with but one bedroom.

Given such grounds for discontent, it is not surprising that Harbury
labourers were active supporters of agricultural trade unionism in
the 1870s.[33]

Only in the rural areas of Northumberland and Durham did Hunter
consider the cottages to be 'very much what they should be – a ground
floor with a windowless loft. . . . Some cots have the . . . luxury of a
passage through to the back door, and into it the door of each room
opens. In nearly every case there was all the comfort which fixtures and
furniture can give.'[34] In reaching this conclusion he differed from an
earlier report by the agricultural writer James Caird. In 1851 Caird
had described Northumbrian labourers' cottages as 'most discreditable';
the family and pig lodged 'in too many cases, under the same roof',
and went 'out and in by the same door' as the human residents. The
cow house was divided 'only by a slight partition wall from the single
apartment which serves for kitchen, living and sleeping room, for all
the inmates'.[35] The situation was aggravated by the 'bondager' system
which prevailed in the county, since if a male labourer had no suitable
female relative available, he had to hire an outsider to give assistance.
In the middle of the century there were households like that of Gilbert
Piercy of Branxton, who lived with his wife, six children and a twenty-
three-year-old resident bondager, and James Grey of the same parish,
who lived with a wife, two children and a bondager, each within the
confines of a small cottage.[36] With such arrangements it is not surprising that charges of immorality were widespread. Only on the
estates of the Duke of Northumberland and the Marquess of Waterford
did Caird consider housing conditions to be satisfactory.

Beyond Northumberland's special circumstances, however, other
critics of rural dwellings pinpointed hazards to morals and health which
overcrowding created. According to the *Morning Chronicle* of 28 October
1850, incest was common, while in speaking to some of the 'unfortunate
females' who gained a living by prostitution the reporter was struck

with the fact that in many cases they belonged to large families, the members
of which were in the habit of sleeping together in one crowded apartment.
'I had four sisters and three brothers,' said one of them to me, 'when I left
home; my eldest brother was seventeen; there were but two beds on the
floor for the children and we used all to sleep there together, and it is to that
more than anything else, that I can trace my ruin.

Seven years later the *Saturday Review* launched a still more savage attack on the moral shortcomings of overcrowded rural areas. The Buckinghamshire village of Chesham was its particular target. Here the trial of a local shoemaker for the murder of his wife led to the disclosure that village women were in the habit of administering drugs to themselves in order to produce miscarriages, while adultery was rife: 'Fornication and adultery, incest and murder, abortion and poisoning – all are tangled together in one hideous web of sin and horror', declared the *Review*. This, in its opinion, was the level of cottage life when 'the practice of abortion is treated as the habit of rural society.' It called upon religious and educational bodies to redress the balance by engaging in 'domestic missions to the worse than heathen of our villages and towns at home'.[37]

John Glyde, writing of Suffolk in the mid-1850s, shared many of these views. He claimed that although the towns had been thought of as 'the great centres of vice and crime' and the residents of villages as 'an unsophisticated and harmless population', in practice such descriptions gave a false impression: 'vice and sorrow have settled upon our agricultural population, and heathenism and crime have culminated, where it would be least expected'.[38]

Just how widespread these problems actually were it is not easy to decide. Middle-class critics, particularly journalists, were likely to be attracted by salacious stories of the misdoings and misdemeanours of labouring families. Certainly, such events did occur, but it is worth remembering that in many large households it was common for the older children to lodge with neighbours whose own offspring had left home and who could offer spare accommodation. Furthermore, in the case of most girls employment as resident domestic servants would take them away from home when they had reached the age of about thirteen. Only in parts of rural Wales, where the custom of 'bundling', or courting in bed, still survived, were Victorian moral fears probably justified. In the 1840s the chaplain to the bishop of Bangor complained that the householders of Anglesey tacitly agreed, when hiring servants, to provide opportunities for fornication. Two decades later the archdeacon of St David's claimed that 'bastardy was common, unchastity . . . the rule' among farmhouse servants in south Wales.[39] However, this is partly explained on the practical grounds that where their future husbands were small farmers who would require the help of children in tilling their holding it was important for women to prove their fertility before the marriage took place.

Apart from these sexual implications, poor housing was blamed for encouraging drunkenness; men, it was said, were driven to the public house by the uncomfortable condition of their home. Philanthropists pressed for cottage improvement and the promotion of temperance societies as the twin solutions to this problem. It became the custom in a number of villages to discourage the consumption of alcohol at village festivals and particularly at the harvest suppers held by farmers. Instead the clergyman or squire would seek to substitute a non-alcoholic harvest festival, at which, as at Pavenham in Bedfordshire during the early 1860s, stimulants were 'banished entirely, and with the happiest results, as the dinner . . . fully proved'.[40] In Norfolk, too, efforts were made to end the tradition of holding harvest suppers at public houses or in barns, where uncontrolled drinking was the order of the day.[41] But in general the endeavours of the temperance reformers met with limited success only, and until the end of the Victorian era prosecutions for drunkenness and associated assaults remained features of village life, and beer and tobacco were condemned as 'the cankerworms' which caused a man to 'fool away' his rent.[42]

However, that spirit of earnest endeavour which encouraged some mid-century landlords to seek to overcome the moral shortcomings of labouring people by promoting various schemes of social improvement also showed itself in their attitudes towards the administration of their estates. As James Caird pointed out in the title of his 1849 pamphlet *High Farming, under Liberal Covenants*, it was improved tillage that would prove *The Best Substitute for Protection*. He assured agriculturalists faced with the uncertainties of Corn Law repeal that their condition was far from hopeless, provided they seized their opportunities. In the case of landlords like Earl Fitzwilliam, Lord Althorp, the Duke of Bedford and Philip Pusey, Caird was preaching to the converted. Even in the 1820s Althorp had gone to the length of setting up a laboratory in his rooms in the Albany in order to acquaint himself with the new science of agricultural chemistry, while both he and Fitzwilliam devoted much time and attention to cattle breeding.[43] Indeed, during the 1840s Althorp (now Earl Spencer) wrote several articles on the latter subject, and after the death of his wife agriculture was said to have become the 'consuming passion' of his life. A few months before his own death in 1845 he appeared at the Royal Agricultural Society's show yard at Shrewsbury in his shirt sleeves to help push livestock into the sheds.[44]

In the eighteenth century there had, of course, been agricultural reformers, but in the immediate post-war years some of the impetus for experimentation and improved tillage was lost. After 1840 that enthusiasm revived and was carried farther than ever before. 'Improvement' became the order of the day: drainage schemes were completed, new buildings erected, machinery purchased and work on crop rotations and stock breeding carried out. The Duke of Northumberland spent £500,000 on improvements to his estate, though for the small return on capital of about 2.5 per cent. And the seventh Duke of Bedford carried his interest in the principles of stock-rearing so far that he permitted Woburn Park farm to become a centre for feeding experiments for the Rothamsted experimental station during the 1850s.[45]

In helping to spread these new ideas the agricultural societies played a significant role. As a writer on Norfolk agriculture pointed out in the 1840s, they provided a vital link between theory and practical knowledge, 'with just so much of sociableness as secures the free interchange of thought and opinion'.[46] Like the old Board of Agriculture itself (which had been wound up in 1822), the societies made little progress during the difficult post-war years, but from the 1840s they increased rapidly in size and importance. Particularly significant was the setting up, in 1838, of the Royal Agricultural Society of England (or the English Agricultural Society, as it was known until 1840). As early as 27 June 1838 – within about a month of its first meeting – the Society proposed prizes for essays on such topics as the 'Best Mode of Keeping Roots', 'Improved Rural Economy abroad', 'Insects Prejudicial to Plants' and many others.[47] It also began to make plans for prizes to be offered at its first show, which was held at Oxford in 1839.

When the Society was founded none of its promoters foresaw the importance of the mechanical department, but that soon changed. At the show held at Gloucester in 1853 2000 implements were exhibited; at the third show in 1841 there had been only 312, though even in 1843 Ransome's, the well-known firm of Suffolk machine makers, were proudly proclaiming the growing number of implements they had on the market. No longer were farmers and landowners reliant on the products of local blacksmiths; instead they could purchase specialist machinery. In the early 1840s Ransome's employed nearly 1000 craftsmen on the manufacture of ploughs, subsoil ploughs, scarifiers, harrows drills, rakes, rollers, mole ploughs, threshers, winnowers, seed dressers, feed mills, chaff and turnip cutters. Equipment was modified to suit differing soil types, crops and husbandry methods, and more than 300 varieties of plough alone were offered for sale.[48] Specialized machinery operators were recruited by the agricultural contractors who were now beginning to appear, their numbers jumping from 55 in 1851 to 1441 (including 236 machine proprietors) ten years later.[49] Alongside them were the general labourers, who were expected to mind machines as part of their daily routine. It was an indication of the changing times that in 1849 the East Suffolk Agricultural Association offered a prize of £3 to the man who kept 'in the best working order, his employer's drilling, horse hoeing, chaff-cutting, threshing, grinding and general agricultural machinery'.[50]

By the mid-1850s tenant farmers had taken over from the large proprietors as major purchasers of machinery. A contemporary considered at that time that the business of manufacturers had doubled since 1851, while from Buckinghamshire came a report that the 'most astounding revolution' had taken place in threshing machines. Formerly only a few horse machines had been used in the county: 'now there are several portable steam engines, which do their work admirably. These steamers are let out at 25s. or 30s. a-day and are constantly employed.' The shortage of labour during the Crimean War, of which railway builders also complained, helped the introduction of steam-threshing machines: 'This improved method of threshing is very opportune', wrote C. S. Read in 1855, 'for hand-threshing wheat had become almost impossible, and labourers do not now covet using the flail on Spring corn.'[51]

Other improvements could be carried through without the use of expensive implements, by changing the techniques of hand harvesting. In southern Britain the scythe and the bagging-hook became the predominant tools for cutting wheat, while in northern Britain the scythe replaced the sickle on all grains. The scythe was much faster to use than either the sickle or the reap-hook, and it therefore reduced labour costs. Opponents of the scythe argued 'that it was inefficient on a laid crop and that to abandon the sickle was to sacrifice neatness and grain-saving to speed and expediency'.[52] But by the middle of the century commercially minded farmers were weighing the respective merits of the two and more and more were coming down in favour of the scythe. In Norfolk the substitution of mowing for reaping shortened the harvest by 'at least a week . . . increased the quantity of straw, and consequently enlarged the quantity of farm-yard manure, now rendered doubly valuable by the system of high feeding'.[53] To William Dickinson, writing on farming in east Cumberland in 1852, the scythe was 'yearly becoming more of a harvest tool as people [got] acquainted with its uses and merits'. He noted that in the previous year the Carlisle District Farmers' Club had discussed the rival advantages of scythe and sickle, and that a farmer present had estimated the cost of mowing his grain with a scythe at 5s. 5d. per acre and of reaping with a sickle at 8s. 9d. per acre: 'There are other circumstances in favour of the scythe; for mowing need not be retarded in dewy mornings or during slight rain; the additional straw is of value; and the crop is ready for the stack three or four days earlier than when cut with the sickle.'[54]

Fertilizers, too, were more widely adopted by the new generation of 'high' farmers, while the active competition of rival manufacturers of the new products helped to popularize them: 'Many men who would not listen to the lectures of professors, or read the articles of chemical experts, were worried by persistent agents for the sale of patent manures into giving them a trial.' Their increasing use led to what has been called the 'second agricultural revolution' and improved yields of both grass and crops. Indirectly they also encouraged cleaner farming, since a man who had paid £10 a ton for manure was unwilling to waste half its value on wet, ill-drained land: 'Manure and drainage acted and reacted upon one another: the one encouraged the other.'[55]

With this greater expenditure, cost-conscious farmers grew anxious about the payment of compensation for unexhausted improvements, should they be required to leave their holdings at short notice. It is significant that it was in these years that the tenant rights issue came to the fore, and a Select Committee on agricultural customs reported in 1848. Although there was no statutory regulation of landlord–tenant relations until the final quarter of the nineteenth century, in many areas satisfactory local arrangements were made; Lincolnshire was a pioneer in this regard. A Bedfordshire farmer, William Bennett, told the Select Committee of the difficulties faced by those for whom customary compensation had not been established:

the landlord who lets his farm from year to year . . . is at liberty at any time to dismiss his tenant; and if there should be any misunderstanding, or if he should not go the right way at an election, or talk too freely of the injury of game, or in any other way offend the landlord, he can get rid of him, and there is no call upon him for compensation; the landlord can get rid of him with perfect impunity at the end of six months.[56]

A Northumberland auctioneer and commission agent pointed to the losses which could be incurred over fixed machinery, such as the massive steam-powered threshing machines which were common in that county. Although the outgoing tenant was in theory entitled to remove them, he rarely did so, and the incoming man was reluctant to pay much to take them over: 'I have seen a machine repaired to the amount of upwards of £100 two years before, sell for £40 at leaving.'[57] It was to end these uncertainties that James Caird enthusiastically advocated a return to the leasing of farms, since this practice had, in many areas, been abandoned in the post-war agricultural depression.

But apart from difficulties over compensation, it must not be forgotten that there were countless agriculturalists who were held back from improvement purely by their innate conservatism and lack of education. In the Vale of Gloucester, where the soil suffered from phosphate deficiency and overluxuriant hedgerows, Caird commented on the decreasing yields: 'Water stagnates in the soil, the industry of the farmer is paralysed, the energy of the labourer deadened, – nothing seems to thrive but the gigantic trees, whose roots in the smaller fields cover nearly their whole substratum like a network.' In 1861 the northern part of the Isle of Wight was described as 'a century behind-hand in practical agriculture' by the *Journal of the Royal Agricultural Society*, while a year earlier the same publication had commented on the deficiencies in the reaping and mowing machinery of Berkshire. It was in these circumstances that enthusiastic landlords and their agents could help by influence and example. Christopher Haedy, auditor to the Duke of Bedford, commented in 1842 on the lack of progress among tenant farmers in Devon and noted with approval that the estate's local agent was doing 'all he can to teach them. Making manure, growing green Crops, and keeping Cattle in the winter, all points they were wholly defective in'. He was in favour, too, of the Duke evicting bad tenants, since he considered this 'a salutary warning' to the rest.[58] In Berkshire Philip Pusey took a similar lead in introducing new agricultural implements and cropping methods; local farmers profited by avoiding his mistakes and adopting those innovations which he found successful.[59] In Essex the land agent and farmer John Oxley Parker was a firm advocate of mixed farming to counterbalance the county's old preoccupation with grain growing. As early as 1845 he also bought a tile-making machine for drainage work on his own farm; purchases of other implements followed shortly afterwards.[60]

The growing demand for meat and dairy produce from a larger, more affluent urban population helped to ensure the prosperity of the livestock producer. Even the agricultural labourer, as Caird noted, was occasionally able to 'indulge himself' with a meat dinner, or to season his dry bread with 'a morsel of cheese'.[61] And in the north of England the labourer's diet was likely to be a good deal better than that. High wool and hide prices meant that farmers who concentrated on animals and dairying enjoyed the best of both worlds, with good returns for the products of both live and dead stock. The rearing districts, located largely in the north and west, benefited from this, but the arable areas, too, shared in the gain, as farmers moved away from a concentration on grain growing towards mixed farming. As E. L. Jones has written, the strength of mixed farming in these years lay in

its special ability to accommodate a varying ratio of cereal to livestock product prices. . . . The system was an integrated one in which, if cereal prices were thought to be comparatively unremunerative, grain could be held back from the market and fed to the fatting stock in the hope of better returns from this quarter. There were certainly spells in the 'fifties when wheat was cheap enough for a little of it to be fed to animals.[62]

The new railway network speeded up the dispatch of livestock to market, thereby avoiding the serious weight losses and difficult travel incurred in sending them 'on the hoof' or by canal. In pre-rail days four shorthorns from Durham, destined for the English Agricultural Society's show at Oxford in 1839, had to walk from Kirklevington in that county to Hull; they travelled from thence by boat to London, were transhipped to a barge which took them by canal to Aylesbury and walked from there to Oxford, which was itself a distance of about twenty-one miles. One imagines they hardly looked their best on their arrival.[63] Ordinary livestock marketing presented similar, if less extreme, problems. A Norfolk farmer told Caird that a sheep lost 7 pounds in weight and 3 pounds inside fat, and a bullock 28 pounds, during a journey 'on the hoof' to London. In his view these losses represented upwards of £600 a year.[64] But in the new era cattle and sheep could be loaded on to trucks in the morning and reach London in the afternoon. Animal feed could be dispatched cheaply and easily by the same means, while it was now easier to select the optimum moment at which to sell. Many local trading connections were, however, undermined. Pastoral farmers in Bedfordshire bemoaned the fact that they had lost the main advantage of being relatively close to the London market. Now they faced competition from graziers in Leicestershire and Northamptonshire, who could send their animals to the capital by rail.[65]

Although cattle and sheep still walked across England to the major markets and fairs, the long-distance droving trade was in decline by the middle of the century. With its gradual disappearance, marketing centres also changed. Those which gained in importance were at the rail heads, like Craven Arms and Ludlow, which catered for livestock from north and mid-Wales, or Crewe and Banbury for cattle imported from Ireland.[66] As early as 1846 Captain Laws, a railway director, informed a parliamentary Select Committee that 'so far from the Graziers having any thing to do with driving Cattle 100 or 150 Miles, they will not do it at all, but they will get them upon the Railway and convey them to Market, and come back again; we allow always a Man to go in charge of Two Waggons for the safety of the Cattle themselves, and to return free'. Nevertheless, Laws thought that despite the expansion of trade, at that date a majority of animals was still being driven by road. Pigs were the exception. They 'always come to us, as they are bad Travellers'.[67] Within a year or two, however, the railways had made giant advances in the share of animals and other agricultural produce which they carried, and this was reflected in the growing general importance of goods traffic in their financial results. In 1845 freight contributed 36 per cent of the gross receipts of the nation's railways; by 1848 it had jumped to 43 per cent.[68]

Landowners, too, benefited from this new form of communication. Not only were they able to dispose of land on favourable terms to the railway companies while construction was in progresss but also those farm holdings with good rail access could be let at higher rentals. This was recognized in 1863 by a Select Committee of the House of Lords, when they heard evidence that 'about seven per cent [on the rental] would be a moderate estimate of the benefit that all the land within five miles of a railway station . . . would receive'. In addition the contribution made to local rates by the companies was often substantial. At the small Buckinghamshire village of Pitstone, which was crossed by the track of the London and Birmingham railway (later the London and North-Western) from the late 1830s, the railway was paying nearly 30 per cent of the total rates up to forty years later. Other parishes benefited in a similar manner.[69]

For the agricultural labourer, also, conditions began to show modest improvement in these mid-century years, though (particularly in the southern and south midland counties) they still left much to be desired. Nonetheless, benefits started to accrue from the new programme of cottage building embarked upon by 'improving' landlords, while, more important, cash wages moved upwards. In 1851 James Caird indicated the wide regional differences which persisted in the sums earned. The highest wage rate he encountered in his 1850–1 tour was 15s. per week, offered in parts of Lancashire; the lowest, 6s. a week, he found in south Wiltshire. In the northern counties wage rates were generally higher, thanks to

the proximity of manufacturing and mining enterprise. . . . The influence of manufacturing enterprise is thus seen to add 37 per cent. to the wages of the agricultural labourers of the Northern counties, as compared with those of the South. The line is distinctly drawn at the point where coal ceases to be found, to the south of which there is only one of the counties we visited in which the wages reach 10s. a week, Sussex.

He attributed this to the fact that well-to-do residents of Brighton and other Sussex coastal resorts provided alternative employment for local labourers.[70] Even within the high-wage counties there were considerable differences, emphasizing the local nature of most internal migration.[71] A report on Cheshire in 1844 suggested that 'in the vicinity of manufacturing or large towns, wages [were] nearly 20 per cent higher than in many parts of the interior, or in the south, south-western, and south-eastern districts', though to counterbalance this rent and food prices were higher in the former area than in the latter.[72]

Another closely related factor influencing wage rates was the emergence of labour shortages in some districts, thanks partly to the effect of migration but also to the labour-intensive tillage methods in vogue among improving farmers and landowners. C. S. Read, writing in 1858 of a scarcity of labourers in parts of west Norfolk, attributed this development not so much to population decrease as to the enlarged demand for workers to hoe and lift potatoes and turnips and to harvest the heavier crops now being grown.[73] At the same time migration to the towns clearly had a role to play, and it is noticeable that in the Midlands population falls first became apparent in parishes 'contiguous to the main line of the London and North-Western Railway'.[74] As early as 1836 there were claims that the migration opportunities offered by the railways had brought full employment to south-west Bedfordshire.[75] Overall, the number of those working on the land fell during the 1850s; the decline among indoor farm servants of both sexes was particularly notable. The drop in their numbers, continuing a trend which emerged in the Napoleonic wars, was not compensated for by the small increase in male farmers, bailiffs, shepherds and outdoor labourers (see Table 8).

However, if the availability of alternative employment outside agriculture and reductions in the supply of labour strengthened the bargaining power of the worker vis-à-vis his employer and helped to raise wage rates, these were not the only factors influencing pay levels.

Table 8 *Argicultural employment in England and Wales at the 1851 and 1861 censuses of population*

Occupation	1851 census	1861 census
Males		
Farmers and graziers	226,515	226,957
Farm bailiffs	10,561	15,698
Agricultural labourers (outdoor)	908,678	914,301
Shepherds	12,517	25,559
Farm servants (indoor)	189,116	158,401
Females		
Farmers and graziers	22,916	22,778
Agricultural labourers (outdoor)	44,319	43,964
Farm servants (indoor)	99,156	46,561
Total	1,513,778	1,454,219

SOURCES: 1851 Census, PP 1852–3, vol. 88, pt 1, and 1861 Census, PP 1863, vol. 53, pt 1.

The age and skill of the man himself had a role to play, as had the financial resources of his employer. Differences in the amount offered by farmers could be found within the same village. Presumably, the man who paid the most had the widest choice of workers, but given the conditions of underemployment which existed in some (though, as we have seen, not all) rural areas, labourers who were dissatisfied with their master's terms had no alternative but to accept them or to move away altogether. John Glyde described the situation in Suffolk in the mid-1850s:

Inquiries in the Bosmere and Hartismere Hundreds convinced us that in those districts the farmers generally paid 1s. or 1s. 6d. a-week less than the farmers of the Sanford Hundred, although they commonly brought their corn to the same market. Thus, in March 1853 we find by our 'notes' that the wages of farm labourers were at Wyverstone, 7s. 6d.; Bacton, 8s. and 8s. 6d.; Bricet, 8s.; Henley, 8s. 6d.; Hintlesham, 8s. 6d. and 9s.; Washbrook, 9s.; Bentley, 10s. Farmers in the same parish are often not uniform in the rate of wages. In one parish near the town of Ipswich we found one farmer paying 10s. a-week to his horsemen and laborers, a second paid 9s. to his horsemen and 8s. to his laborers, and a third 8s. 6d. a-week to both, without further privileges. Of two farmers whose land adjoined those last mentioned, though they lived in another parish, one paid 9s. to horsemen and allowed nine bushels of malt in the year, whilst the other paid the same wages and allowed the horsemen malt, two loads of wood, and cottages rent free.[76]

Significantly, in the village of Wyverstone, where wage rates were lowest, seventy-seven out of the parish's total male population of 173 were engaged as agricultural labourers or farm servants in 1851, while fourteen were farmers with holdings ranging from 1.5 acres to over 300[77] (see Table 7, p. 226).

Stockmen were normally paid more than general labourers because of their special skills and the fact that they had to work on Sundays to feed the animals, but even among the 'general' men the sums paid varied with the individual's own abilities, the amount being reduced as workers grew old. Wage rates at Viscount Dillon's model farm at Ditchley, Oxfordshire, for the week ending 17 October 1856 (see Table 9) give an idea of pay differences.[78] The basic rates earned could,

Table 9: *Daily wage rates at Ditchley model farm*

	s.	d.
James Hall, Cow Man	2	0
Isaac Iles, Carter	1	10
Edwd. Tidecombe, Carter	1	10
Charles Cross, Shepherd	1	10
Thos. Hitchcock – thatching*	1	10
John Hitchcock – thatching*	2	3
Wm. Painting	1	8
John Winter	1	8
James Rook	1	8
Wm. Humphries	1	2
Job Benfield	1	2
Thos. Moulden, ploughboy		9
Charles Corbett, ploughboy		8
Philip Sturdy		6
Irishman	1	8
Irishman	1	8
Irishman	1	8
Girl picking up Potatoes		6
Girl picking up Potatoes		6

*The two thatchers were normally paid at 1s. 8d. per day, as were most general labourers on this farm.

of course, be supplemented by piecework or contract earnings, notably at harvest and at spring hoeing, while stockmen often received a lump sum at Michaelmas or at Lady Day, when their annual agreements came to an end. In the Axminster union of Devon, where basic wages in the quarter ending Christmas 1860 were put at 8s. a week, it was estimated that these could be increased to 10s. or 12s. by task work, while in the Garstang district of Lancashire a basic 13s. a week could be pushed up to 18s. as a result of piecework. Elsewhere, though, groups of contract workers might be brought in for these piecework tasks – as on the Ditchley farm during July 1857, when there were payments to 'G. Packford & Company for Howing 11 a. 2 r. 22 p. of Swedes at 5/- per acre' and to David Biles and company for mowing 218 acres of grass at 3/6 per acre. Neither company leader was a regular employee of the farm. Clearly, then, these 'extra' tasks were not available to all workers, and in any case they applied on a seasonal basis only. They could also be more than counterbalanced, in the case of day labourers, by men being laid off without pay during the winter when work was short or by lower rates being paid in those difficult months. It is significant that the Axminster labourers considered that despite piecework earnings their actual pay averaged 'only 7s. per week' throughout the year.[79]

Yet these individual wage differences notwithstanding, it is apparent that the 1850s and 1860s saw an overall improvement in the sums paid. If the rates for the whole country are averaged out, thereby eliminating the important regional variations, the basic farm wage had risen from 9s. 7d. in 1850–1 to around 11s. 7d. a decade later and to 12s. 5d. by the end of the 1860s. Even in the low-wage rural south-west the advance was from 7s. 9d. to 10s. 6d. between the early 1850s and the later 1860s. Although retail prices rose over the period, wages managed to keep ahead (see Table 10).

Table 10 *Index of wages and prices, 1850–65*[80]

Year	Agricultural wages (England and Wales)	Average retail prices
1850	100	100
1862	125	111
1865	125	107

SOURCE: J. P. Dunbabin, 'Communications: the "revolt of the field"', *Past and Present*, no. 27 (April 1964), p. 112.

Nevertheless, even with this progress life for most labouring families remained difficult. When Caird visited south Wiltshire at the beginning of the 1850s he was curious to discover how one man and his family could survive on 6s a week, since in this case the children were too young to earn anything on their own account. For his breakfast, the Wiltshire labourer had

flour with a little butter, and water 'from the tea-kettle' poured over it. He takes with him to the field a piece of bread and (if he has not a young family, and can afford it) cheese to eat at mid-day. He returns in the afternoon to a few potatoes, and possibly a little bacon, though only those who are better off can afford this. The supper very commonly consists of bread and water. The appearance of the labourers showed, as might be expected from such meagre diet, a want of that vigour and activity which mark the well-fed ploughmen of the northern and midland counties. Beer is given by the master in hay-time and harvest.[81]

In some cases vegetables from the garden or potatoes from a strip planted in the farmer's field would help to eke out supplies, but save for the greater prominence of potatoes, the diet showed little improvement on that recorded for southern labourers by Sir Frederic Eden in the mid-1790s. Even in Bedfordshire, which was not in the lowest wage band, a woman born in 1850 remembered the poverty and deprivation of her early years. Her father, a milker, earned 7s. a week, and she often saw him

come home at night and sit down to eat a piece of bread ... and put a bit of lard on it, and pepper and salt to it. We used to have boiled onions almost every day to eat to our potatoes instead of meat, for there was eight of us to live, and I know I was glad to get enough to go off to a farm house at Riseley to get a good living ... my Brothers went to plough with a piece of bread and a red herring many a day.[82]

These experiences were very different from those of farm servants whom Caird encountered in the north of Derbyshire in 1851:

For breakfast they have porridge, then bread and cheese. They take with them to the field each man his pint of ale, and as much bread and cheese as he likes. At one o'clock they have dinner, which is either bacon, beef, or mutton, and pudding, with small beer *ad libitum*. At seven o'clock they have supper of milk porridge, then bread and cheese. . . . During harvest they have a quart of ale per day.[83]

The availability of alternative employment in manufacturing industry, urban transport and the mining industry induced northern farmers to offer these better terms to their workers, since only thus could they retain them (see Appendix 4 for additional budgets).

Fuel was another problem in the southern counties until the coming of the railways eased coal distribution. In Cornwall gorse and heather were cut to provide firing, while in Wiltshire cottagers burned peat when they could afford it. Coal, carried in sacks on the backs of ponies or donkeys, was used only by the blacksmiths.[84]

However, apart from aiding in the distribution of fuel and agricultural produce and in the migration of country people, the railways had a further important function, for whilst they were under construction during the mid-century years they provided work for unemployed or underemployed men in southern England. This was the case in south Devon during the 1840s, where labourers were attracted to the work by the higher wages offered. Sadly, many lacked the stamina needed to carry out the heavy tasks involved and they were forced to give up. Others, shocked at the lawless, migratory life led by the navvies, refused 'to submit to what they conceived a degradation, of working upon the works'.[85] But a number persisted, and others were taken on as brickmakers or tree fellers to meet the railways' insatiable demand for bricks and timber.[86]

The navvies' presence disrupted the communities through which they passed, and the incumbent of Cassington, Oxfordshire, was not alone when in 1854 he attributed falling attendance at church to the fact that cottagers had been corrupted by having 'as lodgers rail-road labourers for about 3 years, many of them being irreligious and vicious persons'. The farm workers had been 'much demoralized by the Railroad labourers who have so long resided with them, and five Public and Beer Houses in so small a Parish have their usual bad effects upon the morals of our young men'.[87] But at least railway construction brought temporary prosperity to many village communities by creating new jobs.

Given the economic pressures faced by rural families in the middle of the nineteenth century – even after the small improvements in living standards, which were being achieved – it is not surprising that children were sent to work as early as possible to help eke out a scanty parental income. At the 1851 census of population about 6000 boys under the age of ten were employed full-time as agricultural labourers, shepherds and farm servants (out of a total of 1,110,000 males so occupied).[88] But the number working on a part-time, unrecorded basis was far greater. As an assistant commissioner commented in 1843, in the context of child employment in the south-west: 'Boys begin to be regularly employed in farm-work as early as 7 in some few instances, but generally at 9 or 10.' Prior to that they would be kept away from school, bird scaring, watching cattle in the fields, getting wood for the fire, potato planting, stone picking, weeding, and taking part in hay and corn harvests. A strong boy of ten or eleven was thought capable of leading 'horses at plough.... As he gets to 13, 14 or 15, and his strength increases, he begins to hold the plough, and also to attend to the stable; at this age he also begins to help the carter, and he is allowed to drive the team.'[89] As we saw in the discussion about school attendance, it was only in the pastoral northern counties, where parental income was greater and the opportunities for early employment more limited, that recruitment of child labour was restricted. By contrast, it reached its highest level of exploitation in the arable eastern counties, notably Lincolnshire, Huntingdonshire, Norfolk, Cambridgeshire, Suffolk and, to a lesser degree, Northamptonshire, Bedfordshire and Nottinghamshire, where the public gang system prevailed.

Thanks to the success of fen drainage in bringing into cultivation extensive new tracts of land, a large labour force was needed to till the soil. Yet as in the Deeping fen in Lincolnshire, regular day labourers were 'almost unknown' in the area, and cottage accommodation in the vicinity of the new farms virtually non-existent, so although the horse work on the farms in the mid-1860s was carried out by resident farm servants, the remainder of the tasks were performed by 'catchwork' labourers and gangs of women and children brought in from villages and market towns several miles away.[90] At Castle Acre in Norfolk, where the gang system had become established early, it was reported in 1843 that children as young as four or five were employed, sometimes walking five, six or seven miles to their work, and then, if it rained, having to walk back again without earning anything. The gang masters had great power over the children they recruited, and beatings and ill-treatment were the lot of those youngsters who did not keep pace with the rest. According to the vicar of Castle Acre, 'no gang of wretched slaves beneath the sweltering sun of the tropics, could materially fall beneath the generality of persons thus assembled together in intellectual debasement and moral depravity'.[91] A mother admitted that her children's hands were 'so blistered pulling the turnips that I've been obliged to tie them up every night this winter. Pulling turnips blisters the hands very much; they're obliged to pull them up; they must not take turnip-cromes (a sort of fork), for fear of damaging the turnips.'[92] And she added: 'I never heard any one who did not say they disliked it.'

For their efforts the younger children earned a paltry 3d. or 4d. a day; up to 9d. a day was paid to the older ones. Yet so great were the pressures of family poverty that they continued to work, despite the adverse effect on their health and the possible moral dangers posed. One man, whose daughter, aged eleven, had worked for two years in a gang and whose back had been strained by stone picking, openly declared: 'Ganging is what leads 'em into so many bad ways; that's what causes . . . girls to be out of nights, when they ought to be at home.'[93] Many ganging girls became prostitutes, and illegitimate births were common among them. Yet it was not until 1867 that the Agricultural Gangs Act tried to combat some of the worst abuses. It made eight the minimum age for employment; it outlawed gangs of mixed sex; and it required gang masters to be licensed by the magistrates.

Unfortunately, these restrictions applied only to public gangs, which moved around from farm to farm. Private gangs recruited by a single farmer on his own account were not covered, nor were children employed elsewhere in agriculture. As the rector of Brandistone wrote in 1855:

Till Norfolk is made sensible of the vast importance of educating her children and showing at least an equal interest in *them* as she now does in fattening oxen and sheep, on which no labour is spared, she may rest assured that her present agricultural grandeur, achieved by her reckless inattention to the well-being of her labouring classes will, ere long, draw her into a still deeper abyss of immorality and vice.[94]

A few years earlier Charles Kingsley had made much the same point in his novel *Alton Locke*, when he contrasted a flock of highly bred, overfed, fat sheep with the two 'half-starved shivering' children 'who were their slaves'. The youngsters – 'little wretches with blue noses and white cheeks, scarecrows of rags and patches, their feet peeping through bursten shoes twice too big for them' – were engaged in cutting up turnips. But so cold was it that the turnips had frozen and they could not turn the handle of the cutter. Their hands were purple with chilblains and 'they were so sorefooted they could scarcely limp'.[95] These two unfortunates had many real-life counterparts, and the isolated, monotonous days they spent scaring birds or tending animals made them dull-witted and tongue-tied – the archetypal 'chawbacons' beloved of cartoonists.

But if labourers' children worked long hours on the land, particularly in the southern and eastern counties, much the same applied to the offspring of small farmers. As one Cumbrian smallholder observed, he expected his sons to begin to assist with farm work 'as soon as they [could] crawl'.[96] Even by better-off agriculturalists hard work was required. William Clift of Bramley, Hampshire, whose father farmed about 190 acres, remembered the stringent regime he had to follow when he began work on the family holding in the early 1840s:

Our time for rising was 4.30 in the summer, and shortly after 5 in winter. Before breakfast we had all the cattle to feed; and after breakfast (which we took at 6 in the summer, and about 6.30 in the winter) we started, with the

carters, to our work for the day. We had breakfast by . . . rushlight in
winter. . . .

Out early in the field, we set to work till luncheon time. My two eldest
brothers, Thomas and Daniel, were the two carters, John was seedsman, and
I harrow-boy. It was our general practice to have our luncheon in the field
when out with the horses. It usually consisted of bread and cheese, with
small beer, which was brewed at home specially for that purpose, and which
we carried to the field in wooden bottles. We always drank from a wooden
bottle, first the carters and then the boys. . . . A piece of good hay was laid
down to each horse for his lunch at the same time. . . . We used to stop from
twenty minutes to half-an-hour for luncheon, never more. Then on to work
. . . till three o'clock, when the teams 'shot off', except the harrow-boy's team,
which was left behind the others to finish up the day's work properly. . . .
I thought mine was the hardest job in the field: I had to keep my harrows
clean, and stay after the others had gone home to finish the work up all close.
Furrows had to be struck and made clear for the water to get off in case there
came a shower in the night.[97]

From Michaelmas to Christmas William's eldest brother, Thomas,
took corn to sell in Reading each week, and this meant he had to leave
home at midnight on Friday in order to arrive in good time for the
Saturday market. Horses and waggon set off in style for their journey,
for the carters took great pride in their teams. The horses' tails were
neatly plaited and tied with coloured braid, and most of them wore
bells. According to Clift, a team 'going away from home, was not
reckoned in first-class style unless furnished with bells. The bells were
fixed in iron frames by leather hoops, and the frames were fixed to the
two hames of the horse. . . . Each set of bells was tuned harmoniously.'

In the early Victorian countryside, then, as in the eighteenth century,
agriculture provided the principal employment for men and boys,
while for women and girls the main outlet lay in domestic service. In
1851 one in every four women in employment was a servant, and the
majority of them were country girls, who would start their working
life in the households of local clergymen, small tradespeople or farmers,
where wages were low but where they could learn the rudiments of
their duties.[98] Nevertheless, in all communities rural crafts and industries had a significant role to play, often in support of, or in association
with, agriculture. For despite the advances made in internal communications and mass-production techniques in some industries, up to the
middle of the nineteenth century the craftsman managed to retain his
central position in village life and with it the independence that running
a small business could bestow.

Often crafts ran in families, with son succeeding father on the same premises. A number of tradesmen, too, like their Georgian predecessors would take on a whole variety of jobs, according to the vagaries of seasonal employment or to supplement their income. Thus in Bedfordshire around one-third of those owning village brickworks were also farmers.[99] Elsewhere a thatcher might turn to hay trussing for the summer season or a hurdle maker to repairing carts and waggons, while pig killing, teeth drawing or the doctoring of farm livestock provided profitable sidelines for other men. At Bramley William Clift remembered that James Gosling, who kept the 'Three Pigeons' beerhouse, was also a shoemaker and preacher: 'On Sundays he combined preaching with beer-selling, opening his premises from two o'clock to three for business purposes, and from three to five o'clock to hold a religious service.' Then there was the Bramley baker, who combined this trade with that of grocer, bacon curer, corn merchant and farmer.[100] Joseph Arch, the future agricultural trade union leader, combined work as a prize-winning hedgecutter with employment as a carpenter's labourer for a friend: 'Then my skill at hurdle-making and gate-hanging would come in handy at odd times. Being a good all-round man I was never at a loss for a job.'[101]

As in earlier decades, it was customary for workers in many districts to leave their home parish in the late summer to take part in the harvesting of a community some distance away whose grain ripened earlier or later than that at home. Labourers from Bramley, for example, went into south Hampshire for a fortnight's harvest work before the local corn was ready and then travelled into a more backward county, like Wiltshire, to get another two or three weeks' work when the Bramley harvest was finished.[102] Migratory Irish workers, as on Viscount Dillon's estate, added to the harvest labour in several districts. This was no new development, but from the 1840s their mobility and the size of their catchment areas were increased by the railways. Many went by train from Lancashire to the fens and the eastern counties.[103] At Whittlesford in Cambridgeshire Mr G. N. Maynard remembered groups of ragged Irishmen arriving each year with their wives to help get in the harvest. They worked hard during the week but on Sundays clubbed together to buy beer. Then returning to the 'shade of some friendly hedge row or tree . . . would drink – confusion to the Saxon, and redress to the wrongs of Ould Ireland'.[104] By the late 1850s the peak of the Irish migrations had passed, as the population of Ireland itself fell, thanks to the effects of famine, epidemic disease, and emigration in the 1840s. Increasing numbers of migrants were also diverted into non-agricultural work and became, like the men of Leinster, semi-permanent migrants.

Within the major trades village craftsmen like blacksmiths had to be ready to turn their hands to a whole range of specialist tasks, from shoeing a horse and repairing agricultural implements to plugging holes in leaking cooking pans or even ringing pigs to prevent them from grubbing up the floor of the sty. A similar versatility was expected of the village mason or carpenter. According to Walter Rose, whose family kept a carpenter's shop at Haddenham, Buckinghamshire, there was no field for miles around 'but had its gate that sooner or later would need repair: no farmer who did not need his new cow-cribs, sheep-troughs, or ladders. No house, from the vicarage to the labourer's cottage, but had at some time or other a defect in its woodwork for which the services of our men would be required.'[105]

Alongside these were villagers with smaller skills, like the mole catcher, the herbalist and the pedlar. Among the women were dressmakers, laundresses, who worked for the families of the squire, parson and larger farmers, midwives, and nurses. Often, though, women gave nursing care to one another without any fee or reward: 'those best acquainted with the working classes in villages agree that the sympathy of the poor is the best alleviator of the sufferings of the poor', wrote John Glyde in the mid-1850s.[106] There were, too, a few women who kept small shops, where bread, shoes, tea, cheese, tapes, ribbons, bacon, coffee and other commodities were offered for sale in comfortable disarray.

In some districts cottage industries or small factories still provided employment for villagers, particularly the women and children, for although textile production had been hard hit by industrial developments in the north of England, there were a few communities in which domestic clothmaking survived. Until the end of the Crimean War those living in the east of Norfolk were able to do weaving for Norwich manufacturers. A middle man brought the yarn and took away the completed lengths of cloth, though his deductions for expenses and for defects in the work left a mere pittance for the weavers.[107] Pillow lacemaking was carried on in the south midlands and Devon; straw plaiting, for the hat and bonnet trade, around Luton and Dunstable; glovemaking in the south-west, Worcestershire and Herefordshire; hand knitting in the Yorkshire dales; hosiery work in the east Midlands; and net making or 'braiding' on the East Anglian, Dorset and Cornish coasts. There were many other examples.

Among the parishes heavily involved in domestic industry was

Little Horwood in Buckinghamshire, where there were sixty-five women of varying ages engaged in lacemaking in 1851 and nine working as plaiters (out of a total population of 339 – see Table 7), while at Sherrington in the same county there were 170 lacemakers out of a total female population of 419. Thirty-five of these were under the age of fifteen, and some were aged a mere seven or eight years. The oldest workers were in their eighties.[108] About nineteen of the men at Sherrington made mats, another well established domestic trade which occupied many workers in the parish during the eighteenth century. Elsewhere, notably in south Bedfordshire, central and south-east Buckinghamshire and Hertfordshire, it was plaiting which provided the major employment. By 1851 80 per cent (or nearly 22,000) of the total workers in the plait trade lived in the south-east Midlands, over 10,000 of them in south Bedfordshire alone. Even men would plait as a secondary occupation when demand was brisk, though in the view of many critics this 'busy' season had its less desirable side, encouraging 'vacant minds, dirty cottages, neglected children and illegitimate births'.[109]

The Lakeland was the main centre of another rural industry – the making of bobbins to supply the needs of cotton, woollen, silk and linen factories all over Britain. The industry was conducted in small factories, and in 1844 it was reported that so great was demand that 'not enough hands [could] be got for the orders coming in'. At that date Cumbrian bobbin establishments could be counted in dozens, but in a decade or two they were to be counted in scores. Crook in Westmorland, where fourteen men were engaged as bobbin turners and borers in 1851, was one community so involved (see Table 7). The simpler bobbins were made from local coppice wood, which was cut into slices of a few inches' diameter and then formed into smaller cylinders, which were immediately afterwards dried out in a kiln or drying room. Later the centre of each cylinder was bored and the ends of the holes cleared, usually by a boy working a machine with a rotating bit: 'skilled operators, usually adult, submitted the bobbin to more accurate turning and smoothing or bevelling, after which the product might also be polished with beeswax or dyed'.[110]

Ultimately all of these trades were to come under pressure as industrialization spread its tentacles ever more widely. But in the middle of the nineteenth century much of the old self-sufficiency still survived in rural communities. The village wheelwright, blacksmith, miller and carpenter were able to satisfy most local needs, while virtually every parish had its tailor, its dressmaker and its shoemaker. For those seeking more specialized purchases or a little variety there were the market towns which could be visited on foot or by carrier's cart. For the farmer and smallholder these little towns provided a ready outlet for the grain, dairy produce, fruit, poultry and meat which were not disposed of on larger contracts, just as they had done a century earlier. Only to sophisticated outsiders, like R. S. Surtees's fictional Mr Sponge, did they appear narrow and unsatisfactory. One small town encountered by Mr Sponge was 'Barleyboll', which 'had a pond at one end, an inn in the middle, a church at one side, a fashionable milliner from London, a merchant tailor from the same place, and a hardware shop or two where they also sold treacle, Dartford gunpowder, pocket-handker-chiefs, sheep-nets, patent medicines, cheese, blacking, marbles, mole-traps, men's hats, and other miscellaneous articles'.[111]

In the decades that lay ahead this already crumbling self-sufficiency was to disappear altogether, as the growth of the railway network, the arrival of cheap newspapers and the general improvement in internal communications made country people aware of the opportunities – both economic and social – which lay beyond the boundaries of their own parish. Some emigrated to the United States or Australasia; others moved to industrial centres within Britain itself. In many respects, therefore, these mid-century years were ones of transition, as the old order inexorably gave way to the new. A symptom of this was the fact that from the 1820s to the 1850s the rural population was growing relatively slowly – by around 28 per cent in the course of those thirty years – at a time when the number of people living in England and Wales as a whole increased by approximately 50 per cent, though not until the later 1860s did it cease to grow at all.[112] Again, at the census of 1851 the urban population of Britain for the first time exceeded that living in rural areas. By 1861 these urban dwellers outnumbered their rural counterparts in the ratio of five to four.[113] Thereafter the trend continued, until at the time of Queen Victoria's death less than a quarter of the population lived in country districts. The close-knit, narrow, rural world of the eighteenth and early nineteenth centuries had vanished for ever under the impact of the acquisitive drives and class divisions which characterized industrial society.

It was among the agricultural labourers that the greatest changes were apparent. While the number of farmers remained roughly the same, the size of the work force they employed began to fall signifi-cantly from the 1850s. In the towns the real wages of unskilled workers might be about the same as in the villages, while housing conditions were often worse, but the *opportunities* for economic advance beckoned

– and, most important, the social and political pressures of squire and parson were absent. True, the towns 'had their own forms of oppression for . . . working people', but 'there was nothing quite equal to the deadweight of custom and tradition in the countryside'.[114] It was the 'pull' of wider opportunities, combined with the 'push' effect of discontent with conditions at home, which induced the rural exodus of the second half of the nineteenth century. An analysis of that movement, however, falls outside the scope of the present study. Suffice it here to point out that the first absolute decline in county population totals started in Wiltshire in England and Montgomery in Wales during the 1840s and spread to Cambridgeshire, Huntingdonshire, Norfolk, Rutland, Somerset and Suffolk in England, and Anglesey, Brecknock and Cardiganshire in Wales in the following decade. The more rural an area was, the more likely it was to suffer a heavy outflow of population.[115] That was the message of Victorian Britain. As such, it was the inevitable product of the decades of agricultural and industrial change which linked the world of George III with that of his granddaughter and which ensured the final toppling of agriculture from its age-old position of economic dominance.

Appendix 1 Labouring people's budgets in the 1780s

Accounts of the Expences and Earnings of Labouring Families in the Parish of Barkham in the County of Berks, taken at Easter 1787*

Weekly Expences of a Family, consisting of a Man and his Wife, and five Children, the eldest eight years of age, the youngest an Infant.

	s.	d.
FLOUR: 7½ gallons, at 10d. *per* gallon	6	3
Yeast, to make it into bread, 2½d.; and salt 1½d.		4
Bacon, 1 lb. boiled at two or three times with greens: the pot-liquor, with bread and potatoes, makes a *mess* for the children		8
Tea, 1 ounce, 2d.; – ¾ lb. sugar, 6d.; ½ lb. butter or lard, 4d.	1	0
Soap, ¼ lb. at 9d. *per* lb.		2¼
Candles, ⅓ lb. one week with another at a medium, at 9d.		3
Thread, thrum, and worsted, for mending apparel, &c.		3
Total	8	11¼

*From David Davies, *The Case of Labourers in Husbandry* (London, 1795), pp. 8, 10, 15, 18.

I

Weekly Earnings of the Man and his Wife, viz.

The man receives the common weekly wages 8 months in
    the year

By task-work the remaining 4 months he earns something
    more: his *extra* earnings, if equally divided among the 52
    weeks in the year, would increase the weekly wages about

The wife's common work is to bake bread for the family,
    to wash and mend ragged clothes, and to look after the
    children; but at bean-setting, haymaking, and harvest,
    she earns as much as comes one week with another to
    about

	s.	d.
The man receives the common weekly wages	7	0
By task-work extra	1	0
The wife earns about		6
Total	8	6
Deficiency of earnings		5¼

*Weekly Expences of a Family, consisting of a Man and his Wife,
with four small Children, the eldest under 6 years of age, the
youngest an Infant.*

	s.	d.
Flour, 6 gallons, at 10d. per gallon	5	0
Yeast, 2d. – salt 1½d.		3½
Bacon 1 lb.		8
Tea, 1 ounce, 2d. – sugar, ¾ lb. 6d. – butter, ½ lb. 4d.	1	0
Soap, ¼ lb. 2¼d. – candles, ⅓ lb. 3d. – thread, &c. 3d.		8¼
Total	7	7¾

Weekly Earnings of the Man and his wife, viz.

The husband, if he has constant health and constant
    employment, earns on an average

The wife, like No. 1, does not earn above

	s.	d.
The husband earns on an average	8	0
The wife does not earn above		6
Total	8	6
Surplus of earnings		10¼

[However, to this had to be added *annual* outgoings, viz. rent of a cottage and garden, estimated at £2 for a family; fuel, being cut on the common, from 10s. to 12s. – say 10s.; clothing – £3 10s. for a man, wife and three children; lying-in, one year with another, 10s.; casualties, including sickness, loss of time thereby, and burials, estimated at 10s. This made a sum of £7. When these items were taken into account *both* families had a deficiency of earnings, amounting to £8 16s. 9d. per annum for the *first* family and £5 2s. 7d. for the *second*.]

Clothing

1. The *man's:* wear of a suit *per annum* 5s.; wear of a working jacket and breeches 4s.; two shirts 8s.; one pair of stout shoes nailed 7s.; two pair of stockings, 4s.; hat, handkerchief, &c. 2s. Sum £1 10s.
2. The *wife's:* wear of gown and petticoats 4s.; one shift 3s. 6d.; one pair of strong shoes 4s.; one pair of stockings 1s. 6d.; two aprons 3s.; handkerchiefs, caps &c. 4s. Sum £1.
3. The *children's:* their clothing is (usually) partly made up of the parents' old clothes, partly bought at second-hand: what is bought (supposing *three* children to a family) cannot well be reckoned at less than £1: where there are more than three children, 7s. may be added; and where there are fewer, 7s. may be deducted, for each. – Let the whole be estimated at *£3 10s.* for clothing for *family*.

Note. Very few poor people can afford to lay out this sum in clothes; but they should be enabled to do it: some cottagers breed a few fowls, with which they buy what sheets and blankets they want: but those who live in old farmhouses are seldom allowed (to use their own words) *to keep a pig or a chick.*

Appendix 2 Paternalism and social policy on the landed estate:

Wrest Park, Bedfordshire, in the early nineteenth century

The following are extracts from letters written by Lewis Harrison, the estate steward at Wrest Park, Silsoe, to his employer, Baroness Lucas.* They are all written in the third person.

Letter dated 8 April (c. 1807)

Mr. H[arrison] has increased the wages of two or three of the Labourers as they had less than the farmers give. Those who receive milk remain as before. Very few of the poor have the advantage of procuring milk for their families, and Mr. H. cannot help suggesting that the Tenants should be compelled to sell them a certain quantity. It is a great hardship upon the poor of Silsoe &c., not to be able to purchase either milk, coals, or small beer: Mr. Harrison would be happy to point out to Lady Lucas means in her Ladyship's power, to enable the poor people to buy those necessaries in future and which he will mention in London.

Mr. Harrison has lately brought to conviction & punishment, three more wood stealers, one of whom he is sorry to say, is a humble tenant to her Ladyship. His name is Webb of Clophill, & Mr. Harrison in consequence gave him a legal notice to quit at Michaelmas, which Lady Lucas may confirm or not as she thinks proper. The only penalty was a fine of ten shillings each and expenses. . . .

Letter dated 1 November 1808

. . . I have long since found out a person to supply your Ladyship with malt – the man lives at Westoning. I preferred him to either of the Ampthill or Shefford Malsters on account of his having two votes at

*At Bedfordshire Record Office, L30/11/132/6, L30/11/132/36 and L30/11/132/62 respectively.

command, which he voluntarily assured me should be at your Lady-ship's disposal. . . .

The late Underkeeper (Wilmore) was released from his miseries this morning, an event not to be regretted by any one. His life was a burden to the poor man, as well as to your Ladyship and to the Charitable Society of which he was a member. . . .

I have lately enlarged the nursery at the back of the kitchen garden, in order to sow a great quantity of Crab seed & hawthorn for the numberless hedgerows required on the Estate. . . .

Letter dated 26 November 1809

. . . While on the subject of brewing, Mr. Harrison takes the liberty of suggesting to her Ladyship, that it would be a comfort to the greater part of the Inhabitants of Silsoe & others (particularly to the House-keepers who do not brew their own) if Carter [a publican] was obliged to sell his own, brewed from *malt* & *hops* – it is a real evil, that so many Brewers in the County amass large fortunes at the expence of the public – The Duke of Bedford will not suffer his publican tenants to sell any other than their own brewing, and if Lady Lucas thought proper to desire Carter to do the same, her fiat would be instantly obeyed – He once mentioned to Carter, that her Ladyship wished something of the kind, & told him, how much it would answer an Innkeeper's purpose. He made objections on account of the want of brewhouse & utensils, which in plain English meant that he was getting as rich as a Jew without trouble, expence, or inconvenience and would like to go on as usual – indeed he is becoming so independent, that his charges are enormous, & his manners uncivil to almost everyone – he has been a bad Tenant to the house (which he has had many years *for nothing*) having neglected to white wash or paint the sitting rooms in a neat or comfortable manner.

If her Ladyship thought proper to write Carter a note, that on reletting the Inn, with more land, she should expect him not to sell any more Brewers beer, & should desire her Steward to see that her wishes were carried into effect, all difficulties would instantly vanish. . . .

Mr. Harrison is going to a Magistrate to morrow to prosecute some Woodstealers, who have had the assurance to go with a ladder, hatchet, & saw to the Warren Wood, & lop the large branches off the timber – he hopes a more exemplary punishment, than has been before inflicted, will take place. . . . They are very old offenders (four in number) to one of whom her Ladyship gave four or five pollard trees to build him a Cottage, & which he has since had notice to quit, for being detected in the middle of the night upon his masters Walnut tree – he has not attended to his notice, but Mr. H. will consult Mr. Ware as to the best measures to be pursued with him. . . .

Appendix 3 *Extracts from the diary of the Rev. W. C. Risley, vicar of Deddington, for 1838*[*]

Like many other clergymen, Risley was also a justice of the peace. Frequently in rural areas the beneficed clergyman was the only person of educational and social standing in the community. The property qualification for a justice of the peace was raised in 1774 from £40 to £100, and there were many 'open' parishes where the incumbent was one among the very few thus qualified. South Lindsey, Lincolnshire, was one area where the shortage of gentry meant that clergymen were pressed into service as magistrates. In 1824 clergymen and squarsons outnumbered plain squires on the bench by 18 to 15; in 1856, laymen just had the advantage, at 24 to 20
James Obelkevich, *Religion and Rural Society: South Lindsey, 1825–1875* (Oxford, 1976), 32.

14th April: . . . Sent Edmund to Banbury for D. Newton the Neithrop Constable who came over in the course of the day when I offered him this parish & Great Barford – he promised to return his answer yea or nay on Monday next. Sent for two young lads Osborne & Thos. Matthews & reprimanded them for misbehaving themselves in the Churchyard yesterday evening. Matthews, & the other for pelting on the leads of the Church. . . .
15th April: . . . Had a Letter from D. Newton this Evening accepting our offer of becoming our policeman. . . .
16th April: . . . Attended a meeting at Adderbury relative to the selection of a Police man for Adderbury East & West, Milton, & Little Barford – all the respectable persons nearly were present. . . when they deputed me to write to Henry Barnes of Chipping Norton & offer him 63 guineas per annum to undertake the situation. He is 2nd man at Cg. Norton & came from London. Wrote this Evening on my return home – & ordered my Groom to take the Letter the first thing in the morning. . . .

*At the Bodleian Library, MS D.D. Risley, CI 3, vol. 5.

17th April: . . . Edmund went to Chipping Norton & Barnes the Policeman came over & I sent him down to Mr. W. Gardner at Adderbury. . . . A man named Miller one of the Policemen at Oxford called to know if I could & would recommend him to fill a situation in this District as such, I told him I had recommended him & would do so again – but at present there was no opening for him – but that the people at Bloxham would shortly want a policeman & I advised him to offer himself to them. . . .

20th April: The Vestry was adjourned till two o Clock at the Kings Arms I presided & . . . Daniel Newton was chosen our Policeman at a guinea a week payment – he was also deputed to superintend the Mendicity Office & its duties . . . & to live in the house. . . .

14th May: Sent two boys of the ages of 15 & 16 to prison for 3 weeks for having set fire to a cottage at Little Barford by the improper use of gunpowder & injuring the same to the amount of £5 or £6 – Names *Tims & Hiorns*.

18th May: . . . Went up to Mr. Field's to hear a vagrancy case from Adderbury. Dismissed the woman with a reprimand, & some advice as to her future Conduct. . . .

19th May: Heard a case of injuring fences or hedge *pulling* against two women Coles & Payne, ordered Cole to pay 3s. & Payne 2s. . . .

26th May: . . . Heard two cases of Vagrancy from Adderbury against a married woman named Sarah West, & a young woman named Mary Waitman – committed them both to prison, West for 3 months & Waitman for 1 month. West had been convicted before of the same misdemeanour. . . .

30th May: On my return home found Miller the Adderbury Policeman waiting for me to hear a poaching case, Jas. Gibbs of this place was caught taking up 15 Night Lines or eel ties, he was found at the same spot yesterday & cautioned not to repeat it on the same ground & water – Mr. H. Stilgoe's of Adderbury grounds. . . . Committed him for two months in default of the payment of the five pounds penalty awarded against him according to the Act. . . .

4th June: . . . Sent for Newton the policeman to beg that he would defer flogging young Calcott of Hempton till he had seen Mr. Lechmore again from me. . . .

6th June: . . . Committed two young lads to prison – John Calcott for trial at the Sessions for felony at Great Barford – & Wm. Major of Deddington for wilful damage to Wm. Pullen's mowing grass – 14 days . . . A brother of Henry Mullington's of Little Tew called about bailing his brother committed by me for trial at

Sessions for felony – I gave my Consent in writing for his admission to bail. . . .*

8th June: . . . Granted a summons to young Mr. Hall of Barford against his servant man for leaving his place for 3 days & going to Sutton Club. . . .

11th June: . . . Granted a warrant against David Wrightson of Aynhoe for injuring in a very cruel & barbarous manner his master's horse Mr. James Griffin of the same place – Committed him to prison for 1 month & hard labour. . . .

13th June: . . . Baster the policeman called to get an order signed for conveying a prisoner to Gaol. [These policemen were employed by the parishes concerned as 'professionals', as opposed to the old parish constables.]

*At the Quarter Sessions held on 2 July 1838 John Calcott (or Colcott) aged ten was sentenced to a month's imprisonment in the House of Correction and 'during that time to be once whipped' for having stolen 'ten pence in copper money, the property of Joseph Morrey, of Great Barford'. Henry Mullington, aged twenty, was acquitted at the same sessions with having stolen three faggots at Great Tew. Oxfordshire Record Office, QSP. I 12.

Appendix 4 *Labouring people's budgets in the 1840s and 1850s*

The income and expenditure of J. Allen, a labourer from Bolton Percy, near York, his wife Jane and five children, for the period 1 March 1841 to 28 February 1842

Allen's basic daily rate of 2s. 4d. was above the average for agricultural labourers at this date; his wife was paid 8d. or 10d. according to season, and his boy 6d. or 8d.

Income, 1 March 1841 to 28 February 1842

	£	s.	d.
Man	36	4	4
Wife	8	8	10
Boy	5	18	7
Total	50	11	9

Expenditure, 1 March 1841 to 28 February 1842

	£	s.	d.
Flour	19	0	5
Yeast		11	7
Soap		17	5
Sugar	1	18	6½
Coffee and Tea	1	11	5
Candles		14	6½
Oatmeal		7	11½
Bacon		4	8
Milk	1	6	4
Butter	1	0	7¼
Meat	4	17	1
Eggs		2	0
Black currants and raisins		1	6
Potatoes		17	9
Salt			11½
Treacle		3	6½
Brimstone			2
Apples		2	8
Rice			8
Cheese		3	0
Coal	1	18	2
Cotton		9	8½
Worsted		5	0½
Rent	4	0	0
Children's schooling		6	0
Clothing club (4d. per week)		17	4
Miscellaneous*	5	10	10
Total	47	9	10¾

*'Miscellaneous' items included leather for shoes, print for dresses, £2 5s. paid to the tailor, 1s. 10d. for a sweeping brush, 11d. for a prayer book and 1s. for gloves. Expenditure on flour accounted for about two-fifths of the total.

SOURCE: Calculated from accounts in *Reports of Special Assistant Poor Law Commissioners on The Employment of Women and Children in Agriculture*, PP 1843, vol. 12, pp. 302–6. (There are errors of addition in the subtotals printed in the 1843 volume.)

Weekly budget of a Suffolk labourer and his wife (no children)
c. 1850

Income		£	s.	d.
	Weekly wages		8	0

Expenditure

		£	s.	d.
	1 stone of flour		1	10
	½ lb. of butter			6
	1 lb. of cheese			7½
	1½ oz. of tea			4½
	½ lb. of sugar			2
	Rent of cottage		2	0
			5	6
	Balance for sundries*		2	6
			8	0

*'Sundries' would have to cover clothing, shoes and any meat, bacon or milk purchased.

SOURCE: James Caird, *English Agriculture in 1850–51*, 2nd edn (London, 1968), p. 147.

Prices in the Stamford area, on the borders of Lincolnshire, Leicestershire and Northamptonshire, in 1770, when Arthur Young visited the district, and in 1851,* when James Caird did so

	1770		1851	
	s.	d.	s.	d.
Beef, per lb.		3		5½
Mutton, per lb.		3		5
Butter, per lb.		6	1	0
Pork, per lb.	n.a.			5
Milk, per quart	n.a.			2
Bread, per lb.		2		1¼
Wheat, per quarter	41	4	40	0
Labourers' wages per week	6	0	10	0
Women at weeding corn and haymaking	n.a.		8 or 1	0 } per day

*The basic wage here was appreciably higher than that quoted for Suffolk.

	1770	1851
	s. d.	s. d.
Boys who can plough per week	n.a.	5 0 (without food)
Cottage rents	20 0 (with an acre of land)	30 0 on great estates, with 1 rood of land; 80 0 in open villages, with small garden.
Average produce of wheat on good sandy loam	20 bushels	28 bushels
Rent per acre of farms	5s. to 7s.	20s. to 30s.

SOURCE: James Caird, *English Agriculture in 1850–51*, p. 407.

Wages paid to labourers on a farm of 400 acres in Nottinghamshire for the year ending 25 March 1861

No.	Days employed	Wages received	Average per day	Year's receipt, incl. for family	Average week in year	Remarks
		£ s. d.	£ s. d.	£ s. d.	£ s. d.	
1	313	28 12 0	1 10	43 1 0½	16 11	Cowman, with rent-free cottage and garden, milk, fuel &c. and paid to board a servant
2	293	38 13 0	2 7½	52 19 11	1 0 4½	}
3	303	37 0 2	2 5¼	52 13 4	1 0 3	
4	291¼	39 11 3	2 8½	41 13 10	16 0½	
5	304½	37 6 5	2 5¼	37 6 5	14 4¼	} Regular Labourers
6	298¼	37 5 7	2 6¼	37 5 7	14 4	
7	304	35 11 8	2 4	35 11 8	13 8	
8	301½	32 16 8	2 2	32 16 8	12 7½	
9	246	29 2 8	2 4¼	29 2 8	13 6½	}

NOTES: 'More than four times the number of labourers' were employed in 1861 on this farm than had been the case 'in and previous' to 1825. Total income was clearly influenced by regularity of employment and contribution of family.

The men were employed partly on day rates and partly by the piece, hence the variations in pay, so that no. 4, with 291¼ days' work receives more than no. 5, who has worked 304½ days, excluding any family contribution. Piecework often enabled men to boost their pay considerably.

A quart of table beer was allowed to each man daily, with ale at hay time and harvest and when employed in extra work. Two old men were also employed on the farm at the average wage of about 10s. each per week.

The wages of women were 10d. a day and 1s. 6d. a day for harvest work.

SOURCE: John Parkinson, 'On improvement in agriculture in the County of Nottingham since the Year 1800', *Journal of the Royal Agricultural Society of England*, vol. 22 (1861), p. 164.

Notes and References

1 The rural community at the end of the eighteenth century

1 Arthur Young, *A Six Months' Tour Through the North of England*, 2nd edn (London, 1771), vol. 4, pp. 364, 372.
2 John Byng, *The Torrington Diaries* (1789), ed. C. Bruyn Andrews (London, 1935), vol. 2, pp. 9–10.
3 David Levine, *Family Formation in an Age of Nascent Capitalism* (New York, San Francisco, London, 1977), p. 4; Phyllis Deane and W. A. Cole, *British Economic Growth 1688–1959* (Cambridge, 1964), p. 166.
4 J. D. Chambers, *The Workshop of the World* (London, 1961), p. 22.
5 T. S. Ashton, *An Economic History of England: The 18th Century* (London, 1972), p. 18.
6 B. A. Holderness, 'Personal mobility in some rural parishes of Yorkshire', in *Yorkshire Archaeological Journal*, vol. 42, pt 168 (1970), p. 451.
7 Deane and Cole, pp. 119–22.
8 C. F. Kuchemann, A. J. Boyce and G. A. Harrison, 'A demographic and genetic study of a group of Oxfordshire villages', in Michael Drake (ed.), *Applied Historical Studies* (London, 1973), p. 211. For details of Colyton, see A. E. Wrigley, 'A note on the life-time mobility of married women in a parish population in the later eighteenth century', in *Local Population Studies*, no. 18 (Spring 1977), p. 28.
9 J. H. Bettey, *Rural Life in Wessex 1500–1900* (Bradford-on-Avon, 1977), p. 101; Byng, vol. 1 (London, 1934), p. 99.
10 Michael Anderson, *Family Structure in Nineteenth Century Lancashire* (Cambridge, 1971), p. 83.
11 Ashton, p. 18.
12 William Marshall, *The Rural Economy of the Midland Counties*, 2nd edn (London, 1796), vol. 1, p. 35.
13 Young, vol. 1, p. 46.
14 James Woodforde, *The Diary of a Country Parson 1758–1802*, ed. John Beresford (London, 1967), p. 145.

15 'George Paston' [Emily M. Symonds], *Side-lights of the Georgian Period* (London, 1902), p. 245.

16 Henry Gunning, *Reminiscences of the University, Town and County of Cambridge from 1780* (London, 1854), vol. 1, p. 100.

17 M. W. Flinn, *British Population Growth 1700–1850* (London, 1970), p. 17.

18 D. E. C. Eversley, 'The home market and economic growth in England, 1750–80', in E. L. Jones and G. E. Mingay (eds), *Land, Labour and Population in the Industrial Revolution* (London, 1967), p. 252.

19 W. Wachter, E. A. Hammel and P. Laslett, *Statistical Studies of Historical Social Structure* (New York, San Francisco, London, 1978), pp. 78–9. (The highly technical character of this book is likely to limit its use for most students.)

20 Levine, p. 11; R. B. Outhwaite, 'Population change, family structure and the good of counting' (review article), *Historical Journal*, vol. 22, no. 1 (1979), p. 235.

21 F. M. L. Thompson, 'The second Agricultural Revolution, 1815–1880', *Economic History Review*, 2nd series, vol. 21, no. 1 (April 1968), p. 63; E. L. Jones, *Seasons and Prices* (London, 1964), pp. 108–9.

22 Ashton, pp. 31–2.

23 Marshall, vol. 2, pp. 21–2.

24 Gunning, pp. 168–72.

25 Thus *The Times* of 22 February 1797 contains an advertisement by a vendor of an estate at Brothertoft in Lincolnshire comprising 1120 acres and with a thriving business in the sale of woad: 'On the north, this estate is bounded by the river Witham, opening navigable communications with the Lincoln, the Trent, and the Yorkshire rivers: on the south and south west, it is bounded by the North-forty-foot drain, opening a navigable communication with Bourn and Boston. On private canals belonging to the estate, the produce is shipped at the barn door, and the estate is intersected by a turnpike road.'

26 Arthur Young, *A Six Weeks' Tour Through the Southern Counties of England and Wales* (London, 1768), pp. 259–60.

27 Naomi Riches, *The Agricultural Revolution in Norfolk*, 2nd edn (London, 1967), p. 28.

28 Allan B. Crossman, *The Buckinghamshire Posse Comitatus, 1798* (Leicester University M.A. dissertation, 1971), p. 15.

29 William Marshall, *The Rural Economy of Norfolk*, 2nd edn, vol. 2, (London, 1795), pp. 267–8.

30 Fay Godwin and Shirley Toulson, *The Drovers' Roads of Wales* (London, 1977), pp. 13, 16, 20, 119, 224–6.

31 J. H. Clapham, 'The Transference of the Worsted Industry from Norfolk to the West Riding', *Economic Journal*, vol. 2 (1910), p. 199.

32 Peter Pownall's Farm Diary, 1782–1815, at Reading University Library, CHE 1/1/1.

33 John and Joseph Lamb's Farm Diary 1774–1798, at Reading University Library, OXF. 14/3/1.

34 Marshall, *The Rural Economy of the Midland Counties*, vol. 2, p. 159.

35 David Baker, *The Inhabitants of Cardington in 1782* (Bedfordshire Historical Record Society, vol. 52, 1973), pp. 25–6.

36 See, for example, Felicity A. Palmer, *The Blacksmith's Ledgers of the Hedges Family of Bucklebury, Berkshire, 1736–1773* (University of Reading, Research Paper no. 2, Institute of Agricultural History, 1970), pp. 5, 6. This blacksmith also did work for the parish, as in 1773, when he sent a bill of 6d. to the constable for mending stocks.

37 C. S. Orwin, 'Agriculture and rural life', in A. S. Turberville (ed.), *Johnson's England*, vol. 1 (Oxford, 1965), pp. 289–90.

38 Adam Smith, *The Wealth of Nations*, vol. 1 (London: Everyman's Library edn, 1950), pp. 8–9.

39 Baker, p. 25.

40 J. D. Chambers and G. E. Mingay, *The Agricultural Revolution 1750–1880* (London, 1966), p. 103.

41 William Marshall, *The Rural Economy of Gloucestershire*, vol. 2, 2nd edn (London, 1796), p. 159.

42 Marshall, *The Rural Economy of Norfolk*, vol. 2, pp. 177–8, vol. 1, p. 39.

43 Riches, p. 152.

44 G. E. Mingay, *English Landed Society in the Eighteenth Century* (London, 1963), pp. 20, 22.

45 Sir Frederic M. Eden, *The State of the Poor* (London, 1797), vol. 3, pp. cccxxxix–cccl, 769. W. Hasbach, *A History of the English Agricultural Labourer* (London, 1966), pp. 142–7.

46 Marshall, *The Rural Economy of the Midland Counties*, pp. 287–8.

47 Nathaniel Kent, *Hints to Gentlemen of Landed Property* (London, 1775), p. 238.

48 Arthur Young, *The Farmer's Tour Through the East of England*, vol. 1 (London, 1771), pp. 161–2.

49 C. Stella Davies, *The Agricultural History of Cheshire 1750–1850* (Manchester: The Chetham Society, 1960), vol. 10, 3rd series, p. 18. For details of leases at Holkham see, for example, Holkham Letter Book, correspondence of Francis Blaikie, steward, Leases of 11 May and 20 October 1819 on MS Film 707 at Bodleian Library.

50 See Holkham leases of 11 May and 20 October 1819, Bodleian Library, MS Film 707.

51 Robert Dossie, *Memoirs of Agriculture*, vol. 3 (London, 1782), entry under 1771.

52 Dorothy Marshall, *English People in the Eighteenth Century* (London, 1969), p. 120.

53 Stanley Ayling, *George The Third* (London, 1972), p. 207. *Annals of Agriculture*, vol. 32 (1799), pp. 61–76. This article was concerned with

improvements carried out by a well-known Surrey farmer named Ducket during the 1790s.

54 Minute Book of the Board of Agriculture B VI, at Museum of English Rural Life, Reading, entry for 16 April 1799 and *Annals of Agriculture*, vol. 30 (1798), pp. 13–14.

55 Paul Nunn, 'Aristocratic Estates and Employment in South Yorkshire 1700–1800', in Sidney Pollard and Colin Holmes (eds), *Essays in the Economic and Social History of South Yorkshire* (South Yorkshire County Council, Sheffield, 1976), pp. 37–8.

56 Nunn, p. 38.

57 Jane Austen, *Mansfield Park* (London: Collins Classics edn, 1953), p. 60.

58 J. L. Hammond and Barbara Hammond, *The Village Labourer*, vol. 1 (London: Guild Books edn, 1948), p. 31. William Marshall, *The Rural Economy of Yorkshire*, vol. 1 (London, 1788), pp. 20, 258.

59 G. E. Fussell and Constance Goodman, 'The housing of the rural population in the eighteenth century', *Economic History*, January 1930, p. 75.

60 André Parreaux, *Daily Life in England in the Reign of George III* (London, 1969), p. 22.

61 Nunn, p. 39, for details of South Yorkshire households.

62 Parreaux, pp. 36–7.

63 Young, *A Six Months' Tour Through the North of England*, vol. 1, p. 29 and vol. 3, pp. 340, 343. P. Mantoux, *The Industrial Revolution in the Eighteenth Century* (London, 1955), p. 186.

64 B. Cozens-Hardy (ed.), *Mary Hardy's Diary* (Norfolk Record Society, vol. 37, 1968), entries for 5 January 1779 and 1 February 1783.

65 Quoted in Ivy Pinchbeck, *Women Workers and the Industrial Revolution 1750–1850* (London, 1969), p. 38.

66 Pinchbeck, p. 8.

67 Pamela Horn, 'The Dorset dairy system', *Agricultural History Review*, vol. 26, pt 2 (1978), pp. 100–1, 105.

68 Young, *A Six Months' Tour Through the North of England*, vol. 3, p. 135.

69 Duncan Bythell, *The Handloom Weavers* (Cambridge, 1969), p. 58.

70 Ashton, p. 98.

71 R. N. Salaman, *The History and Social Influence of the Potato* (Cambridge, 1949), p. 497.

72 Farm accounts for Steventon Farm, Steventon, Berkshire, at Reading University Library, BER 16/1/1.

73 Alexander Fenton, *Scottish Country Life* (Edinburgh, 1976), p. 215.

74 Ashton, p. 207. Ashton notes that employers 'and even banks, had to pay suit to retailers, turnpike-keepers, and others whose businesses enabled them to accumulate stocks of small change'.

75 Farm diary for farm at Poxwell, Dorset, 1781–1783, at Reading University Library, DOR 8/1/1, and lease of farm at Poxwell by James Wood, 1776, which describes Wood as 'late of Muston but now

of Poxwell . . . Yeoman'. The property involved was a large one.
Lease at Dorset Record Office, D69/T3. I am indebted to the Dorset
County archivist for help in tracing this.

76 David Davies, *Case of Labourers* (London, 1795), p. 38.
77 Young, *A Six Months' Tour Through the North of England*, vol. 1, p. 50,
    and Joyce Godber, *John Howard the Philanthropist* (Bedfordshire County
    Council pamphlet, 1977), p. 4.
78 Fussell and Goodman indicate some of the variations in rural housing
    at this time.
79 *Jackson's Oxford Journal*, 7 December 1793 and 1 February 1794.
80 Eden, *The State of the Poor*, vol. 1, p. 527.
81 Salaman, p. 492.
82 Arthur Young, Jr, 'Relief of the poor in Sussex', *Annals of Agriculture*,
    vol. 28 (1797), pp. 255–7.
83 Eden, vol. 1, p. 555.
84 Ashton, p. 13.

2 The pressures of war

1 R. N. Salaman, *The History and Social Influence of the Potato* (Cambridge,
   1949), p. 499.
2 John Byng, *The Torrington Diaries* (1789), ed. C. Bruyn Andrews
   (London, 1935), vol. 4, p. 43. The comments were written on 4 June
   1794 about Eltesley in Cambridgeshire.
3 Sidney Pollard and David W. Crossley, *The Wealth of Britain 1085–1966*
   (London, 1968), pp. 183–4.
4 T. S. Ashton, *Economic Fluctuations in England 1700–1800* (Oxford,
   1959), p. 167; Charles Hadfield, *British Canals* (London, 1959), pp.
   39–40.
5 J. D. Chambers and G. E. Mingay, *The Agricultural Revolution 1750–
   1880* (London, 1966), p. 99; J. A. Yelling, *Common Field and Enclosure
   in England 1450–1850* (London, 1977), p. 194.
6 M. W. Flinn, *An Economic and Social History of Britain since 1700*
   (London, 1963), p. 92.
7 Salaman, p. 496.
8 Farm diary of Peter Pownall, at Reading University Library, CHE
   1/1/1.
9 Rosalind Mitchison, 'The old Board of Agriculture (1793–1822)',
   English Historical Review, vol. 74 (1959), p. 47. See also the Minute
   Books of the Board at Museum of English Rural Life, Reading. The
   Rough Minute Book entry for 20 March 1798, for example, reveals
   that the Board had accepted two sacks of 'kidney potatoes' from one
   enthusiast. These were subsequently distributed among those interested in experimenting. Rough Minute Book, BI, and Minute Book,
   BVI, entry for 11 December 1798.

10 *First Report from the Select Committee on the Waste, Uninclosed, and Unproductive Lands of the Kingdom*, PP 1795, vol 1, p. 46.

11 Salaman, pp. 505–11.

12 Lucas Papers at Bedfordshire Record Office, L30/11/215/90, letter dated 30 March 1800.

13 Lucas Papers, L30/11/215/106 and L30/11/215/110, dated 11 January 1801 and 29 March 1801 respectively.

14 *Jackson's Oxford Journal*, 27 August 1796.

15 Salaman, p. 513.

16 Walter M. Stern, 'The bread crisis in Britain, 1795–96', *Economica*, vol. 31 (May 1964), p. 182.

17 *Jackson's Oxford Journal*, 1 August 1795.

18 On 6 March 1795, for example, Parson Woodforde entertained some of his friends to a lavish meal of 'a Couple of Boiled Chicken and Pigs Face, very good Peas Soup, a boiled Rump of Beef very fine, a prodigious fine, large and very fat Cock-Turkey rosted, Maccaroni, Batter Custard Pudding with Jelly, Apple Fritters, Tarts and Raspberry Puffs. Desert, baked Apples, nice Nonpareils, brandy Cherries and Filberts. Wines, Port & Sherries, Malt Liquors, Strong Beer, bottled Porter &c.'

19 Correspondence at the Public Record Office, HO 42/35/139.

20 Stern, p. 171.

21 J. Stevenson, 'Food riots in England, 1792–1818', in R. Quinault and J. Stevenson (eds), *Popular Protest and Public Order* (London, 1974), p. 41.

22 E. P. Thompson, 'The moral economy of the English crowd in the eighteenth century', *Past and Present*, no. 50 (February 1971), p. 112.

23 Thompson, p. 102.

24 E. P. Thompson, 'The crime of anonymity', in D. Hay, P. Linebaugh and E. P. Thompson (eds), *Albion's Fatal Tree* (London, 1975), p. 279.

25 Correspondence at the Public Record Office, HO 45.61, letter from mayor of Bideford, dated 8 January 1801.

26 Alan Booth, 'Food Riots in the north-west of England 1790–1801', *Past and Present*, no. 77 (November 1977), pp. 96–7; Stevenson, p. 45.

27 B. Cozens-Hardy (ed.), *Mary Hardy's Diary*, vol. 37 (Norfolk Record Society, 1968), entries for 17 and 21 December 1795.

28 Stevenson, p. 52, for example, suggested only seven food riots in the whole country in August 1795, whereas Booth has eight in the north-west alone; similarly, in October 1795 Stevenson has one in the whole country, while Booth has four in the north-west. See also Stern, p. 172, with six food riots in the whole country in August 1795 and one in October in the same year. Other months have similar discrepancies.

29 Correspondence at Public Record Office, HO 42/35/219.

30 Quotations from J. L. Hammond and Barbara Hammond, *The Village Labourer*, vol. 1 (London, Guild Books edn, 1948), p. 117.

31 *Jackson's Oxford Journal*, 22 August 1795.

32 At Standlake in Oxfordshire, for example, a baker from the nearby small town of Woodstock claimed that he was prevented from taking away flour he had purchased by a magistrate living in the village. As he wrote angrily to the Home Secretary: 'Why the stoppage of circulating Corn and Four sho$^{d \cdot}$ take place at a parish where plenty is to be had I cannot guess.' Correspondence at the Public Record Office, HO 42/35/407, letter dated 14 August 1795.

33 See letter from William Baker dated 10 July 1795 at Public Record Office, HO 42/35/129.

34 *Jackson's Oxford Journal*, 30 April 1796.

35 John Duncumb, *General View of the Agriculture of the County of Hereford* (London: Board of Agriculture, 1805), p. 136. Duncumb was secretary of the Herefordshire Agricultural Society, which had been established in 1797.

36 Quoted in Chambers and Mingay, p. 119.

37 Elizabeth Crittall (ed.), *The Victoria History of the County of Wiltshire*, vol. 4 (London, 1959), p. 81.

38 E. L. Jones, *The Arable Depression after the Napoleonic Wars and the Agricultural Development of the Hampshire Chalklands* (Nottingham University BA dissertation, 1958), p. 25.

39 James Woodforde, *The Diary of a Country Parson 1758–1802* (Oxford: World's Classics, 1967 edn), entry for 7 August 1796, p. 531.

40 *Autobiography of Joseph Mayett* (manuscript, n.d.) at Buckinghamshire Record Office, D/X371, pp. 16–17. Mayett was born in 1783.

41 Alexander Fenton, *Scottish Country Life* (Edinburgh, 1976), pp. 161–2.

42 Agreements for Ilderton Farm, Northumberland, at Reading University Library, NORTHUM 7/1/1.

43 Pamela Horn, *Labouring Life in the Victorian Countryside* (Dublin, 1976), pp. 69–70.

44 The Ilderton blacksmith was to have 'three Pounds ten Shillings for every pair of Horses kept, to be properly shoed winter & summer for the year, & in proportion for less than a year, to include all repairs of Harrows, Plows & Carts – as well as sharping & laying Plows & Harrows – . . . new work to be paid for. Wheels hooping at 1/- pr. pair, 6d. pr. Hr. for hammered work & 7d. for screwed work . . . to have a Cow & Horse among the hinds Cows – & he to [have] what coarse Hay he wants where I point out for which he pays £6 pr. year, a House, & 900 yards of drills for potatoes – finds a Bondager at 8d. per day except Howing Hay & Harvest for which he is to have 1/- per day. Spins 2 lb. of Lint – & leads his own Coals, brings up a Clecken of Ducks or Chickens.' Agreements for Ilderton Farm, Northumberland, at Reading University Library: Agreement for 1813–14.

45 *Jackson's Oxford Journal*, 24 January 1795.

46 Roger Wells, 'The revolt of the south-west, 1800–1801: a study in English popular protest', *Social History*, no. 6 (October 1977), p. 718. Lord Sheffield's scheme for providing cheap flour was discussed in the *Annals of Agriculture*, vol. 29 (1797), pp. 468–70.

47 Chambers and Mingay, p. 120.

48 Dr Michael Turner, lecturing on 'Landownership and parliamentary enclosure' at a conference organized by the Agricultural History Society on 2 December 1978.

49 William Marshall, *The Rural Economy of Yorkshire*, vol. 1 (London, 1788), p. 98.

50 Glenn Hueckel, 'Relative prices and supply response in English agriculture during the Napoleonic wars', *Economic History Review*, 2nd series, vol. 29, no. 3 (August 1976), p. 412.

51 Yelling, p. 194.

52 Dr Michael Martin, lecturing on 'The small landowner and parliamentary enclosure: some Warwickshire evidence' at a conference organized by the Agricultural History Society on 2 December 1978.

53 F. M. L. Thompson, 'The second Agricultural Revolution, 1815–1880', *Economic History Review*, 2nd series, vol. 21, no. 1 (April 1968), p. 63. Peter D. Linneman, 'An econometric examination of the English parliamentary enclosure movement', *Explorations in Economic History*, vol. 15, no. 2 (April 1978), p. 224.

54 Arthur Young, 'General Enclosure', *Annals of Agriculture*, vol. 38 (1801), p. 214.

55 Quoted in Hammond and Hammond, vol. 1, pp. 78–9.

56 Robert Nye (ed.), *William Barnes: A Selection of his Poems* (Oxford, 1972), pp. 40–2.

57 M. K. Ashby, *Joseph Ashby of Tysoe 1859–1919* (Cambridge, 1961), pp. 281–2.

58 John Billingsley, 'Uselessness of commons to the poor' in *Annals of Agriculture*, vol. 31 (1798), p. 31. See also Olga Wilkinson, *The Agricultural Revolution in the East Riding of Yorkshire* (East Yorkshire Local History Society pamphlet no. 5, 1956), p. 18, for another example of this viewpoint.

59 Joan Thirsk, *English Peasant Farming* (London, 1957), pp. 212–13, 217.

60 Jack L. Purdum, 'Profitability and timing of parliamentary land enclosures', *Explorations in Economic History*, vol. 15, no. 3 (July 1978), p. 325.

61 Lucas Papers, L/30/11/132/30, letter dated 9 February 1808. As the steward enthusiastically declared: 'No one can inclose at so little expence . . . on account of having so great a quantity of wood fit for little else, & the carriage for little or nothing.'

62 Michael E. Turner, 'Parliamentary enclosure and landownership change in Buckinghamshire', *Economic History Review*, 2nd series, vol. 28, no. 4 (November 1975), pp. 568.

63 John Chapman, 'Land purchase at enclosure: evidence from West Sussex', *Local Historian*, vol. 12, no. 7 (1977), pp. 337–41. For discussion of the regional variations in enclosure practice, Dr John Chapman, 'Regional variations in parliamentary enclosure', a lecture given at a conference organized by the Agricultural History Society on 2 December 1978.

64 Crittall, vol. 4, p. 67.

65 Bernard Reaney, *The Class Struggle in 19th Century Oxfordshire*, History Workshop Pamphlet, no. 3, 1970, *passim* for a discussion of the Otmoor riots. For the Wilbarston riots, Hammond and Hammond, vol. 1, p. 73.

66 Chambers and Mingay, p. 92.

67 Enclosure of waste land held by the Tollemache family in thirty-five Cheshire villages led to an increase of holdings from 363 in 1790 to 403 in 1821. Other Cheshire estates followed a similar trend. C. Stella Davies, *The Agricultural History of Cheshire 1750–1850* (Manchester: The Chetham Society, 1960), 3rd series, vol. 10, pp. 14–15.

68 Crittall, vol. 4, p. 67.

69 Purdum, p. 319, estimates the return on enclosure of five Manors he studied in Nottinghamshire to vary between 6 and 31 per cent. He attributes some of the variation to the fact that where land reorganization had taken place *prior* to enclosure the benefits associated with enclosure itself would be smaller. Fencing costs were also greater than parliamentary and legal fees in many cases, so access to cheap timber was a significant factor (p. 324).

70 Lucas Papers at Bedfordshire Record Office, L.30/11/132/29, letter dated 11 January 1808.

71 Lucas Papers, L.30/11/132/30, letter dated 9 February 1808.

72 Michael E. Turner, 'Enclosure commissioners and Buckingham parliamentary enclosure', *Agricultural History Review*, vol. 25, pt 2 (1977), p. 128.

73 G. E. Mingay, 'The eighteenth-century land steward', in E. L. Jones and G. E. Mingay (eds), *Land, Labour and Population in the Industrial Revolution* (London 1967), p. 10.

74 Mingay, p. 12.

75 Hammond and Hammond, vol. 1, p. 164.

76 Wells, p. 715.

77 Crittall, vol. 4, pp. 170–1.

78 J. de L. Mann, *The Cloth Industry in the West of England from 1640 to 1880* (Oxford, 1971), p. 137.

79 William Page (ed.), *The Victoria History of the County of Suffolk*, vol. 2 (London 1907), p. 270.

80 Pamela Horn, 'Child workers in the pillow lace and straw plait trades of Victorian Buckinghamshire and Bedfordshire', *Historical Journal*, vol. 17, no. 4 (1974), p. 781.

81 Posse Comitatus returns for Buckinghamshire at Buckinghamshire Record Office, L/P/6.

82 Allan B. Crossman, *The Buckinghamshire Posse Comitatus, 1798* (Leicester University MA dissertation, 1971), p. 45. In 1798 Hanslope also had four male lacemakers, six lace dealers and a pillow maker as well.

83 Quoted in Horn, 'The Buckinghamshire Straw Plait Trade in Victorian England', from *Records of Bucks*, vol. 19, pt 1 (1971), p. 43.

84 Arthur Young, *General View of the Agriculture of the County of Hertford-shire* (London: Board of Agriculture, 1804), p. 223.

85 Pamela Horn, *Labouring Life in the Victorian Countryside*, p. 108.

86 M. W. Flinn, *An Economic and Social History of Britain Since 1700* (London, 1963), p. 101.

87 Ivy Pinchbeck, *Women Workers and the Industrial Revolution 1750–1850* (London, 1969), p. 62.

88 Fenton, pp. 50, 54; E. L. Jones, 'The Agricultural Labour Market in England, 1793–1872', *Economic History Review*, 2nd series, vol. 17, no. 2 (December 1964), p. 323.

89 *Annals of Agriculture*, vol. 39 (1803), pp. 29–30, discussing the Woburn Agricultural Meeting in June 1802.

90 E. J. Hobsbawm and George Rudé, *Captain Swing* (London, 1969), pp. 359–60.

91 The constitutional associations were designed to 'aid and support the Magistrates in the firm and steady Execution of the Laws, and to stand by, and assist in quelling all Riots, Insurrections, and Tumults' (*Jackson's Oxford Journal*, 5 January 1793). Encouragement was given to the burning in effigy of Tom Paine, the author of the revolutionary tract *The Rights of Man*, who was seen as spreading dangerous doctrines. At Stadhampton in Oxfordshire the *Oxford Journal* of 26 January 1793 reported that after the effigy had been burnt 'Bread, Cheese, and Ale were distributed among the Populace in great Abundance. *God Save the King* echoed through the whole village.'

92 Defence of the Realm Returns, 1798, at Hampshire Record Office, B/XVII a/5/3.

93 Ibid.

94 Quoted in *People and Places: An East Anglian Miscellany: Trumpington* (Lavenham, 1973), p. 54.

95 Helen Darbishire (ed.), *Journals of Dorothy Wordsworth* (London: World's Classics edn, 1958), p. 58; A. S. Turberville (ed.), *Johnson's England* (Oxford, 1965 edn), p. 39.

96 Alan F. Cirket, *Samuel Whitbread's Notebooks, 1810–11, 1813–14* (Bedfordshire Historical Record Society, vol. 50, 1971), p. 88.

97 *Jackson's Oxford Journal*, 28 March 1795.

98 Defence of the Realm returns at Hampshire Record Office, B/XVII a/5/3.

99 R. W. S. Norfolk, *Militia, Yeomanry and Volunteer Forces of the East*

Riding 1689–1908 (East Yorkshire Local History Society pamphlet no. 19, 1965), p. 27.

100 Correspondence at the Public Record Office, HO 42/34/377. For the Lower Slaughter advertisement, see *Jackson's Oxford Journal*, 17 December 1796.

101 M. K. Ashby, *The Changing English Village 1066–1914* (Kineton, 1974), pp. 178–9 and George Eliot, *Adam Bede* (London: Everyman's Library edn, 1960), p. 45.

102 See return at Public Record Office, PC 1/37, A.114. At nearby Dartford, of twenty-five balloted two served in their own right – a 'gentleman' and a 'surgeon'; one man defaulted and was fined £15. The others found substitutes; Sir John Dixon Dyke, baronet of Lullingstone, for example, sent one of his farm servants aged nineteen. Another man, in the 'brewery business', also sent one of his employees. Of the twenty-two substitutes, eleven were labourers and three were husbandmen or farm servants. See at the same reference.

103 'George Paston' [Emily M. Symonds], *Side-lights of the Georgian Period* (London, 1902), p. 247.

104 Information and Complaints of John Gough of Princes Risborough, taken on oath, 22 August 1803, at Buckinghamshire Record Office, L/V: 6/4.

105 *Jackson's Oxford Journal*, 26 November 1796.

106 Cozens-Hardy, entry for 12 December 1796.

107 Returns of Maintenance of families of substitutes in Oxfordshire Militia at Oxfordshire Record Office, L/M IX/i/1.

108 Oxfordshire Militia records at the Bodleian Library, Oxford, MS.Oxf. Dioc.Pp.c.173, pp. 58, 165.

109 See, for example, J. M. Davenport, *Sketch of the History of the Oxfordshire Militia* (Oxford, 1869) for an account of the activities of one county militia.

110 J. W. Tibble and Anne Tibble (eds), *The Prose of John Clare* (London, 1951), pp. 46–7.

111 Tibble and Tibble, p. 50.

112 Autobiography of Joseph Mayett at Buckinghamshire Record Office.

113 Stevenson, pp. 47–8. For an account of a riot by the Oxfordshire militia near Newhaven in April 1795, see Pamela Horn, 'A Sussex mutiny', *Sussex Life*, vol. 14, no. 6 (June, 1978), pp. 30–1. The men were protesting over their inadequate rations and poor pay, and five of them were eventually executed for their part in the 'mutiny'. William Cobbett in 1809 also took up the case of militiamen at Ely who mutinied over the question of deductions from their pay. The ringleaders were tried by court-martial and were sentenced to a flogging – which, to Cobbett's anger, was carried out by some German troops who were on garrison duty in England; see G. D. H. Cole, *The Life of William Cobbett* (London, 1924), pp. 150–1.

114 Norfolk, p. 32.
115 Militia records at the Public Record Office, HO50.23, letter dated
     18 May 1795 from Herbert Foley.
116 *Annual Register*, vol. 39 (1797), section on 'History of Europe', p. 257.
117 For an account of the invasion, see Commander E. H. Stuart Jones,
     The Last Invasion of Britain (Cardiff, 1950), *passim*. The French landed
     on the evening of Wednesday, 22 February and surrendered on 24
     February. See also *Pembrokeshire Antiquities: Reprints from the Anti-
     quaries Column in the Pembroke County Guardian* (Solva, 1897), pp. 63–7 at
     Tenby Public Library. On 8 March 1797 the Duke of Portland wrote
     to Captain Allen of Brecon, assuring him that it had given 'His
     Majesty much pleasure, to observe the spirit and alacrity, with which the
     Brecon Volunteers, and Supplementary Militia of that County, in
     common with every description of Persons in the Neighbourhood, have
     come forward to oppose the progress of the Enemy'. On the previous
     day the Duke had made arrangements for the Brecon men to receive
     'the Marching Guinea' for their activities. See Home Office corres-
     pondence at Public Record Office, HO 43.9, 4, 29.

3   The post-war world

1 *Report from the Committee on the Depressed State of the Agriculture of the
   United Kingdom*, PP 1821, vol. 9, p. 26.
2 *Gentleman's Magazine*, vol. C, pt 2 (October, 1830), p. 362.
3 L. P. Adams, *Agricultural Depression and Farm Relief in England 1813–
   1852* (London, 1965), p. 48. (First edition published in 1932.)
4 *Hansard*, 1st series, 1815, vol. 30, cols. 96–7. As early as 1813 a protectionist Bill had been proposed but had been unsuccessful.
5 *Hansard*, 1st series, 1815, vol. 30, cols. 198–9.
6 *Report from the Committee on the Depressed State of the Agriculture of the
   United Kingdom*, PP 1821, vol. 9, p. 5.
7 L. S. Pressnell, *Country Banking in the Industrial Revolution* (Oxford,
   1956), pp. 348, 474.
8 Quoted in Joan Thirsk and J. Imray (eds), *Suffolk Farming in the
   Nineteenth Century* (Suffolk Record Society, 1958), vol. 1, p. 23.
9 Thirsk and Imray, p. 23.
10 Account book of Joseph Falkner, wheelwright, ploughwright, etc., at
   Museum of English Rural Life, Reading, D62/104.
11 *Report from the Committee on the Depressed State of the Agriculture of the
   United Kingdom*, p. 72 (evidence of Mr John Lake).
12 C. Stella Davies, *The Agricultural History of Cheshire 1750–1850* (Manchester: The Chetham Society 1960), 3rd series, vol. 10, pp. 125–6.
13 Quoted in Thirsk and Imray, p. 92.
14 *Report from the Select Committee on Agriculture*, PP 1833, vol. 5, Q 2509,
   2458–71.

15 *Report from the Select Committee on Agriculture*, Q 2524.

16 *Report from the Select Committee on Agriculture*, Q 12848–53 (evidence of George Smallpiece, part owner-occupier and part tenant of a 1000-acre mixed farm).

17 John Prebble, *The Highland Clearances* (London, 1963), p. 138.

18 Alexander Fenton, *Scottish Country Life* (Edinburgh, 1976), p. 25.

19 Prebble, pp. 120, 207; James Hunter, *The Making of the Crofting Community* (Edinburgh, 1976), pp. 16–17.

20 E. L. Jones, *The Arable Depression after the Napoleonic Wars and the Agricultural Development of the Hampshire Chalklands* (BA Dissertation, Nottingham University, 1958), pp. 41–2.

21 *Report from the Committee on the Depressed State of the Agriculture of the United Kingdom*, p. 49.

22 *Jackson's Oxford Journal*, 9 March 1816.

23 *The Agricultural State of the Kingdom* (Board of Agriculture, 1816), report from Edmund Jones, p. 103. The Board played little part in the post-war world and was wound up in 1822.

24 Davies, p. 99.

25 B. E. Howells and K. A. Howells, *Pembrokeshire Life: 1572–1843* (Pembrokeshire Record Society, 1972), p. 95.

26 Farm diary of Little Somborne Farm, King's Somborne, Hampshire, 1815–1867, at Reading University Library, HAN 11/2/1.

27 William Cobbett, *Rural Rides*, vol. 1 (London: Everyman's Library edn, 1948), pp. 116–17.

28 Farm diary of Little Somborne Farm, at Reading University Library.

29 *Report from the Select Committee on Agriculture*, PP 1833, vol. 5, Q 5781–2 (evidence of Joseph Lee of Malpas).

30 F. M. L. Thompson, *English Landed Society in the Nineteenth Century* (London, 1963), p. 231.

31 *Report from the Select Committee on Agriculture*, Q 6171.

32 The statement on the Duke of Grafton's farms is preserved at Northamptonshire Record Office, G.4285.

33 Thomas W. Coke to Messrs Gurney, letter dated 12 January, 1821, in Holkham estate letter books, at Bodleian Library, MS Film 707.

34 R. A. C. Parker, *Coke of Norfolk* (Oxford, 1975), pp. 148–9.

35 Letters from Thomas Beckett, Woburn steward, to W. G. Adam, the Bedford estate's London steward, dated 31 July 1831 (R3/3691) and 21 April 1833 (R3/3753), at Bedfordshire Record Office.

36 Letter from Francis Reynolds, tenant of Heath Farm, Chippenham, R 55.7.11 and Particulars as to the Farms Vacant on the Chippenham Estate, 1836, R 55.7.11, at Cambridge Record Office.

37 Thompson, p. 197.

38 Peter Mathias, *The First Industrial Nation* (London, 1969), p. 71.

39 *Report from the Select Committee on Petitions Complaining of Agricultural*

Distress &c., PP 1820, vol. 2, p. 124 (evidence of John M. Bligh, an owner-occupier and land agent).

40   Ibid., p. 118 (evidence of Robert C. Harvey, a farmer and miller).

41   Ibid. (evidence of William Dowding).

42   John Fisher, *The Political Plough* (introduction by Travis L. Crosby (London, 1974), pp. 14–15. (This pamphlet was first published in 1821.)

43   Holkham estate letter books, vol. 1, at Bodleian Library, MS Film 706, letters dated 9 January and 15 February from Francis Blaikie, the Holkham steward, and 15 March 1817 from A. Wilson of the Woburn estate to Blaikie.

44   E. L. Jones, *The Development of English Agriculture 1815–1873* (London, 1968), p. 15

45   Thompson, p. 236.

46   George Sturt, *William Smith: Potter and Farmer: 1790–1858* (Firle, 1978), pp. 66–7, 176. (The book was first published in 1919.)

47   Farm diary of Mr Paul, Bottisham Place, Bottisham, Cambridgeshire, at Reading University Library, CAM 6.2.1.

48   James Obelkevich, *Religion and Rural Society: South Lindsey 1825–1875* (Oxford, 1976), p. 57.

49   Farm diary of Mr Paul of Bottisham Place, entry for 15 July 1834.

50   E. J. T. Collins, 'Migrant labour in British agriculture in the nineteenth century', *Economic History Review*, 2nd series, vol. 29, no. 1 (February 1976), pp. 44–5.

51   *Reports of Special Assistant Poor Law Commissioners on the Employment of Women and Children in Agriculture*, PP 1843, vol. 12, p. 175.

52   Collins, p. 53.

53   J. D. Chambers and G. E. Mingay, *The Agricultural Revolution 1750–1880* (London, 1966), p. 129.

54   E. J. Hobsbawm and George Rudé, *Captain Swing* (London, 1969), p. 73. For the Sussex evidence of unemployment and underemployment, see N. Gash, 'Rural unemployment 1815–34', *Economic History Review*, vol. 6, no. 1 (October 1935), pp. 90–1, 93.

55   Cobbett, vol. 1, p. 266.

56   *Report from the Committee on the Depressed State of the Agriculture of the United Kingdom* (1821), p. 39. (evidence of Robert C. Harvey, farmer and miller; Harvey had also given evidence in the previous year to the *Select Committee on Petitions Complaining on Agricultural Distress &c*).

57   A. J. Peacock, *Bread or Blood* (London, 1965), p. 27.

58   Cobbett, vol. 2, pp. 120–1.

59   Cobbett, vol. 1, pp. 58–9. In Sussex he also noted with approval that women and children were employed in shaving hop-poles: 'Little boys and girls shave hop-poles and assist in other coppice work very nicely' (ibid., p. 63).

60   J. D. Marshall, 'Nottinghamshire labourers in the early nineteenth century', *Transactions of the Thoroton Society*, vol. 64 (1960), p. 69.

61 J. D. Marshall, 'The Lancashire rural labourer in the early nineteenth century', *Transactions of the Lancashire and Cheshire Antiquarian Society*, vol. 71 (1961), pp. 90–1. The development of turnpike roads and canals also helped to even out wages in Lancashire between the industrial and agricultural areas of the county. A 'series of townships on or near the Leeds and Liverpool Canal . . . and others on the Lancaster Canal . . . were all reported as paying the same rate in 1833, namely 2s. a day' (ibid., p. 104).

62 E. L. Jones, 'The agricultural labour market in England, 1793–1872', *Economic History Review*, 2nd series, vol. 17, no. 2 (December 1964), p. 327; Marshall, 'Nottinghamshire labourers in the early nineteenth century', p. 66.

63 Gash, pp. 92–3.

64 Peacock, p. 69.

65 Peacock, p. 70.

66 Reports of disorders, etc., in 1822 at the Public Records Office, HO 40/17, item 86. There are several letters from other correspondents concerning the 1822 disturbances at this reference.

67 Hobsbawm and Rudé, p. 84.

68 Hobsbawm and Rudé, p. 85.

69 Farm diary of Little Somborne Farm, King's Somborne, at Reading University Library (entry for 1830).

70 *Hansard*, 3rd series, vol. 2 (1830), col. 71 (debate on 23 December 1830).

71 G. D. H. Cole, *The Life of William Cobbett* (London, 1924), pp. 364–71; Asa Briggs, *William Cobbett* (Oxford, 1967), p. 56.

72 Hobsbawm and Rudé, p. 91.

73 Gash, p. 93.

74 Barbara Kerr, *Bound to the Soil* (London, 1968), pp. 108–10; Hobsbawm and Rudé, p. 189.

75 Hobsbawm and Rudé, p. 169; Sturt, p. 218.

76 Home Office Correspondence at the Public Record Office, HO 43.39, letter from Sir Robert Peel to the Marquess of Camden dated 18 October 1830 (162).

77 Ibid., 169, Sir Robert Peel to the Marquess of Camden, 22 October 1830. On 29 October S. M. Phillipps of the Home Office wrote to Sir E. Knatchbull, Bt, stating that Mr Maule, the Solicitor of the Treasury, would be at Maidstone on the following Monday 'for the purpose of conferring with the Magistrates as to the best mode of obtaining information and disposing of five Police Officers, who will be sent down to Maidstone to obey directions'. There were many other letters on the subject.

78 Farm diary of Little Somborne Farm, King's Somborne (entry for 1830).

79 Mary R. Mitford, *Our Village*, vol. 5 (London, 1832), pp. 6–9.

80   *Gentleman's Magazine*, vol. C, pt 2 (1830), p. 638.
81   Anne Digby, *Pauper Palaces* (London, 1978), p. 98.
82   Hobsbawm and Rudé, p. 125.
83   Hobsbawm and Rudé, pp. 262–3.
84   W. H. Hudson, *A Shepherd's Life* (Tisbury, 1978), pp. 144–5.
85   Thomas Banting, MS notes on Filkins and other parishes (n.d., *c.* 1887–95), at the Bodleian Library, MS Top.Oxon.e.220, p. 9.
86   Peacock, pp. 129, 133, 174–6.
87   *First Report from the Select Committee on the State of Agriculture*, PP 1836, vol. 8, pt 1, Q 1598 (evidence of John Rolfe, a farmer and valuer from Beaconsfield). See also *Third Report*, PP 1836, vol. 8, pt 2, Q 13,172 (evidence of T. Boniface of Climping, Sussex, a farmer).
88   *Report from the Select Committee on Agriculture*, PP 1833, Q 1238 (evidence of Robert Hughes, land agent and surveyor).
89   Hudson, p. 146.

4   The relief of the poor

1   Advertisement in *Jackson's Oxford Journal*, 24 December 1796.
2   Letter from the Poor Law Commission to Thame Union, Oxfordshire, dated 27 November 1838, in MH 12/9733 at the Public Record Office. The letter was written in response to an appeal by the Thame guardians for guidance as to what could be done to aid 'poor industrious labourers in employment with large families in view of the high price of bread'.
3   Anne Digby, *Pauper Palaces* (London, 1978), p. 122.
4   Overseers' book for Sibford Gower at the Bodleian Library, MS D.D.Sibford Gower b.1.
5   J. S. Taylor, 'The impact of pauper settlement 1691–1834', *Past and Present*, no. 73 (November 1976), p. 51.
6   Digby, *Pauper Palaces*, p. 90.
7   Michael E. Rose, 'Settlement, removal and the new Poor Law', in Derek Fraser (ed.), *The New Poor Law in the Nineteenth Century* (London, 1976), p. 27.
8   Frederic M. Eden, *The State of the Poor*, vol. 3 (London, 1797), p. 781.
9   Eden, vol. 3, pp. 743–4.
10   Overseers' Accounts for Eynsham, 1764–1806, at the Bodleian Library, MS D.D.Par.Eynsham b.15.
11   Quoted in J. H. Bettey, *Rural Life in Wessex 1500–1900* (Bradford-on-Avon, 1977), p. 121.
12   David Williams, *A History of Modern Wales*, 2nd edn (London, 1977), p. 201.
13   James Woodforde, *The Diary of a Country Parson 1758–1802*, ed. John

Beresford (London: World's Classics edn, 1967), p. 295.

14 T. F. Teversham, *History of Sawston*, pt 2 (Cambridge, 1947), p. 188.

15 M. K. Ashby, *The Changing English Village 1066–1914* (Kineton, 1974), p. 235.

16 Norman Longmate, *The Workhouse* (London, 1974), p. 27.

17 Digby, *Pauper Palaces*, p. 36.

18 Digby, *Pauper Palaces*, p. 2.

19 Digby, *Pauper Palaces*, p. 32.

20 Eden, vol. 2, p. 220.

21 Roger A. E. Wells, *Dearth and Distress in Yorkshire 1793–1802* (University of York, Borthwick Papers, no. 52, 1977), p. 17.

22 Wells, p. 19.

23 *The Poor Law in Gloucestershire* (Gloucester: Gloucestershire Record Office, 1974), document 16.

24 J. D. Marshall, *The Old Poor Law 1795–1834* (London, 1968), p. 41.

25 *Select Committee on the Poor Laws*, PP 1817, vol. 6, p. 19, noted that parochial farms had been established in the parishes of Benenden and Cranbrooke; see also Elizabeth Melling (ed.), *Kentish Sources: The Poor* (Maidstone: Kent County Council, 1964), p. 150.

26 M. K. Ashby, *Joseph Ashby of Tysoe 1859–1919* (Cambridge, 1961), p. 278.

27 Ashby, p. 277.

28 *Reports of Special Assistant Poor Law Commissioners on the Employment of Women and Children in Agriculture*, PP 1843, vol. 12, p. 112.

29 Minutes of the Magistrates in Petty Sessions for the Three Hundreds of Aylesbury, 1800–1803, at Buckinghamshire Record Office, PS/AY/M/1.

30 *Jackson's Oxford Journal*, 11 October 1794. At Sibford Gower, for example, an entry of men 'on the Round' first appears in the overseers' book in 1787.

31 Williams, *A History of Modern Wales*, p. 201.

32 Select Committee on Labourers' Wages, PP 1824, vol. 6, p. 7.

33 At Lidlington in Bedfordshire, for example, annual expenditure jumped from £134 in the early 1780s to £719 by 1807–8, while at Sutton in Cheshire the increase was from between £90 and £150 in the pre-war period to £695 by 1816. See Joyce Godber, *History of Bedfordshire* (Bedfordshire County Council, 1969), p. 416; C. Stella Davies, *The Agricultural History of Cheshire 1750–1850* (Manchester: The Chetham Society, 3rd series, vol. 10, 1960), p. 87.

34 D. A. Baugh, 'The cost of poor relief in south-east England, 1790–1834', *Economic History Review*, 2nd series, vol. 28, no. 1 (February 1975), p. 60.

35 R. Salmon, 'On the practice of employing the labouring poor as rounds

men or perhaps more properly as overseers pass men, or home vagrants', manuscript report, 1816, at Bedfordshire Record Office, R3/2119.

36 Report by Edward Gulson to the Poor Law Commissioners, 27 May 1835, at the Public Record Office, MH 32.28.

37 Baugh, p. 64. The hundreds of Uttlesford, Clavering and Freshwell in Essex initiated allowance scales as late as 1826.

38 Baugh, p. 64.

39 Marshall, p. 39.

40 Anthony Brundage, *The Making of the New Poor Law* (London, 1978), p. 9.

41 Ashby, p. 282. Miss Ashby notes that there were at that time forty-five men and boys in receipt of relief, in addition to girls and women. Later in the same year the overseers sent a number of small Tysoe children in a waggon to a cotton factory at Guyscliffe, twenty miles away, to be apprenticed there.

42 Derek Fraser, *The Evolution of the British Welfare State* (London, 1973), p. 38.

43 Marshall, p. 41.

44 Autobiography of Joseph Mayett at Buckinghamshire Record Office, D/Z 371, pp. 90–1.

45 S. G. Checkland and E. O. A. Checkland (eds), *The Poor Law Report of 1834* (Harmondsworth: Penguin Books edn, 1974), p. 161.

46 Williams, *A History of Modern Wales*, p. 203.

47 Report by W. J. Gilbert on Buckinghamshire at Public Record Office, MH 32.26, dated 9 June 1835.

48 Report by W. J. Gilbert on Devon at Public Record Office, MH 32.26, dated 24 June 1836.

49 Correspondence and notes of Henry Russell on Poor Law matters at the Bodleian Library, MSS Eng.Letters c. 175, p. 96.

50 Marshall, p. 33.

51 *Royal Commission on the Poor Laws*: Appendix B, Answers to Questions Circulated in Rural Districts, pt 5, PP 1834, vol. 34, 376e.

52 S. Webb and B. Webb, *English Poor Law History*, Pt 2: *The Last Hundred Years*, vol. 1, (London, 1929), p. 113.

53 Anne Digby, 'The labour market and the continuity of social policy after 1834: the case of the eastern counties', *Economic History Review*, 2nd series, vol. 28, no. 1 (February 1975), p. 71.

54 Taylor, p. 53, for a discussion of changes in the settlement laws. Henley Poor Law Union Minute Book, 1837–8 at Oxfordshire Record Office, T/G IV/i/3, entry 31 October 1837, for the case involving Bix and Henley.

55 Joan Thirsk, *English Peasant Farming* (London, 1957), p. 295.

56 Digby, *Pauper Palaces*, p. 89.

57 B. A. Holderness, '"Open" and "close" parishes in England in the

eighteenth and nineteenth centuries', *Agricultural History Review*, vol. 20, pt 2 (1972), p. 130.

58 Anne Digby, 'The rural Poor Law', in Fraser, *The New Poor Law in the Nineteenth Century*, p. 150.

59 W. J. Gilbert to the Poor Law Commissioners, 7 August 1835, at the Public Record Office, MH 32.26.

60 Digby, 'The rural Poor Law', pp. 150–1.

61 Brundage, p. 93.

62 *Jackson's Oxford Journal*, 3 October 1835.

63 John Glyde, Jr, *Suffolk in the Nineteenth Century* (London, 1856), p. 187.

64 Digby, *Pauper Palaces*, p. 220. At the Depwade union workhouse at Pulham St Mary high surrounding walls with corner sentry posts had to be built which had loopholes in them so that armed watchmen could be deployed.

65 Records of Kendal Poor Law Union at Public Record Office, MH 12.13581, letter from assistant commissioner W. J. Voules to the Poor Law Commission, 28 May 1836.

66 Nicholas C. Edsall, *The Anti-Poor Law Movement 1834–44* (Manchester, 1971), p. 30.

67 Edsall, p. 38.

68 Digby, *Pauper Palaces*, p. 223.

69 Edsall, p. 41.

70 David Williams, *The Rebecca Riots* (Cardiff, 1971), p. 139.

71 David Roberts, 'How cruel was the Victorian Poor Law?', *Historical Journal*, vol. 6 (1963), p. 105.

72 Digby, 'The rural poor law', pp. 159–60.

73 Henley Poor Law Union Minute Book, 1835–6, at Oxfordshire Record Office, T/G. IV/i/1.

74 Duncan Bythell, *The Handloom Weavers* (Cambridge, 1969), pp. 249–50.

75 *Appendix to Fourth Report of the Poor Law Commission*, PP 1837–8, vol. 28, p. 135.

76 Records of Kendal Poor Law Union, 1839–42, at Public Record Office, MH 12.13582. Letter from W. H. S. Hawley to the Poor Law Commission, dated 24 October 1842.

77 Digby, 'The labour market and the continuity of social policy', p. 71.

78 Michael E. Rose, 'The allowance system under the new Poor Law', *Economic History Review*, 2nd series, vol. 19, no. 3 (December 1966), p. 613.

79 Calculated from Appendix to *Sixteenth Report from the Select Committee to Inquire into the Administration of the Relief of the Poor*, PP 1838, vol. 18, pt 1, p. 33.

80 Digby, 'The labour market and the continuity of social policy', p. 72.

81 Ibid., p. 73.

82 For the application from the Boston guardians, see records at Public Record Office, MH 12.6633, letter dated 2 February 1847, and for

K

Crediton, MH 12.2198, letter from Poor Law Commission dated 18 May 1847, permitting out-relief to the able-bodied in that union.

83 Digby, 'The rural Poor Law', p. 160; Digby, 'The labour market and the continuity of social policy', p. 77.

84 Digby, 'The rural Poor Law', p. 162; Rose, 'The allowance system under the new Poor Law', p. 607.

85 S. Webb and B. Webb, *English Poor Law Policy* (London, 1963 edn), p. 141.

86 Digby, 'The rural Poor Law', p. 155.

87 However, the attempts to arrest absconders were by no means always successful. On 11 October 1843 the clerk to the Crediton union reported to the Poor Law Commission that over the period 1839–43, thirty-seven persons had absconded, leaving their wives of children chargeable; of these, five had been apprehended, nine had been reunited with their families without being apprehended, and twenty-three were apparently still at large: MH 12.2198 at Public Record Office.

88 Longmate, p. 138.

89 Digby, *Pauper Palaces*, p. 165.

90 For an account of the Andover affair, see, for example, Longmate.

91 Melling, p. 138.

92 Overseers' Accounts for Eynsham, 1764–1806, entry for 28 March 1791.

93 For details of the Boston union contracts in 1847, see MH 12.6633 at Public Record Office. On 9 February in that year the medical officer for the Boston district had asked the Poor Law Commission if extra payments could be made for compound fractures of the arm, 'as is the case in compound fractures of the leg', over and above the 'one pound for single fracture of the arm' already allowed. The secretary of the Commission replied coldly on 15 February: 'I am to inform you that those fees mentioned in the Commissrs.' order are the only fees provided for Medical Officers in addition to their salaries.'

94 Return from the Clerk to the Guardians of Crediton Union, 18 December 1847, at Public Record Office, MH 12.2198. For details of the Bicester union policy, see minute books at Oxfordshire Record Office.

95 Ruth G. Hodgkinson, *The Origins of the National Health Service* (London, 1967), pp. 107–8.

96 Hodgkinson, p. 14.

97 *Report of the Select Committee on Medical Relief*, PP 1854, vol. 12, Q 1570.

98 Ibid., Q. 1376.

99 Hodgkinson, p. 12.

100 Records of Chipping Norton Poor Law Union at Public Record Office, MH 12.9637, letter from Poor Law Commissioners dated 4 March 1837.

101 *Reports of Special Assistant Poor Law Commissioners on The Employment of*

Women and Children in Agriculture, PP 1843, vol. 12, p. 238.

102 *Second Report of the Poor Law Commission*, PP 1836, vol. 29, pt 1, p. 267.
103 Ibid., p. 266.
104 Fraser, p. 46.
105 Phyllis Deane and W. A. Cole, *British Economic Growth 1688–1959* (Cambridge, 1964), p. 143.

5 **Village institutions**

1 John Hurt, *Education in Evolution* (London, 1971), p. 120, quoting the comments of one of Her Majesty's Inspectors of Schools.
2 George Crabbe, 'The Borough' (1810).
3 Quoted in Pamela Horn, *The Victorian Country Child* (Kineton, 1974), p. 131.
4 Thomas W. Laqueur, *Religion and Respectability* (London, 1976), p. 49.
5 Rex C. Russell, *A History of Schools and Education in Lindsey, Lincoln-shire 1800–1902*, pt 2 (Lindsey County Council Education Committee, 1965), p. 19.
6 R. M. Grier, *John Allen: A Memoir* (London, 1889), pp. 102–3.
7 Richard D. Altick, *The English Common Reader* (Chicago, 1957), p. 147.
8 Derek Robson, *Some Aspects of Education in Cheshire* (Manchester: Chetham Society, 1966), 3rd series, vol. 13, p. 96.
9 Ibid.
10 Robson, pp. 113–14.
11 Eric E. Rich, *The Education Act 1870* (London, 1970), p. 56.
12 See school returns at the Bodleian Library, Oxford, MS Oxf. Dioc.Pp. d.707.
13 Quoted in J. Stuart Maclure, *Educational Documents: England and Wales 1816–1968* (London, 1972), p. 19.
14 Autobiography of Joseph Mayett, manuscript (n.d.) at Buckinghamshire Record Office, D/X371, 1.
15 Quoted in Pamela Horn, *Education in Rural England 1800–1914* (Dublin, 1978), p. 116.
16 Horn, *Education in Rural England*, p. 35.
17 James Obelkevich, *Religion and Rural Society: South Lindsey 1825–1875* (Oxford, 1976), p. 169. For the Devon example, see Roger R. Sellman, *Devon Village Schools in the Nineteenth Century* (Newton Abbot, 1967), p. 26.
18 Horn, *Education in Rural England 1800–1914*, pp. 51–2.
19 Rich, p. 53; Anne Digby, *Pauper Palaces* (London, 1978), p. 183.
20 *Report of the Annual Meeting of the Diocesan Association of Schoolmasters in the Diocese of Oxford* (Oxford 1857), p. 38.
21 Quoted in Richard Johnson, 'Educational policy and social control in early Victorian England', *Past and Present*, no. 49 (November 1970), p. 112.

22   *Hansard,* 3rd series, 1847, vol. 91, cols. 1012, 1017.

23   Grier, p. 105.

24   *Minutes of the Committee of Council on Education for 1845,* PP 1846, vol. 32, p. 298.

25   J. Lawson, *Primary Education in East Yorkshire 1560–1902* (East Yorkshire Local History Society, 1959), Pamphlet no. 10, p. 22.

26   A. Platts and G. H. Hainton, *Education in Gloucestershire: A Short History* (Gloucestershire County Council, 1954), p. 69.

27   *Minutes of the Committee of Council on Education for 1854–55,* PP 1854-5, vol. 42, p. 479. For the earlier comment, see P. H. J. H. Gosden, *How They Were Taught* (Oxford, 1969), p. 23.

28   Horn, *Education in Rural England, 1800–1914,* p. 162; Sellman, p. 19.

29   Quoted in Lawson, p. 21.

30   *Report of Commissioners of Inquiry into the State of Education in Wales,* pt 1, PP 1847, vol. 27, p. 32.

31   *First Report of the Royal Commission on the Employment of Children, Young Persons and Women in Agriculture,* PP 1867–8, vol. 17, report by Mr Culley on Bedfordshire, p. 522. For the Bedfordshire men the proportion was 35 signing with a mark in 1865, as opposed to the average for England of 22.5. For details of the earlier literacy position, see Lawrence Stone, 'Literacy and Education in England 1640–1900', *Past and Present,* no. 42 (February 1969), p. 122.

32   H. C. Barnard, *A History of English Education from 1760* (London, 1966), p. 71.

33   Thomas Hughes, *Tom Brown's Schooldays* (London, Nelson's Classics edn, n.d.), pp. 118–19.

34   Grier, pp. 20–1.

35   *Jackson's Oxford Journal,* 4 July 1795. For an account of the Clergy Daughters' School, see Winifred Gérin, *Charlotte Brontë* (Oxford, 1967), pp. 1–12.

36   Hughes, pp. 55–6; C. R. Davey (ed.), *Education in Hampshire and the Isle of Wight* (Winchester: Hampshire Archivists' Group Publication no. 3, 1977), identifies Twyford School as that attended by Thomas Hughes and described in his novel.

37   Obelkevich, p. 54.

38   Ronald Fletcher, *The Parkers at Saltram 1769–89* (London, 1970), p. 128.

39   Lucas Papers at Bedfordshire Record Office, letter dated 11 January 1808; L.30/11/132/29; see also letter dated December 1809, L.30/11/132/63.

40   Joseph Arch, *The Story of His Life Told by Himself* (London, 3rd edn, n.d. [1898]), pp. 53–4.

41   Diaries of the Rev. W. C. Risley at the Bodleian Library, vol. 11, 1843, MS D.D.Risley c.67. Entries for 9 October, 12 October, 6 December and 18 December 1843.

42 Margaret F. Thorp, *Charles Kingsley 1819–1875* (Princeton NJ, 1937),
    p. 33; Susan Chitty, *The Beast and the Monk* (London, 1974), p. 96.
43 *Jackson's Oxford Journal*, 17 January 1835.
44 Obelkevich, p. 64.
45 Jesse Collings, *Land Reform* (London, 1906), pp. 71–2.
46 *The Labourer's Friend* (issued by the Labourer's Friend Society, 1833),
    p. 1.
47 Ibid., p. 49.
48 Ibid., p. 280.
49 A. C. Todd, 'An answer to poverty in Sussex', *Agricultural History
    Review*, vol. 4 (1956), pp. 48–9.
50 L. Marion Springall, *Labouring Life in Norfolk Villages 1834–1914*
    (London, 1936), p. 36.
51 Arthur W. Ashby, *Allotments and Small Holdings in Oxfordshire* (Oxford,
    1917), p. 31; J. L. Green, *The Yeomen of England and Small Holdings in
    Land* (London n.d. [*c.*1892]), p. 13.
52 Quoted in Margaret Fuller, *West Country Friendly Societies* (University
    of Reading, 1964), p. 7.
53 Fuller, pp. 10–11.
54 Fuller, pp. 42, 44.
55 Richard Hine, 'Friendly societies and their emblems', in *Proceedings of
    the Dorset Natural History and Antiquarian Field Club*, vol. 59 (1928),
    p. 118.
56 Fuller, p. 87.
57 Hampshire Friendly Society, Minutes of the Proceedings of the Board
    of Management, 1825–38 (vol. 1), at the Society's office in Winchester,
    entries for 4 April 1826 and 3 August 1833.
58 Hampshire Friendly Society, Minutes; for example, on 18 October
    1825 there were eight examples of assurances for the endowment of a
    daughter or a son. This was a fairly typical admission picture. At the
    same time there were nineteen men and women who joined on their
    own account. They comprised seven servants, four labourers, two
    schoolmasters, two dressmakers, and a shoemaker, a gardener, a
    carpenter and a laundress.
59 P. H. J. H. Gosden, *The Friendly Societies in England 1815–1875* (Man-
    chester, 1961), pp. 31, 42; Fuller, p. 25.
60 Fuller, p. 110.
61 *Jackson's Oxford Journal*, 11 May 1771.
62 James Woodforde, *The Diary of a Country Parson 1758–1802*, ed. John
    Beresford (London: World's Classics edn, 1967), entry 9 May 1771,
    p. 74.
63 Marjorie Reeves, *Sheep Bell and Ploughshare* (Bradford-on-Avon, 1978),
    pp. 43–4.
64 W. Ravenscroft, 'Secession from the Church of England', *Milford-on-
    Sea Record Society Occasional Magazine*, vol. 5 (November 1912), p. 39.

65 Dorothy Marshall, *John Wesley* (Oxford, 1965), p. 26.

66 William M. Thackeray, *Vanity Fair* (London: Oxford University Press edn, n.d.), p. 113 (this volume in the Oxford Thackeray series was based on the revised edition of 1864); David Cecil, *A Portrait of Jane Austen* (London, 1978), p. 69.

67 Eric J. Evans, 'Some reasons for the growth of English rural anti-clericalism, *c.* 1750-*c.* 1830', *Past and Present*, no. 66 (February 1975), p. 100. For details of Hakewell's position, see Diana McClatchey, *Oxfordshire Clergy 1777-1869* (Oxford, 1960), pp. 42, 53. For the national figures of non-resident clergy, see Owen Chadwick, *Victorian Miniature* (London, 1960), p. 10.

68 E. H. Stuart Jones, *The Last Invasion of Britain* (Cardiff, 1950), p. 25.

69 William Dickinson, *Cumbriana or Fragments of Cumbrian Life* (London, 1875), pp. 128, 140.

70 McClatchey, pp. 138-9.

71 McClatchey, p. 43.

72 McClatchey, p. 45.

73 Quoted in McClatchey, pp. 90-1. For the Davies quotation, see document 7 of the Davies MSS. in the Cole Collection at Nuffield College, Oxford.

74 Consistory Court Papers at Northamptonshire Record Office, X 953, bundle 12 (case involving Robert Chapman, rector of Braybrooke and John Everett, yeoman of Braybrooke, in 1799). A consistory court is the principal ecclesiastical court of a diocese, in which the chancellor or official principal sits as judge. From his sentence an appeal lies to the archbishop of the province.

75 Chadwick, p. 90.

76 Chadwick, p. 99-101.

77 Evans, 'Some reasons for the growth of English rural anti-clericalism', p. 100.

78 Ibid.

79 Evans, 'Some reasons for the growth of English rural anti-clericalism', p. 104.

80 McClatchey, p. 182.

81 Eric J. Evans, *The Contentious Tithe* (London, 1976), p. 26.

82 A. Driver and W. Driver, *General View of the Agriculture of the County of Hampshire* (London, 1794), p. 33.

83 Evans, *The Contentious Tithe*, p. 22.

84 Barbara Kerr, *Bound to the Soil* (London, 1968), p. 177. This cleric was subsequently able to obtain some of his tithes in kind or at a money composition even more favourable to himself. Neither provision endeared him to his farmer parishioners.

85 Case involving William Maris, rector of St Peter's, Wallingford, and a Quaker, Stephen Green, at Berkshire Record Office, P/S/W/B/5/1/1 (1809 and 1811).

86 Evans, *The Contentious Tithe*, p. 29.
87 *Hansard*, 3rd series, 1836, vol. 31, cols. 207, 698. Lord John Russell, in moving the introduction of the Bill, called tithes 'a penalty on skill, a heavy mulct on those who expended the most capital and displayed the greatest skill in the cultivation of the land' (col. 186).
88 Evans, *The Contentious Tithe*, pp. 130–1.
89 Stanley Ayling, *John Wesley* (London, 1979), pp. 91, 247, 256.
90 Arthur Warne, *Church and Society in Eighteenth Century Devon* (Newton Abbot, 1969), p. 28.
91 W. Bardsley Brash, *Methodism* (London, 1928), p. 165; Ayling, *John Wesley*, p. 310.
92 *Bedford St Paul's Methodist Circuit Class Book* (Bedfordshire County Record Office, 1977), pp. 73–7, provides the basis of the calculations.
93 Obelkevich, pp. 243–4.
94 Brash, p. 179.
95 George Eliot, *Adam Bede* (London: Everyman's Library edn, 1976), pp. 28–9.
96 Obelkevich, p. 227. Bourne and Clowes were expelled from membership in 1808 and 1810 respectively, and it was in March 1810 that the Camp Meeting Methodists became a distinct community. Brash, p. 172.
97 B. Cozens-Hardy (ed.), *Mary Hardy's Diary* (Norfolk Record Society, vol. 37, 1968), entry for 10 April 1795.
98 E. P. Baker (ed.), *Bishop Wilberforce's Visitation Returns for the Archdeaconry of Oxford in the year 1854* (Oxfordshire Record Society, vol. 35, 1954), pp. 36, 63.
99 Obelkevich, p. 162.
100 Pamela Horn, *Labouring Life in the Victorian Countryside* (Dublin, 1976), p. 15. Alan Everitt, 'Nonconformity in country parishes', in Joan Thirsk (ed.), *Land, Church and People* (Reading: Museum of English Rural Life, 1970, for British Agricultural History Society), pp. 189–90
101 Everitt, p. 196.
102 Ibid.; see also P. G. Rogers, *Battle in Bossenden Wood* (London, 1961), for an account of Tom and his followers.
103 Warne, pp. 100–2.
104 Thorp, pp. 29–30; Chitty, p. 94.
105 Reeves, p. 136.
106 John Bossy, *The English Catholic Community 1570–1850* (London, 1975), pp. 173, 330.
107 Obelkevich, pp. 239.
108 Obelkevich, p. 195. In the Bedford St Paul's Methodist Circuit in 1796 there were seven local preachers. The occupations of six of them are known: they were a farmer, a shoemaker, a clerk, a chimney sweep, a weaver and a labourer. By 1806 there were twenty-two local preachers apparently serving in this circuit; unfortunately their occupations are

not available. The number of members in the Bedford Circuit had now reached 908. *Bedford St Paul's Methodist Circuit Class Book*, pp. 166–7.

109 Arch, pp. 19–20.
110 Mrs M. C. Balfour, 'Legends of the Lincolnshire cars' in *Folk-Lore*, vol. 2 (1891), p. 257.
111 Balfour, p. 259.
112 The Rev. J. C. Atkinson, *Forty Years in a Moorland Parish* (London 1891), pp. 99–100.
113 Obelkevich, pp. 305–6.
114 *Gentleman's Magazine*, vol. 21 (1751), p. 186, and vol. 55, pt 2 (1785), entry for July.
115 Chadwick, p. 86.
116 Balfour, p. 260.
117 Obelkevich, p. 273. Warne, pp. 33–4 also mentions the problem of those who wished to be confirmed twice.
118 Christina Hole, *English Sports and Pastimes* (London, 1949), p. 97.
119 Christina Hole (ed.), *Witchcraft at Toner's Puddle, 19th C.* (Dorset Record Society, Publication no. 2, 1964), pp. 4–8.
120 *Folk-Lore*, vol. 5 (1894), 336–7, and vol. 6 (1896), p. 127.
121 In Devon, Herefordshire and Sussex, farmers and labourers would, for example, assemble as Christmas to wassail the apple trees, so that they would bear a good crop in the coming season: 'A bad wassailing is *sure* to be followed by a defective crop.' In Sussex it was also common to nail up a horseshoe reversed, in the belief that this would diminish the power of any witches who might enter the house or would even prevent their admission: The Rev. T. W. Horsfield, *The History and Antiquities of Lewes and its Vicinity*, vol. 2 (Lewes, 1824), p. 267.

6   Crime and punishment

1 J. L. Hammond and B. Hammond, 'Poverty, crime, philanthropy', in A. S. Turberville (ed.), *Johnson's England*, vol. 1 (Oxford, 1965), pp. 327–8.
2 Rev. H. Worsley, *Juvenile Depravity* (London, 1849), quoted in J. J. Tobias, *Nineteenth-Century Crime: Prevention and Punishment* (Newton Abbot, 1972), pp. 16–17.
3 Douglas Hay, 'Property, authority and the criminal law' in Douglas Hay, Peter Linebaugh, E. P. Thompson (eds), *Albion's Fatal Tree* (London, 1975), p. 19.
4 Hay, p. 18.
5 Hay, p. 41.
6 Hay, p. 43.
7 David Jones, 'Thomas Campbell Foster and the rural labourer: incendiarism in East Anglia in the 1840s', *Social History*, vol. 1 (January 1976), pp. 28, 30.

8 James Caird, *English Agriculture in 1850–51*, 2nd edn (London, 1968) pp. 467–8. (The book was first published in 1852.)

9 Jones, p. 5.

10 E. P. Thompson, 'The crime of anonymity', in Hay *et al.*, p. 261. In an examination of 284 letters or handbills (anonymous and hand-written) printed in the *London Gazette* over the period 1750–1811 Thompson shows that arson or arson and murder combined provided the most common threat (pp. 258–9).

11 Home Office Correspondence at the Public Record Office, HO 61.1, letters dated 9, 13 and 26 December 1821, from B. Dashwood; also HO 43/31, letter from Home Office to Dashwood, 10 December 1821, promising to advertise the reward and pardon in the *London Gazette*.

12 Margaret F. Thorp, *Charles Kingsley 1819–1875* (Princeton NJ, 1937), p. 30.

13 Piers Brendon, *Hawker of Morwenstow: Portrait of a Victorian Eccentric* (London, 1975), pp. 67, 123.

14 Phyllis Deane, *The First Industrial Revolution* (Cambridge, 1965), p. 206. For an instance of the military being used to back up customs officers, see, for example, '1776, 1876', magazine section of the *Regimental Journal of the 1st The Queen's Dragoon Guards*, vol. 3, no. 4 (1976), p. 355. This notes that in one week during June 1785 parties from the Queen's Dragoon Guards based in Hampshire helped in three separate incidents, leading to the seizure of large quantities of illicit liquor, including 40 gallons of wine, 242 gallons of rum, 91 gallons of brandy, and 136 gallons of gin.

15 David Williams, *The Rebecca Riots* (Cardiff, 1971), p. 46.

16 John Fielding, *The Farmer's Guide Through Fairs and Markets or A Sure Way to Preserve their Property from the attempts of a Low Set of Gamblers* (pamphlet, Nantwich, 1775), pp. 15–16.

17 'Guarding the Horse Mails, 1794–1823', vol. 1, records at the Post Office Record Office, Post 10.8, letter from C. Saverland, Surveyor, dated 13 August 1796, and his journal entry for August 1796.

18 Letter from the Treasury dated 16 December 1801, agreeing that armed guards be carried into 'immediate effect'; the Post Office was to report after a year on the effectiveness of the guarding policy (in PO 10.8).

19 Edmund Vale, *The Mail-Coach Men of the Late Eighteenth Century* (London, 1960), p. 263.

20 Quoted in T. A. Critchley, *A History of Police in England and Wales 900–1966* (London, 1967), p. 69.

21 *Royal Commission on a Constabulary Force*, PP 1839, vol. 19, pp. 21–2, 58.

22 E. P. Thompson, *Whigs and Hunters* (London, 1975), p. 255.

23 Ronald Fletcher, *The Parkers at Saltram 1769–89* (London, 1970), p. 23.

24 Hon. Grantley Fitzhardinge Berkeley, MP, *A Pamphlet in Defence of the Game Laws* (London, 1845), pp. 46–7.

25 Roger Longrigg, *The English Squire and His Sport* (London, 1977), p. 154.

26 George M. Trevelyan, *The Life of John Bright* (London, 1913), p. 124; E. W. Bovill, *English Country Life 1780–1830* (London, 1962), p. 158.

27 F. M. L. Thompson, *English Landed Society in the Nineteenth Century* (London, 1963), p. 138.

28 Letter from Thomas Bennett, the Woburn steward, to C. Haedy, the London steward, 25 December 1841, R3/4488/1, Bedford estate at Bedfordshire Record Office.

29 Circular to tenants, 10 February 1818, in Holkham Letter Books, MS Film 706 at Bodleian Library, and letter from Henry Shepherd of Wighton to Francis Blaikie, estate steward, dated 27 January 1819, in Holkham Letter Books, MS Film 707 at Bodleian Library.

30 Charles P. Chevenix-Trench, *The Squire and the Poacher* (London, 1967), p. 125.

31 Deputations of Gamekeepers 1797–1809, at Hampshire Record Office, entries for July to September 1798.

32 St Katherine's Chapter Minute Book 1775–93, at Cathedral Archives and Library, Canterbury, entry for Midsummer 1788, p. 354.

33 P. B. Munsche, 'The game laws in Wiltshire 1750–1800', in J. S. Cockburn (ed.), *Crime in England 1550–1800* (London, 1977), p. 217.

34 Munsche, p. 214

35 Bovill, p. 175.

36 Bovill, pp. 176–8.

37 Chevenix-Trench, p. 135.

38 Letter from Joseph Pawsey, steward, to Lady Lucas, dated 10 June 1800, in Lucas Papers at Bedfordshire Record Office, L.30/11/215/98.

39 Quoted in Bovill, p. 184.

40 A. J. Peacock, 'Village radicalism in East Anglia, 1800–50', in J. P. D. Dunbabin (ed.), *Rural Discontent in Nineteenth-Century Britain* (London, 1974), p. 51.

41 Henry P. Delme, *v.* William Richards the younger and John Abbott, at Hampshire Spring Assizes, 1818, document at Hampshire Record Office 5M51/174.

42 William Cobbett, *Rural Rides*, vol. 1 (London: Everyman's Library edn, 1948), pp. 151–2.

43 *Hansard*, 2nd series, vol. 19, 6 May 1828, col. 365.

44 *Hansard*, 3rd series, vol. 78, 27 February 1845, col. 72.

45 *Select Committee on the Game Laws*, PP 1846, vol. 9, pt 1, p. 258.

46 Chester Kirby, 'The attack on the English game laws in the forties', *Journal of Modern History*, vol. 4 (1932), p. 34.

47 Trevelyan, p. 125.

48 Joseph Arch, *The Story of His Life Told by Himself*, ed. the Countess of Warwick (London, 3rd edn, n.d. [1898]), pp. 159–61.

49 John Glyde Jr, *Suffolk in the Nineteenth Century* (London, 1856), p. 155.

50 James Hawker, *A Victorian Poacher*, ed. Garth Christian (Oxford, 1978), p. xii.

51 Hawker, p. xv.

52 Douglas Hay, 'Poaching and the game laws on Cannock Chase', in Hay *et al.*, p. 194.

53 Table Showing Number of Persons Committed for Trial or Bailed in England and Wales and Offences with which they stood charged, PP 1849, vol. 54.

54 Rules of Aldermaston, Wasing and Padworth Association for the Prosecution of Felons, 1800, at Berkshire Record Office, D/P3/28/1; see also the similar Rules for the Thatcham Association, also for 1800, at the Record Office, D/P3/28/1.

55 Midgham Constables' Accounts 1741–79, at Berkshire Record Office, D/P130c/9.

56 Minutes of the East Hendred Association for the Protection of Property, at Berkshire Record Office, D/P66/28/1.

57 Old Calendars of Prisoners, at Oxfordshire Record Office, QSP I/1.

58 Ibid. and broadsheet describing the man's death. He was born in the village of Stanton St John in 1749 and so was barely thirty when he was executed on 22 March 1779.

59 *Hansard*, 2nd series, 1823, vol. 9, cols. 397–404. Sir James also contrasted the situation in France, where there were only six crimes punishable by death. This debate on the Criminal Laws was held on 21 May 1823.

60 J. J. Tobias, *Crime and Industrial Society in the Nineteenth Century* (London, 1967), p. 213.

61 A Return of the Persons convicted in England and Wales in the Years 1823, 1824 and 1825 of stealing sheep, before whom and whether left for execution or reprieved, PP 1826, vol. 24; and a similar Return for stealing horses, also in PP 1826, vol. 24.

62 *Hansard*, 3rd series, 1832, vol. 11, cols. 948–9. Ewart noted that in England overall, while nearly 1400 sentences of death had been imposed in 1830, executions amounted to forty-six.

63 *Hansard*, 3rd series, 1832, vol. 13, col. 202.

64 Williams, p. 57.

65 *Royal Commission on a Constabulary Force, First Report*, PP 1839, vol. 19, p. 5.

66 Ibid., p. 263.

67 Cuddesdon Constables' Accounts, at Bodleian Library, MS D.D.Par. Cuddesdon c.6.

68 Williams, p. 57.

69 *First Report of the Royal Commission on a Constabulary Force*, p. 257.

70 Ibid., p. 263.

71 *Second Report from the Select Committee on the Police*, PP 1852–3, vol. 36, Q 2778.

72 Basingstoke Constable's Diary, at Hampshire Record Office, 8M 62/22 and 8M 62/23.

73 Arch, p. 150.

74 S. Webb and B. Webb, *English Prisons under Local Government* (London, 1922), p. 31.

75 John Howard, *The State of the Prisons* (London: Everyman's Library edn, 1929), p. 202. (The first edition of Howard's book appeared in 1777. He started his investigations when he was appointed Sheriff of Bedford in 1773.)

76 Howard, p. 2.

77 Joyce Godber, *John Howard the Philanthropist* (Bedfordshire County Council, 1977), p. 9.

78 Quoted in Webb and Webb, p. 55.

79 Giles Playfair, *The Punitive Obsession* (London, 1971), p. 76.

80 E. Melling (ed.), *Crime and Punishment: Kentish Sources IV* (Maidstone: Kent County Council, 1969). pp. 240-1.

81 Miscellaneous correspondence on prisons at Public Record Office, HO 20/1 and *Hansard*, 2nd series, 1822, vol. 7, cols 1-51, 518; See also J. Stevens Cox, *Ilchester Gaol and House of Correction*, Ilchester Historical Monographs No. 4 (Ilchester, 1949 pamphlet), pp. 89-90.

82 Webb and Webb, pp. 73-5.

83 *Minutes of Evidence Before the Select Committee on Gaols and Houses of Correction*, PP 1835, vol. 11, evidence of the Earl of Chichester, p. 70.

84 Tobias, p. 206; Playfair, pp. 81-2.

85 *Appendix to Evidence Before the Select Committee on Gaols and Houses of Correction*, PP 1835, vol. 11, p. 120.

86 Webb and Webb, p. 131.

87 'The king of the Norfolk poachers', in Lilias Rider Haggard (ed.), *I Walked by Night* (Ipswich, 1974), pp. 41-3. (This book was first published in 1935.)

7 Politics and protectionism: 1830s-1850s

1 Anthony Trollope, *Framley Parsonage* (London, 1957 edn), p. 84.

2 Dorothy Marshall, *Industrial England 1776-1851* (London, 1973), p. 64; J. L. Hammond and B. Hammond, *The Village Labourer*, vol. 1 (London: Guild Books edn, 1948), p. 13.

3 Holkham Letter Books, Circular to the Tenantry sent by Francis Blaikie, steward and dated 12 May 1817. MS Film 706 at Bodleian Library. Shortly afterwards Blaikie and Coke made arrangements to sell lifehold interests in certain of the cottages to some of the more politically reliable tenant farmers so that they might themselves obtain 'Freehold qualifications to vote for County Members'; see Memorandum describing a meeting held with some of the tenants on 31 May 1817.

4 Michael Brock, *The Great Reform Act* (London, 1973), p. 22.

5   Brock, p. 23.
6   George Herbert, *Shoemaker's Window* (Chichester, 1971 edn), p. xvi.
7   Brock, p. 26.
8   *Hansard*, 2nd series, vol. 8, 1823, col. 1254.
9   E. L. Jones, *The Arable Depression after the Napoleonic Wars and the Agricultural Development of the Hampshire Chalklands* (BA dissertation, Nottingham University, 1958), p. 56.
10 E. W. Bovill, *English Country Life 1780–1830* (London, 1962), p. 71.
11 Quoted in Travis L. Crosby, *English Farmers and the Politics of Protection, 1815–52* (Hassocks, 1977), p. 58.
12 *Hansard*, 2nd series, vol. 7, 1822, col. 62.
13 Letter from the Rev. Edward Marshall of Iffley to his son, at Oxfordshire Record Office (n.d. [1831]), XV/xv/1/j.
14 David Spring, 'Ralph Sneyd: Tory country gentleman', *Bulletin of the John Rylands Library*, vol. 38, no. 2 (March 1956), p. 537.
15 Quoted in Jones, pp. 100–1.
16 Brock, p. 125.
17 Ibid.
18 David C. Moore, *The Politics of Deference* (Hassocks, 1976), p. 104.
19 Joyce Godber, *History of Bedfordshire* (Bedfordshire County Council, 1969), p. 408.
20 Norman Gash, *Politics in the Age of Peel* (London, 1964), p. 154.
21 Quoted in Roger Cook, 'Changes in parliamentary representation in Hampshire 1832–1867', typescript (n.d.), at Hampshire Record Office, p. 37.
22 C. J. F. Atkinson, *Recollections from a Yorkshire Dale*, 2nd edn (London, 1935), p. 48.
23 David Spring, *The English Landed Estate in the Nineteenth Century: Its Administration* (Baltimore, Md., 1963), p. 131. Martin unenthusiastically described his electoral duties in 1852 as 'a sad obstacle to business', though he pursued them conscientiously enough.
24 Philip Pusey's election expense accounts 1832–4, at Berkshire Record Office, D/EBp.02/1.
25 J. K. Hedges, *The History of Wallingford*, vol. 2 (London, 1881), p. 203.
26 Papers of a Wallingford election agent, at Berkshire Record Office, D/EH 09.
27 F. M. L. Thompson, *English Landed Society in the Nineteenth Century* (London, 1963), p. 277.
28 Letter from Thomas Bennett, the Woburn steward, to W. G. Adam, the London steward, dated 21 April 1833, in Russell papers, at Bedfordshire Record Office, R3/3753.
29 Quoted in Moore, p. 294.
30 Gash, p. 239.
31 David Williams, *The Rebecca Riots*, 2nd edn (Cardiff, 1971), p. 31.

32   Williams, p. 31.
33   Williams, p. 32.
34   Williams, p. 33.
35   Thompson, p. 198.
36   R. J. Olney, *Lincolnshire Politics 1832–1885* (Oxford, 1973), p. 35.
37   Olney, p. 33.
38   James Obelkevich, *Religion and Rural Society: South Lindsey 1825–1875* (Oxford, 1976), p. 34.
39   Olney, p. 42.
40   J. A. Perkins, 'Tenure, tenant right, and agricultural progress in Lindsey, 1780–1850', *Agricultural History Review*, vol. 23, pt 1 (1975), p. 9.
41   Perkins, p. 9.
42   Richard W. Davis, *Political Change and Continuity 1760–1885: A Buckinghamshire Study* (Newton Abbot, 1972), p. 175.
43   Rev. J. C. Atkinson, *Forty Years in a Moorland Parish* (London, 1891), pp. 17–18.
44   Thompson, pp. 201–2.
45   Gash, p. 182.
46   Olney, p. 44.
47   John Morley, *The Life of William Ewart Gladstone*, vol. 1 (London, 1908), p. 178.
48   Moore, pp. 257–8.
49   Risley diaries, at the Bodleian Library, vol. 5, MS D.D.Risley CI3, entries for 18 and 26 May 1838.
50   Pamela Horn, *Education in Rural England 1800–1914* (Dublin, 1978), pp. 190–1.
51   *The Martyrs of Tolpuddle 1834–1934* (London: Trades Union Congress General Council, 1934), p. 8; Joyce Marlow, *The Tolpuddle Martyrs* (London, 1971), p. 42.
52   Home Office, Letter Books 1833–4, HO 43/44, 378; see also *The Martyrs of Tolpuddle*, p. 172.
53   *The Martyrs of Tolpuddle* (reprint of handbill), p. 12.
54   Home Office, Letter Books 1833–4, HO 43/44, 492.
55   George Loveless, *The Victims of Whiggery* (London: The Central Dorchester Committee, n.d., 8th edn [1837]), p. 8.
56   Quoted in *The Martyrs of Tolpuddle*, p. 118.
57   *Hansard*, 3rd series, 1834, vol. 22, col. 725.
58   *Hansard*, 3rd series, 1834, vol. 23, col. 313.
59   Marlow, pp. 192–3, 223.
60   Pamela Horn, *Joseph Arch* (Kineton, 1971), pp. 18–21, 44.
61   Home Office correspondence, letter from two JPs, dated 23 July 1839, HO 40/42.
62   Asa Briggs (ed.), *Chartist Studies* (London: Papermac edn, 1962), p. 177.
63   Briggs, p. 178.

64 Home Office correspondence, letter from Mr Maundry of Trowbridge to Mr Parker of Stroud, HO 40/42.
65 Briggs, p. 289.
66 Briggs, pp. 216–17. For a fictional account of a Chartist meeting in a village, see Charles Kingsley, *Alton Locke* (London, 1889 edn), pp. 203–14. (This book was written in 1849.)
67 Alice M. Hadfield, *The Chartist Land Company* (Newton Abbot, 1970), p. 16.
68 Hadfield, p. 41.
69 Briggs, p. 329.
70 Quoted in Williams, p. 150.
71 *The Courier*, 17 October 1832.
72 Crosby, p. 89.
73 Crosby, pp. 103–4.
74 Williams, p. 153. For mention of the position in Cheshire and Lancashire, see J. D. Chambers and G. E. Mingay, *The Agricultural Revolution 1750–1880* (London, 1966), p. 153.
75 For details of Acland's activities in Suffolk, see Home Office correspondence, HO 40/56, letter and enclosure from H. B. Bence, a Suffolk JP, dated 22 May 1840; see also Norman McCord, *The Anti-Corn Law League* (London, 1958), pp. 57, 74.
76 Joseph Arch, *The Story of His Life Told by Himself* (London, 3rd edn, n.d. [1898]), p. 10.
77 Archibald Prentice, *History of the Anti-Corn Law League*, vol. 2 (London, 1853), pp. 381–2.
78 Crosby, p. 115.
79 Crosby, p. 123.
80 Olney, p. 117.
81 Crosby, p. 129.
82 Crosby, pp. 132–3.
83 David C. Moore, 'The Corn Laws and high farming', *Economic History Review*, 2nd series, vol. 18, no. 3 (December 1965), p. 554.
84 Crosby, p. 137.
85 Thompson, pp. 134–5.
86 E. A. Wasson, 'The third Earl Spencer and agriculture, 1818–1845', *Agricultural History Review*, vol. 26, pt 2 (1978), p. 97.
87 B. Disraeli, *Lord George Bentinck* (London, 1905 edn), pp. xxx–xxxi, xxxvi.
88 David Cannadine, 'Aristocratic indebtedness in the nineteenth century: the case re-opened', *Economic History Review*, 2nd series, vol. 30, no. 4 (November 1977), p. 629; J. K. Fowler, *Echoes of Old Country Life* (London, 1892), pp. 159–62. Fowler also states that Chandos let his farms at low rent in order 'to pose as the farmers' friend'.
89 Cook, pp. 32–3.
90 Crosby, p. 174.

91 Christ Church estate records, MS Estates 72.286, at Christ Church Library.

92 Christ Church estate records, MS Estates 59.357, at Christ Church Library.

93 Woburn estate Letter Book 1850–3, R 4/7, pp. 7, 9.

94 Woburn estate Letter Book, 1850–3, p. 67 (report on Bedfordshire and Buckinghamshire Tenants, dated 7 November 1850).

95 Spring, p. 192.

96 Susan Fairlie, 'The Corn Laws and British wheat production, 1829–76', *Economic History Review*, 2nd series, vol. 22, no. 1, (April 1969), p. 103.

97 Crosby, pp. 187–8.

98 Quoted in Chambers and Mingay, p. 157.

8 The rural community in the mid nineteenth century

1 David Spring, 'Ralph Sneyd: Tory country gentleman', *Bulletin of the John Rylands Library*, vol. 38, no. 2 (March 1956), pp. 539–40.

2 *Morning Chronicle*, 28 October 1850, on labouring life in Hertfordshire, Bedfordshire, Huntingdonshire and Cambridgeshire.

3 See J. Bateman, *The Great Landowners of Great Britain and Ireland*, 4th edn (London, 1883).

4 G. E. Mingay, *Enclosure and the Small Farmer in the Age of the Industrial Revolution* (London, 1968), p. 16. *1851 Census Report*, PP 1852–53, vol. 88, pt 1, p. lxxviii.

5 Pamela Horn, *Labouring Life in the Victorian Countryside* (Dublin, 1976), p. 11.

6 *Morning Chronicle*, 19 January 1850; census return for Crook at the Public Record Office, HO 107.2441.

7 Census Return for Kentmere in 1851 at the Public Record Office, HO 107.2441.

8 William Dickinson, *Essay on the Agriculture of East Cumberland* (Carlisle, 1853), p. 41; census return for Grey's Forest in 1851, at the Public Record Office, HO 107.2422.

9 N. L. Leyland and J. E. Troughton, *Glovemaking in West Oxfordshire*, Oxford City and County Museum Publication no. 4 (1974), pp. 11–12.

10 James Obelkevich, *Religion and Rural Society: South Lindsey 1825–1875* (Oxford, 1976), p. 12; Horn, *Labouring Life in the Victorian Countryside*, p. 8.

11 Post Office Records, PO 58/12.

12 Secretary's Minutes at the Post Office Record Office, Post 35/17, entry for 13 March 1831. However, there were also such entries as that for 18 April 1830: 'Let Mr. Johnson appoint Lord Shaftesbury's Man on the first opportunity.'

13 F. E. Baines, *Forty Years at the Post-Office* (London, 1895), p. 19.

14 Norman Gash, *Politics in the Age of Peel* (London, 1964), pp. 346, 351.

15 P. W. Kingsford, *Victorian Railwaymen: The Emergence and Growth of Railway Labour, 1830–1870* (London, 1970), pp. 7, 90.

16 E. L. Jones, 'The agricultural labour market in England, 1793–1872', *Economic History Review*, 2nd series, vol. 17, no. 2 (December 1964), p. 331. Horn, *Labouring Life in the Victorian Countryside*, pp. 86–7.

17 George Osbaldeston, *Squire Osbaldeston: His Autobiography*, ed. E. D. Cuming (London, 1926), p. 3.

18 David Cannadine, 'Aristocratic indebtedness in the nineteenth century: the case re-opened', *Economic History Review*, 2nd series, vol. 30, no. 4 (November 1977), p. 630.

19 C. S. Orwin and E. H. Whetham, *History of British Agriculture 1846–1914* (London, 1964), pp. 92–3; see also David Spring, *The English Landed Estate in the Nineteenth Century: Its Administration* (Baltimore, Md., 1963), p. 52.

20 Russell papers, at Bedfordshire Record Office, Letter Book 1850–3, R 4/7, 56.

21 J. W. Burgon, *Lives of Twelve Good Men*, vol. 2 (London, 1889), p. 378.

22 Burgon, p. 373.

23 Owen Chadwick, *Victorian Miniature* (London, 1960), p. 71.

24 Joyce Godber, *History of Bedfordshire* (Bedfordshire County Council, 1969), p. 467.

25 Russell papers at Bedfordshire Record Office, Letter Book 1848–9, R 4/6, 34, 36, 52, 134, 143. The quotation appears in a letter written on 31 May 1848.

26 Obelkevich, pp. 36–7.

27 Chadwick, pp. 103–5.

28 Allan Jobson, *Victorian Suffolk* (London, 1972), p. 45.

29 Christ Church estate records, MS Estates 81.133, letter dated 13 January 1852.

30 Christ Church estate records, MS Estates 81.168, letter dated 19 November 1853.

31 *Report by Dr Hunter on the Dwellings of Agricultural Labourers in Seventh Report of the Medical Officer of the Privy Council*, PP 1865, vol. 26, p. 135.

32 David C. Moore, *The Politics of Deference* (Hassocks, 1976), p. 9.

33 Pamela Horn, *Joseph Arch* (Kineton, 1971), p. 44; *Report by Dr. Hunter on the Dwellings of Agricultural Labourers*, p. 277.

34 *Report by Dr. Hunter on the Dwellings of Agricultural Labourers*, p. 187.

35 James Caird, *English Agriculture in 1850–51*, 2nd edn (London, 1968), p. 389. (First published in 1852.)

36 Census return for Branxton in 1851, at Public Record Office, HO 107.2422.

37 *Saturday Review*, vol. 3, no. 72 (14 March 1857), pp. 239–40.

38 John Glyde, Jr, *Suffolk in the Nineteenth Century* (London, 1856), p. 146.

39 Pamela Horn, *The Rise and Fall of the Victorian Servant* (Dublin, 1975), p. 136.

L

40 *Bedford Times*, 24 July 1858, 24 September 1861.

41 L. Marion Springall, *Labouring Life in Norfolk Villages 1834–1914* (London, 1936), p. 71.

42 Glyde, p. 359.

43 Spring, p. 543.

44 E. A. Wasson, 'The third Earl Spencer and agriculture, 1818–1845', *Agricultural History Review*, vol. 26, pt 2 (1978), pp. 91, 94.

45 Godber, p. 469.

46 Richard N. Bacon, *The Report on the Agriculture of Norfolk* (London, 1844), pp. 138–9.

47 Minute Book of the English Agricultural Society (later Royal Agricultural Society of England), at Museum of English Rural Life, Reading, BI 10. At its meeting on 10 December 1838 it proposed to correspond with agricultural, horticultural and other scientific societies at home and abroad, in order to collect information. The 'diffusion of Agricultural information' was to be 'one of the most important means' by which the Society would achieve its objectives.

48 Orwin and Whetham, p. 7.

49 Jones, 'The agricultural labour market in England, 1793–1872', p. 333.

50 Jobson, p. 33.

51 Quoted in J. R. T. Hughes, *Fluctuations in Trade, Industry, and Finance* (Oxford, 1960), p. 223.

52 E. J. T. Collins, *Sickle to Combine* (Museum of English Rural Life: University of Reading, 1969), p. 14.

53 Bacon, p. 409.

54 Dickinson, pp. 18–19.

55 R. E. Prothero (later Lord Ernle), *English Farming Past and Present*, 2nd edn (London, 1917), p. 367. F. M. L. Thompson, 'The second agricultural revolution, 1815–1880', *Economic History Review*, 2nd series, vol. 21, no. 1 (April 1968), p. 70.

56 *Report of the Select Committee on Agricultural Customs*, and *Minutes of Evidence*, PP 1847–8, vol. 7, Q.1938. Bennett was interviewed on 23 March 1848.

57 Ibid., Q 4894 (interview on 4 May 1848).

58 Spring, *The English Landed Estate*, p. 75.

59 Caird, p. 112.

60 J. Oxley Parker, *The Oxley Parker Papers* (Colchester, 1964), pp. 142–3.

61 Caird, p. 518, noted that whereas in 1840 a stone of flour cost the labourer 2s. 6d., he could purchase it in 1850–1 for 1s. 8d.: 'good Congou tea in 1840 was, exclusive of duty, 2s. 6d. per lb., and is now only 1s.; and the same quality of sugar which then cost him 6d. per lb., can be had now for 3½d.' Caird thought that 'the principal articles of . . . consumption' had fallen in price by 'upwards of 30 per cent'.

62 E. L. Jones, *The Development of English Agriculture 1815–1873* (London, 1968), pp. 20–1.

63 'The farming activities of the third Earl Spencer', *Northamptonshire Past and Present*, vol. 3 (1961), p. 47.

64 Caird, p. 169.

65 Nigel E. Agar, *Employment and Community in Bedfordshire and Hertfordshire in the Nineteenth Century* (Ph.D. thesis, University of East Anglia, 1979), p. 13.

66 Orwin and Whetham, p. 27.

67 *Select Committee on the Railways*, PP 1846, vol. 13, Q 1446–8 (interview on 21 May 1846).

68 J. H. Clapham, *An Economic History of Modern Britain*, vol. 1 (Cambridge, 1939), p. 400.

69 *In Pitstone Green There is a Farm* (Pitstone Local History Society, 1979); Caird, p. 125.

70 Caird, p. 511–12. W. F. Karkeck, 'On the farming of Cornwall', *Journal of the Royal Agricultural Society of England*, vol. 6 (1845), p. 458.

71 A. Redford, *Labour Migration in England 1800–1850*, 2nd edn (Manchester 1964), p. 190.

72 William Palin, 'The farming of Cheshire', *Journal of the Royal Agricultural Society of England*, vol. 5 (1844), p. 87.

73 Jones, 'The agricultural labour market in England, 1793–1872', p. 328.

74 Ibid., p. 328.

75 Agar, p. 99.

76 Glyde, p. 348.

77 Census return for Wyverstone in 1851, at Public Record Office, HO 107.1795.

78 Viscount Dillon's estate, Ditchley model farm wages, DIL I/e/2a, at Oxfordshire Record Office.

79 *Average Rate of Weekly Earnings of Agricultural Labourers in the Unions of England and Wales for the Quarters ending Michaelmas and Christmas, 1860*, PP 1861, vol. 50.

80 J. P. D. Dunbabin, 'Communications: the "revolt of the field"', *Past and Present*, no. 27 (April 1964), p. 112; Horn, *Labouring Life in the Victorian Countryside*, p. 259.

81 Caird, pp. 84–5.

82 *Bedford Times*, 15 April, 1910 ('The "good" old times').

83 Caird, p. 395.

84 W. H. Hudson, *A Shepherd's Life* (Tisbury, 1978), p. 46.

85 *Select Committee on Railway Labourers*, PP 1846, vol. 13, Q 895, 309.

86 Agar, p. 134; Godber, p. 512.

87 E. P. Baker (ed.), *Bishop Wilberforce's Visitation Returns for the Archdeaconry of Oxford in the year 1854*, vol. 35 (Oxfordshire Record Society, 1954), p. 28.

88 Pamela Horn, *The Victorian Country Child* (Kineton, 1974), p. 94. By 1861 these young workers numbered over 7500; not until the 1871 census did their numbers fall sharply.

89   *Reports of Special Assistant Poor Law Commissioners on the Employment of Women and Children in Agriculture*, PP 1843, vol. 12, report by Mr A. Austin on the counties of Wilts, Dorset, Devon and Somerset, pp. 28–30.

90   *Sixth Report of the Children's Employment Commission*, PP 1867, vol. 16, p. vii.

91   Rev. J. H. Bloom, *Notices, Historical and Antiquarian of the Castle and Priory of Castleacre* (London, 1843), p. 307.

92   *Reports of Special Assistant Poor Law Commissioners*, report by Mr Denison on the counties of Suffolk, Norfolk and Lincoln, p. 275.

93   Ibid., pp. 276–7.

94   Springall, p. 44.

95   Charles Kingsley, *Alton Locke* (London, 1889), pp. 201–2. (Kingsley wrote the book in 1849, as the book's preface indicates (xlii).)

96   Horn, *The Victorian Country Child*, p. 82.

97   *The Reminiscences of William Clift of Bramley* (Basingstoke, 1908), pp. 16–20.

98   John Burnett (ed.), *Useful Toil* (London, 1974), p. 137; Horn, *The Rise and Fall of the Victorian Servant*, pp. 32–4, 47–8.

99   Agar, p. 134.

100   Clift, pp. 31, 35.

101   Joseph Arch, *The Story of His Life Told by Himself*, 3rd edn (London, n.d. [1898]), p. 63.

102   Clift, p. 64.

103   E. J. T. Collins, 'Migrant labour in British agriculture in the nineteenth century', *Economic History Review*, 2nd series, vol. 29, no. 1 (February 1976), pp. 50, 52.

104   Maynard MSS., vol. 4, R 58/5/5, at Cambridgeshire Record Office (written *c*. 1881).

105   Walter Rose, *The Village Carpenter* (London, 1952), p. 37.

106   Glyde, p. 359.

107   Springall, p. 63.

108   Census returns for 1851 for Little Horwood, at Public Record Office, HO 107.1722, and Sherrington, HO 107.1723.

109   Charles Freeman, *Luton and the Hat Industry* (Corporation of Luton Museum and Art Gallery, 1953), p. 13; see also Pamela Horn, 'Child workers in the pillow lace and straw plait trades of Victorian Buckinghamshire and Bedfordshire', *Historical Review*, vol. 17, no. 4 (1974), pp. 782–3, for consideration of the spatial distribution of the lace and plait trades in these two counties.

110   J. D. Marshall, *Old Lakeland* (Newton Abbot, 1971), p. 147.

111   R. S. Surtees, *Mr. Sponge's Sporting Tour* (London: World's Classic edn, 1958), p. 208. (This book was first published in 1853.)

112   S. G. Checkland, *The Rise of Industrial Society in England 1815–1885* (London, 1964), p. 33.

113 Checkland, p. 33.
114 John Saville, *Rural Depopulation in England and Wales 1851–1951* (London, 1957), p. 20.
115 Saville, pp. 53–5; Agar, pp. 221, 224.

Bibliography

Manuscript collections

Agreements for Ilderton Farm, Northumberland, at Reading University Library

Agriculture, Minute Books of the Board of, at Museum of English Rural Life, Reading

Aldermaston, Wasing and Padworth Association for the Prosecution of Felons, Rules, 1800, at Berkshire Record Office

Thomas Banting, *Notes on Filkins and other parishes*, at the Bodleian Library, Oxford

Basingstoke constable's diary 1853–4, at Hampshire Record Office

Bottisham Place, Cambridgeshire, farm diary, at Reading University Library

Buckinghamshire Returns of the Posse Comitatus, 1798, at Buckinghamshire Record Office

Chippenham estate records, at Cambridgeshire Record Office

Christ Church, Oxford, estate records in the Library at Christ Church

Consistory Court, Papers of Peterborough, at Northamptonshire Record Office

Roger Cook, *Changes in Parliamentary Representation in Hampshire 1832–1867*, at Hampshire Record Office

Cuddesdon constables' accounts, at Bodleian Library, Oxford

David Davies MSS in the Cole Collection, Nuffield College, Oxford

Defence of the Realm Returns, 1798, at Hampshire Record Office

Viscount Dillon: Ditchley model farm wages books, at Oxfordshire Record Office

Eynsham, Oxfordshire, overseers' accounts, at Bodleian Library, Oxford

Joseph Falkner, wheelwright, ploughwright, etc., account book, at Museum of English Rural Life, Reading

Gamekeepers, Deputations of, 1797–1809, at Hampshire Record Office

Duke of Grafton's returns of Northamptonshire farms, at Northamptonshire Record Office

Greg correspondence *re* pauper apprentices, at Manchester Central Reference Library

Hampshire Friendly Society minute books, at headquarters of the Hampshire and General Friendly Society at Winchester

Holkham estate, Norfolk, letter books, on microfilm at the Bodleian Library Oxford

Home Office Correspondence (including Home Secretary's Letter Books), at Public Record Office

John and Joseph Lamb, Oxfordshire, farm diary 1774–98, at Reading University Library

St Katherine's chapter minute books, at Cathedral Archives and Library, Canterbury.

Little Somborne, Hampshire, farm diary, at Reading University Library

Lucas papers, at Bedfordshire Record Office

Rev. Wm. Mairis v. *Stephen Green*: tithe case, at Berkshire Record Office

Joseph Mayett, *Autobiography of,* at Buckinghamshire Record Office

Midgham constables' accounts, 1741–1779, at Berkshire Record Office

Militia records, at the Public Record Office

Minutes of the English Agricultural Society (later the Royal Agricultural Society of England), at the Museum of English Rural Life, Reading

Minutes of the Magistrates in Petty Sessions for the Three Hundreds of Aylesbury, 1800–3, at Buckinghamshire Record Office

Oxford Militia records, at the Bodleian Library, Oxford

Oxfordshire Militia returns of maintenance of families of substitutes, at Oxfordshire Record Office

Poor Law Commission records, at the Public Record Office

Poor Law Union minute books, at various County Record Offices

Population: 1851 Census Returns, at the Public Record Office

Post Office records, at the Post Office Record Office, London

Peter Pownall's farm diary, Cheshire, 1782–1815, at Reading University Library

Poxwell, Dorset, farm diary, 1781–3, at Reading University Library

Prisons, miscellaneous correpondence on, at the Public Record Office

Philip Pusey's election expense accounts, 1832–4, at Berkshire Record Office

Reports of disorders in 1822, at Public Record Office

Returns of Cavalry Force Ballots in Sub-Divisions of Kent, 1797, at Public Record Office

Rev. W. C. Risley, Deddington, Oxfordshire, diaries of, at Bodleian Library, Oxford

Henry Russell of Swallowfield: correspondence on Poor Law matters, 1830s, at the Bodleian Library, Oxford

Russell papers: the Duke of Bedford's estate papers, at Bedfordshire Record Office

Sibford Gower, Oxfordshire, constables' book, at the Bodleian Library, Oxford

Sibford Gower, Oxfordshire, overseers' book, at the Bodleian Library, Oxford

Rev. Thomas Stevens, account books, at Berkshire Record Office

Wallingford election agent, papers of, at Berkshire Record Office

Whittlesford, Cambridgeshire: Maynard MSS, at Cambridgeshire Record Office

Official reports and publications

(PP=Parliamentary Papers)

Agricultural Customs, Select Committee on, PP 1847–8, vol. 7

Agricultural Labourers, Average rate of Weekly Earnings of, in Quarters ending Michaelmas and Christmas, 1860, PP 1861, vol. 50

Agriculture, Select Committee on, PP 1833, vol. 5

Children, Young Persons and Women in Agriculture, Royal Commission on the Employment of, PP 1867–8, vol. 17; 1868–9, vol. 13

Children's Employment Commission, Sixth Report of, PP 1867, vol. 16

Constabulary Force, Royal Commission on, PP 1839, vol. 19

Depressed State of the Agriculture of the United Kingdom, Select Committee on, PP 1821, vol. 9

Education in Wales, Reports of Commissioners of Inquiry into the State of PP 1847, vol. 27

Education, Minutes of the Committee of Council on, from 1839 (annually)

Game Laws, Select Committee on, PP 1846, vol. 9

Gaols and Houses of Correction, Select Committee on PP 1835, vol. 11

Hansard

Labourers' Wages, Select Committee on, PP 1824, vol. 6

Medical Officer of the Privy Council, Seventh Report of, PP 1865, vol. 26

Medical Relief, Select Committee on, PP 1854, vol. 12

Persons Committed for Trial and Bailed in England and Wales and Offences with which they stood charged, PP 1849, vol. 54

Persons Convicted in England and Wales for Stealing Sheep and Horses, 1823–5, Returns of, PP 1826, vol. 24

Petitions Complaining of Agricultural Distress, &c., Select Committee on, PP 1820, vol. 2

Police, Select Committee on, PP 1852–3, vol. 36

Poor Law Commission, Annual Reports of

Poor Laws, Royal Commission on, PP 1834, vol. 34

Poor Laws, Select Committee on, PP 1817, vol. 6

Railway Labourers, Selec tCommittee on, PP 1846, vol. 13
Railways, Select Committee on, PP 1846, vol. 13
Relief of the Poor, Sixteenth Report from the Select Committee to Inquire
    into the Administration of, PP 1838, vol. 18, pt 1
State of Agriculture, Select Committee on, PP 1836, vol. 8
Waste, Uninclosed and Unproductive Lands of the Kingdom, Select Com-
    mittee on, PP 1795, vol. 1
Women and Children in Agriculture, Reports of Special Assistant Poor Law
    Commissioners on the Employment of, PP 1843, vol. 12

Newspapers and journals

Annals of Agriculture
Annual Register
Bedford Times
Folk-Lore
Gentleman's Magazine
Jackson's Oxford Journal
Journal of the Royal Agricultural Society of England
Labourer's Friend
Milford-on-Sea Record Society occasional magazines
Morning Chronicle
The Times

Periodical articles

D. A. Baugh, 'The cost of poor relief in south-east England, 1790–1834',
    Economic History Review, 2nd series, vol. 28, no. 1 (February 1975)
Alan Booth, 'Food riots in the north-west of England 1790–1801', *Past and
    Present*, no. 77 (November 1977)
David Cannadine, 'Aristocratic indebtedness in the nineteenth century: the
    case re-opened', *Economic History Review*, 2nd series, vol. 30, no. 4 (Nov-
    ember 1977)
John Chapman, 'Land purchase at enclosure: evidence from West Sussex',
    Local Historian, vol. 12, no. 7 (1977)
J. H. Clapham, 'The transference of the worsted industry from Norfolk to
    the West Riding', *Economic Journal*, vol. 20 (1910)
E. J. T. Collins, 'Migrant labour in British agriculture in the nineteenth
    century', *Economic History Review*, 2nd series, vol. 29, no. 1 (February
    1976)
Ann Digby, 'The labour market and the continuity of social policy after
    1834: the case of the eastern counties', *Economic History Review*, 2nd
    series, vol. 28, no. 1 (February 1975)
J. P. D. Dunbabin, 'Communications: the "revolt of the field"', *Past and
    Present*, no. 27 (April 1964)

Eric J. Evans, 'Some reasons for the growth of English rural anti-clericalism, *c.* 1750–*c.* 1830', *Past and Present*, no. 66 (February 1975)

Susan Fairlie, 'The Corn Laws and British wheat production, 1829–76', *Economic History Review*, 2nd series, vol. 22, no. 1 (April 1969)

Norman Gash, 'Rural unemployment 1815–34', *Economic History Review*, vol. 6, no. 1 (October 1935)

Richard Hine, 'Friendly societies and their emblems', *Proceedings of the Dorset Natural History and Antiquarian Field Club*, vol. 49 (1928)

B. A. Holderness, ' "Open" and "close" parishes in England in the eighteenth and nineteenth centuries', *Agricultural History Review*, vol. 20, pt 2 (1972)

B. A. Holderness, 'Personal mobility in some rural parishes of Yorkshire, 1777–1822', *Yorkshire Archaeological Journal*, vol. 42, pt 168 (1970)

Pamela Horn, 'Child workers in the pillow lace and straw plait trades of Victorian Buckinghamshire and Bedfordshire', *Historical Journal*, vol. 17, no. 4 (1974)

Pamela Horn, 'The Buckinghamshire straw plait trade in Victorian England', *Records of Bucks*, vol. 19, pt 1 (1971)

Pamela Horn, 'The Dorset dairy system', *Agricultural History Review*, vol. 26, pt 2 (1978)

Pamela Horn, 'A Sussex mutiny', *Sussex Life*, vol. 14, no. 6 (June 1978)

Glenn Hueckel, 'Relative prices and supply response in English agriculture during the Napoleonic Wars', *Economic History Review*, 2nd series, vol. 29, no. 3 (August 1976)

Richard Johnson, 'Educational policy and social control in early Victorian England', *Past and Present*, no. 49 (November 1970)

David Jones, 'Thomas Campbell Foster and the rural labourer: incendiarism in East Anglia in the 1840s', *Social History*, vol. 1 (January 1976)

E. L. Jones, 'The agricultural labour market in England, 1793–1872', *Economic History Review*, 2nd series, vol. 17, no 2 (December 1964)

W. F. Karkek, 'On the farming of Cornwall', *Journal of the Royal Agricultural Society of England*, vol. 6 (1845)

Eric Kerridge, 'Arthur Young and William Marshall', *History Studies*, vol. 1, pt 2 (1968)

Chester Kirby, 'The attack on the English game laws in the forties', *Journal of Modern History*, vol. 4 (1932)

Peter D. Linneman, 'An econometric examination of the English parliamentary enclosure movement', *Explorations in Economic History*, vol. 15, no. 2 (April 1978)

J. D. Marshall, 'The Lancashire rural labourer in the early nineteenth century', *Transactions of the Lancashire and Cheshire Antiquarian Society*, vol. 71 (1961)

J. D. Marshall, 'Nottinghamshire labourers in the early nineteenth century', *Transactions of the Thoroton Society*, vol. 64 (1960)

J. M. Martin, 'The small landowner and parliamentary enclosure in Warwickshire', *Economic History Review*, 2nd series, vol. 32, no. 3 (August 1979)

Rosalind Mitchison, 'The old Board of Agriculture (1793–1822)', *English Historical Review*, vol. 74 (1959)

David C. Moore, 'The Corn Laws and high farming', *Economic History Review*, 2nd series, vol. 18, no. 3 (December 1965)

R. B. Outhwaite, 'Population change, family structure and the good of Counting', *Historical Journal*, vol. 22, no. 1 (1979)

William Palin, 'The farming of Cheshire', *Journal of the Royal Agricultural Society of England*, vol. 5 (1844)

J. A. Perkins, 'Tenure, tenant right, and agricultural progress in Lindsey, 1780–1850', *Agricultural History Review*, vol. 23, pt 1 (1975)

Jack L. Purdum, 'Profitability and timing of parliamentary land enclosures', *Explorations in Economic History*, vol. 15, no. 3 (July 1978)

David Roberts, 'How cruel was the Victorian Poor Law?', *Historical Journal*, vol. 6 (1963)

Michael E. Rose, 'The allowance system under the new Poor Law', *Economic History Review*, 2nd series, vol. 19, no. 3 (December 1966)

David Spring, 'Ralph Sneyd: Tory country gentleman', *Bulletin of the John Rylands Library*, vol. 38, no. 2 (March 1956)

Walter M. Stern, 'The bread crisis in Britain, 1795–96', *Economica*, vol. 31 (May 1964)

Lawrence Stone, 'Literacy and education in England 1640–1900', *Past and Present*, no. 42 (February 1969)

'Sweet Auburn', *Saturday Review*, vol. 3, no. 72 (14 March 1857)

J. S. Taylor, 'The impact of pauper settlement 1691–1834', *Past and Present*, no. 73 (November 1976)

E. P. Thompson, 'The moral economy of the English crowd in the eighteenth century', *Past and Present*, no. 50 (February 1971)

F. M. L. Thompson, 'The second agricultural revolution, 1815–1880', *Economic History Review*, 2nd series, vol. 21, no. 1 (April 1968)

A. C. Todd, 'An answer to poverty in Sussex', *Agricultural History Review*, vol. 4 (1956)

M. E. Turner, 'Enclosure commissioners and Buckingham parliamentary enclosure', *Agricultural History Review*, vol. 25, pt 2 (1977)

M. E. Turner, 'Parliamentary enclosure and landownership change in Buckinghamshire', *Economic History Review*, 2nd series, vol. 28, no. 4 (November 1975)

E. W. Wasson, 'The third Earl Spencer and agriculture, 1818–1845', *Agricultural History Review*, vol. 26, pt 2 (1978)

Roger Wells, 'The revolt of the south-west, 1800–1801: a study in English popular protest', *Social History*, no. 6 (October 1977)

A. E. Wrigley, 'A note on the life-time mobility of married women in a parish population in the later eighteenth century', *Local Population Studies*, no. 18 (Spring 1977)

Printed books and pamphlets (excluding novels)

Adams, L. P., *Agricultural Depression and Farm Relief in England 1813–1852*, London: Frank Cass & Co. Ltd, 1965

Agricultural State of the Kingdom, London, Board of Agriculture, 1816

Altick, Richard D., *The English Common Reader*, Chicago: University of Chicago, 1957

Anderson, Michael, *Family Structure in Nineteenth Century Lancashire*, Cambridge: Cambridge University Press, 1971

Arch, Joseph, *The Story of His Life Told by Himself*, 3rd edn, London: Hutchinson, n.d. [1898]

Ashby, Arthur W., *Allotments and Small Holdings in Oxfordshire*, Oxford: Clarendon Press, 1917

Ashby, M. K., *The Changing English Village 1066–1914*, Kineton: Roundwood Press Publishers Ltd, 1974

Ashby, M. K., *Joseph Ashby of Tysoe*, Cambridge: Cambridge University Press, 1961

Ashton, T. S., *Economic Fluctuations in England 1700–1800*, Oxford: Clarendon Press, 1959

Ashton, T. S., *An Economic History of England: The 18th Century*, London: Methuen & Co., 1972

Atkinson, Rev. J. C., *Forty Years in a Moorland Parish*, London: Macmillan, 1891

Ayling, Stanley, *George The Third*, London: Collins, 1972

Ayling, Stanley, *John Wesley*, London: Collins, 1979

Bacon, Richard N., *The Report on the Agriculture of Norfolk*, London: Ridgways & Chapman Hall, 1844

Baines, F. E., *Forty Years at the Post-Office*, London: Richard Bentley & Son, 1895

Baker, David, *The Inhabitants of Cardington in 1782*, Bedfordshire Historical Record Society, vol. 52, 1973

Baker, E. P. (ed.), *Bishop Wilberforce's Visitation Returns for the Archdeaconry of Oxford in the Year 1854*, Oxfordshire Record Society, vol. 35, 1954

Barnard, H. C., *A History of English Education from 1760*, London: London University Press, 1966

Barnes, William, *A Selection of Poems*, ed. Robert Nye, Oxford: Carcanet Press Ltd, 1972

Bateman, J., *The Great Landowners of Great Britain and Ireland*, 4th edn, London: Harrison, 1883

Bedford St Paul's Methodist Circuit Class Book, Bedfordshire County Council, 1977

Berkeley, Hon. Grantley Fitzhardinge, MP, *A Pamphlet in Defence of the Game Laws*, London: Longman, Brown, Green & Longman, 1845

Bettey, J. H., *Rural Life in Wessex 1500–1900*, Bradford-on-Avon: Moonraker Press, 1977

Bloom, Rev. J. H., *Notices, Historical and Antiquarian, of the Castle and Priory at Castleacre*, London: Pelham Richardson, 1843

Bonser, K. J., *The Drovers*, London: Macmillan, 1970

Bossy, John, *The English Catholic Community 1570–1850*, London: Darton, Longman & Todd, 1975

Bovill, E. W., *English Country Life 1780–1830*, London: Oxford University Press, 1962

Brash, W. Bardsley, *Methodism*, London: Methuen & Co., 1928

Brendon, Piers, *Hawker of Morwenstow: Portrait of a Victorian Eccentric*, London: Jonathan Cape, 1975

Briggs, Asa (ed.), *Chartist Studies*, London: Macmillan 1962

Brock, Michael, *The Great Reform Act*, London: Hutchinson, 1973

Brundage, Anthony, *The Making of the New Poor Law*, London: Hutchinson, 1978

Burgon, J. W., *Lives of Twelve Good Men*, 2 vols, London: John Murray, 1889

Burnett, John, *Useful Toil*, London: Allen Lane, 1974

Byng, Hon. John, *The Torrington Diaries*, ed. C. Bruyn Andrews, 4 vols, London: Eyre & Spottiswoode, 1934–8

Bythell, Duncan, *The Handloom Weavers*, Cambridge: Cambridge University Press, 1969

Caird, James, *English Agriculture in 1850–51*, 2nd edn, London: Frank Cass & Co. Ltd, 1968

Carlyle, A. J., and Carlyle, R. M. (eds), *The Poetical Works of George Crabbe*, London: Oxford University Press, 1914

Cecil, David, *A Portrait of Jane Austen*, London: Constable, 1978

Chambers, J. D., *The Workshop of the World*, London: Oxford University Press, 1961

Chambers, J. D., and Mingay, G. E., *The Agricultural Revolution 1750–1880*, London: Batsford Ltd, 1966

Checkland, S. G., and Checkland, E. O. A. (eds), *The Poor Law Report of 1834*, Harmondsworth: Penguin, 1974

Checkland, S. G., *The Rise of Industrial Society in England 1815–1885*, London: Longman, 1964

Chevenix-Trench, Charles P., *The Squire and the Poacher*, London: Longman, 1967

Chitty, Susan, *The Beast and the Monk*, London: Hodder & Stoughton, 1974

Cirket, Alan F. (ed.), *Samuel Whitbread's Notebooks, 1810–11, 1813–14*, Bedfordshire Historical Record Society, vol. 50, 1971

Clift, William, *The Reminiscences of William Clift of Bramley*, Basingstoke: Bird Bros, 1908

Cobbett, William, *Rural Rides*, 2 vols, London: J. M. Dent & Sons Ltd, 1948

Cockburn, J. S. (ed.), *Crime in England 1550–1800*, London: Methuen & Co. 1977

Cole, G. D. H., *The Life of William Cobbett*, London: Collins, 1924

Collings, Jesse, *Land Reform*, London: Longmans, Green & Co., 1906

Collins, E. J. T., *Sickle to Combine*, Museum of English Rural Life, University of Reading, 1969

Cozens-Hardy, B. (ed.), *Mary Hardy's Diary*, Norfolk Record Society, vol. 37, 1968

Critchley, T. A., *A History of Police in England and Wales 900–1966*, London: Constable, 1967

Crittall, Elizabeth (ed.), *The Victoria History of the County of Wiltshire*, vol. 4, London: Oxford University Press, 1959

Crosby, Travis L., *English Farmers and the Politics of Protection, 1815–52*, Hassocks: Harvester Press Ltd, 1977

Darbishire, Helen, (ed.), *Journals of Dorothy Wordsworth*, London: Oxford University Press, 1958

Davenport, J. M., *Sketch of the History of the Oxfordshire Militia*, Oxford, 1869

Davies, C. Stella, *The Agricultural History of Cheshire 1750–1850*, Manchester: The Chetham Society, 3rd series, vol. 10, 1960

Davies, David, *The Case of Labourers in Husbandry*, London: G. G. and J. Robinson, 1795

Davis, Richard W., *Political Change and Continuity 1760–1885: A Buckinghamshire Study*, Newton Abbot: David & Charles, 1972

Deane, Phyllis, *The First Industrial Revolution*, Cambridge: Cambridge University Press, 1965

Deane, Phyllis, and Cole, W. A., *British Economic Growth 1688–1959*, Cambbridge: Cambridge University Press, 1964

Dickinson, William, *Cumbriana or Fragments of Cumbrian Life*, London: Whittaker & Co., 1875

Dickinson, William, *Essay on the Agriculture of East Cumberland*, Carlisle: A. Thurnam, 1853.

Digby, Anne, *Pauper Palaces*, London: Routledge & Kegan Paul, 1978

Disraeli, B., *Lord George Bentinck*, London: A. Constable & Co., 1905

Dossie, Robert, *Memoirs of Agriculture*, vol. 3, London: C. Nourse, 1782

Driver, A., and Driver, W., *General View of the Agriculture of the County of Hampshire*, London: Board of Agriculture, 1794.

Dunbabin, J. P., *Rural Discontent in Nineteenth-Century Britain*, London: Faber & Faber, 1974

Duncumb, John, *General View of the Agriculture of the County of Hereford*, London: Board of Agriculture, 1805

Eden, Sir Frederic M., *The State of the Poor*, 3 vols, London: J. Davis, 1797

Edsall, Nicholas C., *The anti-Poor Law Movement 1834–44*, Manchester: Manchester University Press, 1971

Evans, Eric J., *The Contentious Tithe*, London: Routledge & Kegan Paul, 1976

Fenton, Alexander, *Scottish Country Life*, Edinburgh: John Donald Publishers, 1976

Fielding, John, *The Farmer's Guide Through Fairs and Markets*, Nantwich: J. Bromley, 1775

Fisher, John, *The Political Plough*, London: Hugh Evelyn, 1974

Fletcher, Ronald, *The Parkers of Saltram, 1769–89*, London: British Broadcasting Corporation, 1970

Flinn, M. W., *An Economic and Social History of Britain Since 1700*, London: Macmillan, 1963

Flinn, M. W., *British Population Growth 1700–1850*, London: Macmillan, 1970

Fowler, J. K., *Echoes of Old Country Life*, London: Edward Arnold, 1892

Fraser, Derek, *The Evolution of the British Welfare State*, London: Macmillan, 1973

Fraser, Derek (ed.), *The New Poor Law in the Nineteenth Century*, London: Macmillan, 1976

Freeman, Charles, *Luton and the Hat Industry*, Luton: Museum and Art Gallery, 1953

Fuller, Margaret, *West Country Friendly Societies*, University of Reading, 1964

Gash, Norman, *Politics in the Age of Peel*, London: Longman, 1964

Gaskell, Elizabeth C., *The Life of Charlotte Brontë*, London: Oxford University Press, 1961

George, Dorothy, *England in Transition*, Harmondsworth: Penguin, 1953

Glyde, John, Jr, *Suffolk in the Nineteenth Century*, London: Simpkin, Marshall & Co., 1856

Godber, Joyce, *John Howard the Philanthropist*, Bedfordshire County Council, 1977

Godber, Joyce, *History of Bedfordshire*, Bedfordshire County Council, 1969

Godwin, Fay, and Toulson, Shirley, *The Drovers' Roads of Wales*, London: Wildwood House, 1977

Gosden, P. H. J. H., *How They Were Taught*, Oxford: Basil Blackwell, 1969

Gosden, P. H. J. H., *The Friendly Societies in England 1815–1875*, Manchester: Manchester University Press, 1961

Grier, R. M., *John Allen: A Memoir*, London: Rivington, 1889

Grigg, David, *The Agricultural Revolution in South Lincolnshire*, Cambridge: Cambridge University Press, 1966

Gunning, Henry, *Reminiscences of the University, Town and County of Cambridge from the Year 1780*, 2 vols, London: George Bell, 1854

Hadfield, Alice M., *The Chartist Land Company*, Newton Abbott: David & Charles, 1970

Hammond, J. L., and Hammond, Barbara, *The Village Labourer*, 2 vols, London: Guild Books, 1948

Hasbach, W., *A History of the English Agricultural Labourer*, London: Frank Cass & Co., 1966

Hawker, James, *A Victorian Poacher*, ed. Garth Christian, Oxford: Oxford University Press 1978

Hay, Douglas, Linebaugh, Peter, and Thompson, E. P. (eds), *Albion's Fatal Tree*, London: Allen Lane, 1975

Hedges, J. K., *The History of Wallingford*, 2 vols, London: Wm. Clowes & Sons, 1881

Hobsbawm, E. J., and Rudé, George, *Captain Swing*, London: Lawrence & Wishart, 1969

Hodgkinson, Ruth G., *The Origins of the National Health Service*, London: The Wellcome Historical Medical Library, 1967

Hole, Christina (ed.), *Witchcraft at Toner's Puddle, 19th C.*, Dorset Record Society, Publication no. 2, 1964

Hole, Christina, *English Sports and Pastimes*, London: Batsford, 1949

Horn, Pamela, *Joseph Arch*, Kineton: Roundwood Press Publishers, 1971

Horn, Pamela, *Education in Rural England, 1800–1914*, Dublin: Gill & Macmillan, 1978

Horn, Pamela, *Labouring Life in the Victorian Countryside*, Dublin: Gill & Macmillan, 1976.

Horn, Pamela, *The Rise and Fall of the Victorian Servant*, Dublin: Gill & Macmillan, 1975

Horn, Pamela, *The Victorian Country Child*, Kineton: Roundwood Press Publishers, 1974

Horsfield, Rev. T. W., *The History and Antiquities of Lewes and its Vicinity*, 2 vols, Lewes: J. Baxter, 1824

Howard, John, *The State of the Prisons*, London: J. M. Dent & Co., 1929

Howells, B. E., and Howells, K. A., *Pembrokeshire Life: 1572–1843*, Pembrokeshire Record Society, vol. 1, 1972

Hudson, W. H., *A Shepherd's Life*, Tisbury: The Compton Press, 1978

Hughes, J. R. T., *Fluctuations in Trade, Industry and Finance*, Oxford: Clarendon Press, 1960

Hunter, James, *The Making of the Crofting Community*, Edinburgh: John Donald, 1976

Hurt, John, *Education in Evolution*, London: Hart-Davis, 1971

In Pitstone Green There is a Farm, Pitstone Local History Society pamphlet, 1979

Jobson, Allan, *Victorian Suffolk*, London: Robert Hale, 1972

Jones, E. H. Stuart, *The Last Invasion of Britain*, Cardiff: University of Wales Press, 1950

Jones, E. L., *The Development of English Agriculture 1815–1873*, London: Macmillan, 1968

Jones, E. L., *Seasons and Prices*, London: George Allen & Unwin, 1964

Jones, E. L., and Mingay, G. E. (eds), *Land, Labour and Population in the Industrial Revolution*, London: Edward Arnold, 1967

Kent, Nathaniel, *Hints to Gentlemen of Landed Property*, London: J. Dodsley, 1775

Kerr, Barbara, *Bound to the Soil*, London: John Baker, 1968

'King of the Norfolk Poachers', *I Walked by Night*, ed. Lilias Rider Haggard, Ipswich: Boydell Press, 1974

Kingsford, P. W., *Victorian Railwaymen*, London: Frank Cass & Co., 1970

Laqueur, L. Thomas, *Religion and Respectability*, New Haven & London: Yale University Press, 1976

Lawson, J., *Primary Education in East Yorkshire 1560–1902*, East Yorkshire Local History Society Publication no. 10, 1970

Levine, David, *Family Formation in an Age of Nascent Capitalism*, New York, San Francisco, London: Academic Press, 1977

Leyland, N. L., and Troughton, J. E., *Glovemaking in West Oxfordshire*, Oxford City and County Museum, Publication no. 4, 1974

Lobel, Mary (ed.), *Victoria County History of Oxfordshire*, vol. 6, London: Oxford University Press, 1959

Longmate, Norman, *The Workhouse*, London: Temple Smith, 1974

Longrigg, Roger, *The English Squire and his Sport*, London: Michael Joseph, 1977

Loveless, George, *The Victims of Whiggery*, London: Central Dorchester Committee, 8th edn, n.d. [1837]

McClatchey, Diana, *Oxfordshire Clergy 1777–1869*, Oxford: Clarendon Press, 1960

MacClure, J. Stuart, *Educational Documents: England and Wales 1816–1968*, London: Methuen, 1972

McCord, Norman, *The Anti-Corn Law League*, London: George Allen & Unwin, 1958

Mann, J. de L., *The Cloth Industry in the West of England from 1640 to 1880*, Oxford: Clarendon Press, 1971

Mantoux, Paul, *The Industrial Revolution in the Eighteenth Century*, London: Jonathan Cape, 1955

Marlow, Joyce, *The Tolpuddle Martyrs*, London: André Deutsch, 1971

Marshall, Dorothy, *English People in the Eighteenth Century*, London: Longmans, 1969

Marshall, Dorothy, *Industrial England 1776–1851*, London: Routledge & Kegan Paul, 1973

Marshall, Dorothy, *John Wesley*, Oxford: Oxford University Press, 1965

Marshall, J. D., *Old Lakeland*, Newton Abbot: David & Charles, 1971

Marshall, J. D., *The Old Poor Law 1795–1834*, London: Macmillan, 1968

Marshall, William, *The Review and Abstract of the County Reports to the Board of Agriculture*, 5 vols, York: Wilson & Sons, 1818

Marshall, William, *The Rural Economy of Gloucestershire*, 2 vols, 2nd edn, London: G. Nicol, 1796

Marshall, William, *The Rural Economy of the Midland Counties*, 2 vols, London: G. Nicol, 1st edn, 1790; 2nd edn, 1796

Marshall, William, *The Rural Economy of Norfolk*, 2 vols, 2nd edn, London: G. Nicol, 1795

Marshall, William, *The Rural Economy of Yorkshire*, 2 vols, London: T. Cadell, 1788

Martyrs of Tolpuddle, London: Trades Union Congress General Council, 1934

Mathias, Peter, *The First Industrial Nation*, London: Methuen, 1969

Melling, Elizabeth (ed.), *Crime and Punishment: Kentish Sources*, Maidstone: Kent County Council, 1969

Melling, Elizabeth (ed.), *Kentish Sources: The Poor*, Maidstone: Kent County Council, 1964

Mingay, G. E., *Enclosure and the Small Farmer in the Age of the Industrial Revolution*, London: Macmillan, 1968

Mingay, G. E., *English Landed Society in the Eighteenth Century*, London: Routledge & Kegan Paul, 1963

Mitford, Mary, *Our Village*, vol. 5, London: Whittaker, Treacher & Co., 1832

Moore, David C., *The Politics of Deference*, Hassocks: Harvester Press, 1976

Morley, John, *The Life of William Ewart Gladstone*, 2 vols, London: Edward Lloyd, 1908

Norfolk, R. W. S., *Militia, Yeomanry and Volunteer Forces of the East Riding 1698–1908*, East Yorkshire Local History Society, Pamphlet no. 19, 1965

Obelkevich, James, *Religion and Rural Society: South Lindsey, 1825–1875*, Oxford: Clarendon Press, 1976.

Olney, R. J., *Lincolnshire Politics, 1832–1885*, Oxford: Oxford University Press, 1973

Orwin, C. S., and Whetham, E. H., *History of British Agriculture 1846–1914*, London: Longmans Green & Co., 1964

Osbaldeston, George, *Squire Osbaldeston: His Autobiography*, ed. E. D. Cuming, London: Bodley Head, 1926

Page, William (ed.), *The Victoria History of the County of Suffolk*, vol. 2, London: Archibald Constable, 1907

Palmer, Felicity, *The Blacksmith's Ledgers of the Hedges Family of Bucklebury, Berkshire 1736–1773*, University of Reading, Research Paper no. 2, Institute of Agricultural History, 1970

Parker, J. Oxley, *The Oxley Parker Papers*, Colchester: Benham & Co., 1964

Parker, R. A. C., *Coke of Norfolk: A Financial and Agricultural Study 1707–1842*, Oxford: Clarendon Press, 1975

Parreaux, André, *Daily Life in England in the Reign of George III*, London: George Allen & Unwin, 1969

'George Paston' [Emily M. Symonds], *Side-lights of the Georgian Period*, London: Methuen, 1902

Peacock, A. J., *Bread or Blood*, London: Victor Gollancz, 1965

Pembrokeshire Antiquities, Solva: H. W. Williams, 1897

Pinchbeck, Ivy, *Women Workers and the Industrial Revolution 1750–1850*, London: Frank Cass & Co., 1969

Platts, A., and Hainton, G. H., *Education in Gloucestershire*, Gloucestershire County Council, 1954

Playfair, Giles, *The Punitive Obsession*, London: Victor Gollancz, 1971

Plumb, J. H., *The Commercialisation of Leisure in Eighteenth-century England*, University of Reading, 1973

Pollard, Sidney, and Crossley, David W., *The Wealth of Britain 1085–1966*, London: Batsford, 1968

Pollard, Sidney, and Holmes, Colin (eds), *Essays in the Economic and Social History of South Yorkshire*, Sheffield: South Yorkshire County Council, 1976

Poor Law in Gloucestershire, Gloucester: Gloucestershire Record Office, 1974

Prebble, John, *The Highland Clearances*, London: Secker & Warburg, 1963

Prentice, Archibald, *History of the Anti-Corn Law League*, 2 vols, London: W. & F. G. Cash, 1853

Prothero, R. E. (later Lord Ernle), *English Farming Past and Present*, 2nd edn, London: Longmans, Green & Co., 1917

Quinault, R., and Stevenson, J., *Popular Protest and Public Order*, London: George Allen & Unwin, 1974

Reaney, Bernard, *The Class Struggle in 19th Century Oxfordshire*, Oxford: History Workshop, Pamphlet no. 3, 1970

Reeves, Marjorie, *Sheep Bell and Ploughshare*, Bradford-on-Avon: Moonraker Press, 1978

Rich, Eric E., *The Education Act, 1870*, London: Longman, 1970

Riches, Naomi, *The Agricultural Revolution in Norfolk*, 2nd edn, London: Frank Cass & Co., 1967

Robson, Derek, *Some Aspects of Education in Cheshire*, Manchester: Chetham Society, 3rd series, vol. 13, 1966

Rose, Michael E., *The English Poor Law 1780–1930*, Newton Abbot: David & Charles, 1971

Rose, Walter, *The Village Carpenter*, London: Country Book Club, 1952

Russell, Rex C., *A History of Schools and Education in Lindsey, Lincolnshire, 1800–1902*, Lindsey County Council Education Committee, 1965

Salaman, R. N., *The History and Social Influence of the Potato*, Cambridge: Cambridge University Press, 1949

Saville, John, *Rural Depopulation in England and Wales, 1851–1951*, London: Routledge & Kegan Paul, 1957

Sellman, Roger R., *Devon Village Schools in the Nineteenth Century*, Newton Abbot: David & Charles, 1967

Smith, Adam, *The Wealth of Nations*, 2 vols, London: J. M. Dent & Sons, 1950

Spring, David, *The English Landed Estate in the Nineteenth Century: Its Administration*, Baltimore, Md: Johns Hopkins Press, 1963

Springall, L. Marion, *Labouring Life in Norfolk Villages 1834–1914*, London: George Allen & Unwin, 1936

Sturt, George, *William Smith: Potter and Farmer, 1790–1858*, Firle: Caliban Books, 1978

Teversham, T. F., *A History of Sawston*, 2 vols, Cambridge: Crampton, 1947

Thirsk, Joan (ed.), *Land, Church and People*, Reading Museum of English Rural Life, 1970, for British Agricultural History Society

Thirsk, Joan, *English Peasant Farming*, London: Routledge & Kegan Paul, 1957

Thirsk, Joan, and Imray, J., *Suffolk Farming in the Nineteenth Century*, Suffolk Record Society, vol. 1, 1958

Thompson, E. P., *The Making of the English Working Class*, London: Victor Gollancz, 1963

Thompson, E. P., *Whigs and Hunters*, London: Allen Lane, 1975

Thompson, F. M. L., *English Landed Society in the Nineteenth Century*, London: Routledge & Kegan Paul, 1963

Thorp, Margaret F., *Charles Kingsley 1819–1875*, Princeton, NJ: University Press, 1937

Tibble, J. W., and Tibble, Anne (eds), *The Prose of John Clare*, London: Routledge & Kegan Paul, 1951

Tobias, J. J., *Crime and Industrial Society in the Nineteenth Century*, London: Batsford, 1967

Tobias, J. J., *Nineteenth-Century Crime: Prevention and Punishment*, Newton Abbot: David & Charles, 1972

Trevelyan, George M., *The Life of John Bright*, London: Constable & Co., 1913

Turberville, A. S. (ed.), *Johnson's England*, 2 vols, Oxford: Clarendon Press, 1965

Vale, Edmund, *The Mail-Coach Men of the Late Eighteenth Century*, London: Cassell, 1960

Wachter, K. W., Hammel, E. A., and Laslett, P., *Statistical Studies of Historical Social Structure*, New York, San Francisco, London: Academic Press, 1978

Warne, Arthur, *Church and Society in Eighteenth-Century Devon*, Newton Abbot: David & Charles, 1969

Watt, Ian A., *A History of the Hampshire and Isle of Wight Constabulary 1839–1966*, Hampshire & Isle of Wight Constabulary, 1967

Webb, S., and Webb, B., *English Prisons under Local Government*, London: Longmans, Green & Co., 1922

Webb, S., and Webb, B., *English Poor Law History*, Part 2: *The Last Hundred Years*, London: Longmans & Co., 1929

Webb, S., and Webb, B., *English Poor Law Policy*, London: Frank Cass & Co., 1963

Wells, Roger A. E., *Dearth and Distress in Yorkshire, 1793–1802*, University of York, Borthwick Papers, no. 52, 1977

White, Gilbert, *The Natural History of Selborne*, London: J. M. Dent & Sons, 1966

Wilkinson, Olga, *The Agricultural Revolution in the East Riding of Yorkshire*, East Yorkshire Local History Society, Pamphlet no. 5, 1956

Williams, David, *A History of Modern Wales*, 2nd ed., London: John Murray, 1977

Williams, David, *The Rebecca Riots*, Cardiff: University of Wales Press, 1971

Woodforde, James, *The Diary of a Country Parson 1758–1802*, ed. John Beresford, London: Oxford University Press, 1967

Yelling, J. A., *Common Field and Enclosure in England 1450–1850*, London: Macmillan, 1977

Young, Arthur, *A Six Months' Tour Through the North of England*, 4 vols, 2nd edn, London: W. Strahan, 1771

Young, Arthur, *A Six Weeks' Tour Through the Southern Counties of England and Wales*, London: W. Nicoll, 1768

Young, Arthur, *The Farmer's Tour Through the East of England*, 4 vols, London: W. Strahan, 1771

Young, Arthur, *General View of the Agriculture of the County of Hertfordshire*, London: Board of Agriculture, 1804

Theses

Agar, Nigel E., *Employment and Community in Bedfordshire and Hertfordshire in the Nineteenth Century*, PhD thesis, University of East Anglia, 1979

Crossman, Allan B., *The Buckinghamshire Posse Comitatus, 1798*, MA dissertation, Leicester University, 1971

Jones, E. L., *The Arable Depression after the Napoleonic Wars and the Agricultural Depression of the Hampshire Chalklands*, BA dissertation, Nottingham University, 1958

Novels

Austen, Jane, *Mansfield Park*, London: Collins, 1953

Eliot, George, *Adam Bede*, London: J. M. Dent & Sons, 1960

Goldsmith, Oliver, *The Vicar of Wakefield*, London: Readers' Library Publishing Co., n.d.

Hardy, Thomas, *The Mayor of Casterbridge*, London: Pan 1953

Hughes, Thomas, *Tom Brown's Schooldays,* London: Nelson & Sons, n.d.

Kingsley, Charles, *Alton Locke*, London: Macmillan, 1889

Surtees, R. S., *Mr. Sponge's Sporting Tour*, London: Oxford University Press, 1958

Thackeray, William, *Vanity Fair*, London: Oxford University Press, n.d.

Trollope, Anthony, *Framley Parsonage*, London: Oxford University Press, 1957

Index